HAREM HISTORIES ❖

HAREM HISTORIES

Envisioning Places and Living Spaces

Marilyn Booth, editor

DUKE UNIVERSITY PRESS Durham & London 2010

© 2010 Duke University Press
All rights reserved

Printed in the United States of America on acid-free paper ♾
Designed by Jennifer Hill
Typeset in Adobe Jenson Pro by Tseng Information Systems, Inc.

Library of Congress Cataloging-in-Publication Data appear
on the last printed page of this book.

CONTENTS

INTRODUCTION

Marilyn Booth

 In 1909, Demetra Vaka Brown (1877–1946), a Greek ethnic subject of the Ottoman Empire, published *Haremlik: Some Pages from the Life of Turkish Women*. Writing in English for a primarily North American audience, she drew cleverly on her insider/outsider position to present the harem to readers who probably felt that they already knew what the word meant, even if they had little idea of its social realities for women of the empire or of how "the life of Turkish women" might have changed over time. Vaka Brown—who had lived, worked, and married in the United States—returned to her native Constantinople, now Istanbul, to visit Turkish Muslim friends and to sketch the interiors of their lives for the citizens of her new country. She started with the interior of, as she put it, the "Old Serai . . . dark and mysterious as the crimes committed within its walls."[1] She could count on an audience: to use the word *harem* in a book title was to lure readers with an image often assumed by Western European or American observers to be characteristic of an entire society or a vast stretch of territory in the East.[2] That Vaka Brown was in some sense a "native informant"—someone who socially as well as physically crossed and blurred the inner/outer divide that the word *harem* seemed to signal—enhanced her authority for readers, as she manipulated her representation of private spaces for public political, international, and domestic aims.

If Vaka Brown exploited the drawing power of the harem as an image of exoticism and mystery for her North American friends and readers, she also sought to complicate that image for her readers, contrasting it with the "hatred and scorn" she had heard Americans express toward Turkey, as they assured her that Turkish "women [were] miserable creatures."[3] The "harems" she visits in her book are often monogamous households; if they are polygynous, they are portrayed as harmonious communities of women, who may speak flawless French, enjoy the outdoors, have a cosmopolitan aesthetic sense, and confound the visitor with blunt, smart questions about Euro-American assumptions of what "freedom" and "ambition" involve. They offer, in other words, an image of the harem as a domestic scene that would be congenial and familiar—if quite possibly disappointing in its lack of exoticism—to upperclass female North American readers. For this audience, the harems in her book also offer a haven of hospitality and grace: unhurried meals, fine textiles, good company, pleasing gardens, and the time and sense to enjoy them. "I had lived so long in a civilized country," mused Vaka Brown with canny irony, "that I had forgotten how much more civilized, in some respects, uncivilized Turkey is."[4] Her genteel construction of a few upperclass Turkish households was also pointedly deconstructive of Western Orientalist presuppositions about the harem—and, by extension, about what that institution was thought by Westerners to prove about Turkish society, and Muslim-majority societies in general.

Equally disorienting for an Anglophone reader might have been the comment of another traveler and writer, Zeyneb Hanoum (a pen name), after a visit to Britain's Parliament. Addressing a friend in her 1913 book, *A Turkish Woman's European Impressions*, Zeyneb Hanoum exclaimed: "But, my dear, why have you never told me that the Ladies' Gallery is a harem? A harem with its latticed windows! The harem of the Government! . . . How inconsistent are you English! You send your women out unprotected all over the world, and here in the workshop where your laws are made, you cover them with a symbol of protection."[5] Zeyneb Hanoum and Vaka Brown were consciously writing against a persistent Western, and particularly masculine, eroticization of the harem that stood in for a sweeping judgment of the societies it was thought to order. As Reina Lewis vividly puts it: "For men, the harem woman trapped in a cruel polygamous sexual prison was a titillating but pitiful emblem of the aberrant sexuality and despotic power that characterized all that was wrong with the non-Christian Orient."[6] The burden of representation that Vaka Brown and Zeyneb Hanoum were trying to shoulder, even as they exploited the commercial potential of the harem, led another Ottoman subject, who belonged to a slightly later generation and who became a prominent official in the early Turkish republic, to call for jettisoning the term entirely. Asked how English women could help Turkish women, Halide Edib Adivar (1884–1964) said: "Ask them to delete for ever that misunderstood word 'harem,' and speak of us in our Turkish 'homes.'"[7]

These "counter-travel" books, whose authorship is sometimes in doubt, sought, sometimes ambiguously, to undo accumulations of Euro/American imagery that unambiguously placed "Eastern" women in an envisioned harem of Western making. Yet, the appeal of those imagined harems offered by Western travelers remained strong. European women traveling to Istanbul or Cairo sometimes expressed disappointment that the domestic reality they witnessed did not fulfill expectations raised by the armchair harems of Anglophone or Francophone travel literature and the visual imagery of eighteenth- and nineteenth-century European Orientalist art. Even today, these texts and images continue to shape popular views of the harem, particularly in societies that produced this art and literature but also, in some cases, among Middle Easterners. Scholars worldwide have been busy dissecting Orient-scapes and explicating them as politically loaded and romantically infused products of European and American minds, pens, and ambitions over time. Yet, in the West, images and attitudes that the discourses and images of Orientalism shaped continue to saturate assumptions about Middle Eastern, Arab, Muslim, and Eastern women, and to underlie judgments about their societies. After all, in "Western" as well as "Eastern" societies, representations of women's bodies and the spaces they should, might, or do inhabit have carried heavy symbolic burdens, often standing in for particular political agendas, representing perceived social problems, evoking justifications for war, or bearing the weight of "moral" campaigns. As we shall see, the imagined, represented, and experienced space of the harem — in its wide range of meanings and manifestations — has been one of these sites of symbolic representation available for various uses.

Harem Histories offers a series of historically specific and wide-ranging examples of institutions and images that the term *harem* has encompassed across geographical spaces and over centuries. Our emphasis is on the concept/institution/image of the harem as shaped and represented *within* societies of the Middle East and North Africa, while we also attend to its representational and political uses by visitors to and observers of these societies. The genesis of this project was a conference organized by Professors Nasser Rabbat and Heghnar Watenpaugh at the Massachusetts Institute of Technology in May 2004, on "The Harem in History and Imagination," funded by the Aga Khan Program for Islamic Architecture at MIT. Some essays in this volume were written for that conference; more of them have been solicited since.[8] How, we ask collectively, has the harem, and understandings of gendered space in the societies where the harem structured women's and men's lives, been represented *within* societies of which it was a historical part? How successfully can one even define the word *harem*? Moreover, how can a range of architectural scapes and literary-political discourses that have shaped the spatial practices of gender-specific segregation, but that have not always been explicitly known as "the harem," be linked to this term that sometimes seems both ubiquitous and elusive? This collection of essays explores the harem as social institution, architectural framework, and representational figure both in Muslim-majority societies and in Euro/American imaginations. It considers the harem not as a static space but as a historically changing and geographically and socially variable concept which helps us to understand broader notions of gendered space in Muslim-majority cultures. The harem is just a starting point.

What do we—the contributors to this book—mean by *harem*? First and foremost, we suggest its variability, as we recognize its allusive power, not only in the West but also in societies where the term had institutional meanings and still has political purchase. In Egypt, for example, writing in 1987, the veteran feminist and journalist Amina al-Sa'id used the term as a metaphorical base line when she argued, in the popular monthly magazine *al-Hilal*, that in the difficult post-1967 political and economic circumstances of Egypt, women were paying the price for Egyptians' perceived sense of failure. She titled her article: "Are Women Returning to the Age of the Harem?"[9]

If, for al-Sa'id, "harem" was a shorthand way to encapsulate the loss of "all that [women] have gained through the past sixty years of their struggle,"[10] including public political rights as well as changes in family law and educational and work opportunities; if, for Vaka Brown, it was a space of female community constructed explicitly to counter dominant Euro/American notions of "harem" as a place of incarceration and sexual free-for-all; and if, for writers and groups of people whom we shall meet in this book, it meant certain (but varying) patterns of social and familial arrangements and their spatial correlates, it is possible at least to note some specific circuits of meaning that the word connotes. The semantic field of the Arabic word *harīm* is hardly what one would expect against the backdrop of Hollywood films or European paintings of odalisques—or even Amina al-Sa'id's political metaphor. İrvin Schick addresses some basic definitional origins in chapter 3 of this book. Nevertheless, and risking repetition, it is perhaps useful to offer some immediate linguistic pointers. The Arabic verbs *harama* and *harrama* mean "to deprive" and "to forbid," but they are not specifically gendered; they have no a priori connotation of "depriving" or "forbidding" women space or movement. On the contrary, with the word *harem* women, children, and closely related men are placed within the space that is "forbidden." The semantic field of these verbs' associated nouns ranges from "that which is forbidden" or "that which is illegal" (*harām*) to a female spouse or a sacred enclave (*haram*). The mosque precinct in Mecca is "the noble Sanctuary" (*al-haram al-sharīf*), while Mecca and Medina, the two holiest cities of Islam, are "the two harams." Colloquially, *haraam 'alayk* means "shame on you!" (literally, "it is forbidden to you"), while *hariimi*, in its contemporary and utterly secular sense, is an adjective referring to women's items, such as women's clothing. Harīm can refer both to an inviolable space that women and only close male relatives can enter, and to woman or wife (in the singular or plural). As an institution, the concept denotes a certain arrangement of domestic space that has been common to a wide variety of Islamicate societies across many centuries. It is not limited to any single architectural or class-defined elaboration of that concept—for example, the imperial harem which is so often gestured to in European paintings. To insist on the latter would be to retain a stereotypical and narrow idea of the harem, a notion that this book challenges.

Persistent representations of the harem have tended to highlight particular and spectacular applications while passing over the more mundane and socially variable phenomena to which the term has been attached. In the very recent past, Euro/American dictionary definitions, or thesaurus groupings, of the word *harem*, as Judy Mabro notes, had little to do with the meanings of the Arabic term; rather, they house *harem* with *impurity* or *love-nest*—synonymous meanings only within an ahistorical lexicon of Anglophone usage.[11]

That the focus of Euro/American scholarship on the harem has been on Euro/American representations of it is understandable. Pre-twentieth-century Western travel writings about the region, which helped to crystallize popular notions of the harem, are perennially popular texts for analysis by scholars and in college courses focused on cultural encounter. The visual impact of European art, known to so many of us through art history courses and museum tours, has left its mark on many an imagination. Yet, as Mohja Kahf reminds us, the harem as an almost ubiquitous element in Western representations of the Oriental Other was not part of Europe's earliest representations of this particular Orient, but rather emerged some time after the European medieval period, and after Europeans had already become aware of, and were representing, Arab and Muslim-majority societies to themselves.[12] And in Enlightenment Europe, the harem became a resonant image of political authoritarianism—the opposite of the reign of individual rights that Enlightenment thinkers argued ought to undergird legitimate political sovereignty. The harem took on a representational life of its own within the political debates and social tensions of Western societies in transition.

This volume includes essays that focus on European culture as a repository of harem representations. A larger number of chapters, though, tackle indigenous representations of home spaces and their significance for how men and women, girls and boys, were bodily distributed in social space, from early Islamic Mecca to early-twentieth-century Cairo. Some chapters also address the awareness of Arab and Turkish intellectuals of what observers from the West saw—or what they thought they saw, or understood—when they gazed at the walls of a house in, say, Cairo, Istanbul, or Tunis. Thus, one theme that threads through these essays is the intimate interrelatedness of "West" and "East" through encounters within and around the harem, whether in the elite sociabilities of precolonial Tunis or in historical novels published in Istanbul and Cairo from the late nineteenth century on, and popular among a rapidly broadening readership as literacy became more common. One has only to read the Arabic press of late-nineteenth-century Cairo, for instance, to find high degrees of awareness and sensitivity among the literate urban populace about how they were seen in the metropolises of Europe and North America. Arab, Turkish, and Persian writers of fiction and essays looked to the West (generalized as *al-Gharb*, in Arabic) for literary models and ideas about social organization, but at the same time, they criticized the filters through which their own societies were represented, and they asserted their own representational abilities. They also recognized how complicated and truly transcultural are human disseminations of cultural artifacts—how circuitous are the paths down which images travel. In her biography and critical study of the Egyptian poet ʿAʾisha Taymur (1840–1902), the Lebanese writer Mayy Ziyada (1886–1941) noted that she had read with pleasure the serialized 1901 Arabic version of a novel allegedly written in English by a Turkish woman, Layla Hanım—whose father, Khalil Pasha Sharif, had been a minister of the Ottoman Empire. "I have absolutely no doubt," said Ziyada of this novel, "that it describes the 'harim' of Istanbul in those days more truthfully than everything written by the Europeans on this subject."[13]

When discussing the harem, a key concept (and methodological underpinning) to consider is that of *spatial thinking*. Thinking about space not as passive or neutral or natural in its familiar contours, but rather as humanly formed and as a powerful shaper of human identities and understandings, has led scholars to consider how people in groups organize themselves physically and formatively around gender. The formulations of Gaston Bachelard, Henri Lefebvre, Yi-Fu Tuan, Edward Soja, and others have emphasized the relationships between humans' constructed spaces and lived experiences, along with the significance of intimate embodiments—how people have lived and used their bodies—and the way we think about and construct the spaces in which we live and move.[14] The pioneering work of Shirley Ardener, Dolores Hayden, and Doreen Massey energized feminist scholars to consider not only how built environments have corresponded to existing social assumptions about certain spaces as specific to females or males and the genders' appropriate roles, but also how architecture itself fixes and sustains these understandings and practices over time—in other words, how the construction of spaces helps to *form* gender identities. Daphne Spain, for example, suggests that segregated spaces in the home, in educational institutions, and throughout work sites—as well as the geographical distancing of "female" from "male" space—have been significant as they have distanced women from valued nodes of knowledge that underwrite social hierarchies.[15]

These scholars' work also makes it clear that segregated gendered spaces have not been the exclusive property of Muslim-majority societies—a point that Leila Ahmed drives home in her memoir of growing up in Egypt and moving to England for her university education. Newly ensconced at the University of Cambridge, she wondered whether all-female Girton College was not "the harem perfected," with the positive associations of camaraderie in a female community that the term carried for her.[16] Ahmed's metaphoric use of "harem" echoes that of some European women, travelers following in the energetic footsteps of Lady Mary Wortley Montagu (1689–1762), who traveled to Istanbul and wrote about it for audiences back in England in her celebrated and posthumously published *Turkish Embassy Letters* (1763). Elite women such as Montagu and other travelers lived at the beginning of the transition to an industrialist capitalist economy that separated home from workplace and loudly proclaimed the home as the proper space for women. If some European male commentators thought that their female compatriots ought to be thankful that they did not live within the physical constraints of elite Muslim homes (as these male travelers represented them), some of their female peers (Montagu, for instance, and later Vaka Brown) saw aspects to value in the female-run spaces of domestic life in the Arab or Turkish city. Montagu felt that veiled and supposedly secluded Turkish women had more freedom—in the anonymity she saw as guaranteed by the "portable harems" of their all-enveloping street clothes—than did most European women of her day. These traveling and writing women may also have realized that referencing the harem could silence criticism of ways by which European or American women were spatially (and otherwise) constrained.

Today, issues of space and the body remain central, even critical, across Muslim-majority societies and Muslim communities, and one can trace these issues historically back to the concept and practice of the harem in its many, many variations. Likewise, spatial and bodily imagery remain central to the politics of East-West encounter. Among Muslims, some contemporary interpretations of how Islam should be lived emphasize the need to reestablish gender-defined spatial boundaries, whether by encouraging women to stay home or by asserting the importance of covering and hiding the female body. (This is not to deny that women have many reasons to wear the *hijab*, and that in most Muslim communities they have choices about whether to do so. Nor is it to deny that issues of domesticity and dress are also important elsewhere and in other faith communities—for example, among some communities in the United States.) Today's republication of medieval treatises and *fatwas* (juridical opinions on issues of daily life) in glossy yet highly affordable editions sold on the street throughout the Arab world focus noticeably on women's comportment and their spatial disposition, as do contemporary biographies of famous women that explicitly position women in the home as earlier biographies did not.[17] The Moroccan scholar and activist Fatima Mernissi sees this phenomenon as a response to a collective identity crisis: "Muslims in search of identity put the accent on the confinement of women as a solution for a pressing crisis. Protecting women from change by veiling them and shutting them out of the world has echoes of closing the community to protect it from the West."[18] Ironically, among Western non-Muslims, this "accent" risks resurrecting the old stereotype of Muslim women as synonymous with the harem—even if the dominant Western stereotype of the harem produces images of "undress" more than it does that of the covered body, as Joan DelPlato shows in her chapter.

English-language writings on the harem have tended to fall into three categories. First are memoiristic evocations, personal meditations, and travelogues.[19] These include recent republications of earlier works such as those of Vaka Brown, Zeyneb Hanoum, and others, which gave readers and travelers an allegedly indigenous view of harem culture, although some authorship has been challenged.[20] Second are discussions of the harem as a trope in European and American cultures, as represented in these societies' visual arts and literature (including travelogues), often as part of a larger study of aspects of Orientalism (in the sense of collective representations developed in the West of North African and Asian populations as essentially different and inferior, as outlined particularly by Edward Said and further developed by many other scholars).[21] The third group consists of historical treatments of the harem as a set of institutions in particular historical contexts[22] or theorizations of the harem within institutional and discursive parameters defined by Islam and Muslim-majority societies, which focus on the languages, archives, and specific histories of the Middle East (while also sometimes considering, as do works in the first group, the fantasies that the harem has evoked in Orientalist discourses).[23]

This volume builds on the insights and archival work of these and other scholarly publications. But we hope to undo, or at least to question, what appears to be a division of representational labor that has marked most literature on the harem. Studies focused on Islamicate societies (the third group above) have understandably tended to focus on the harem as a historically documentable institution. Those focused on artistic and literary representations—the harem as image—have generally emphasized Orientalist texts (including visual arts and film) that "look in on" the region. This volume, however, emphasizes representations of gendered space and the harem (and gendered space *as* the harem) produced *in* and *by* the societies of which they are a part—while questioning exactly what *in* and *by* might mean, in times and places already constituted by perpetual cultural motion. The temporal and geographical focus of the essays includes the early Arab Islamic heartland, the medieval Islamic Empire, the middle and late Ottoman Empire, and modern Turkey, Egypt, Syria, and Tunisia—as well as nineteenth-century Europe.

Thus, this volume focuses also on the harem as metaphor—and often as a hovering, implicit institution that signified women's relations to domestic and public space even when the harem itself as an identifiable part of a household with identifiable inhabitants was not, not yet, or no longer operative (as in Amina al-Sa'id's use of the term in the late twentieth century). Moving from representations of the earliest Islamic society to discourses about early-twentieth-century Egyptian urban space and to late Ottoman photography, the scholars here explore aspects of interrelations between built environments, bodies, and social organization and process.

The book is divided into thematic sections that are also more or less chronological. The first section, "Normative Images and Shifting Spaces," considers gendered space in Islamic contexts through the lenses of normative representations and their shifts through time. In chapter 1, "Early Women Exemplars and the Construction of Gendered Space," we begin with the examination of how notions of women's relations to domestic and public space changed over discrete historical moments, as Asma Afsaruddin examines the representation of the lives of women of the Prophet Muhammad's time who were his associates and became models for women's interactions with and in diverse social spaces. She compares biographical treatments of their lives in different periods for what these life-story constructions "tell us about changing conceptions of women's moral excellence and their public roles in Muslim societies through the late medieval period," reading them in conjunction with conduct manuals of the same eras that spelled out normative behavior for women. Her tracings of these women's portrayals show not only the contingency and historical variation entailed in women's access to public space but also remind us that early Muslim women were community leaders and warriors—an image far from that of the female secluded in the harem, but also one that was muted in later biographical dictionaries concurrent with conduct manuals that emphasized the merit of staying home. (As noted earlier, some of these very same conduct books have been republished in the present and are sold at newsstands to women and men in Cairo and elsewhere in the Arab-speaking world.)

Yet, as Yaseen Noorani reminds us in chapter 2, "Normative Notions of Public and Private in Early Islamic Culture," "public" and "private" are themselves categories that one must subject to historically rigorous scrutiny, thinking through the issue of how people divide up their social lives, and what sorts of value they give to these divisions, and furthermore how concepts of the self govern the relationships of bodies to space. Noorani draws upon Jurgen Habermas's explication of the emergence of the public sphere in eighteenth-century Europe from concepts of the family as the space of "psychological interiority" par excellence, contrasting these understandings of public and private with a very different notion of personhood and household and social space evident in early Islamic literary texts. With their shifting deployments of the Arabic word *harīm* (harem), and the absence of fixed sites specific to discrete social realms and normative statuses, these texts offer a very different model of sociospatial organization than that organized around a public/private distinction. And Noorani reminds us, importantly, that the harīm has not been uniformly coterminous with "women's realm" in Arab-Muslim histories or in the literary imaginaries that have subtended them. As we focus on the relations of gendered subjecthood to home spaces that our other contributors map out, Noorani's work obliges us to work against the residue of assumptions about the harem that we may yet bring to our reading.

Ending this section, İrvin Schick's chapter, "The Harem as Gendered Space and the Spatial Reproduction of Gender," moves away from historical settings to set out some crucial concepts that resonate through Afsaruddin's and Noorani's work as well as through later chapters. Getting us to think about the origins of the term *harem*, as I briefly described them here, Schick conceptualizes the harem as a set of sites crucial to gender construction. Citing a wide range of theorists, and drawing particularly on the work of geographers and others who study the social construction of space, he asks us to scrutinize all of the chapters in this volume for the political implications of a spatial-social practice that separates bodies according to gender, age, and kin relationships, where that separation both illustrates and enables differential social and economic power.

The second cluster of chapters, "Rooms and Thresholds: Harems as Spaces, Socialities, and Law," takes up the analysis of historical spaces and legal discourses. These chapters also incorporate issues of representation and normativity; however, the book's divisions are to some extent artificial, as all chapters range across methodologies, source material, and focuses. It is impossible to study the "lived harem" without attending to the ways it has been represented, whether in Orientalist painting, European travelers' memoirs, Arabic novels, or juridical texts, just as it is crucial to be historically specific. Nadia Maria El Cheikh reiterates this in chapter 4, on lived spaces in Abbasid Baghdad, where she discusses both the harem of Caliph al-Muqtadir (908–932) and the dwellings of urban families, using images culled from chronicles and belletristic collections. In both cases, the multiplicity of spaces recognizable as the harem requires us to take women's exercise of power into account and to see that seclusion was often partial, multivalent, or interrupted. Moreover, the caliphal harem was an enormously complex, polygynous institution, but the urban elite home was not. There, monogamy was more often the norm. The harem emerges not as monolithic but rather as a range of spaces that are anything but impermeable, fixed, or indistinguishable one from the other.

In chapter 5, "Domesticating Sexuality: Harem Culture in Ottoman Imperial Law," Leslie Peirce considers shifts in Ottoman culture during the fifteenth century and the first half of the sixteenth, investigating what they say about changing notions of social space and the disposition of gendered bodies. Peirce examines the *Kanunname-i Osmanî*—the imperial Ottoman book of laws—that successive sultans shaped, as a central codification of normative practice. She asks what edicts about sexual disorder meant for the organization of the household, and how the laws changed over time. Her subtle analysis, which builds on her earlier work on the Ottoman royal harem, scrutinizes criminal statutes and laws about illicit sexual acts for what they tell us about the changing normative status of domestic space as inhabited by a range of ages, statuses, and genders—what she calls "a reading of domestic life from the ground up as viewed from the top down."

Also imagining domestic space as envisioned from the imperial center, in chapter 6 Jateen Lad takes us into the social space of the Ottoman royal household, in an essay and photographs that focus on the eunuch as a liminal figure, a threshold marker whose ability to traverse the spaces of the harem actually highlights the boundaries that divide those spaces from one another. Lad emphasizes that the imperial Ottoman harem was not *a* space but rather a complex sequence of spaces, whereby spatial arrangements themselves might have a disciplinary effect upon the inhabitants. The eunuchs, powerful and revered, were "crucial mediators" and "formidable barriers," and their own situation was simultaneously powerful and abject.

With Julia Clancy-Smith's mid-nineteenth-century Tunisian panorama (chapter 7), we turn away from Istanbul's projection of enclosure and imperial power and toward the creole intersections of North Africa before the time of the European colonies. In "Where Elites Meet: Harem Visits, Sea Bathing, and Sociabilities in Precolonial Tunisia," Clancy-Smith argues that Europeans who resided in and around Tunis partook of the spatial articulations of the ruling system in seeking to implant themselves residentially near the summer palace of the bey, inserting their own social circles into the social life of the local elite, including gendered sociability around sea bathing. Women, both European and Tunisian, were critical to diplomacy as they became part of each other's social worlds. Familiar North African practices that combined socializing and hygienic concerns—and the gendering of space—met the new European interest in traveling for health-related tourism, notably the restorative effects of hot springs. Thus, concerning nineteenth-century Tunis, to see the harem as a space separated off from public life, or as emblematic of an us-them divide, is to not see it at all.

In chapter 8, Heghnar Watenpaugh, scrutinizing the urban space of nineteenth-century Syria as reconstructed by Aleppines in the late twentieth century, finds a nostalgic production of spaces through a focus on the old courtyard house, not only as the scene of contemporary restaurants and the inspiration for the interior arrangement of residential apartments, but as pervading the contemporary rewriting of earlier lives. In particular, she analyzes recent biographies of the writer and salon founder Mariyana Marrash (1848–1919), finding a spatial correlate to those biographies that seems to substitute the home and the duties of hostess for the body, mind, and intellectual productions of this Arab female intellectual. As a nineteenth-century Arab female author becomes the focus for the production of a certain kind of gendered nostalgic discourse that centers on the woman/home equation, the woman herself is occluded. Watenpaugh offers us an instance of how this figure of woman in domestic space can serve political agendas, broadly defined, in the present.

The final group of essays, "Harems Envisioned," analyzes the harem as a set of literary and artistic representations. In chapter 9, "Harem/House/Set," Nancy Micklewright walks us through a series of photographs of Ottoman interiors that both continue and question the conventions of European Orientalist painting. Photographers supplied their European tourist customers in Istanbul with studio versions of the imagined harem as constructed in European art and travel literature, set pieces that allowed them to momentarily enter the harem, albeit a harem that existed mostly in the European imagination. Meanwhile, as Ottoman subjects sought photographic representation of their homes and lives, the results offered cosmopolitan interiors that belied the consistent material markers of the imagined European harem, corresponding more to Demetra Vaka Brown's interested portrayals of elite Ottoman households as blurring East-West boundaries (however artificial those boundaries already were). In chapter 10, "Dress and Undress," Joan DelPlato turns our attention from the sets to the clothed and nude bodies in European paintings of the harem, linking these images to the imperial politics and trade flows that bound western Europe to the Ottoman Empire, as well as showing how images of the harem reverberated against domestic issues of gendered space and gender politics. The erotics of the represented female harem inhabitant, in artworks by Ingres, Maurin, Lewis, and Lane—which DelPlato analyzes against the art-critical commentary and popular travel writing of each artist's milieu—are put into play by the images' suggestive maneuvers with clothing, whether worn or discarded. The details of each representation persuade the viewer to accept the claim that these European gazes into the harem are authentic.

The following three chapters concern fictional representations of the harem as a site that engaged the contemporary political worlds of writers and readers. With Orit Bashkin's analysis of nineteenth-century Arabic historical novels in chapter 11, we turn (again) to indigenous representations of domestic space. Yet here we find a parallel to the case of Ottoman photography: when Concubine J asserts her agency in a historical novel by the prolific Jurji Zaydan (1861–1914), a Syrian writer and journalist in Egypt, the border between indigenous and outsider is not fixed but rather becomes increasingly ambiguous. Zaydan draws on and yet simultaneously seems to critically mimic Orientalist notions of the harem and "Oriental despotism" in order to intervene in the debates of his era concerning gender rights and the shifting alignments of gender and lived space in Egypt and the Ottoman Empire during the nineteenth century and the early twentieth. Bashkin argues that whether Zaydan is taking the stuff of his fictions from medieval Baghdad or contemporary Istanbul, his representations of women in or of the harem (from the sultan's mother to the racialized portrayals of slaves, from Concubine J to her friend, the modern, book-toting Shirin) allegorize political tyranny through the constraints of the gender-segregated household and family structure. It's interesting that Zaydan is writing at precisely the time, the 1890s, when (according to Reina Lewis) Anglophone "harem literature" is at its peak.[24] If this audience was not Zaydan's primary concern, it is likely that a cosmopolitan intellectual of his sort, who drew much of the material for his Arabic journal *al-Hilal* (the crescent) from European sources, was aware of the transnational—but not consistent—symbolic resonance of the harem. (And how fitting it is, then, that it was in this very magazine, nearly a hundred years later, that Amina al-Saʿid used her metaphoric harem as a critical counterpoint to what she saw as gained but threatened by women's rights.)

It may be that it was only in a period when the seclusion of women was beginning to fade—or at least to seem likely to fade in the near future— that writers such as Zaydan (and there were others) could consciously use the harem as a pivotal, questioned space in a changing social landscape. Considering the contemporaneous novels of the Turkish intellectual Ahmet Midhat Efendi, in chapter 12, A. Holly Shissler finds the spaces of domestic life, and the harem as a principle of social organization (as Shissler puts it, "the removal of women from the world and their placement under male protection") to be a central and positive value in these fictions, an institution that "protect[s] the deepest structure of the family from market forces." The middle-class harem—a space very different from that of, say, the imperial palace—is a place where private virtue is learned and practiced, and where morality inheres in individual choices and complementary gendered roles, all to the benefit (the novels argue) of the larger society.

These male reformers, earnestly supporting certain kinds of choices and new types of education for young women—and young men—do not offer the kinds of transgressive thinking about harem spaces that we can find in certain Anglophone memoirs and other texts by women writing around the beginning of the twentieth century—unusual texts that bespeak a bold imaginary yet a lonely path beyond, more than within, the writer's own society, and that (as noted) construct a readership that is not necessarily indigenous. Consider the shape-shifting Melek Hanım (aka Marie de Jean, 1814–73), whose 1872 *Thirty Years in the Harem*, published in the United States, actually features travel across vast swathes of land more than it does home spaces. The author shows Ottoman women gazing out their latticed windows at men, a prelude to direct communication; girls and women wandering around outside on Ramadan nights; and Ottoman princesses donning European clothes and slipping out of the palace, showing that they were able to use the harem visits of European women to their own ends

by masquerading as those women. And Melek Hanım's strongest representation of seclusion comes when she is sent to her mother-in-law's home
in Rome. Meanwhile, she shows how gender hierarchies are modulated by
other hierarchies: the commoner husbands of Ottoman princesses are little
more than prisoners of their wives, and the Ottoman sultan is confined to
his palace and denied access to politically important information.[25] The
text challenges the whole idea of what some Western scholars have labeled
homogeneously as Muslim spaces[26] — as do Zaydan's novels, though in
a very different way. Or, moving from Ottoman Turkey to India under
British rule, consider the feminine utopian fantasy of Rokeya Sakhawat
Hossain, written in English rather than in the Bengali of her controver-
sial essays "The Secluded Ones." In *Sultana's Dream*, men are locked into
the harem, and a fine satire on nationalist rhetoric has the queen asking
the men to enter the zenana (harem) "for the sake of honor and liberty."
The men are shown as disciplined into confinement: the power of custom
obviates the need for policed boundaries. This is a discipline that Fatima
Mernissi, born in 1936, will emphasize, nearly a century later, as she speaks
in her memoiristic novel *Dreams of Trespass* of the socialization of girls
into learning "invisible" boundaries: childhood is a series of boundaries, but
boundaries also create frontiers.[27] In both texts, women's communities are
sustaining, the harem offers refuge to women dealing with conflict in their
lives, and the intimate rooms above the grand salon inhabited by men offer
spaces for creativity. Aunt Habiba's storytelling voice "opens up magic glass
doors, leading to moonlit meadows"[28] — even if the motif of dreaming suggests limitations on action. And in the homes that the young girl inhabits,
the social organization of the patrilineal and patriarchal extended family is
institutionalized architecturally. Yet the younger generation of men has inherited the principles that Ahmet Midhat Efendi (and his Arab counterparts of the late nineteenth century) propagated in their fiction and other
polemics: for Mernissi's father and uncle, monogamy and a preference for
nuclear family space are central to a nationalist outlook.[29]

My chapter, like Shissler's, investigates fictional representations of prostitution, moving into the early twentieth century and south to Cairo. In
the city after the First World War, as represented in the texts I analyze,
"houses" (brothels), the moral opposite of the harem, actually afford young
women more protection than do the cloistered spaces of home. Echoing
Melek Hanım, for these young women, traversing open space is a way to
save oneself. For these characters, dreams become nightmares. In "Between

Harem and Houseboat," I consider prostitution as a textual unveiling of what has gone wrong with the process of becoming modern, in the view of those elites who were producing (and reading) early Ottoman and Arabic fiction. What I call ventriloquized memoirs—where the female and/or subaltern narrator is presented as a memoirist and yet textual clues suggest that this narrator is not the author/authority producing the text—are linked, I argue, to a broadening cultural scene in 1920s Egypt, as more voices joined in a reformist and nationalist discursive ferment. Historicizing these texts against a campaign to end legalized prostitution, I see them as exposing the fiction of protection as represented by the paternal home's secluded and supposedly feminine space, to suggest the failure of the state and of nationalist reformist activism to provide a feasible space and future for young, educated middle-class and elite girls.

In public discourse today, at least in North America, efforts to educate citizens about the histories, multiplicities, and expressive arts of Muslim-majority societies seem constantly undermined by prejudiced, prepackaged, narrow notions of what Islam is. These bundled sets of images, sound bites, and words—jihad, Mecca, harem—have been reshaped into narrower and nonreligious meanings as they have joined the Anglophone lexicon through time, and they often find the starkest and most shorthand representations in gendered images. If the harem no longer saturates public discourse in the West as it once did, its imagined walls hover behind other symbols that carry similar valence for Western audiences. Where once the harem stood in for "Oriental despotism" and Muslim or "Eastern" women's alleged powerlessness, now the veil has become a sign of abjection and silence: as Asma Afsaruddin has put it, "female coveredness has often impressionistically served as a barometer for gauging female subjection";[30] and yet many women have adopted the veil partly because it allows them to respectably assert a stronger public presence, whether in the workforce or through political action. The veil—in its myriad forms, a variety not always recognized in North American discourse—comes to stand for an opacity of understanding that precludes communications between those of different cultural origins, just as it (and the harem) stood for mystery and inaccessibility in the accounts of nineteenth-century travel writers. From Lord Cromer to President George W. Bush, Western male leaders have used "saving the (other) women" as gestures—perhaps sincerely meant— that are also justifications buttressing political and military encroachments across boundaries. And both *veil* and *harem* contain within their symbolic reach the notions of "stripping off" and "penetrating": envisioned acts that encompass connotations of sexual mastery, violent transgression, and colonial triumph, in the face of long-standing stereotypical notions that *veil* and *harem* evoke, of passivity, silence, incarceration, and sensuality. If these are symbols that obscure the varieties of lived experience, we need also to consider them as aspects of experience, but ones that did not work in ways that observers and commentators expected or even "saw."

Thus, if the harem is popularly understood in Europe and North America as a thing of the past, old representations of it, with accumulations of newer and equally gendered images, continue to shadow how the region as a whole is imagined. To take on the ideologically fraught and symbolically loaded word *harem* is to consider the ways in which this institution, with its dynamic histories and myriad manifestations across a range of societies, is fixed in popular imaginations, as well as to confront how understandings of sexual and gender identities shape and represent whole culture areas to each other. The harem as concept and institution reminds us that these representations, within and across cultural areas, are always located in social space and historical time. Taken together, the essays in this volume suggest that the harem is not—in any way, shape, or form—a static concept or an immediately recognizable, repeatable space. It is a varying institutional practice that has shaped the lives of many, and it remains a productive locus for thinking about how gender matters in the ways that human beings make, use, and represent the spaces in which we live out our lives—and think about the lives and spaces of others.

NOTES

Throughout this volume, we transliterate Ottoman Turkish terms according to contemporary Turkish norms. For Arabic, we use the simplest possible system, marking only ʿayn and internal *hamza*, except in the case of *harīm* and occasionally other words for clarity. All translations are mine, unless otherwise indicated.

1 Vaka Brown, *Haremlik*, 2.
2 On the marketing potential of the word *harem* in English-language publications of this period, see Lewis, *Rethinking Orientalism*, chap. 1.
3 Vaka Brown, *Haremlik*, 13.
4 Ibid., 15.
5 Zeyneb Hanoum, *A Turkish Woman's European Impressions*, 194.
6 Lewis, *Rethinking Orientalism*, 13.
7 Quoted in ibid., 45.

8   I am grateful to the organizers for their enthusiastic help as I assumed responsi-
     bility for this project, and I am also indebted to Nasser Rabbat for some felicitous
     turns of phrase in this introduction, inspired by his introduction at the conference.

9   Al-Saʿid, "Hal taʿudu al-marʾa ila ʿasr al-harim?"

10 Ibid., 30.

11 Mabro, *Veiled Half-Truths*, 7.

12 Kahf, *Western Representations of the Muslim Woman*.

13 Ziyada, *ʿAʾisha al-Taymur*, 98.

14 Bachelard, *The Poetics of Space*; Lefebvre, *The Production of Space*; Tuan, *Space and
     Place*; Soja, *Postmodern Geographies* and *Thirdspace*.

15 Ardener, *Women and Space*; Hayden, *The Grand Domestic Revolution* and *Redesign-
     ing the American Dream*; Massey, *Spatial Divisions of Labor*, *Space, Place, and Gen-
     der*, and *For Space*; Spain, *Gendered Spaces*.

16 Ahmed, *A Border Passage*, 181.

17 See Booth, *May Her Likes Be Multiplied*, chap. 8; Booth, "John Stuart Mill . . .
     Islamist?"; Mernissi, *The Veil and the Male Elite*.

18 Mernissi, *The Veil and the Male Elite*, 99.

19 See, for example, Shaarawi, *Harem Years*; Mernissi, *Dreams of Trespass*.

20 See also a collection of excerpts from these sources: Lewis and Micklewright,
     Gender, Modernity and Liberty. For a review of this series, see Booth, "Armchair
     Harems."

21 Malek Alloula's early and influential work remains important and has been joined
     by many more-recent studies. See Alloula, *The Colonial Harem*; DelPlato, *Multiple
     Wives, Multiple Pleasures*; Graham-Brown, *Images of Women*; Lewis, *Rethinking
     Orientalism*; Melman, *Women's Orients*; Yeazell, *Harems of the Mind*.

22 See Lal, *Domesticity and Power in the Early Mughal World*; Peirce, *The Imperial
     Harem* and *Morality Tales*.

23 See Göle, *The Forbidden Modern*; Schick, *The Erotic Margin*; Yeğenoğlu, *Colonial
     Fantasies*.

24 Lewis, *Rethinking Orientalism*, 14.

25 Melek Hanım, *Thirty Years in the Harem*, 12–13, 25, 28–29, 20–21, 182, 41.

26 See for example Spain, *Gendered Spaces*, chap. 2. Spain's move from specific anthro-
     pological examples and geographical sites to general commentary on "Islamic pur-
     dah" is very problematic, especially with her use of the "timeless" present tense and
     her tendency to slip among categories such as Muslim, Arab, and Indian, while
     failing to define what she means by "Islamic nations" (51).

27 Mernissi, *Dreams of Trespass*, chap. 1.

28 Ibid., 19.

29 Ibid., 35.

30 Afsaruddin, "Introduction," 7.

PART I · NORMATIVE IMAGES AND SHIFTING SPACES

The chapters with which we open suggest that in the centuries after Islam emerged, representing spaces as inhabited (or not) by women quickly became, as Asma Afsaruddin puts it in chapter 1, integral to the "highly contested issues" of "women's visibility and activity outside the home." She argues that normative constructions of the figures of the Prophet's female associates, as role models for later women, increasingly emphasized domestic seclusion. In chapter 2, Yaseen Noorani also addresses normative constructions of women's and men's assignment to social space, but he argues that early Islamic literary discourses represent spatial differentiation in terms more of social relationships than of clearly defined spaces. Concepts of the self underlie this emphasis on social relationships, specifically "women's relationship to the man in authority over them." These early discourses do not name the harem as an institution because, Noorani finds, the related form *hurma* is more important, signifying "the sanctity and inviolability of a person or thing." Similarly, in chapter 3, İrvin Schick emphasizes the double significance of *harem* and related words as referring to both spaces and categories of people. All three authors suggest that the harem as a spatial concept cannot be equated with, or even necessarily understood in terms of, concepts of public and private as they have developed in modernity. Moreover, these literary constructions of lived spaces are fluctuating and permeable, even as they section off a sphere of contained space as that of women and the family. The constructions have lasting importance, for the texts that Afsaruddin and Noorani analyze are ones that came to hold revered places as normative texts and as part of the high literature of Arabic tradition.

One question that these chapters implicitly raise—and it is a question that will hover throughout the book—is: how does the representation of space begin to shape the embodiment of its inhabitants? That is, do descriptions and assumptions about what kinds of spaces women or men belong in begin to drape, and reshape, those figures? In the placement of the body, the hand, and the foot, do these writers signal a necessary spatial disposition of the body?

1 • EARLY WOMEN EXEMPLARS AND THE CONSTRUCTION OF GENDERED SPACE

(Re-)Defining Feminine Moral Excellence

Asma Afsaruddin

 Muslim women's presence in what is conventionally described as the public sphere—along with their right to be there—has been a highly fraught issue throughout much of Islamic social and cultural history. It is a question that has occupied the minds of jurists and theologians of different stripes, who sought to clearly demarcate the spatial boundaries of acceptable feminine conduct and determine its legal and moral valence. To judge by biographical literature and advice manuals composed for women after the second century of Islam (the eighth century of the common era), it is clear that women's visibility and activity outside the home became highly contested issues in juridical and theological circles. A literary cult of domesticity apparently grounded in religious texts and hallowed praxis came to be propagated in these circles, and seclusion in the home was promoted as the defining feature of feminine moral excellence. To a considerable extent, the legal and theological hermeneutics of these scholars on this matter were based on appeals to the normative behavioral precedents set by the Sahabiyyat (singular, Sahabiyya), the female Companions of the Prophet Muhammad. As the Prophet's closest female associates and relatives, their conduct and actions as recorded for us in official biographies were deemed to have met with Muhammad's approval, and thus they were held up as morally exemplary and prescriptive for later generations of Muslim women. Biographies through time remain, therefore, an invaluable source for assessing how the Sahabiyyat were invoked as role models through the centuries. Furthermore, they allow us to plot the transformations that occurred in the progressive recounting of these accounts, and to evaluate the significance of these transformations.[1]

As our ensuing discussion demonstrates, early biographers (roughly, those before the fifth/eleventh century) when discussing the lives of the Sahabiyyat showed relatively little concern for general moralizing about the desirability or undesirability of women's access to the public sphere. Instead, early biographers tended to provide a more factual, straightforward recounting of relevant details of the women's lives. After all, the harem did not yet exist in the time of the female Companions, and these early biographers in general showed little inclination to inscribe the restrictions of this later institution onto the bodies of these first-generation Muslim women. It is worthy of note that the Arabic word *harīm* does not occur in these early biographical works. In comparison, biographers writing after the fifth/eleventh century exercised quite a bit of poetic license to ensure that the gendered notions of space that had hardened into near-dogma by their time found anachronistic reflection in the lives of the earliest Muslim women, in order to validate and mandate the institution of the harem.

This chapter focuses on certain prominent female personalities from the first generation of Muslims, considering how the details of their lives — particularly their entry into the public sphere as warriors, relief workers, and religious leaders — are depicted primarily in two major biographical works from different eras. The women selected for this study are not among the Prophet's female relatives and wives, the best-known female Companions, but are lesser-known ones who have earned their right to be in these biographical works through the invocation of specific criteria. This chapter thus deliberately eschews entries on the traditional "First Ladies of Islam," so to speak, since their kinship with Muhammad through blood and marriage would have been the paramount criterion undergirding their selection as Companions and would have automatically guaranteed their inclusion in the biographical works. Two purposes of this study are to determine what specific factors, in the absence of such kinship, contributed to the valorization of these women as distinguished members of the first generation of Muslims, and to investigate whether gender played a significant role in the criteria invoked to assess their moral excellence. Another objective is to plot the transformations occurring over time in the conceptualization of women's roles and their access to the public sphere, which increasingly came to be regarded as an almost exclusively masculine domain.

The two well-known biographical works used in this study are the *Kitab al-Tabaqat al-kubra* (the book of the great generations), by Muhammad Ibn Sa'd (d. 230/844–45),[2] and *al-Isaba fi tamyiz al-sahaba* (the correct apprehension of the distinctive status of the Companions"), by Ibn Hajar al-'Asqalani (d. 852/1449).[3] A third biographical work occasionally referred to herein is *al-Isti'ab fi ma'rifat al-ashab* (grasping the knowledge of the Companions"), by the Cordoban scholar Ibn 'Abd al-Barr (d. 463/1070).[4] Ibn Sa'd lived and worked during the heyday of the Abbasid era (133/750–648/1250) as did Ibn 'Abd al-Barr, although physically and culturally the latter belongs to the Andalusian environment, while Ibn Hajar was a product of the Mamluk era (648/1250–992/1517). These three biographical dictionaries are probably the most frequently consulted works dealing with the Companions and have accordingly played a foundational role in shaping popular perceptions of these moral exemplars who lived in the first century of Islam. Comparing their portrayals of specific Sahabiyyat, I will focus on how certain details of these portrayals were amended or reworked (or not) over time, and what the resulting insights can tell us about changing conceptions of women's moral excellence and their public roles in Muslim societies through the late medieval period.

In conjunction with biographical works, prescriptive manuals composed in the late Seljuk and Mamluk periods which instruct women on "proper" behavior are instructive. Such manuals are highly important indices of societal attitudes concerning women's presence in the public sphere at this time; they allow us to further plot critical transformations in the conceptualization of women's roles when compared to the earliest period of Islam. Tellingly, such manuals, which focused on reinforcing the harem as the locus par excellence for the virtuous female, are not to be found in the earlier period.

TELLING LIVES: WOMEN EMIGRANTS FROM MECCA TO MEDINA

We begin by glimpsing the recorded lives of select women from among the Meccan emigrants to Medina—who are known in Arabic as *al-muhajirat*—many of whom were fleeing from the persecution of the pagan Meccans opposed to the propagation of Islam. The following women are among those who appear in the section in Ibn Sa'd's *Tabaqat* titled "Naming the Women Who Pledged Allegiance from among the Quraysh, Their Allies [*hulafa'ihim*], Their Clients [*mawalihim*], and Relatively Unknown Women from among the Arabs in General [*wa-ghara'ib nisa' al-'arab*]." I will not discuss each biographical entry as a whole but rather will select certain points that I find to be illuminating of the central concerns of this chapter.

Umm Ayman was the nurse and a freedwoman of the Prophet; she later married Zayd b. Haritha, Muhammad's adopted son and freedman. Her exceptionally high standing among the Companions is indicated in the following two *hadiths*.[5] In the first one, an unnamed shaykh from the Banu Sa'd b. Bakr reports: "The Messenger of God, peace and blessings be upon him, used to address Umm Ayman as 'my mother.' And when he would look at her, he would say, 'This lady is what remains of my family [*baqiyyat ahl bayti*].'"[6] The second hadith is reported by Sufyan b. 'Uqba, who said: "The Messenger of God, peace and blessings be upon him, said, 'Whoever wishes to marry a woman from among the dwellers of heaven, let him marry Umm Ayman.'"[7]

Ibn Sa'd highlights Umm Ayman's participation in several of the major battles in early Islam. She was present on the battlefield at Uhud in 4/625, where she is said to have fed the thirsty and nursed the wounded, and she witnessed the battle of Khaybar (7/628) as well. She is also said to have been present at the battle of Hunayn (8/630), where she invoked God's curse on the opposing army, for which she was gently rebuked by the Prophet.[8]

Umm Kulthum bt. 'Uqba's preeminence in early Islam is signaled in the following way. She is said to have accepted Islam in Mecca and given her allegiance (*bay'a*) to the Prophet before the emigration from Mecca to Medina. She is described as having been the first woman to emigrate from Mecca to Medina, escaping immediately after the Prophet. As Ibn Sa'd puts it, Umm Kulthum's particular claim to distinction lies in the fact that "we know of no female Qurayshi other than Umm Kulthum bt. 'Uqba who left her parents as a Muslim woman, emigrating to God and His Messenger."[9]

The dramatic circumstances in which Umm Kulthum made her escape throw into relief her unusual courage, and these circumstances are said to have occasioned the revelation of a specific Qur'anic verse. As related by Ibn Sa'd, Umm Kulthum left Mecca by herself and arrived in Medina at the time of the treaty of al-Hudaybiyya (6/627–28), accompanied at this time by an unnamed man from the tribe of Khuza'a. Her two brothers, al-Walid and 'Umara, who were opposed to her emigration, set out in hot pursuit of her and reached Medina the morning after her arrival. They implored the Prophet to return her to them, according to the terms of the treaty of al-Hudaybiyya. As is well known, those terms stipulated that any Meccan wishing to join the Muslims in Medina would have to be returned to Mecca, whereas anyone from Medina who went over to the Meccans would not have to be returned to the Muslims.[10] On hearing her brothers' request, Umm Kulthum is quoted as responding: "O Messenger of God, I am a woman, and a woman's situation as you know is [similar to] that of the weak. If you were to return me to the unbelievers, they might torture me on account of my religion and I would not be able to endure it." The Qur'anic revelation is then said to have come down, allowing for a special dispensation for the women refugees from Mecca, who would be allowed to remain in Medina after their sincerity of purpose and firm conversion to Islam had been ascertained. This particular Qur'anic verse, part of Surat al-Mumtahana (Qur'an 60:10), says: "O those who believe, whenever believing women come to you as refugees, examine them, God knows best of their faith, so if you recognize them to be believing women, do not send them back to the unbelievers; such women are not lawful for them nor are such men lawful for them."

After this revelation, women were not sent back to Mecca but rather were queried regarding their intentions in emigrating. Ibn Sa'd reports that the Prophet is said to have addressed some of these remarkable women emigrants thus: "Nothing but love for God, His Messenger, and Islam has brought you out [of your homes], and you have not come out [seeking] a husband or wealth." Umm Kulthum's situation thus provides the *sabab al-nuzul* (the occasion of revelation) for this particular verse.[11] Biographical accounts that point to this occasion of revelation in turn highlight Umm Kulthum's exemplary piety and courage.

Umayya[?] bt. Qays accepted Islam after the emigration to Medina and, in the words of Ibn Sa'd, "witnessed Khaybar with the Messenger of God, peace and blessings be upon him." Ibn Sa'd preserves an account from Umayya herself, in which she relates that she, along with a group of women from her tribe, the Banu Ghifar, asked permission of the Prophet to "go out with you to this destination of yours, that is Khaybar, so that we may tend to the wounded and help the Muslims to the best of our ability." The Prophet replied, "With the blessing of God," and therefore she and the other women set off for Khaybar. Umayya is described at this time as a young girl who had just reached puberty. Due to her participation in the battle, she won a share of the booty, which was a necklace that the Prophet himself fastened around her neck.[12]

Umm Sinan al-Aslamiyya accepted Islam and gave her allegiance to the Prophet after the *hijra*. When she offered her allegiance, she relates, Muhammad glanced at her hand and remarked that women should not alter the appearance of their hands—an incident that I will discuss further below. She is reported as saying that only women who were apparently past marriageable age would emerge for the Friday congregational prayer (*al-jumʿa*) and the two ʿId prayers in her time.[13] This remark is noteworthy, for it highlights an interesting paradox in some of these depictions of the Sahabiyyat: apparently women who enthusiastically departed for the battlefield primarily populated by men did not [or could not] attend congregational prayers in the Prophet's mosque, a point to which we will return later.

Umm Sinan is also said to have requested permission to go to Khaybar with the Prophet, primarily to tend the sick and the wounded. The Prophet granted permission in practically the identical words spoken to Umayya, telling Umm Sinan: "Go with the blessing of God." When she expressed a preference to be with the Prophet rather than with members of her tribe (*qawmiha*), he told her: "Be with Umm Salama, my wife." This statement makes it clear that Umm Salama also accompanied the Prophet to Khaybar.[14]

Kuʿayba bt. Saʿd al-Aslamiyya gave her allegiance to the Prophet after the emigration to Medina, and she is said to have had a tent set up for her in the mosque at Medina, where she tended to the sick and the wounded. Saʿd b. Muʿadh is said to have received treatment at her hands after he was wounded at Khandaq, until he died. Kuʿayba is also said to have been present at Khaybar.[15] This additional example of a woman being present on the battlefield suffices to show that this was not an exceptional activity for the Sahabiyyat.

Compared to the above accounts, it is interesting to note the case of Umm Kabsha, who is described by Ibn Saʿd simply as a "woman from [the tribe of] Qudaʿa." She is said to have accepted Islam (we may assume somewhat late, since the time period is not specifically mentioned and early conversion was a matter of pride) and related a hadith from the Prophet. The reason her entry particularly catches our eye is that she is said to have requested permission from the Prophet to go into battle with him (*an taghzu* ma'ahu), and he refused. She then implored: "O Messenger of God, I will take care of the wounded and tend to the sick." But the Prophet told her: "Stay behind, so that people may not say that Muhammad fights alongside women."[16] Ibn Saʿd does not mention which specific battle provides the backdrop to this account. However, when we look at Ibn Hajar's entry on Umm Kabsha, we find more details regarding the event which allow him, and us, to evaluate the significance of this report and its subtext. We shall return to this important subject later.

Sometimes the entries on individual women are very short, but they convey the most relevant details about the life and justify the woman's inclusion in these works. Umm Habiba bt. Nabati al-Asadi earns only one sentence from Ibn Saʿd, in which he states that she accepted Islam, pledged allegiance to the Prophet, and emigrated to Medina along with other family members. Short and pithy though this entry is, it clearly establishes this subject's claim to priority or precedence in Islam (in Arabic, sabiqa), a very important concept in early Islam, about which more will be said later.

THE WOMEN OF MEDINA

The Ansar, or "helpers" of the Meccan emigrants in Medina, were those living in and around Medina who accepted Islam either before or soon after 622 CE, the year the hijra to Medina began, and they included quite a number of celebrated females. Like many of the muhajirat, these women helpers win their place in the biographical collections on account of their personal piety and meritorious deeds.

Nusayba bt. Kaʿb was better known as Umm ʿUmara, a celebrated figure from the Banu Najjar. Ibn Saʿd devotes what amounts to three and a half pages of print to the recounting of her exploits. According to him, Umm ʿUmara gave her allegiance to the Prophet on the night of ʿAqaba,[17] and eventually witnessed several key events of early Islam: she was present at the battles of Uhud (4/625), al-Hudaybiyya (6/627–28), Khaybar (7/628), Hunayn (8/630), and al-Yamama (12/633–34). At Uhud, she was with her husband, Ghaziyya b. ʿAmr, and her two sons. Ibn Saʿd tells us that the valiant Umm ʿUmara had headed for Uhud with the intention of quenching the thirst of the combatants but soon found herself fighting against the enemy. In the course of the battle, she is said to have sustained twelve wounds to her body, inflicted by either a spear or a sword.

Ibn Saʿd includes a detailed account from Umm ʿUmara, who confided the following details to another woman, Umm Sa'id, when the latter asked her precisely what had happened on that day. According to Umm 'Umara, she had gone out to the battlefield in the early part of the day, carrying her waterskin for the thirsty, and worked her way through the battlefield until she reached the Prophet. As the tide of the battle began to turn against the Muslims, she remained by the side of the Prophet and began to fight, defending him with a sword and a bow and arrow, until she was severely injured. Umm Sa'id then comments on the deep gash that she observed across Umm 'Umara's shoulders and asked the latter to identify her assailant. Umm 'Umara replied that it was Ibn Qumay'a, fighting on the pagan Meccan side and shouting: "Point out Muhammad to me, for I will not have succeeded if he escapes!" Umm 'Umara was among the group of people who converged on the Prophet to defend him, as a consequence of which she suffered severe wounds. She makes it clear, however, that she was able to get in a few good thrusts herself at Ibn Qumay'a, but, as she comments ruefully, "the enemy of God had on two plates of armor."[18] The Prophet himself commented on Umm 'Umara's valor: "Indeed the position of Nusayba bt. Ka'b today is higher than the position of such-and-such people [*fulan wa-fulan*]." She is also said to have lost a hand at al-Yamama during the battle fought against the false prophet Musaylima from the Banu Hanifa, after the fall of Mecca in 9/630. She heard hadiths from the Prophet and transmitted from him. Umm 'Umara's stature remained high among the early Muslims after the Prophet's death; it is said that Abu Bakr would frequently inquire about her after he became caliph.[19]

It should be pointed out that there is another female Ansari Companion with the name of Umm 'Umara, who is distinguished from the first by being called Umm 'Umara al-Ansari. Ibn Sa'd does not refer to her in his biographical work, but Ibn Hajar does in his. According to Ibn Hajar, Umm 'Umara al-Ansari is the female Companion who remarked to the Prophet regarding the Qur'anic revelations up to that point: "I see that everything pertains to men; I do not see the mention of women." Subsequently the following verse was revealed: "Indeed those who submit to God and accept the true Faith; who are devout, sincere, patient, humble, charitable, and chaste; who fast and are ever mindful of God—on these, both men and women, God will bestow forgiveness and a rich reward" (Qur'an 33:35).[20] According to Ibn Sa'd, it was actually Umm Salama, the Prophet's wife, who had remarked that women had not been specifically mentioned so far in the revelations. Ibn Sa'd records her comment as part of the occasion of revelation for this verse.[21] We will return to Umm 'Umara shortly.

The entry on Umm Waraqa bt. 'Abd Allah b. al-Harith follows a pattern that we have now come to expect. Ibn Sa'd mentions in the first sentence of this entry that Umm Waraqa accepted Islam, gave her allegiance to Muhammad, and related hadiths from him. She is said to have memorized the Qur'an, and the Prophet asked her to lead her household in prayer (*ta'umm ahl dariha*).[22] She also hired a (male) caller to prayer (muezzin; in Arabic, *mu'adhdhin*). The Prophet visited her frequently, and he conferred on her the epithet "the martyred woman" (*al-shahida*). At the battle of Badr, Umm Waraqa entreated Muhammad to let her accompany him to the battlefield and tend the wounded so that "perhaps God may grant me martyrdom [*shahada*]." The Prophet assured her that God would grant her martyrdom. Ibn Sa'd further records that Umm Waraqa continued to lead the members of her household in prayer until two servants, a male and a female, who were under her charge murdered her during 'Umar's caliphate and fled. They were brought back by 'Umar and crucified, being the first to suffer this fate in Medina. 'Umar is then said to have remarked that "the Messenger of God spoke the truth when he used to say, 'let us go and visit al-Shahida.'"[23]

Most of the other entries on the Ansari women are fairly short. Like their Muhajiri counterparts, the Ansari women are introduced with their names going back usually to their paternal great-great-great-grandfather, with their mother's name listed thereafter. (Sometimes a woman is identified immediately after her patronymic, that part of her name which identifies her as the daughter of so-and-so, or as the sister or other relative of someone already known to the reader. The names of the husbands of these women are frequently, but not always, given; the same holds for the names of their siblings.) The basic information always included in this kind of entry is that the Sahabiyya under discussion accepted Islam and gave her allegiance to the Messenger of God, acts that establish her individual moral and political agency. When her acceptance of Islam was very early or historically significant in some other way, this fact is underscored. For example, Layla bt. al-Khatim is identified by Ibn Sa'd as the first woman to give her allegiance after the Prophet arrived in Medina, along with her two daughters and two granddaughters.[24] Among the Muhajirat, Asma' bt. Abi Bakr, for example, is described as having accepted Islam early (*asolamat qadiman*), a point of distinction that established her precedence in Islam and her moral excellence.[25]

FROM IBN SA'D'S NARRATIVES TO IBN HAJAR'S ENTRIES

We will now turn our attention to Ibn Hajar's biographical work, composed in the ninth/fifteenth century, to scrutinize its entries on the women introduced above. Comparing them to Ibn Sa'd's entries, we find that many of the accounts in Ibn Hajar's *al-Isaba* are taken almost verbatim from Ibn Sa'd. Ibn Sa'd's third/ninth-century work is specifically mentioned by Ibn Hajar as one of the most important sources for his compilation. Therefore, Ibn Hajar, like Ibn Sa'd, documents each woman's priority in accepting Islam and doing so out of sincere conviction, her individual bay'a to the Prophet, her emigration from Mecca to Medina, and, when applicable, her transmission of hadith(s) from Muhammad. These biographical details clearly establish each woman's sabiqa—that is, her priority in conversion and service to Islam in its early period. The criteria invoked to justify the inclusion of these female Companions in these biographical accounts of illustrious personages from the earliest period of Islam, are basically the same as those invoked in the case of the male Companions of the same period.

Women, like men, are described as participating in these momentous and very public events. Gender appears to have made no perceptible difference in the set of criteria invoked to gauge the moral excellence and precedence of the Companions. Male and female Companions are equally assigned moral excellence on the basis of commonly accepted criteria of priority and prominence in service to Islam. Sabiqa was a powerful, highly emotive term, based on Qur'anic verses such as Surat al-Tawba, 9:100, which states: "God is satisfied with those who preceded foremost [*al-sabiqun al-awwalun*] from among the Muhajirun and the Ansar and those who followed them in charity and they are pleased with Him, and He has prepared for them gardens below which flow rivers where they will dwell forever; that is the great victory." Two other verses that emphasize this notion of sabiqa are Surat al-Waqi'a, 56:10–12, which states: "Those who precede are the ones who precede [*al-sabiqun al-sabiqun*], they are those who will be brought near [to God] in the gardens of bliss"; and Surat al-Hadid, 57:10, which states: "Those among you who spent and fought before the victory are not of the same rank [as others] but greater in rank than those who spent and fought afterwards." These verses were deployed to assign the greatest moral excellence and precedence to the Companions of the Prophet in general. Sabiqa was grounded in early and sincere conversion to Islam, emigration to Medina, and giving one's pledge to the Prophet, particularly during the meeting at 'Aqaba (621 CE) or during the Hudaybiyya episode. It was also grounded in meritorious loyalty to the Prophet and the cause of Islam, often expressed in service on the battlefield.

These biographical entries on the female Companions clearly assign independent agency and initiative to them in making the decisions that they did. The entries clearly indicate the women's personal choice in accepting Islam and explicitly state that they individually and vocally gave allegiance to the Prophet. Like the comparable entries for the male Companions, the biographical accounts of the female Companions make the women the chief protagonists.

However, when we compare the minutiae of specific entries on certain female Companions, we find Ibn Hajar deviating occasionally from Ibn Sa'd's presentations. As slight as they may seem, such rhetorical deviations are highly revealing of how societal conceptions of women's agency and proper conduct in the public realm came to be progressively defined and restricted in the late medieval Muslim world, and how these later conceptions came to be inserted into the biographies of the earliest Muslim women. Establishing such a mimetic continuity legitimated restrictions placed on women's agency and their increasing domestication or separation from men.

For example, in comparing Ibn Sa'd's and Ibn Hajar's entries on our heroic female warrior, Umm 'Umara or Nusayba bt. Ka'b, I found different emphases on different events. In his three-and-a-half-page entry, Ibn Sa'd mentions her pledge to the Prophet and her participation in many of the key events of early Islam. He then relates four variant accounts of her valiant defense of the Prophet during the battle of Uhud that emanate from different sources. Ibn Sa'd also reports that she was responsible for disseminating the hadith, according to which the Prophet said: "When someone eats in front of a fasting person, the angels pray for him—that is, the fasting person—or bless him."[26]

Ibn Hajar provides these basic details as well in his entry on Umm 'Umara but emphasizes different details. His entry is only about a quarter as long as Ibn Sa'd's. Given Ibn Hajar's special interest in hadith and its transmitters,[27] it is not surprising to see that he foregrounds the report relating Umm 'Umara's transmission of the hadith regarding eating before a fasting person. Like Ibn Sa'd, he then goes on to document Umm 'Umara's witnessing of the early major events in Islam. When Ibn Hajar reaches the part where she is waiting to offer her allegiance to the Prophet, he dwells on the fact that the men offered their allegiances by directly taking the Prophet's hand into their own. Umm 'Umara's husband, whose name is given as 'Araba b. 'Amr,[28] then draws the Prophet's attention to the presence of Umm 'Umara and another woman, Umm Mani'a, who were waiting to declare their allegiance. 'Araba said directly to the Prophet: "These are two women who came with us to declare their loyalty to you." The Prophet replied: "I have [already] taken their pledges according to the pledges I took from you; for indeed I do not shake hands with women."[29]

This incident does not appear in Ibn Sa'd's entry on Umm 'Umara/Nusayba bt. Ka'b. He does list an Umm 'Umara in his prefatory section on the women companions, where he recounts the anecdote concerning her and Umm Mani'a. But since he does not include this report under Nusayba's name, it is clear that he understood them to be two different individuals. Ibn 'Abd al-Barr also indicates the possibility of two women sharing the *kunya*[30] Umm 'Umara, leading to confusion regarding their exact identities.[31] Ibn Hajar, however, conflates these two women without apparently being aware of this problem, resulting in interesting consequences for the portrayal of Nusayba. Ibn Hajar's insertion of this account of how Umm 'Umara's allegiance was taken—and I deliberately use the passive voice here—diminishes her full agency in the commission of this act, contrary to what we are led to understand from several accounts in Ibn Sa'd's work about women offering their allegiance. Umm 'Umara's presence, together with Umm Mani'a's, and her intention are made known to the Prophet through the mediation of a man, Umm 'Umara's husband; the two women appear to have remained silent during the entire procedure. Their femaleness and thus their different status seem to be underscored here, and we sense that there is an attendant diminution in the value attached to a woman's individual pledge of allegiance.

The way women offered allegiance is in fact an important issue for some of our biographers and necessitates a digression here. At the beginning of his section on women in the *Tabaqat*, Ibn Sa'd includes in a fairly lengthy excursus references to the special modes of allegiance given by the female Companions to the Prophet. According to Ibn Sa'd, in some instances Muhammad is said to have accepted the bay'a from women with his hand draped in a garment (presumably to avoid skin-to-skin contact)—according to some accounts, specifically a yellow garment, or in other accounts, a cloak (*burda*). When women took the oath of allegiance, they had to swear that they would not associate anything with God, steal, commit fornication, kill their children, or lie.[32] In one instance, the women specifically asked the Prophet if he would shake their hands. He demurred, saying he did not shake hands with women, and that his speaking to a single woman was like his speaking to a hundred women. According to another account, when the Prophet arrived in Medina, several women accepted Islam and wished to give their allegiance to him. Ibn Sa'd reports that the women said: "O Messenger of God, our men have given their allegiance to you and we wish to do the same." The Prophet then called for a pitcher of water, dipped his hand into it, and passed the pitcher around to the women, each of whom did likewise.[33] From these and other variant accounts, it is clear that women were expected to give their allegiances to the Prophet separately from the men and that their public pledge of allegiance did matter, even though their mode of offering it apparently differed from that of the men. There seems to be some difference of opinion about whether allegiance should be given in an individual manner or en masse. The reports that the women gave their allegiance individually are more numerous; and that this was the preferred mode is suggested by the accounts that go to the trouble of pointing out how this could be effected without physical contact between the Prophet and the Sahabiyyat.

In fact, the individual accounts of the female Companions offering their allegiance sometimes belie Ibn Sa'd's editorial comments which, in deference to the sensibilities of his third/ninth-century (presumably chiefly male) audience, seek to establish a degree of physical distance between Muhammad and the Sahabiyyat. A case in point is the aforementioned Umm Sinan al-Aslamiyya, who is clearly depicted in all three of the biographical works consulted as personally giving her allegiance to the Prophet, which clearly involved some gesture with her bare hand, since he remarks on its appearance.[34]

To return to Ibn Hajar: after the bay'a episode that he recounts in the entry on Umm 'Umara, we then lamely proceed to a single account of her bravery on the battlefield, her valiant defense of the Prophet and the serious wounds that she suffered, and the Prophet's awareness of her martial prowess. The fulsome prophetic praise that Umm 'Umara earned as a consequence, reported by Ibn Sa'd—to the effect that Muhammad declared her to have the highest status of all Muslims on the day of Uhud—is not repeated by Ibn Hajar. Coming on the heels of the allegiance episode in which Umm 'Umara plays the role of the silent spectator, this single account of her valor in Ibn Hajar's entry falls relatively flat, compared to the four breathtaking accounts of her exploits recorded by Ibn Sa'd.

Ibn Hajar's other entries on individual women show similar slight alter-

ations or shifts in emphases or nuances that are significant for tracing a specific evolution in societal conceptions of feminine propriety and conduct,
including their public and visible roles in the Muslim community. One instance where the differences between Ibn Sa'd's and Ibn Hajar's treatment
of the women's biographical material become quite obvious has to do with
women's participation in the battles of early Islam, a very public and traditionally masculine domain. We finally see a resolution in Ibn Hajar's biographical work with regard to what has clearly become a highly sensitive
issue in Umm Kabsha's case. To briefly refresh our memories, Ibn Sa'd describes Umm Kabsha simply as "a woman from [the tribe of] Quda'a," who
requested the Prophet's permission to take part in an unnamed battle. The
permission was denied, and Ibn Sa'd leaves it at that. Ibn Hajar, however,
makes of this event a cause célèbre. In his version of this report, Umm
Kabsha asks for permission to go out with such and such an army [*fi jaysh
kadha wa-kadha*]; again, as we can see, there is no reference to a specific
battle. The Prophet responds categorically by simply saying: "No." At this
point, Umm Kabsha pleads with him and explicitly states that she does
not want to fight but only to tend the wounded and provide water. (In Ibn
Sa'd's account, she is not quoted as saying that she would not fight.) The
Prophet then replies: "I would have given you permission were it not for
the fact that it would become an established precedent [*sunna*], and thus it
would be said that such and such a female [*fulana*] had gone out [to battle].
So stay behind."[35]

Ibn Hajar then points out that the content of this single report is at odds
with another report referred to earlier, which mentions that Umm Sinan
al-Aslamiyya had been granted permission to go to the battlefield. The only
way to reconcile these two reports with their contradictory implications
is to maintain, according to Ibn Hajar, that the hadith concerning Umm
Kabsha abrogates [*nasikh*] the hadith concerning Umm Sinan. Ibn Hajar
states that the reason for this abrogation is due to the later provenance of
the Umm Kabsha report, which refers to an incident that occurred after
the conquest of Mecca [*al-fath*] in 9/630. Since the Umm Sinan report has
Khaybar as the backdrop and another report refers to the battle of Uhud,
both of which were earlier, the later report after the fath, according to Ibn
Hajar, must be considered to have superseded the earlier two.

How Ibn Hajar comes to know the historical context of the Umm Kabsha report is not explained. Ibn Sa'd, as I mentioned before, does not indicate a precise chronology for this report. Choosing the period after the

conquest of Mecca as the historical locus for this report makes possible the implication that women's participation in battles before the fall of Mecca was unobjectionable because everyone—male and female—had to contribute to the defense of Islam under the dire circumstances in which the small community of Muslims found itself at that time. After the fall of Mecca, such participation could be dispensed with, as Islam became the predominant religion in the Arabian peninsula and then a world civilization. By locating the Umm Kabsha report in the period after the fath, Ibn Hajar seems to want to underscore the fact that specific historical exigencies in the early period had made women's participation in certain battles necessary, perhaps even desirable. Once these exigencies ended, such participation was not only undesirable but downright objectionable. The fact that Umm Kabsha is cited in Ibn Hajar's version as specifically disavowing armed combat and desiring only to aid the wounded and the thirsty is also very significant. Ibn Hajar leaves no doubt in the reader's mind that it was not potentially a combatant's role that was being denied to Umm Kabsha, but rather her physical presence itself on the battlefield, for even the most humanitarian of purposes.

In this discussion of abrogation of reports, Ibn Hajar does not refer to, or perhaps conveniently does not remember, the case of Umm 'Umara, who is said to have lost a hand at al-Yamama, a battle that was fought after the fall of Mecca in 12/633–34. However, both Ibn Sa'd and Ibn Hajar mention this historical detail about Umm 'Umara in their entries on her. One would be justified in remonstrating here that surely the conduct of a well-known Sahabiyya who had fought in a clearly identified battle after the fall of Mecca should have more of a bearing on Ibn Hajar's discussion of this sensitive issue than the case of Umm Kabsha, especially since the historical details about the latter are dubious at best. The Umm Kabsha episode, therefore, cannot provide a firm basis from which to derive categorical conclusions about the chronology involved, and this would also affect its status as an abrogating report. Ibn Hajar, however, appears to have clearly made up his mind regarding the latter-day propriety of women's presence on the battlefield—and by extension, in the public sphere in general—and therefore produces only the Umm Kabsha episode as a proof-text in defense of this position.

Given what we might describe as Ibn Hajar's propensity to look askance at women's presence on the battlefield as evident in the al-Isaba fi tamyiz al-sahaba, we should not be surprised that he chooses to make this point again in his carefully edited entry on Umm Waraqa, the Sahabiyya who had suffered a tragic fate at the hands of her servants. This event is reported and further embellished by Ibn Hajar; what catches our eye, however, is his omission of the following significant detail. Whereas Ibn Sa'd records that Umm Waraqa had led her household (which, since we are not told otherwise, must have consisted of male and female members) in prayer at the express request of the Prophet, Ibn Hajar makes no mention of this matter. He records rather that she asked the Prophet's permission to hire a male muezzin. Further doctoring on Ibn Hajar's part of the older version recorded by Ibn Sa'd becomes evident when the former launches into an explanation of the sobriquet "the martyred woman," conferred on Umm Waraqa by the Prophet. Ibn Hajar foregrounds the account of her asking Muhammad's permission to take part in the battle of Badr as a nurse; in his rendition of this event, the Prophet explicitly forbids her, using Qur'anic diction: "Remain [*qirri* or *qarri*][36] in your house; for indeed God will grant you martyrdom [in another way]." In case the import of this directive is lost on the reader at the first iteration, Ibn Hajar supplies a variant account in which Muhammad is quoted as counseling her even more bluntly: "Sit in your home [*uq'udi fi baytiki*], for indeed God will grant you martyrdom *in your house*" (emphasis added).[37] The tragic denouement to Umm Waraqa's life then teleologically falls into place: a woman can achieve the enviable status of a martyr by remaining (and only by remaining) within her home and carrying on her usual domestic activities, like the supervision of her servants.[38] Writing earlier in the fifth/eleventh century, in his entry on Umm Waraqa, Ibn 'Abd al-Barr relates that the Prophet responded in the following way to her plea to join him at Badr: "God will indeed grant you martyrdom, and remain [*qarri/qirri*] in your house, for you are [will be] a martyr"; this is similar but not identical to what Ibn Hajar records. Ibn 'Abd al-Barr does not record the second prophetic statement given by Ibn Hajar, which points to Umm Waraqa's own home as the site of her future martyrdom.[39] It is worth bearing in mind that Ibn Sa'd does not record the Prophet's injunction to "remain in your house," in response to Umm Waraqa's entreaty; in fact, the only prophetic response he records is Muhammad's assurance to her that she would indeed achieve martyrdom. Ibn Sa'd's version does not rule out the possibility that Umm Waraqa did accompany the Prophet to the battlefield; Muhammad's prescient statement simply presages her tragic end but does not express disapproval of her potential presence at Badr.

Given that we are now able to detect a certain editorial proclivity on Ibn Hajar's part, it is not surprising that Umm Waraqa's function as the imam of her household, mentioned by Ibn Sa'd and Ibn 'Abd al-Barr, goes unreported by him as well. Traditionally, superior knowledge of the Qur'an, which in itself is a hallmark of religious piety, confers moral excellence and, often, leadership status on the individual in various circumstances. This again is broadly in accordance with the principle of sabiqa, as defined above. This has been true for the leader (caliph or imam) of the Muslim polity in particular, particularly for the Rightly Guided Caliphs, as it has been for prayer leaders and other leaders in more circumscribed situations.[40] Ibn Sa'd refers to Umm Waraqa's memorization of the entire Qur'an and indicates that this qualification was the reason for her appointment as prayer leader for her household. The implication is clear: her superior knowledge of the Qur'an placed her ahead of the male members of her family in this respect, and a male relative could not trump her in this regard simply by virtue of being male. Ibn Hajar retains the reference to her memorization of the Qur'an—a laudable achievement for any Muslim, male or female— but denies her any recognition that may have ensued from this noteworthy achievement. Religious knowledge may not be denied to the female, of course, but she must not develop "uppity" notions on account of it—for example, believing herself thereby able to lead prayers for her mixed household. Elision of this inconvenient fact allows Ibn Hajar to document the life of this female Companion without allowing her to set a precedent for what appears by his time to be undesirable feminine activity.

That Ibn Hajar should construe some of the reports as he does and tailor their content to bring them into alignment with certain social expectations and sensibilities is explained by his cultural environment. In the Seljuk and Mamluk periods, theologians began to compose elaborate manuals explicating the parameters of proper feminine conduct. Essentially prescriptive in nature, such works dispensed advice on specific topics to contemporary women without necessarily invoking the lives of female Companions as models of emulation. One such manual is the *Ahkam al-nisa'* by the Hanbali theologian Ibn al-Jawzi (d. 597/1201), from the Seljuk period. Two chapters in particular in this work refer to the desirability of women cloistering themselves in their homes: chapter 26 is titled "Cautioning Women from Going Outside the Home" (*tahdhir al-nisa' min al-khuruj*), and chapter 27 is called "Mention of the Merit of [Staying] Home for Women" (*fi dhikr fadl al-bayt li-'l-mar'a*).[41] Ibn al-Jawzi begins chapter 26 by counseling women to avoid going out as much as possible. If a woman should be obliged to go out, she should do so only after obtaining her husband's permission, and she should be attired in shabby, unattractive clothes. She should try to wend her way through empty areas, avoiding busy thoroughfares and market-places. She should be careful not to have her voice heard in public, and if she should walk in the streets, she should stick to the sides and not walk in the middle of them.[42] In chapter 27, Ibn al-Jawzi records a report (not a prophetic one) in which the Companion 'Abd Allah Ibn Mas'ud remarks that if a woman emerges from her home, and her family members ask her, "Where are you headed?" and she replies, "I am going out to visit the sick" or "to pay my respect to a deceased person's family," then she is accompanied by the devil. Ibn Mas'ud is further quoted as saying that the woman instead finds favor in the sight of God by staying within the confines of her home and worshipping the Almighty.[43]

A miscellany of droll reports and "wise" counsel regarding women, titled *Akhbar al-nisa'* and attributed to another Hanbali theologian, Ibn Qayyim al-Jawziyya (d. 751/1350), from the eighth/fourteenth century, drives home the point that such attitudes had become firmly entrenched by the Mamluk period, at least among certain theologians. Even though the attribution of this work to Ibn Qayyim has been doubted,[44] the social and cultural attitudes toward women reflected in this work are much more typical of the post-Abbasid period. According to the author of *Akhbar al-nisa'*, a certain Bedouin Arab who is described as being quite concerned with women [*dha hamm bi-hinna*] said the ideal woman was, among other things, inclined "to stick to her home, valued among her relatives, [and] self-effacing."[45] In another chapter devoted to "the perfidy of women" (*ghadr al-nisa'*), the author records the following hadith without an *isnad* or any indication of its reliability: "Consult with women and do the opposite of what they recommend; for indeed in opposing them is blessing [*al-baraka*]."[46] It is note-worthy that such misogynistic counsel represents a dramatic departure from the report recorded by Ibn Sa'd, for example, about the most prominent Companions who sought 'A'isha's advice after Muhammad's death, particularly on the inheritance shares [*al-fara'id*].[47]

Reading such manuals makes us aware of the strong disjunction between the active, public, humanitarian roles played by Muslim women of the first generation—as depicted in Ibn Sa'd's *al-Tabaqat al-kubra*, for example—and the considerably diminished public roles imagined for Seljuk and Mamluk women. This disjunction is further reinforced by the fact that the earlier *Ahkam al-nisa'* work attributed to Ibn Hanbal from the third/ninth century is a much shorter work (at least according to the printed edition currently available)[48] and does not similarly emphasize women's seclusion in their homes. The majority of the chapters have to do with purity rituals and personal hygiene for women, modest clothing, and the permissibility of marital relations with the *ahl al-kitab*. One chapter that deals with the propriety of women's emergence from their homes has to do with the performance of the congregational prayer during the two 'Ids, the festivals after the month of Ramadan and after the completion of the pilgrimage during the month of Dhu 'l-Hijja.[49] It is significant that this chapter includes two reports, both attributed to Ibn Hanbal, which merely record his personal opinion on this matter. In both these reports, Ibn Hanbal (on being queried about this issue) expressly states that in his time he could not approve of such a custom, since women represented a source of distraction [*li-annahunna fitna*]. In contrast to the tone adopted by Ibn al-Jawzi in his manual, Ibn Hanbal records his opinion on the propriety of women going out for the 'Id prayers as just that: his personal opinion contingent on the specific historical circumstances of his time. His opinion is not undergirded by a prophetic or companion hadith to establish its authoritativeness; thus it may not be interpreted as a binding injunction for women in general. We may assume that Ibn Hanbal, a renowned traditionist and the compiler of a highly respected hadith collection—or the author of the *Ahkam* who ascribes these views to him—would not have hesitated to back up his opinion with a prophetic or companion report, if he had known of any. That he did not do so is a fair enough indication that there was none in circulation in his time, or at least none that he deemed reliable that would fit this context.[50]

One may be reminded at this point of the previously mentioned statement of Umm Sinan al-Aslamiyya, in which she affirms—according to Ibn Sa'd—that essentially only elderly women would take part in the Friday and 'Id congregational prayers during the time of the Prophet. As I commented earlier, this statement is rather peculiar within Ibn Sa'd's work, since so many of the female Companions he describes are so visibly active outside their homes. Why the apparent restraint on attending public congregational prayers when one could with apparent ease, as in the case of Umm Sinan and others, go off to the very masculine arena of the battlefield? The statement's peculiarity is compounded by the fact that women's presence in the mosque at Medina is documented in various sources, and we have prophetic reports recorded in authoritative hadith collections that expressly permit *all* (not just elderly) women to attend congregational prayers. A particularly well-attested hadith states, "Do not prevent God's female servants from attending the mosques of God."[51] Such paradoxes confirm that the process of "editing" the lives of Muslim women from the first generation and thus their roles as exemplars in mediating gendered issues of a later period was already under way in Ibn Saʿd's time.

By the Seljuk period, it clearly appears, therefore, that etiquette manuals composed for women, and literary and biographical works composed about women, came to place a disproportionate emphasis on the desirability of feminine seclusion when compared with earlier works on the same subject. This becomes most evident in the case of the *Ahkam al-nisa'* literature, when we compare the earlier work attributed to Ibn Hanbal from the third/ninth century to the work attributed to Ibn Qayyim in the Mamluk period. Appropriate reports, mostly companion reports, are sometimes affixed to the counsel dispensed to women in the later works, as we saw above, to establish its prescriptive nature.

I am not suggesting that this "progression" from women's greater access to the public sphere in the early centuries to a more circumscribed one in the later period is a strictly linear one, or that it exactly mirrors social realities (more on this point a little later). More comprehensive diachronic research, beyond the purview of this chapter, would be required before we could possibly claim to fully understand what was going on in the premodern period concerning gender. Women's public activities must have ebbed and flowed contingent on their surrounding sociopolitical circumstances and on their own socioeconomic status. One can only speculate at this point, but it is not unreasonable to assume that political and social turmoil in the Islamic world during the Seljuk and Mamluk periods had a considerable bearing on the shaping of distinctive attitudes at those times, at least in certain scholarly circles, toward women's mobility outside the home. The Seljuk period had already witnessed the depredations of the Crusaders, and the Mamluks had to do battle with the Mongols and deal with the havoc left in their wake. In such periods of social and political instability, societies often tend to turn inward and focus on regulating the domestic sphere, concentrating particularly on the public comportment of women, as a way to ward off uncontrollable change from without.[52] In such circumstances, men who are accustomed to running their own lives and their communities suddenly find themselves deposed from such positions of authority by other, more powerful men or find their power contested by rival forces. Tightening their hold over their women and restricting the latter's access to the public sphere allow the men to maintain the illusion of still being in control of their lives and of staving off undesirable change, at least on the home front.

Of course, the *Ahkam/Akhbar al-nisa'* works in themselves do not establish that women's social and economic roles were considerably curtailed in the Mamluk period; on the contrary, we have scholarly studies that document women's notable participation in certain economic, civic, and scholarly activities during this and the previous Seljuk periods.[53] What these manuals with their strident content do suggest is that feminine seclusion came to be regarded as a desideratum in certain influential circles and held up at least as a model to be emulated, very likely as a reaction to the greater participation of Mamluk women in the public sphere. Thus the existence of such works may serve instead as attestations of women's actual "transgressive" presence outside the home in this period, against which certain scholars felt obligated to construct ostensibly religious sanctions. Against this backdrop, Ibn Hajar seems to be participating in corroborating and disseminating an idealized image of the decorous, well-bred, and sequestered Mamluk lady in his rereading of the earlier biographical material of some of the Sahabiyyat.[54]

It is clear from this study that many women from the first generation of Muslims played robust and prominent public roles in their society. Recognition of these roles finds ample documentation in medieval biographical collections. Our survey firmly establishes that it was primarily these women's exemplary piety, their devotion to the Prophet, and their virtuous actions paralleling those of men which justified their inclusion in these collections of the earliest exceptional Muslims, and that gender did not significantly influence the choice of criteria in evaluating the moral excellence of the male and female Companions in the early period (roughly before the fifth/eleventh century). Common standards of moral excellence exemplified in the term *sabiqa*, which established the precedence of the Companions in meritorious service to Islam, were invoked equally for men and women in the early period. Recognition of the greater moral excellence of some of the Sahabiyyat and thus their precedence over other Muslims is codified, for example, in reports that guarantee paradise to them. As we know, there is a very well-known hadith that promises paradise to ten prominent early Companions, the *'ashara al-mubashshara*, all of whom are men.[55] In the biographical dictionaries, however, we find entries on individual women from among the Companions, like Umm Ayman, who are also promised Paradise for their exceptional standing within Islam. Such biographical entries make clear that certain pious women had also been singled out by the Prophet as destined for heavenly reward on a par with the ten distinguished male Companions, even though their names are not grouped together on a convenient list to indicate their enhanced status, as is the case for their masculine counterparts.

Gender, however, clearly leaves its imprint in the way some of the earlier biographical accounts are reread and their narrative strands sifted and reconstituted by later compilers, in order to conform to certain views on the proper roles of women that had taken hold of the (male) Muslim social imaginary by the later medieval period—particularly in regard to women's activities in the public sphere. The *salaf*, the men and women of the first generation, were regarded as the pious forebears of Muslims everywhere and as the moral exemplars of the *umma*. Muslims strove to model their conduct on that of the pious forebears; strict sexual segregation that characterized late medieval Muslim societies was seen as being based on the social mores established by the salaf themselves, in accordance with their correct interpretation of religious prescriptions. The virtuous Muslim woman from the Abbasid period on, closeted in a circumscribed world of female relatives and companions and close male relatives, could thus imagine herself to be replicating the world of her pious female predecessors of the first century of Islam, thanks to the editorial intrepidity of certain biographical compilers. Through the excision of inconvenient details jarringly incongruous with the carefully crafted image of the female salaf, Ibn Hajar brings the biographical accounts of specific women, who were otherwise perfectly exemplary, into line with late medieval constructions of virtuous feminine identity.

Although never fully erasing mention of women's participation in the building of the early Muslim community and frequently paying handsome homage to them, later narratives—in tandem with sociocultural developments of the period—do nevertheless attenuate to a considerable extent the public, vital roles of these women and the full range of their activities, including in the religious sphere. Careful reading and comparisons of these valuable historical documents allow us, however, to restore full agency to these prominent women and to reconstruct the considerable impact of their diverse activities, valorized in their contemporary milieu.

NOTES

This chapter is adapted from an earlier version, "Reconstituting Women's Lives: Gender and the Poetics of Narrative in Medieval Biographical Collections," *Muslim World* 92, nos. 3–4 (2002): 461–80. I thank the editors of *Muslim World* for granting me permission to publish this article in its revised form. All translations are mine, unless otherwise indicated.

1 Ruth Roded considers the changing representation of individual female figures in Arabic biographical dictionaries in *Women in Islamic Biographical Collections*. Marilyn Booth, in *May Her Likes Be Multiplied*, discusses the use of premodern biographical dictionaries by more recent writers, and the changing representations of famous women from premodern to modern biographical compendiums and sketches.

2 For whom, see the *Encyclopaedia of Islam* (henceforth referred to as *EI²*), 3:922–23.

3 For whom, see ibid., 3:776–78.

4 For whom, see ibid., 3:674.

5 Hadiths are accounts of words and deeds traditionally attributed to the Prophet. Although they do not have the standing of divine revelation, and are therefore not included in the Qur'an itself, they constitute the second principal textual source for Islamic beliefs and the Muslim way of life.

6 Ibn Sa'd, *al-Tabaqat al-kubra*, 8:179.

7 Ibid.

8 Ibid., 8:180.

9 Ibid., 8:183.

10 For these terms, see Ibn Hisham, *al-Sira al-nabawiyya* (the Prophet's life), 2:784. See also the article "Al-Hudaybiyya," *EI²*, 3:539.

11 Al-Tabari in his Qur'an commentary *Jami 'a al-bayan fi ta'wil al-qur'an* (the compendium of eloquence concerning interpretation of the Qur'an), 12:66–67, does not refer to Umm Kulthum specifically in his explication of this verse but cites authorities who understood it to refer to women emigrants in general. Another exegete, al-Wahidi, refers to the case of a different woman, named Subay'a bt. al-Harith al-Aslamiyya, as occasioning the revelation of this verse; see his *Asbab al-nuzul* (the causes of revelation), 357. However, Ibn Sa'd does not relate Qur'an 60:10 to Subay'a in his entry on her (*al-Tabaqat al-kubra*, 8:224).

12 Ibn Sa'd, *al-Tabaqat al-kubra*, 8:228.

13 Ibid., 8:227.

14 Ibid.

15 Ibid., 8:226–27.

16 Ibid., 8:237–38.

17 For this event, which took place in 621 CE right before the hijra, see Ibn Hisham, *al-Sira al-nabawiyya* 1:299–300. See also "Sahaba," *EI²* 8:828; and "Akaba," *EI²* 1:314.

18 Ibn Sa'd, *al-Tabaqat al-kubra*, 8:303–4.

19 Ibid., 8:305.

20 Ibn Hajar, *al-Isaba fi tamyiz al-sahaba*, 8:262.

21 Ibn Sa'd, *al-Tabaqat al-kubra*, 8:334–35.

22 See Ahmed, *Women and Gender in Islam*, 61. Ahmed points out further that 'A'isha and Umm Salama had acted as imams for women during the Prophet's lifetime. However, 'Umar, the second caliph, apparently saw fit to appoint a male prayer leader for the women during his reign.

23 Ibn Sa'd, *al-Tabaqat al-kubra*, 8:334–35.

24 Ibid., 8:255.

25 See ibid., 8:200. The phrase *aslama* or *aslamat qadiman* occurs with some regularity in Ibn Sa'd's work in order to highlight the exceptional merit of those Companions, male and female, who accepted Islam very early. For a discussion of the early religious and social significance of these twin concepts of precedence and moral excellence (*sabiqa* and *fadl* or *fadila*, respectively), see Afsaruddin, *Excellence and Precedence*.

26 Ibn Sa'd, *al-Tabaqat al-kubra*, 8:306.

27 He is the author of several *rijal* works (works which assess the probity of individual transmitters of hadith), including the well-known *Tahdhib al-tahdhib*.

28 Ibn Sa'd gives his name as Ghaziyya b. 'Amr; Arabic orthography would allow the first name to be read as either Ghaziyya or 'Araba.

29 Ibn Hajar, *al-Isaba fi tamyiz al-sahaba*, 8:262.

30 A woman's *kunya* is the appellation identifying her as the mother of (usually) her oldest male child.

31 Ibn 'Abd al-Barr, *al-Isti'ab fi ma'rifat al-ashab*, 4:503.

32 See Qur'an 60:12.

33 Ibn Sa'd, *al-Tabaqat al-kubra*, 8:8.

34 For Ibn Sa'd's entry, see the preceding note. For the other two, see Ibn 'Abd al-Barr, *al-Isti'ab fi ma'rifat al-ashab*, 4:495; and Ibn Hajar, *al-Isaba fi tamyiz al-sahaba*, 8:244.

35 Ibn Hajar, *al-Isaba fi tamyiz al-sahaba*, 8:270.

36 The usage of this word here evokes Qur'an 33:33, "*wa-qarna fi buyutikunna*," commonly translated as "remain in your [feminine plural] homes." The imperative *qarna* remains problematic, however, since it is irregular and in its form here cannot categorically be linked to the verbs *qarra* or *waqara*, which would connote "to remain" and "to behave with dignity," respectively. For a brief discussion of this, see Stowasser, *Women in the Qur'an, Traditions, and Interpretation*, 172, note 79. Ibn Hajar's usage of the etymologically related imperative *qarri/qirri* shows that he has made up his mind regarding the contested semantics of this verse.

37 Ibn Hajar, *al-Isaba fi tamyiz al-sahaba*, 8:289.

38 This position is reflected in the *tafsir* literature in general. See, for example, Ibn Kathir (d. 775/1373), *Tafsir al-qur'an al-'azim* (commentary on the majestic Qur'an) 3:482, where he interprets Qur'an 33:33 as counseling the Prophet's wives "to remain in their homes."

39 Ibn 'Abd al-Barr, *al-Isti'ab fi ma'rifat al-ashab*, 4:519.

40 See Afsaruddin, "The Excellences of the Qur'an."

41 Ibn al-Jawzi, *Ahkam al-nisa'* (regulations pertaining to women), 68–71.

42 Ibid., 70.

43 Ibid., 72.

44 Basim Musallam (*Sex and Society in Islam*, 61) chooses to attribute this work to Ibn al-Jawzi without stating a reason. Hilary Kilpatrick ("Some Late 'Abbasid and Mamluk Books about Women," 69–75) also doubts its attribution to Ibn Qayyim but does not suggest another possible author.

45 [Ibn Qayyim al-Jawziyya?], *Akhbar al-nisa'* (information about women), 12.

46 Ibid., 103.

47 Ibn Sa'd, *al-Tabaqat al-kubra*, 8:52–53.

48 Ibn Hanbal, *Ahkam al-nisa.'*

49 Ibid., 46–47.

50 For an exercise in isnad analysis of what G. H. A. Juynboll terms "woman-demeaning sayings" attributed to the Prophet, see his "Some *Isnad*-analytical Methods Illustrated on the Basis of Several Woman-demeaning Sayings from *Hadith* Literature." This article indicates the possible problems with the reliability of such reports, particularly their provenance.

51 This hadith is recorded by al-Bukhari, Muslim, Abu Da'ud, Ibn Maja, al-Darimi, Malik b. Anas, and Ibn Hanbal; see Wensinck, *Concordance et indices de la tradition Musulmane* 1:123.

52 See Lutfi, "Manners and Customs of Fourteenth-Century Cairene Women," 101 and note 8, where she refers to al-Maqrizi, *al-Khitat al-Maqriziyya* (the Maqrizi plans) for evidence of such sentiments in the Mamluk period; and Ahmed, *Women and Gender*, 120. See also Mernissi, *The Veil and the Male Elite*, 99–100. This is hardly a phenomenon restricted to Muslim societies, though. Third world nationalist movements in general and recent Christian fundamentalist movements have focused on the regulation and "purification" of the private, domestic sphere on the assumption that this would then lead to national or social regeneration. See Jayawardena, *Feminism and Nationalism in the Third World*; Hunter, *Evangelicalism: The Coming Generation*; Rose, "Christian Fundamentalism."

53 See, for instance, Lutfi, "Manners and Customs of Fourteenth-Century Cairene Women," where she discusses in detail the contents of the work *al-Madkhal ila tanmiyat al-a'mal bi-tahsin al-niyyat* (entry into the flourishing of deeds with pure intentions), by the Mamluk scholar Ibn al-Hajj (d. 737/1336–37). In this work, Ibn al-Hajj shows himself to be clearly influenced by Ibn al-Jawzi's earlier prescriptive work on women and similarly rails against the public roles of women, which they appear to have carried on undaunted. For documentation of women's economic and other social activities during the Mamluk period, see, for example, 'Abd al-Raziq, *La femme au temps des Mamlouks en Egypte*; Lutfi, "Al-Sakhawi's *Kitab al-Nisa'*"; Petry, "Class Solidarity versus Gender Gain"; Chapoutot-Remadi, "Femmes dans la ville Mamluke"; Fay, "Women and Waqf." For Mamluk women's prominent roles in religious scholarship, see Afsaruddin, "Knowledge, Piety, and Religious Leadership."

54 This discourse would continue into the later period (and indeed continues today,

in the wake of Islamic resurgent movements): see Khouri, "Drawing Boundaries and Defining Spaces." It should also be pointed out that all Mamluk scholars did not regard women's nondomestic activities with a jaundiced eye. The well-known Mamluk scholar Shams al-Din Muhammad b. 'Abd al-Rahman al-Sakhawi (d. 1497), a student of Ibn Hajar, wrote the *Kitab al-Nisa'* (the book of women), the name popularly given to the last volume of his encyclopedic biographical work known as *al-Daw' al-lami' li-ahl al-qarn al-tasi'a* (the brilliant light belonging to the people of the ninth century), which remains one of the best sources for recovering the multiple, public roles played by women in the Mamluk period especially, particularly as scholars and teachers—a number of whom al-Sakhawi studied with and whose accomplishments he remembers with admiration and gratitude: see Afsaruddin, "Knowledge, Piety, and Religious Leadership."

55 See the entry on al-'ashara al-mubashshara in *EI²*, 3:674.

2 • NORMATIVE NOTIONS OF PUBLIC AND PRIVATE IN EARLY ISLAMIC CULTURE

Yaseen Noorani

Any attempt to understand early Islamic practices of female segregation or seclusion must take into account what normative notions were behind these practices. The Arabic poetic and literary tradition is an important source in this regard. Classical Arabic *adab* literature, with its abstract, conventional, and stylized modes of depiction, tells us very little about actual social practices. It tells us a great deal, however, about the normative notions that were operative in imagining and portraying moral and social order, and their legitimation of political authority. In particular, it shows that envisioning gender relations and gendered space in a specific manner was central to the representation of order and authority. The enormous body of poetic and expository discourses that deploy and redeploy these structures of representation establishes a normative model of gendered space that had a substantial presence within the literate culture. The widespread reproduction of this model seems to suggest that it continued to hold meaning and relevance in terms of its relation to actual social practices. In any case, such a model certainly provides key evidence of how literate elites thought about and imagined gendered space.

I will argue that the normative notions of gendered space operative in the texts that I consider do not correspond to the modern normative division between public and private. Whereas the modern division entails a private domestic sphere that is a preconstituted, role-defined space, the gendered space of early Islamic literary texts is a relational space defined by status. The modern division posits a private family domain consisting of roles and relations, including romantic love, which naturally generate public values. This private domain is thus internal to the public order. The representation of gendered space I will examine, however, makes passionate desire external to communal order, which comes into being only through the mastery and control of desire. Just as the elite male individual achieves self-integration and thus social virtue through his mastery of a fiery interiority consisting of chaotic desire, so does the social order constitute itself through men's mastery and control of the women under their authority. In this sense women, insofar as their womanhood is concerned, are extensions of the male person, in that his control over them signifies his successful control over himself, and thereby brings social order into being. Women, therefore, come into the communal order not through their enactment of this order, but through their obedience to it, which entails the confinement of their womanhood.

Yet this relation does not define feminine social roles nor imply any specific domain of the "private." The notion of the "harem" in Western contexts, even scholarly ones, is often conceived as the Muslim form of the private sphere. The problem with this way of looking at things is that it assumes a structural parallel between Islamic and modern Western societies in terms of the division of social realms. The difference is believed to lie only in the ideals of domesticity and womanhood that are operative in the Muslim private sphere. I will contend, however, that no notion of the harem as a space occupied by women or associated with a social role was of importance in Arabic texts in the first five centuries of Islamic history. This suggests that even in much later periods, when the term acquired a gendered and spatial association in some contexts, we should be wary of equating such associations with a private sphere.

To contrast more fully the notions of gendered space I am proposing here with the modern public/private division, it is useful to consider an account of this division that shows the public nature of private family life in bourgeois ideology. In *The Structural Transformation of the Public Sphere*, Habermas argues that the private sphere emerged in eighteenth-century

England, France, and Germany in connection with the rise of the bourgeois conjugal family in that period. The environment of the bourgeois conjugal family, made possible by the economic autonomy of the head of the family in the sphere of the market, fostered an ideal of humanness specific to this new social form. The self-representation of the conjugal family as a community created voluntarily through love that nurtured the inner development of its members gave rise to a conception of humanity as "the emancipation of an inner realm, following its own laws, free from extrinsic purposes of any sort."[1] This new psychological interiority—which found its expression in the eighteenth-century profusion of intimate letters, epistolary novels, diaries, and the like—is the core element of the notion of privateness. In this notion, the private sphere is the realm of humanity, freedom, and love, the domain of life in which human beings are to seek happiness. Habermas argues further that the public sphere, which he defines as "a sphere of ongoing participation in rational-critical debate concerning public authority," arose as the "expansion and at the same time completion of the intimate sphere of the conjugal family."[2] It was the outward manifestation, in other words, of "the subjectivity of the privatized individual."[3]

As would be expected, the normative notion of privacy that Habermas explicates in this account—that of a domestic sphere in which the conjugal family produces and nurtures the publicly oriented humanity of its members—is not relevant to early Islamic representations of social activity and fulfillment. Family life finds scarcely any depiction in early Islamic texts, and all the less so as a realm of freedom and humanity. There is little evidence that such a unit as the conjugal family was even conceived of as a social category or a miniature society.[4] It cannot be claimed that such a notion was completely absent, for there are occasional proverbs, poetic verses, and other dicta indicating an appreciation of self-contained familial fulfillment.[5] And it cannot be discounted that among certain nonelite urban groups— merchant families, for instance—such an ideal may have loomed large in personal aspirations. Yet this was clearly not a significant normative ideal, nor even a distinctly developed concept, in the dominant discourses of the first four or five Islamic centuries.

Another conception of the public and private that seems to be of limited applicability to the early Islamic context is that of Greek and Roman antiquity, touched upon by Habermas and others. According to Habermas, in antiquity the domain of the household (*oikos*) was a domain of necessity, the site where economic and sexual social reproduction took place under

the unfettered dominance of the master. The realm of humanity and freedom was the public arena, in which male citizens deliberated and took decisions concerning common affairs (*politeia, res publica*) and competed in the
display of virtue: "Just as the wants of life and the procurement of its neces-
sities were shamefully hidden inside the *oikos*, so the *polis* provided an open
field for honorable distinction."[6] The designation of the private as the realm
of nature and necessity and the elevation of the public display of virtue resembles early Islamic norms. Yet the forms taken by these two domains in
Greek and Roman antiquity are not present in the early Islamic context.[7]
While it may be argued that there were some kinds of public political de-
liberation in the early Muslim polity—as seen, for instance, in the extensive
political oratory during the early civil wars, or in the politico-theological
struggles of the early Abbasid period—there apparently was, on the other
side of the equation, no Islamic equivalent of the oikos, the self-sufficient
household as center of economic production as well as social reproduction.[8] Moreover, even a more minimal conception of the household as an
integrated site of life activity makes only limited appearance; just as often,
a person's house (*manzil, bayt, dar*) appears as simply a building.[9] This does
not mean that the household did not exist, but it suggests that "household"
was not a key concept or representational category. And this eliminates the
possibility of a normative private sphere based on the model put forward
by Habermas for antiquity.

The absence of a well-delineated sphere defined by its private nature in
any of the above senses raises the possibility that such a site did not exist
in early Islamic culture. Certainly, we should resist any urge to insist upon
one. It is worthy of note that the Western idea of the harem is in many ways
parallel yet antithetical to the bourgeois ideal of private domesticity. The
harem is conceived of as a private space defined by concupiscence rather
than love and sentiment; indolence and excess rather than thrift; confinement rather than freedom; and sensual pleasure rather than spiritual fulfillment. In regard to the Ottoman court, Leslie Peirce argues that it is a myth
to regard the harem as "an Islamic manifestation of the Western conception of the public/private dichotomy."[10] Moreover, even though the Arabic word *harīm* has come in recent centuries to have the sense of women's
space, as well as being a polite synonym for *women*, this does not always
appear to have been the case.

Textual evidence from the first five centuries of Islamic history indicates that the terms *haram* and *harīm* rarely referred to a space occupied

by women.[11] Since early Islamic times, if not before, the primary meaning of the term *haram* has been a sanctum of prohibitive status, denoting particularly the mosques of Mecca, Medina, and Jerusalem. The term *harīm* can have a similar sense and also signifies that which is most precious and must be defended at all costs. Both of these terms are at times used, in texts of the earlier centuries, to refer to the wife or wives and other womenfolk of a man. The word *harīm* had this sense mainly in set phrases signifying the total desecration of an individual and his household, such as *ujtiha al-harim wa subiya al-atfal* (the womenfolk were violated and the children abducted).[12] More frequently, the related word *huram* and even its singular form *hurma* (the sanctity and inviolability of a person or thing) were used to mean someone's wife or women. Although the terms *haram* and *harīm* acquire a spatial sense in their reference to holy sites, they are almost never used in the early period to signify part of a household.[13] I believe that this is the case because their usage to signify a woman or women derives not from any spatial idea, but from the hurma, the sanctity and inviolability, of the women's relationship to the man in authority over them. Indeed, these terms are apparently used in this meaning most often in contexts touching upon a man's status in respect to the women so designated.[14]

We may be led to conclude from these considerations that a public/private framework is inapplicable in the understanding of early Islamic norms, or even those of later periods. Peirce concludes that "a dichotomy of public/commonwealth/male and private/domestic/female does not work for early modern Ottoman society." Similarly, Elizabeth Thompson questions the value of "dichotomous models of public and private" for research in Middle Eastern history.[15] In other words, these terms are not applicable so long as we transmit to our attempted analyses the preconstituted normative content inhering in the terms. It should be possible, however, by keeping apart the distinct meanings evoked by the terms, to use them in a more precise and productive manner. Of great importance in this regard is an underlying distinction that can be made with respect to the different meanings of the public/private opposition.[16] In one fundamental sense, these terms signify an opposition between that which is visible, open, or accessible to all and that which is concealed. In another fundamental sense, they signify an opposition between that which is collective (including political) in nature, and that which is personal or individual. Many versions of the public/private distinction contain elements of both senses. Conflating the two senses where it is not warranted, however, leads to confusion, because something may be both restricted and collective in nature, or may be accessible to all yet belong to an individual. There are further distinctions that can and should be made in this regard, yet even this rudimentary one is of value because of the greater clarity that it confers.

The conceptual framework of public and private is valuable in that it induces us to examine the normative relationships arising from the relation between subjective interiority and collective order. In what follows, I will identify features of subjective interiority as it is represented in Arabic poetry in its relation to the status of womanhood and gendered space. I have chosen two poems for extended analysis due to their intensive development of the conventional motifs of feminine representation in the context of feminine concealment. These poems, one by 'Umar b. Abi Rabi'a and the other by Ibn Darraj al-Qastali, were composed at least three centuries apart and in different regions of the Islamic world. Despite this, they elaborate a common normative structure of gendered space in complementary manners. For this reason, they offer valuable insights into the normative logic at work in the vast body of poetry that draws on the same body of representational motifs. Poems such as these do not tell us much about the specific regimes of female seclusion and social interaction in effect in their respective societies. We cannot use them to construct a history of social practices. This kind of poetry is invaluable, however, for reconstructing the normative ideals connected with regimes of seclusion as manifested in the first few centuries of elite Islamic culture.

The Arabic panegyric poem and related poetic forms are key to any attempt to understand conceptions connected with private and public in the early Islamic context because the very structure of the panegyric poem links individual desire, in the form of the *nasib*, the love reverie that is the first part of such poems, with the communal manifestation of virtue, in the form of the *madih*, the praise of the ruler or other exalted figure. This latter is in fact akin to the form of publicity that Habermas identifies, in the context of European feudalism, as "representation."[17] The medieval Arabic panegyric makes manifest the praised figure's embodiment of the community through the perfection of its virtues within him. Publicity here is not a social sphere of action or interaction, but an attribute of lordly personages whose legitimacy rests on their claim to represent the community to itself.[18] This attribute is made visible and accessible not so much through the person of its bearer (which may be hidden to all but a few) but by means of rituals, displays, spectacular actions, and the like, including panegyric poems.

The panegyric poem shows us that the virtue embodied in the ruler derives from the management, control, and transformation of the desire that originally held sway. This desire is private in the sense that it belongs to the poet, and in the sense that it ought to be concealed and is revealed only because the poet is unable to suppress it. The normative importance of psychic interiority as erotic desire can be seen throughout literary/ethical *adab* works of the early Islamic period. We may take as an example the fourth-/ tenth-century work *al-Muwashsha*, an exposition of the courtly ideal of *zarf*, "refinement." This ideal, though it seems to comprise nearly all known positive traits, is most consistently identified with eloquence, moral nobility, chastity and generosity.[19] Virtue (*muru'a*) is required for refinement,[20] but so is desire. Passionate love (*hawa*) "is one of the surest norms bearing on [those with rationality], and the firmest proof for whoever contemplates them of the proper constitution of their character and impulses."[21] Moreover, passionate love is "the first door by which the mind opens, and the innermost soul expands; it has a force upon the heart by which the intellect comes to life." For the sages, "no one who is free of passionate love is a cultured man [*adib*]." An alternating emphasis on self-constraint (especially in the form of chastity) and passionate desire is a characteristic feature of works of this nature. Authors who propound the antithesis between passion and the constraining power of reason (*'aql*) on one page celebrate the former on another; and while exhorting their readers to chastity in the strongest terms, they caution that passion is the internal impulse that leads to social abasement and the commission of the gravest, most unpardonable sins. These works give us to understand that desire should be present and evident, yet mastered and concealed, for moral ideals to exist.[22]

The key feature of erotic desire in terms of its social significance and its implications for the status of women is its constitution, in poetic and other representations, outside of social order. A poem by the early Umayyad poet 'Umar b. Abi Rabi'a (644–711 CE), one of the founders of the love poem as an independent genre and perhaps its most celebrated practitioner, provides a striking depiction of the social externality of desire. 'Umar's poetry centers on illicit affairs with noble ladies, whom he often pursues during the pilgrimage at the holy mosque, taking advantage of his residence in Mecca. His poetry is characterized by its narrative richness and vivid dialogues involving the poet's paramours, who take an active role in their erotic adventures with him. The poem I will discuss takes up the pre-Islamic theme of the nocturnal, clandestine penetration of the lover's tribal encampment and personal enclosure, depicted as a fantastically audacious and dangerous undertaking.[23] The poem begins with the poet's complaint of his passion for Nu'm.

> Neither Nu'm's proximity, when she is near, can help you,
> nor can you forget her when she is distant, nor even bear it.
> And another woman who came between us, whose kind
> should stop a man with sense, if only he would think and hold back.
> When I visit Nu'm a relative of hers does not leave off
> glowering so long as I am with her.
> It is unbearable for him that I should alight at her tent;
> he harbors malice toward me, and shows scorn. (lines 4–7)

The relationship with Nu'm apparently has no prospect for permanence or long-term fulfillment. Despite the presence of another woman to whom some social obligation is owed and the menacing hostility of Nu'm's male relatives, the poet is unable to engage his rational faculty of self-restraint. The poem then recounts a previous meeting, providing an opportunity to contrast the two lovers' lifestyles.

> She saw a man who, when the sun beats down,
> is underneath it, and at night is chilled.
> A nomad who wanders the earth, flung
> from desert to desert, matted with dust and disheveled.
> He has no shade atop his mount,
> but that cast over him by his patterned cloak.
> She enjoyed her life in the shade of an apartment
> and the rich greenery of luxuriant gardens,
> and a guardian who provided what she wanted,
> so that nothing was there to keep her awake late at night.
>   (lines 14–18)

These lines establish that the poet starts off from a position outside of society. Unlike the pre-Islamic poems that culminate in communal values, in which the poet's blissful time in the garden with the mistress is the most anterior component of the poem—its paradise lost—here the poet is outside of society before his love adventure, and will be again afterward.

Somewhat abruptly, the poet begins narrating the poem's main episode. One night the poet set off on a journey: "the infatuated lover often undertakes what is fearful" (line 19). He found an uncomfortable hideout near Nu'm's tribal settlement and waited there until the animal herders had withdrawn, the men conversing had retired, and there were no more sounds or lights, wondering how he would manage to find her abode in the dark. Not to worry: "I was guided by her scent that I recognized and the self's passion, which had become nearly visible" (line 24). One can see here that the lovers are in an extreme condition, the condition in which interior desire has escaped its ordinary constraint and enclosure and come out into the open. This exposure of desire is the key feature of the poem. The poet, with great wariness, crawls through the encampment and surprises Nu'm in her tent, the enclosure in which she, as a noble lady, is protected from nature, exertion, and the attentions of the vulgar. "You've disgraced me," she exclaims, biting her fingertips, but then, getting hold of herself, she says: "You are, without a question, my lord as long as you stay" (lines 29, 34). Finally, the poet attains what he has risked his life for, and the two lovers spend a blissful night together.

Unfortunately, the happy pair fail to bestir themselves on time in the morning. They are alarmed when they see signs of daybreak and hear around them sounds of early activity. They find themselves in a grave situation. The poet can come up with no better proposal than to go out, face the tribesmen, and either escape or die. Nu'm rejects this option, as it will confirm the malicious gossip about her; she prefers a course of action that will keep the matter concealed. Deciding to consult her two sisters, "she stood, dejectedly, the blood gone from her face due to grief, tears streaming from her eyes" (line 50). Her sisters are naturally taken aback to find a man in Nu'm's tent, but they quickly recover and come up with a plan: to disguise him in women's clothing and walk surrounding him until he can make his escape. "Our secret will not get out, and he will not be visible" (line 55). He consents. "My shield from those whom I feared was three bodies: two buxom maidens and a girl" (line 56). On reaching safety, they say to him: "Is it your habit to behave so recklessly? Do you not feel shame or restrain yourself or think what you are doing?" (line 58). No answer is provided. The poem ends with a desperate desert journey (rahil) in which the poet describes how his camel nearly dies of thirst in the desert, while he himself appears unperturbed.

This poem's structure contains distinctive features that are illustrative of the nature of desire.[24] These features are the poet's complete integration into feminine society, to the extent that he becomes a woman, and the lack of any praise section at the end, making it appear that the poem is incomplete. These features in fact give the poem a different structure from the pre-Islamic poems that contain the same theme. 'Umar's poem bears resemblance to the *su'luk* or brigand poem, in which the poet remains perpetually outside of the social order in a liminal condition.[25] An indication of this is the appearance of rahil motifs before the main narrative as well as after. This representation is in keeping with 'Umar's love poetry in general, in which the poet is always a loner who has illicit and surreptitious liaisons with women and never becomes a member of male society. What we have, then, is a figure who is permanently liminal, and whose liminal condition centers on an inverse integration into feminine society. Instead of moving from an unrealized, natural condition through a liminal phase of moral purgation that allows the attainment of agency and ascension into the realm of culture, 'Umar's persona moves from the liminal state of wandering in the desert into the countersociety of women and then back again. Ordinarily, the desert journey after the adventure would be the means by which the poet can move to virtuous self-integration, or full masculinity, but here the rahil cannot represent a movement to a fulfilled masculinity. Rather, it reestablishes the poet's position outside of society, characterized by his nearly animal condition of desert endurance, with which the poem began.

The overall effect, then, is the identification of the poet with inner desire, with the secret realm whose control and concealment gives rise to order. The poem establishes that he is led by desire and passion (*shawq wa hawa*), that he has no rational constraining faculty, that he does not feel shame or reflect on what he is doing. And indeed, when the two sisters describe how they will give him their clothes to wear, they say: "He will walk in our midst disguised, so that our secret will not be revealed, nor will he appear" (line 55). In other words, the poet is their secret, the inner self that must be kept hidden. He has achieved his total identification with the inner self by violating an inner sanctum of the tribe, by exposing the secret of the tribe's women. This secret can be recontained only by turning it (him) into a concealed woman. The poet's identification with inner desire and the consequences of this identification indicate the ambivalent nature of the secret inner self. It is like femininity, but it transcends femininity — as we can see from the poet's continual movement: from outside of human society, into female society, and back out again. Within society, the secret inner self must be contained as a woman. Yet within men it is potentially uncontained. The suppression and control of the secret make order and virtue possible, but its very existence implies and indeed demands its release. Perhaps this is why such secrets, as long as they are those of others, are so casually and prolifically revealed in the pages of early Arabic literary texts.

An anecdote connected with the initial appearance of the poem casts further light on the cultural status of the kind of representation it contains.[26] According to a report attested to by a long chain of transmitters, the poem was first recited in the holy mosque of Mecca. The great sage and religious authority of the first generation, Ibn 'Abbas, was providing legal opinions to a group of Kharijites, an early Muslim political faction popularly regarded as religious fanatics, when the poet 'Umar happened by. Ibn 'Abbas asked him to recite something; 'Umar complied and then took his leave. The Kharijites were annoyed, and one of them said: "We've come all the way here to ask you about the permitted and the forbidden, and you listen to this Qurayshi playboy." He then repeated one of the verses of the poem in a garbled manner insulting to the poet. Ibn 'Abbas corrected him, and the Kharijite said: "It looks like you've memorized the whole thing." Ibn 'Abbas proceeded to recite the whole poem, causing those present to marvel at his mental powers. It is clear that the reason this story is reproduced is to attribute to the poem the approval of the highest religious authorities. Those who are scandalized by the poem, or by its recitation in the most holy site of Islam, find themselves placed on the side of the fanatical Kharijites. The great Ibn 'Abbas liked the poem; he memorized it and had no qualms about repeating it in the sacred precinct of God's house. We may conclude from the presence of this kind of narrative that representations like that in this poem were not merely mischievous frivolities but were regarded by many as having a significance worthy of the most exalted religious approval.

If masculine interiority can be hidden, or contained, as a woman, it can then fulfill its internal necessity of appearing and defying any constraint in other guises. In other words, the status of women as a symbol of masculine interiority allows desire to be divided into different manifestations so that it can be both in evidence and constrained. We can examine this idea more fully by looking at a representation from a much later period that gains illustrative power by elaborating the pervasive motifs of feminine representation in a particularly intensive manner. The eminent Andalusian poet Ibn Darraj al-Qastali (958–1030 CE) is unusual in that he frequently addresses and mentions members of his family in his panegyric poems. Picking up on a precedent from the early Abbasid poet Abu Nuwas, Ibn Darraj developed the motif of taking leave of a distraught wife (and sometimes child) before undertaking the long and arduous journey to the ruler. A key work of this kind,[27] a panegyric made for al-Mansur Ibn Abi 'Amir, begins addressed to a woman, presumably Ibn Darraj's wife, whom the poet consoles, insisting that the reward he will receive will outweigh the dangers and hardships of the journey, as well as asserting the moral imperative behind undertaking it: "Do you not know that staying put is death, and that the houses of the impotent are tombs?" (line 3). He describes his parting with her thus:

> When she felt the time of departure approaching
> my fortitude was disturbed by her sighs and moans.
> She beseeched me, invoking our time of affection and passion
> while in the cradle lay a small one with the call of a fawn.
> Speechless yet his utterance
> was expert in locating the self's desires.
> He occupied the forbidden place within hearts
> and was cradled in ornamented arms and bosoms;
> nursed by women of great beauty,
> cared for by women of supreme loveliness.
> I disobeyed in him the self's advocate,
> and turned instead to the hardship of nocturnal journeys.
> The wing of separation lifted me away, while
> the wings of anguished parting took her.
> Though she parted from me jealous of me,
> I guard my resolve from her tearfulness jealously. (lines 9–16)

These lines are followed by a description of the poet's travels through the wilderness, employing the motifs of the desert journey, leading up to the praise of al-Mansur. The section translated performs the function of the nasib, that is, the remembrance of past love. The motifs it contains are those found in the nasib, yet—because the poet is addressing a woman under his authority—the manner in which these lines perform their function is altered.[28]

The significance of lost love from the past in the conventional nasib is that it was not under the poet's control. It came to an end due to fate, as all love must. Otherwise, the poet would still be in the arms of his beloved. The poet gives up love and looks elsewhere for permanent fulfillment because he has found that love cannot provide this. In Ibn Darraj's poem, the situation is different. At the poem's outset the poet has already transcended love. The purpose of the translated lines is to show that this is the case, to show that love is present but has been constrained, so that the poet is already in a position to attach himself to the communal figure of the ruler. In other words, these lines show that the poet has transformed himself by depicting his constrained desire as separate from himself. The poet's former desirous self is shown not as a memory of the past, but as present here and now, in the form of the infant who calls to him. The identification of the infant with the inner self is established in the description. He is not eloquent, like those possessed of reason, but inarticulate. Yet his speech penetrates directly to "the self's desires." He occupies the "forbidden place within hearts"—that is, the site of the secret that must remain hidden. He is thus the self's advocate, the one who speaks for it. He rests upon the bodies of beautiful women, because this is where the desirous self always imagines itself. This verse invokes the motifs connected with childhood as the time of naive, issueless eroticism. The remembrance of past love in the ordinary nasib is, in some respects, a remembrance of childhood, or rather pre-adulthood, the time when one took part in women's society. This is the basis of the set of motifs surrounding the love of the place where one grew up (*watan*).

The infant is not present in this scene by accident; he is there because of his mother. The infant signifies what the lady wants the poet to be: his former desirous self. This is why she appeals to their "time of affection and passion." She does not—or perhaps cannot—realize, however, that the poet cannot simply go back to the cradle. To do so would mean death: the homes of those who stay put are tombs. The poet therefore effects and enforces his separation from his interiority by repudiating the blissful condition of the infant—that is, by leaving the arms of his wife and turning to arduous desert treks in which he is seared by the sun, exposed to death, and so forth. The rigors undergone in the course of desert travel, the courage and resolve shown therein, would reveal to the lady, could she but witness them, that the poet is "impatient when wronged, but steadfast through the pain of hardship," that "hopes are obedient" to his will for glory (lines 21, 29)—in sum, that he is worthy of the ruler's favor. In other words, by protecting himself from the tearful emotional attachment of the lady, by refusing to return to infantile bliss, he demonstrates the moral condition that makes him worthy of attachment to the figure that embodies social virtue. The presence of the lady, therefore, as a female under the poet's authority, allows the representation of the poet's own interiority not as something that he was in the past, but as a state of being that he perpetually masters by keeping his wife under his control.

The poems by 'Umar b. Abi Rabi'a and Ibn Darraj stand out because they contain richer representations of gender relations than do conventional poems, which depict interiority in a more abstract manner. These two poems in fact, to a certain degree, might be seen as creating an incipient delineation of a women's realm in which desire holds sway. There is a kind of space associated with femininity in these two poems. In 'Umar's poem, this space would be the *khidr*, or private enclosure of the lady of high social status, though this word is not used in the poem (another word, *khiba'*, is mentioned instead). The word *khidr* has class as well as erotic connotations. It denotes a kind of woman's space. But it is an extremely abstract term: there is no sense of what this space looks like, how large it is, what it contains, whether it is a living space or simply a sleeping space, and so forth, although it implies a life of leisure. In fact, the word does not seem ever to have denoted a specific spatial form, but merely the status of the space occupied by a noble lady as concealed and off-limits. Ibn Darraj uses the term in some of his poems, addressing his wife (presumably) as *rabbat khidr*, the mistress of a khidr. In addressing her in this fashion, he establishes her status and desirability. In the poem referred to above, Ibn Darraj does not use the term, or any other, in reference to the space occupied by the lady and infant. Yet the idea is clear that to stay with them would be to succumb to desire. This means that they occupy a zone in which desire is dominant, from which the poet distances himself, moving to a zone in which virtue is dominant: the court of the ruler. The zone of desire, however, has no name and no spatial or material depiction. It is an emanation of the lady and the child, rather than a free-standing space with specific characteristics. It is an effect of personal status, rather than a sphere of life for the performance of a specific type of activity.

An emphasis on relations of status and the absence of any substantive notion of a role-defined gendered space is evident as well in other kinds of literary, religious, and legal texts. Literary compendiums like the *'Uyun al-Akhbar* by Ibn Qutayba (d. 889 CE) and *al-'Iqd al-farid* by Ibn 'Abd Rabbih (d. 940 CE) contain lengthy sections on the topic of women, consisting of anecdotes about pre-Islamic and early Islamic figures, prophetic and other dictums, and poetic quotations.[29] Many of these anecdotes focus on the nobility of high-status Arab women as manifested in their obedience and attachment to heroic male authority figures. Others focus on women as objects of desire. Themes of chastity and the control and confinement of women receive much emphasis. Yet these sections on women, despite their numerous subdivisions, contain scarcely an allusion to any kind of household setting or domestic labor. Religious and legal texts emphasize similar themes. The marriage relation is often regarded primarily as a sexual contract. Al-Shafi'i, for example, states that the husband "provides for the expenses of his wife whether she is rich or poor in consequence of his confinement of her to himself for taking pleasure in her and other things, and his restriction of her from others."[30] Wives are obliged to be sexually available whenever their husbands wish.[31] Al-Ghazali makes the "breaking of lust" the primary purpose of marriage after reproduction.[32] It is true that he also includes "management of the household" as a benefit of taking a wife, in that it allows the Muslim to free himself for religious duties, but this hardly creates a domestic ideal. In this regard, it is important to note that husbands are usually regarded in legal texts as financially responsible not only for their wives' daily expenses, including preparation of food, clothing, and housework, but also for the suckling of children.[33] Thus, the gender relationship appears in these kinds of texts as a status relationship that keeps chaotic desire outside of the communal order, rather than a relationship that constitutes a role-defined private sphere.

Generally speaking, early Islamic literary texts create the strong impression that there were in fact no normatively defined spheres of social life. In other words, there is little evidence that there were sharply divided realms of social life that existed both as ideal concepts and social institutions. One gets the impression, rather, that spatial ideas were too abstract to support such divisions. The idea of a social realm like the public or private sphere in bourgeois society is of course metaphorical; such realms do not designate or require an actual geographical space for their location. They are constituted, rather, by divisions between modes of social activity and relation, and their differential aims and values. But these types of activity are associated with a range of environments and venues which are often devoted to a single type of activity and defined in relation to it. Thus, important spaces in society often have a character and meaning deriving from the social realm to which they belong. For this to take place, the structure of spatial representations must support relatively fixed and rich contents. When one thinks of a bank, for instance, one imagines a kind of building, a kind of interior space, as well as the activities that go on there, the kind of people found there, and further, a set of definite meanings associated with banking. It does not seem that in the early Islamic context spatial terms had this kind of pictorial concreteness. The terms do not seem to carry any sense of specificity, of calling to mind actual material sites. Writers often use the singular and plural interchangeably when referring to the same building(s). Also, different words, such as *qasr, dar, bayt*, can be used for the same place, not necessarily even a single building, without much sense that these terms were seen as applying to different types of buildings. Even dictionaries are extremely vague and equivocal about such terms. Moreover, one often doubts whether a writer is actually referring to a specific site or space. For example, when Ibn Darraj calls his wife "rabbat khidr," is there an actual space corresponding to this designation? This loose and abstract use of spatial terms is evident in historical writing as well.[34] The sense, therefore, is that these terms do not designate sites with specific material, spatial, and functional characteristics, but invoke an abstract spatial type or a context-specific status. Spatial ideas of this kind of referential structure imply the absence of rigid spatial distinctions, which makes it unlikely for the spatial metaphor of sharply demarcated social spheres to emerge. This does not mean, of course, that women (or men) did not occupy a defined sphere or spheres of life associated with specific locales. Certainly, their lives must have been spent in certain types of spaces, in which they engaged in typical activities. But it does not appear that any of these spheres had a normative status in elite discourses and representations.

The nature of particular social spaces, and their meaning and value, should therefore be understood more as determined by the status and relations of the people present in them than as independently constituted and already existing. The court of a monarch, for example — his audience — is above all the relation between the monarch and those in his presence. Insofar as it is a space, it emanates from the monarch rather than awaiting his occupation of it. It may be said to be public in the sense that the ruler embodies communal values. But it is also private in the sense that it involves that which should be concealed. The ruler is the ultimate protector and generator of social order, which includes his ensuring that "public" morality is not breached. Yet at the same time, the ruler's audience may involve the exposure of his own interiority. All rulers were expected to have "boon companions," and many had stories circulating about their sexual exploits. When we consider the social realm of male interaction at less exalted levels, it is clear that the court is the model for many forms of social assembly, from those in which social virtue is the dominant theme to those in which the release of individual interiority takes precedence. Again, virtue and interiority, the collective and the secret, are not separable. It should be noted that the nature of sociability in these gatherings—convivial, scholarly, political, or otherwise—is defined by the exclusion of free women.

The ruler and the free woman are the two limit figures of early Islamic representations. There is a kind of symmetry between them in terms of their relation to the social collectivity. In the model of gendered space I have examined here, the concealment of free women defines the nature of the primary relationship that governs their activity. This does not mean that women had necessarily to be physically concealed; it does not imply any specific regime of female seclusion or segregation. It means, rather, that women's relationship with the men in control of them had the concealment of masculine interiority as its primary symbolic function. Control over one's women signified control over one's self, and thereby enabled a society of rational, virtuous agents to exist. Therefore, the relationship of control was both one of concealment and of political generation.

In this sense, control meant primarily control over women's bodies. It is a formal relation that can be established in different ways. Furthermore, it does not determine an ideal of femininity in the manner of the bourgeois notion of the private sphere. It does not set up a specific lifestyle, role, attributes, and purpose as essential to successful womanhood. The relation of physical control, whatever form it takes in a specific social conjuncture, is undeniably decisive and determinative, but beyond that relation, ideals of womanly activity and behavior may not necessarily be specified. It may well have been the case that elite women of this early period, for example, engaged in forms of social assembly, including literary and convivial gatherings, similar to those of men.[35] They certainly engaged in "public" activities such as investment, charity, and so forth, as is well known, and at times they even participated in the representation of collective values through oration and the declamation of panegyric poetry.[36] Therefore, relinquishing rigidly demarcated and content-laden spatial notions in order to focus on the spaces created by the status of persons and the social-symbolic relations among them may make it possible to develop a better understanding of the nature of communal order and social space in different societies and the roles that could be played by women within them.

NOTES

All translations are mine, unless otherwise indicated.

1 Jürgen Habermas, *The Structural Transformation of the Public Sphere*, 47.
2 Ibid., 211, 50.
3 Ibid., 50.
4 There is no term corresponding to the Western *family* in early Islamic writings; such a term did not appear in Arabic until the late nineteenth century. The term *usra* (clan) was little used and limited to the context of praising someone's exalted kinship status. The term *bayt* (house), usually in the plural *buyutat*, could have a similar sense. The term *'a'ila*, which now means family in the sense of the nuclear family, meant dependents in premodern texts and included slaves and servants. On the emergence of this term in its modern meaning in the late nineteenth century, see Asad, *Formations of the Secular*, 231–32.
5 See, for example, al-Raghib al-Isfahani, *Muhadarat al-udaba*, 391, for some of these. Rare but noteworthy is the statement reportedly made by Ziyad b. Abihi (Caliph al-Ma'mun) that the happiest man is "a Muslim man who has a Muslim wife; their means are sufficient for their needs; he is content with her and she with him; he does not know us nor we him" (for this version, see Ibn Hazm, *Tawq al-hamama*, 185).
6 Habermas, *The Structural Transformation of the Public Sphere*, 4.
7 Jeff Weintraub, however, points to a second Roman concept of the public in the notion of imperial sovereignty. This may be more applicable in the early Islamic context. See Weintraub, "The Theory and Politics of the Public/Private Distinction," 10–13.
8 This is due primarily, no doubt, to the intensely urban substrate of early Islamic norms and social forms. The Greek conception of the household was adopted and had a marginal presence in the idea of *tadbir al-manzil* (household management), which is referred to mainly in philosophical works. It is interesting to note that in this context, the word *private*, from the Greek, sometimes made an appearance, as *khass*—which is also the modern translation of this term.
9 A notable reference to the household in its lesser sense under the concept of tadbir al-manzil is that of al-Ghazali, who includes freedom from household management (washing dishes, etc.) as a benefit of marriage. See al-Ghazali, *Ihya' 'ulum al-din*, 2:39–40.
10 Pierce, *The Imperial Harem*, 6.
11 Nadia Maria El Cheikh discusses the paucity of reference to or description of specific quarters for women in the Abbasid royal palace complex in her chapter in this volume. See also Hugh Kennedy, *The Court of the Caliphs*, 160. Shaun Marmon acknowledges that, for the Mamluk period, the term *harim*, in its spatial sense, had no gendered specification, but she seems to argue that the term did indeed designate a sexualized "domestic space." See Marmon, *Eunuchs and Sacred Boundaries in Islamic Society*, 6–10. Yet, while it is true that *Lisan al-'Arab al-Muhit*, Ibn

Manzur's thirteenth-century CE dictionary, gives, as one of the many meanings of this term, the interior of the house that can be locked up (as opposed to the *fina'*, or courtyard), this space would include areas for receiving male guests. In later centuries, the word clearly acquired the additional sense of women's quarters, as is evident, for example, in the writing of the nineteenth-century Egyptian historian al-Jabarti, who makes reference to harīm in this sense throughout his *'Aja'ib al-athar fi al-tarajim wa al-akhbar*.

12 This word was also used in the names of two locations in Baghdad. Al-Harim was an area within Baghdad, comprising about a third of the city, in which the caliphal palaces were located. Al-Harim al-Tahiri was the name of the site of the Tahirid palaces, so called because "anyone who sought protection there was granted it." See Yaqut al-Hamawi, *Mu'jam al-buldan*, 2:250–52.

13 After examining texts up to the eleventh century CE, and conducting database searches, I have come across very few instances in which the term haram clearly refers to the part of a household where women resided, and none in which harīm does so.

14 For some examples, see al-Mas'udi, *Muruj al-dhahab wa ma'adin al-jawhar*, 3:385; al-Jahiz, *al-Bayan wa al-tabyin*, 1:338; al-Isbahani, *Kitab al-aghani*, 13:4800; Ibn 'Abd Rabbih, *al-'Iqd al-farid*, 5:321. The terms hurma, huram, and haram, in the sense of a woman or women belonging to a man, do not seem to appear all that frequently.

15 Peirce, *The Imperial Harem*, 7; Thompson, "Public and Private in Middle Eastern Women's History," 53.

16 This distinction is noted and developed by Weintraub in "Theory and Politics," 5 ff.

17 Habermas, *The Structural Transformation of the Public Sphere*, 7–8.

18 For more on the representation of political figures in early Islamic panegyric, see Stefan Sperl, *Mannerism in Arabic Poetry*; Suzanne Stetkevych, *The Poetics of Islamic Legitimacy*.

19 Al-Washsha', *al-Muwashsha*, 82–83.

20 Ibid., 65.

21 Ibid., 91.

22 For a discussion of the parody of this discourse through the exposure and manipulation of its internal paradox, see Noorani, "Heterotopia and the Wine Poem in Early Islamic Culture."

23 This poem begins "a min ali nu'min anta ghadin fa mubkiru" and is perhaps 'Umar's most famous. See 'Umar b. Abi Rabi'a, *Sharh diwan 'Umar b. Abi Rabi'a*, 92–103. There are many anecdotes regarding it and its reception in Abu al-Faraj al-Isfahani, *Kitab al-aghani*, 1:71–74.

24 I am contrasting the structure of 'Umar's poem with that of tripartite pre-Islamic poems. My understanding of the latter is based on Suzanne Stetkevych, *The Mute Immortals Speak*.

25 On su'luk poetry, see Stetkevych, *The Mute Immortals Speak*, chap. 4.

26 Al-Isfahani, *Kitab Al-aghani*, 1:71–73.

27 Ibn Darraj al-Qastali, *Diwan Ibn Darraj al-Qastali*, 297–304. These lines are also quoted and extolled in Ibn Bassam al-Shantarini, *al-Dhakhira fi mahasin ahl al-Jazira*, 1:83.

28 On the nasib in Arabic poetry and its representation of interiority, see Jaroslav Stetkevych, *The Zephyrs of Najd*.

29 See Ibn Qutayba, *'Uyun al-akhbar*, 4:1–147; Ibn 'Abd Rabbih, *al-'Iqd al-farid*, 7:88–156.

30 Al-Shafi'i, *Kitab al-umm*, 5:300.

31 See, for instance, Ibn Hazm, *al-Muhalla*, 11:237; al-Ghazali, *Ihya' 'ulum al-din*, 2:73.

32 Al-Ghazali, *Ihya' 'ulum al-din*, 2:35–39.

33 See, for instance, Al-Shafi'i, *Kitab al-umm*, 5:298.

34 Robert Hillenbrand, a historian of Islamic art and architecture, discusses the vagueness of descriptions of buildings in medieval Islamic literary sources in *Islamic Architecture*, 26–30.

35 For example, the great Andalusian writer Ibn Hazm tells us that the women with whom he grew up taught him the Qur'an, transmitted a substantial body of poetry to him, and trained him in calligraphy. This implies that women of this class created a social environment among themselves conducive to the cultivation of high levels of literate culture. See Ibn Hazm, *Tawq al-hamama*, 166.

36 I have in mind the orations attributed to women during the early civil wars (656–691 CE) and, much later, the report that two female poets, 'Abida al-Jahniyya and 'Atika al-Makhzumiyya, formally declaimed poems in praise of 'Adud al-Dawla (r. 949–983 CE). See al-Tanukhi, *Nishwar al-muhadara wa akhbar al-mudhakara*, 5:267–70.

Every social community reproduced by the functioning
of institutions is imaginary, that is to say, it is based on
the projection of individual existence into the weft of a
collective narrative.

—ETIENNE BALIBAR, "The Nation Form"

3 • THE HAREM AS GENDERED SPACE AND THE SPATIAL REPRODUCTION OF GENDER

İrvin Cemil Schick

 The word *harem* denotes both the female members of a household and the dedicated spatial enclosure in which they live. The practice of identifying people by the space wherein they dwell or work is
not particularly unusual: one speaks of Highlanders, Europeans, shantytown dwellers, office workers, scullery maids,
stable boys, and so on. But with the harem, it is not the case
that a spatial term is simply used as a qualifier for certain
individuals; instead, one and the same word denotes both a
space and a category of people — and that is rather unusual.
This singular fact offers an important hint about how to approach the harem conceptually, as this chapter does, in the
context of recent theoretical work on the social construction of space and its relation to gender, as well as recent
sociological and ethnographic research on spatiality as the
lived experience of women in various societies.

As is well known, the Arabic root *ḥ-r-m*, from which
harem is derived, conveys the notion of a taboo: it generally
refers to prohibition, unlawfulness, veneration, sacredness,
inviolability.[1] One word derived from this root is *ḥurmat*,
which refers to something held holy and revered, something

which it is one's duty to honor and defend, and in particular a man's wives and family.[2] Another word derived from the same root is *harīm*, which refers to those parts of a house or property whose use is forbidden to all but the rightful owner, such as a well. Certain classical Arabic dictionaries define it specifically as "the part of the house into which one enters and upon which the door is closed,"[3] and it is in this sense of the private quarters of a home that the women's apartments came to be known as the harem.

This root has thus provided Arabic speakers with an axis for the inside-outside dichotomy that is present in some form in virtually all human societies. The harem was contrasted to the central courtyard (*wasat al-dar* in the Maghrib, *hawsh* in the Mashriq) in which social activities involving visitors took place. In Turkish, these two spaces were known as *harem* (or *haremlik*) and *selâmlık*; in Persian, *andarun* and *birun*. But the presence of an inside-outside dichotomy and the overlay of gender upon that dichotomy are two very different matters. Contrary to received opinion, the relegation of Muslim women to the internal half of a bisected space is not clearly mandated by the Qur'an; indeed, although derivatives of the root *h-r-m* occur no fewer than eighty-three times there[4]—referring to dietary laws, prohibitions during the pilgrimage, the holy months, and the sacred precincts of Mecca in which it is forbidden to kill—not once does a derivative refer to women or women's quarters. Rather, this principle is based upon a particular reading of the so-called Verse of the Veil, which says, in part: "And when you ask them [feminine] for something, ask from behind a hijab [veil/curtain]; that makes for greater purity for your hearts and for theirs."[5] Although commentators usually agree that "them" in this verse refers specifically to the Prophet's wives, they have often generalized it to all Muslim women and have taken this verse to ordain that men and women must be spatially segregated.[6] The Verse of the Veil is, incidentally, the origin of the word *purdah*—literally meaning curtain or veil in Persian—that denotes female seclusion in India.

The degree to which sexual segregation is fundamental to Islam has been the subject of some debate. For example, Fatima Mernissi has argued that the Prophet's home in Medina "created a space in which the distance between private life and public life was nullified, . . . in which the living quarters opened easily onto the mosque, and which thus played a decisive role in the lives of women and their relationship to politics."[7] However, there are prophetic traditions (hadiths) that suggest that this practice did not last.

One, for instance, describes how the Prophet stretched a curtain between Safiyya and the people to emphasize that she was his wife; another relates how 'A'isha refused to admit the brother of her foster uncle into her apartment following the revelation of the Verse of the Veil, until the Prophet gave her leave on the grounds of kinship.[8] Whatever the situation may have been at the beginning, it is known that sexual segregation was increased following the death of the Prophet, both under the leadership of Caliph 'Umar b. al-Khattab (r. 634–44 CE), known for his strict views concerning women, and as a result of the growing influence of peoples with whom the Arabs came into contact through military conquest.[9]

I have just used the term *sexual segregation*. I did so as shorthand, for the sake of convenience, but the term is in fact inexact. As is evident from the hadith concerning 'A'isha and the brother of her foster uncle, the principle is not based on sex alone. Adult men and women are allowed to share a common space if they are forbidden (*mahram*) from marrying each other by virtue of kinship—based on consanguinity, colactation,[10] marriage, or sexual union, as explicitly stipulated in the Qur'an.[11] However, it is forbidden (*harām*) for men to enter a space occupied by women other than their kin. Thus, although the universalizing grand paradigm of "rigidly demarcated and mutually impenetrable territories of male versus female inhabitancy" has been convincingly challenged by a number of recent studies,[12] this much is nevertheless true: since most men and women are not each other's kin, the effective consequence of the Verse of the Veil in the way it was interpreted by later commentators was often the creation of two relatively distinct—if not necessarily reciprocally hermetic—subspaces, one occupied primarily by men, the other primarily by women.

Indeed, while the word *harem* is generally associated in the Western mind with polygyny, an image reinforced by accounts of the countless wives and concubines who supposedly peopled the households of men like the Abbasid Caliph Harun al-Rashid (r. 786–809 CE) and the Mughal emperor Akbar (r. 1556–1605 CE), the admittedly scanty quantitative data we have pertaining to the common people do not support this view. A demographic study conducted by Alan Duben and Cem Behar, for instance, has revealed that in late Ottoman Istanbul, only 2.29 percent of all married men were polygynous; among those, furthermore, the average number of wives was only 2.08.[13] Other surveys likewise indicate that the proportion of polygynous households in North Africa and South Asia did not exceed 5 percent. Thus, the harem was much more likely to be a monogamous (albeit extended) family's domestic quarters than a space dedicated to housing multitudes of women. In sub-Saharan Africa, on the other hand, although a much higher proportion of households (Muslim or not) are polygynous—sometimes over 40 percent—harems are uncommon. There, communal ownership of land and the predominance of women in agricultural work make polygyny widespread, but seclusion impractical; by contrast, individual ownership of land and the predominance of male-dominated plow farming in Eurasia and North Africa make seclusion possible, but polygyny undesirable.[14] This underscores the fact that the term *harem* primarily denotes a principle of spatial organization, a system of female seclusion, rather than just polygyny by another name.

Although boundaries could be permeable, and the activities in which men and women engaged within their respective subspaces were not necessarily mutually exclusive, these subspaces were not in any sense symmetric or similarly configured. An apt analogy might be an archipelago in the midst of an ocean, where the islands collectively represent the subspace devoted to women, and the sea the subspace devoted to men. The women's subspace included harems, public baths, saints' tombs and shrines, recreational areas, cemeteries, and so forth; movement between them was carefully regulated, most notably by the practice of veiling, which allowed women to remain ritually "inside" while physically "outside." Although the space in which men circulated was also modulated—notably by homes, mosques, dervish lodges, workplaces, markets, baths, and the like—men were clearly far less restricted than women from the standpoint of spatial dynamics. And, of course, they were not monitored, nor required to veil themselves, when going from one place to another. In short, the subspaces pertaining to men and women were not only separate, they were also unequal.[15]

A question naturally follows: how did this bisected and fundamentally asymmetric spatial arrangement affect the lives of the men and women who inhabited it? More specifically, how did the dissimilarity of their respective subspaces influence the relationship between men and women? What impact did it have on their social differentiation—that is, on the construction and reproduction of gender? Feminist geographers have long stressed the mutually constitutive nature of space and gender, arguing that the differences in the ways men and women experience geography are not only a consequence of gender differences, but are also productive of them.[16] Clearly, there is every justification to interpret the concept of geography in the broadest possible sense, encompassing spatial structures that are not only natural but also artificial, not only physical but also imagined. When viewed in this context, it becomes evident that the harem system has provided a spatial basis for gender difference in many Muslim societies; and since spatial differentiation often coexists with power differentiation, it has as well been implicated in the production and perpetuation of power asymmetries along gender lines.

Let me now turn to the role of the harem in the spatial production and reproduction of gender. I draw my inspiration in part from Teresa de Lauretis, who coined the Foucauldian term *technology of gender* to describe the discursive instruments and strategies by means of which gender is socially constructed and reconstructed.[17] In that sense, I will argue that the harem was and is a technology of gender. In other words, by conceptualizing it primarily as a socially constructed space, often more imagined than physical, I shall attempt to analyze the harem as a site of gender construction. More concretely, I will ask in what manner the spatial configuration called the harem taught female children how to be Muslim women and male children how to be Muslim men. I will not answer this question here, but I will at least make an effort to state the terms of the problem as explicitly as I can.

In taking this somewhat more abstract, not to say theoretical, point of view, I will occasionally venture into a discussion of the relationship between space and gender in non-Muslim societies. This is emphatically not to deny the specificity of the harem system and its cultural and religious ties to Islam. However, it is my belief that many past studies of the harem have suffered from a bit of particularism, and that a certain amount of conceptual cross-pollination would not be such a bad thing at this juncture. We all know, of course, that until frighteningly recent times, Western scholars insisted on viewing the rest of the world through highly Eurocentric lenses. Whether approached from a Christian point of view, as heathens and heretics in need of salvation; from a colonial point of view, as inferior races in need of stewardship and civilization; or from a developmentalist point of view, as primitive savages in need of social and technological modernization, people not of European descent were inevitably represented and analyzed not on their own terms but on those of the Western scholars. During the last three decades, a countercanon has taken shape that aims to overturn many of these preconceived notions and to adopt new paradigms more in line with the realities under study. Needless to say, this is a most welcome development. However, an unintended consequence has been the relative neglect of the exciting theoretical innovations that have recently emerged in cultural theory. I am pleading for a small adjustment, not a whole pendulum swing, to give these innovations their due. A great deal of fascinating feminist analysis has been conducted in the fields of cultural and human geography; yet, although quite relevant to the problem at hand, applications to the institution of the harem have been few and far between.[18]

At the heart of the spatial constructionist approach lies the notion that space is more than either a neutral medium for social practices or their passive resultant; rather, it is and must be analyzed as "an active, constitutive, irreducible, necessary component in the social's composition."[19] Space is constructed through social practices and bears the imprint of the power relations that characterize them; in turn, space inflects social practices, reproducing society and reaffirming the power relations that organize it. As Edward Soja elegantly put it: "The generative source for a materialist interpretation of spatiality is the recognition that spatiality is socially produced and, like society itself, exists in both substantial forms (concrete spatialities) and as a set of relations between individuals and groups, an 'embodiment' and medium of social life itself."[20]

Likewise, Doreen Massey, a pioneer feminist geographer, suggests that the spatial should be viewed not as purely physical but in terms of the social relations it comprises: "Instead . . . of thinking of places as areas with boundaries around, they can be imagined as articulated moments in networks of social relations and understandings, but where a large proportion of those relations, experiences and understandings are constructed on a far larger scale than what we happen to define for that moment as the place itself."[21] And "spatial differentiation, geographical variety, is not just an outcome: it is integral to the reproduction of society and its dominant social relations."[22]

This is, indeed, the key issue. Just as society is not homogeneous, just as the social is partitioned and stratified along the lines of class, gender, race, sexuality, generation, ethnicity, religion, and myriad other factors, so too is space. Moreover, "unequal social relations are both expressed and constituted through spatial differentiation."[23] Michel Foucault dubbed such spatial variegations "heterotopias," arguing that they are defined by particular mechanisms of opening and closing, and change as society changes in ways that mirror its aspirations and fears.[24] The analysis of heterotopias takes us a long way toward understanding the power structures underlying society, for power is intrinsically spatial just as spatiality is imbued with power.[25]

In an interesting study of place and transgression, Peter Stallybrass and

Allon White have written that "the grouping together of sites of discourse, the acceptance and rejection of place, with its laws and protocols and language, is . . . a coding of social identity."[26] The construction of the self, then, is at the same time the construction of a network of places which are constituted by and simultaneously reproduce social cleavages such as gender (e.g., domestic and public), race (e.g., suburb and inner city), or class (e.g., club and pub). More generally, according to Shirley Ardener, "societies have generated their own rules, culturally determined, for making boundaries on the ground, and have divided the social into spheres, levels and territories with invisible fences and platforms to be scaled by abstract ladders and crossed by intangible bridges with as much trepidation or exultation as on a plank over a raging torrent."[27]

Spatial differentiation would have been innocent enough, and hardly worth our attention, if it were not for the enormous difficulty entailed in passing from one subspace to another, and if it were not for the fact that heterotopias provide metonymic road maps that greatly facilitate the oppression of one group of people by another.[28]

This is precisely the topic of David Sibley's incisive analysis of the intimate connections between spatiality and the construction of "outsider groups." As this is a cornerstone of my argument, I am taking the liberty of quoting Sibley at length:

> Space is implicated in the cultural construction of outsiders in two respects. First, marginal, residual spaces . . . confirm the outsider status of the minority. They may be places which are avoided by members of the dominant society because they appear threatening—a fear of the "other" becomes a fear of place . . . The labelling of places as threatening confirms the otherness of the minorities with whom the places are associated, and relegation to marginal spaces serves to amplify deviance . . . A second role for space in the constitution of the outsider group concerns the arrangement of spaces in the built environment. Spatial structures can strengthen or weaken social boundaries, thus accentuating social division or, conversely, rendering the excluded group less visible. In order to understand the role of space in this process, it is necessary to think about space in relation to the exercise of power. Space represents power in that control of space confers the power to exclude . . . [S]pace is an integral part of the outsider problem.[29]

Although Sibley's main focus is the spatial manifestations of racial and sexual difference in Britain, the relevance of his analysis to the case of space and gender in general, and to the harem system in particular, should be clear—if not positively striking. Indeed, since one of the main organizing principles in most societies is gender, it stands to reason that social differentiation along the lines of gender should influence the configuration of space, and that spatial structures should in turn produce and reproduce gender difference, as a pair of examples illustrates.

Consider first the case of the Renaissance architect and theoretician Leon Battista Alberti (1404–72), whose *On the Art of Building in Ten Books* has been immensely influential in European architectural theory. Referring to ancient Greece, he writes that it was "the custom . . . for certain parts of the house, where the women resided, to be out of bounds to all but closest kin. And certainly, to my mind, any place reserved for women ought to be treated as though dedicated to religion and chastity; also I would have the young girls and maidens allocated comfortable apartments, to relieve their delicate minds from the tedium of confinement. The matron should be accommodated most effectively where she could monitor what everyone in the house was doing. But in each case we should abide by whatever may be the ancestral custom."[30]

Note that although Alberti drew his inspiration and legitimacy from antiquity, where the gynaeceum was the norm, he was writing during the fifteenth century. Replace "matron" with "eunuch," and this might just as well be an Orientalist account of a harem. More to the point, the residence as conceived by Alberti is meant not only to *house* women but to *define* them—that is, to transform sexual difference into gender difference. As Mark Wigley notes in his stimulating analysis of Alberti's writings on family and gender, the passage above "participates in the production of the artifact 'woman' by high discourse."[31]

As a second example, consider the emergence and development of suburbia in Britain during the nineteenth century. Prompted by a desire to spatially separate work and home, according to Robert Fishman's *Bourgeois Utopias*, this process was heavily imbricated with changing conceptions of gender and resulted in the spatial isolation of women and their sequestration within the domestic sphere, as well as the domestication of reproductive labor and the elision of communal strategies for dealing with it.[32] Moreover, Fishman demonstrates that this process was driven by the evangelical movement, which set forth the ideal of a "truly Christian family" as a unit turned inward upon itself and held together by strong emotional ties managed by women, a safe haven from the abrasive daily existence of the male provider. The contradictions between premodern London and "the Evangelical ideal of the family provided the final impetus for the unprecedented separation of the citizen's home from the city that is the essence of the suburban ideal."[33] Reviewing this process, Don Mitchell concludes that "once the ideal had been established, and once the family had been remade to fit the landscape even as the landscape was remade to fit the new family, suburbia exploded, becoming, as it were, the *only* option for respectable middle-class life. And this respectability . . . was predicated on the sequestering of women in the domestic sphere. Definitions of femininity—and masculinity—were predicated on finding a spatial form that policed the divide between public and private spheres."[34]

The two examples I have just discussed show how female sequestration was theorized and practiced not in the Muslim world, but in Christian Europe. Let me emphasize once again that I am not for a moment losing sight of the specificity of the Islamic context. The issue I am struggling to address is simply this: we know that the institution of the harem exhibits great variability across both history and geography. Is there anything to be learned from analyses of other gendered constructions of space to help us explain this variability?

For example, Mitchell mentions "the divide between public and private spheres," and this is one of the frameworks within which the harem has been studied. There is in fact good reason to think of the dichotomous spatial arrangement of harem and selâmlık (or andarun and birun) as representative of a private/public cleavage: after all, the harem or andarun was an inner sanctuary for both male and female members of the household, while the selâmlık or birun was a public stage for welcoming and entertaining guests of both sexes. At the same time, as demonstrated in several studies, women routinely engaged in social, economic, and even political activities from behind harem walls, suggesting that the word *private* in the sense commonly given it in the Western context today fails to capture the full range of experiences in which women participated there.[35]

But perhaps it is Western ideas of private and public that need revision, as already argued by several scholars. For instance, Nancy Duncan points out that although the distinction between these two domains is deeply rooted in culture and enshrined in the law, "it is nevertheless unstable and often problematically conflated with related distinctions such as that between domestic or familial autonomy and public spheres."[36] Likewise, Lynn Staeheli notes that "there is no *necessary* reason why actions that are intended to affect broad economic, social, or political relations must be taken in public spaces," and shows that alternative spatial configurations have emerged, blurring the traditional boundaries between public and private: "The shifting constructions of public and private become something to be *explained*, rather than dismissed."[37] Never mind how we might feel about it, the received idea that the public sphere is masculine, worldly, and important, and the private sphere feminine, local, and trivial is simply not sustainable when all the empirical evidence is weighed.

The private/public dichotomy is far from a historical invariant, and the role of spatial practices and representations in its development deserves careful scrutiny. Wigley writes that in the centuries following Alberti's theorization of gendered space, a

> new sense of privacy was gradually produced . . . by redefining the spaces of the house into a complex order of layered spaces and subdivisions of spaces that map a social order by literally drawing the lines between hierarchies of propriety . . . A new kind of space emerged in which distance is no longer the link between two visible objects in space but is the product of a mask whose surface is scrutinized for clues about what lies beyond it but can never simply be seen . . . Architecture was used to effect it as the agent of a new kind of modesty and in so doing played an active part in the constitution of the private subject. It clothed the body in a way that redefined it, at once constructing the body as dangerous and containing the threat.[38]

Some noteworthy parallels exist here between aspects of spatial differentiation in Europe and the concentric spatial configuration (prevalent in many Muslim societies) that constructs the harem as the center—sometimes feminine, and sometimes sacred.[39] The system of embedded courtyards at the Topkapı Palace described by Jateen Lad in this volume is a good example of such a concentric spatial configuration.

Here again, spatial differentiation is not innocent. As Duncan points out: "The public/private dichotomy (both the political and spatial dimensions) is frequently employed to construct, control, discipline, confine, exclude and suppress gender and sexual difference preserving traditional patriarchal and heterosexist power structures."[40]

As the above makes clear, the role of the body in the conceptualization of private and public is quite central to the argument. Indeed, Don Mitchell lays it out very eloquently: "Social space is experienced bodily. It follows, then, that the production of space . . . at the same time serves to produce certain kinds of bodies. Such an abstract idea makes sense, however, only if we understand 'bodies' to be both the physical embodiment of particular people, and a culturally constructed set of ideas and ideals about what is bodily proper for men and women. That is to say, there is an intimate relationship between the social construction (and policing) of space, the cultural construction (and policing) of gender, and the ways we comport ourselves, the experiences we have, and, at least to some degree, the very morphology of our physical bodies."[41]

And the effect goes both ways. John Allen writes that "it is the vast array of spatial practices, from the routine walks and rhythms which endow a place with meaning to the coded gestures, styles and mannerisms which prescribe a certain use for it, that puts both us and power in place."[42] When we imagine space as socially constructed, therefore, we must not think only of ideas, signs, and symbols; space is constructed also through bodily practices, and, needless to say, space in turn conditions bodily practices. At least for contemporary societies and perhaps for historical ones as well, this suggests a promising approach to analyzing the harem as a site of production and reproduction of gender.

A nice example of this approach, though in a Hindu rather than a Muslim context, is the ethnographic work of Seemanthini Niranjana, which focuses on "the spatial axis underlying everyday practices, as well as societal or group reproduction," and on "the 'acts' within which women define their lives and the arenas, events or qualities that mark bodies as female."[43] Niranjana concludes that: "Perceptions of and injunctions surrounding female bodies and female morality . . . are central to the negotiation of space, specifying how identities are consolidated and lived in the course of marking the boundaries of movement and the 'limits' of women's honour . . . [A] very strong spatial narrative governed the lives of people . . . [M]uch of what was said of femininity, sexualization and the female body, as well as the activities of women, was all embodied in this idiom . . . [T]he body, and the modes in which it inhabits space, itself comes to be deployed as a medium through which the 'female' is constituted."[44]

Closer to home, Pierre Bourdieu's classic study of the Kabyle house surely needs no introduction.[45] Though it has been used and abused in more ways than one cares to remember, generalized beyond the bounds of reason and common sense, and criticized for causes both valid and not,[46] this essay was pathbreaking in its attention to the ways in which systems of bodily practices and "incorporated dispositions"—what Bourdieu would later call *habitus*[47]—were related to habitat. He paid special attention to the sexualization and gendering of certain elements of the Kabyle house, and how they were correlated with the practices of the men and women who lived there.

More recently, Traki Zannad Bouchrara conducted ethnographic field-work among Tunisian townswomen (*beldia*), in which she carefully choreographed their corporal dynamics within the traditional home as compared to male corporal dynamics in the public sphere. Noting that "there exists between the human body and urban space a dialectic that, beyond signifying forms, beyond the palpable and the observable, also features a dimension that has the quality of the signified and the symbolic,"[48] she describes a certain complementarity and skew-symmetry—which she characterizes as driven by centrifugal and centripetal forces—between the private and public spaces.

Abdessamad Dialmy, for his part, studied spatial and sexual practices in Morocco. Noting that "built space plays the role of the signifier of a reality of a non-spatial nature," he set forth four modes of relationship between space and sexuality—symbolic, lexical, territorial, and functional—and conducted a field survey focusing on the latter two. As he points out: "The inferior condition of woman is written and signified by the nature and placement of the space which is reserved for her. The same goes for 'male domination,' which is likewise transcribed by the superiority of the masculine places."[49]

There is a rich and growing literature concerning the ways in which women have historically experienced space, and do so today.[50] This literature provides both inspiration and practical hints for studying the harem as a site of gender construction and reproduction.

In conclusion, and as unlikely as the connection between the subject of this volume and the political situation in the world today may seem, we may draw upon the ongoing debates concerning seclusion and veiling within the Islamist political movement—both in Muslim countries and in the Islamic diasporas in the West—to suggest that this focus of debate can and *must* be viewed as an aspect of spatial politics, as a contest over the restructuring of space. Discussing radical Islamist movements such as FIS (Front Islamique du Salut, or Islamic Salvation Front) in Algeria, Dialmy argues:

> The resurgence of Islam as a factor of spatial organization returns to the
> fore the territorial mode as a weapon of combat in the quest for identity

... The Islamist movement cannot remain silent or indifferent before the problematic of space, and particularly that of women's consumption of public space. But can it, despite the progress of modernity, reclaim sexual segregation as a fundamental principle for the social organization of space? ... The commingling of the sexes, which can no longer be circumvented, will henceforth be undermined by the veil and by the organized separation of the sexes at the university, on the beaches, in the bus.[51]

Indeed, as Massey writes: "Particular ways of thinking about space and place are tied up with ... particular social constructions of gender relations ... [C]hallenging certain of the ways in which space and place are currently conceptualized implies also, indeed necessitates, challenging the currently dominant form of gender definitions and gender relations."[52]

In sum, like any social institution, the harem is in essence a representation; and like the history of any social institution, its history is largely that of its representation. But representations of the harem have been multiple and often contradictory, its portrayal ranging from a microcosm of Oriental despotism and the locus of phallocratic oppression, on the one hand, to a space of female autonomy in which Muslim women are able to engage in social, economic, and even political activities unhindered by male domination, on the other hand. Rather than searching for the true essence of the harem in religious texts or historical practices, it may be more fruitful to conceptualize it primarily as a socially constructed space, often more imagined than physical, and to focus on how it has functioned to produce and reproduce gender. Feminist geographers have long stressed the mutually constitutive nature of space and gender, arguing that the differences in the ways men and women experience geography are not only a consequence of gender differences, but are also productive of them. Segregation reproduces itself, as spaces of otherness become not only repositories of others, but producers of alterity as well. At the same time, this necessarily means that the harem is also a site of resistance; indeed, the ongoing political struggle over veiling and seclusion can be viewed as an aspect of spatial politics, a contest over the restructuring of space.

NOTES

All translations are mine, unless otherwise indicated.

1 Ibn Manzur, *Lisan al-'Arab al-muhit*, 615–19.

2 [Al-Jawhari], *Mukhtar al-sihah*, 486; al-Fayruzabadi al-Shirazi, *Qamus al-muhit*, 4:110.

3   Al-Zabidi, *Taj al-'arus min jawahir al-qamus*, 8:240; al-Azhari, *Tahdhib al-lughat*, 5:47.

4   'Abd al-Baqi, *al-Mu'jam al-mufahras li-alfaz al-Qur'an al-karim*, 197–99.

5   Qur'an, *Ahzab* 33:53.

6   Al-Qurtubi, *al-Jami' li-ahkam al-Qur'an*, 14:227. Although the lives of the female companions of the Prophet are deemed paradigmatic by Muslims, they have historically been subjected to reinterpretations in significant ways, as shown by Asma Afsaruddin's chapter in this volume.

7   Mernissi, *The Veil and the Male Elite*, 113.

8   Al-Bukhari, *Sahih*, Nikah 62:22, 89; 40, 166.

9   Ahmed, *Women and Gender in Islam*, 41–78.

10   Colactation is a form of kinship based upon milk — i.e., the act of breast-feeding. It was common among Arab Bedouins — and then across many societies in the region — to have a "milk sibling," someone nursed by the same woman.

11   Qur'an 4:23.

12   Afsaruddin, "Introduction," 3. See also the various other contributions to that interesting volume, edited by Afsaruddin.

13   Duben and Behar, *Istanbul Households*, 148–49.

14   Boserup, *Woman's Role in Economic Development*, 37–52; Goody, "Polygyny, Economy and the Role of Women."

15   In this context, it is still instructive, half a century later, to read the unanimous opinion of the U.S. Supreme Court in the 1954 case of *Brown v. Board of Education*: "Does segregation of children in public schools solely on the basis of race, even though the physical facilities and other 'tangible' factors may be equal, deprive the children of the minority group of equal educational opportunities? We believe that it does . . . We conclude that in the field of public education the doctrine of 'separate but equal' has no place. Separate educational facilities are inherently unequal. Therefore, we hold that the plaintiffs and others similarly situated for whom the actions have been brought are, by reason of the segregation complained of, deprived of the equal protection of the laws guaranteed by the Fourteenth Amendment."

16   See, e.g., Domosh and Seager, *Putting Women in Place*; Massey, *Space, Place, and Gender*; McDowell, *Gender, Identity and Place*; McDowell and Sharp, *Space, Gender, Knowledge*; G. Rose, *Feminism and Geography*.

17   De Lauretis, "The Technology of Gender," 3.

18   A notable exception is Joan DelPlato's study of Orientalist harem paintings informed by the theories of Henri Lefebvre, "Lefebvre's Critique of Space as Interdisciplinary Paradigm." Although I extensively used the "social construction of space" framework in *The Erotic Margin*, my primary concern there was the use of harem imagery in the construction of the "Orient" as a space of otherness, and not the spatial constitution of the harem itself.

19   Keith and Pile, "Introduction, Part 2: The Place of Politics," 36.

20   Soja, *Postmodern Geographies*, 120.

21   Massey, *Space, Place, and Gender*, 154.

22 Massey, *Spatial Divisions of Labor*, 299–300.

23 G. Rose, *Feminism and Geography*, 113.

24 Foucault, "Of Other Spaces."

25 J. Allen, *Lost Geographies of Power*, 159.

26 Stallybrass and White, *The Politics and Poetics of Transgression*, 194.

27 Ardener, Introduction, 2.

28 What I mean by "metonymic road maps" is spatialized representations of society, in which spaces stand in for sets of characteristics associated with them, such as the distinction between suburb and inner city standing in for racial difference. Such representations often provide guidelines for social practices as well as public policies. See, e.g., Entrikin, *The Betweenness of Place*, 43–59, for an analysis of regionalism in this context.

29 Sibley, "Outsiders in Society and Space," 112–113, 116. See also his *Geographies of Exclusion*.

30 Alberti, *On the Art of Building in Ten Books*, 5:149.

31 Wigley, "Untitled," 333. Wigley also provides an interesting discussion of Xenophon's writings on the subject.

32 Fishman, *Bourgeois Utopias*.

33 Ibid., 38.

34 Mitchell, *Cultural Geography*, 129.

35 Hegland, "Political Roles of Aliabad Women"; Peirce, "'The Law Shall Not Languish'"; Marsot, "The Revolutionary Gentlewomen in Egypt"; Yaseen Noorani's chapter in this volume.

36 Duncan, "Renegotiating Gender and Sexuality in Public and Private Spaces," 127.

37 Staeheli, "Publicity, Privacy and Women's Political Action," 609, 605.

38 Wigley, "Untitled," 345.

39 It might be useful to remember that the holy sites of Mecca and Medina are known in Arabic as the Two Harams.

40 Duncan, "Renegotiating Gender and Sexuality in Public and Private Spaces," 128.

41 D. Mitchell, *Cultural Geography*, 217.

42 J. Allen, *Lost Geographies of Power*, 162.

43 Niranjana, *Gender and Space*, 13.

44 Ibid., 31, 15–16.

45 A number of versions of "The Kabyle House or the World Reversed" exist, some more complete than others. An English translation quite close to the French original that appeared in the *Mélanges* in honor of Claude Lévi-Strauss (1970) is included as an appendix in Bourdieu, *The Logic of Practice*, 271–83, 316–19.

46 For a well-deserved rejoinder to this misuse, see Lipstadt, "'There Is [Almost] No Occurrence of the Berber House in This Document.'"

47 Bourdieu subsequently defined *habitus* as "systems of durable, transposable *dispositions*, structured structures predisposed to function as structuring structures, that is, as principles of the generation and structuring of practices and representations which can be objectively 'regulated' and 'regular' without in any way being the product of obedience to rules, objectively adapted to their goals without presup-

posing a conscious aiming at ends or an express mastery of the operations necessary to attain them and, being all this, collectively orchestrated without being the
product of the orchestrating action of a conductor" (*Outline of a Theory of Practice*,
72).

48 Zannad [Bouchrara], *Symboliques corporelles et espaces musulmans*, 13.

49 Dialmy, *Logement, sexualité et Islam*, 13, 16.

50 Some notable examples are: Ardener, *Women and Space*; Deutsch, *Women and the
City*; Hanson and Pratt, *Gender, Work and Space*; Low and Lawrence-Zúñiga, *The
Anthropology of Space and Place*; Momsen and Townsend, *Geography of Gender in
the Third World*; Spain, *Gendered Spaces*; Weisman, *Discrimination by Design*.

51 Dialmy, *Logement, sexualité et Islam*, 24, 78–79. By "the territorial mode," Dialmy
means "the subdivision of space into male, female, and mixed territories."

52 Massey, *Space, Place, and Gender*, 2.

PART II · ROOMS AND THRESHOLDS
Harems as Spaces, Socialities, and Law

If the harem is not named in early representations of "outside" versus "inside" space, such as those analyzed in Part I, how might an accumulation of representations—for example, the anecdotes in adab collections on which Nadia Maria El Cheikh draws in chapter 4 for representations of the harem in Baghdad during the fourth/tenth century—have contributed to specific naming of different spaces? And how might transgressions of gendered divisions between spaces, as described in some of these anecdotes, work to normalize the divisions themselves? Furthermore, what kinds of internal hierarchies does this division of space make possible? How does it position some women vis-à-vis other women? When Montesquieu, in *The Persian Letters* (1721), and other European writers imagined the harem as a seat of power, they assumed that power alignments followed divisions of gender—even when, as in the case of Montesquieu, they were using an estranged view to critique their own European society, and when the physical absence of masculine authority seemed to them to presume a fragmentation of order. How do indigenous representations of harem spaces challenge assumptions about alignments between power and gender? El Cheikh elucidates the power of certain harem women—notably, but not solely, the mother of the caliph— in the politics of the day, and distinguishes the caliph's harem from his subjects' household harems. Like Noorani, El Cheikh contests the equation of the harem with "private" space; and like Schick, she notes that *harīm* and its associated terms often referred to people rather than to specific spaces.

In chapter 5, Leslie Peirce moves westward to Istanbul, seat of the Ottoman Empire, and to a later moment, as she scrutinizes the codification of statutes setting out appropriate social and sexual behavior under successive sultans. Again, place and space were not intrinsically important: being respectable was more about conduct than confinement, but "restricted appearance in public" was a sign of a woman's probity (and of her family's economic and social position). Ottoman regulation of behavior—men's and women's—became increasingly elaborate, interacting with local customary law and changing social patterns. "Harem culture" was not a timeless fixture of Ottoman life but rather a result of these shifting and complex pressures on the society. The harem's variability is just as evident in nineteenth-century Tunis, on the empire's periphery just before formal European colonization, Julia Clancy-Smith finds in chapter 7. Women of elite Tunisian and European families came together there, as Europeans tried to insert themselves into a local culture of sociability. The harem— as in the earlier court culture described by El Cheikh—was a space where political and social power was sought and exercised.

In chapter 6, Jateen Lad explores this political space from a different vantage point, that of eunuchs in the imperial court in Istanbul, again exploring the internal hierarchies that a uniquely elaborate harem generated. In chapter 8, drawing on modern envisionings of a late-nineteenth-century urban intelligentsia household, Heghnar Watenpaugh shows that in the contemporary Middle East, representations of domestic life a century ago do not encapsulate either changes over time or the complexity of women's movement through social spaces, which all of these chapters emphasize.

4 · CALIPHAL HAREMS, HOUSEHOLD HAREMS

Baghdad in the Fourth Century of the Islamic Era

Nadia Maria El Cheikh

 The harem cannot be understood apart from its historical specificity. Although Western observers have decontextualized and fetishized the harem, using misconceptions of it for their own ends,[1] it is not only the Orientalist tradition that is guilty in this connection. Arab critics have also argued that the Arab cultural heritage has been projected as something absolutely exemplary, timeless, and outside history. Abdallah Laroui has pointed to the exaggerated medievalization obtained through quasi-magical identification with the zenith of classical Arabian culture. According to him, the true alienation is this loss of self in the absolutes of language, culture, and the saga of the past, the absolute truths of the medieval world: as he describes it, the language of al-Jahiz, the scholasticism of al-Ash'ari, the mysticism of al-Ghazali.[2] Mohammed Arkoun similarly asserts that "all of the contemporary discourse emerging in Islamic contexts inevitably refers to the emerging period of Islam, and the 'Golden Age' of its civilization used as mythological references to reactivate 'values' — ethical and legal paradigms."[3] Such identification produces what becomes received knowledge. In this context, Arkoun has consequently argued that Arab scholars have the responsibility to "create methodological and epistemological options in order to conquer new territory not only to explore new fields of meaning, but primarily, to initiate new levels of understanding of many inherited issues that remain unexamined."[4] In this chapter, I examine such an "inherited" issue by exploring Abbasid harems in Baghdad during the fourth/tenth century using a variety of well-known historical and literary texts. Surveying sources for relevant references to harems, I set these up in opposition to the atemporal fantasy, promoted by both Arab "Medievalism" and Western Orientalism, which continues to obscure our historical understanding.

This chapter thus challenges both the static, timeless nature of prevailing images of the harem and the tendency in Orientalist literature to refer to "harem" in the singular — as if there were simply one type of harem. I contend instead that there were a variety of living arrangements for women in Islamic households in the Abbasid period. To steer away from conventions and clichés, I undertake a more detailed investigation of harems at a particular historical moment. I discuss the harem of Caliph al-Muqtadir (295–320/908–32), analyzing its structure as well as the social, economic, and political power that a number of harem women were able to exercise. The narratives pertaining to the caliph's reign are particularly useful for such an investigation since the power struggle among the various factions at the court allowed the caliph's mother, along with a number of harem women, to wield political power and influence.

While the model of the complex, polygamous harem complete with multiple wives, concubines, and eunuchs applies to the caliphal harem, it was far removed from most people's lived experiences. Thus, the second part of this chapter discusses household harems. The two adab anthologies of al-Tanukhi (940–94), *Kitab al-Faraj ba'da al-shidda* and *Nishwar al-muhadara wa akhbar al-mudhakara*, are particularly valuable as they contain material pertaining to the social history of this period. Although distinct in intention and content, both belong to a literary genre within adab that was quite popular in the third/ninth and fourth/tenth centuries — namely, compilations of edifying and entertaining anecdotes. Adab has been defined as including the best of what had been said in the form of verse, prose, aphorism, and anecdotes on every conceivable subject which an educated man, an *adib*, is supposed to know. Adab also purports to deal with a wide range of problems in language, literature, and ethical and practical behavior.[5] Such books of anecdotal narratives convey not only historical information but also social values and the art of social conduct.[6]

THE HAREMS: SOME DEFINITIONS

Critics of Orientalism see the harem as a fictional notion, and they point to the inability to establish any kind of truth about "reality" in the harem. One such critic makes the distinction between "real" harems and the harem of European literature, which "is nothing but fantasm, a purely fictional construction onto which Europe's own sexual repressions, erotic fantasies and desire of domination were projected."[7] Fatima Mernissi has similarly differentiated between the historical reality of "her" harem—the one in which she grew up—and the Western harem, which gets its vitality from images created by Western paintings, operas, and ballets, all of which depict the harem as a sexual paradise populated by naked, vulnerable creatures, perfectly happy in their captivity.[8]

The *Encyclopedia of Islam* defines *harīm* as a "term applied to those parts of the household to which access is forbidden, and hence more particularly the women's quarters."[9] Nikki Keddie distinguishes between polygamous elite households with slaves and servants and non-elite households that were most probably monogamous and had no slaves or concubines. In the former, activities of the harem were more complex, but it was not "the den of idleness and voluptuousness depicted from their imaginations by Western painters."[10] Leila Ahmed has defined the harem both as "a system that permits males sexual access to more than one female" and as "a system whereby the female relatives of a man—wives, sisters, mothers, aunts, and daughters—share much of their time and their living space, and further, which enables women to have frequent and easy access to other women in their community."[11] In her introduction to the memoirs of Huda Sha'rawi, a leading Egyptian feminist of the early twentieth century, Margot Badran states that the harem was the part of the house where women and children conducted their daily lives. Upper- and middle-class women lived within the private enclosures of their domestic quarters and veiled their faces when they went out, taking their seclusion with them.[12] Such definitions suggest variety across social space and time, but also a shared core of meaning.

The separation of domestic space into the public quarters and the private family space of the harem does not have an overtly sexual connotation. Recent research on domestic space in Muslim community contexts has generally challenged the notion of rigidly demarcated territories, showing that the private and public spheres shared many points of contact in varying historical circumstances.[13] According to Leslie Peirce, while the institution of the harem derived from notions of sexual propriety, "sexuality was

not the dominant ordering principle within the household."[14] Reina Lewis
has characterized "the segregated domains of Ottoman women as spaces
of political agency and cultural production."[15] In her study on the Safavid
period, Kathryn Babayan has similarly concluded that the harem enjoyed
different layers of meaning within contexts that provided functions and
channels for women to exercise political, religious, and social roles.[16] Rather
than secluding women from the outside world, the harem created a central
role for them in the dissemination of information.[17] Emily Apter has defined the harem as a place where women gather and speak to each other.
She has highlighted the ambivalence of harems as spaces that can protect
and nurture women as well as imprison them.[18]

Hugh Kennedy has pointed out that the term *harīm* is seldom used in
Abbasid sources. The texts refer to the caliph's *huram*—his women and
others under his control. (Huram comes from the same root as harīm.)
Thus, the reference is to a group of people rather than to a physical location
such as a particular building.[19] Al-Mas'udi (d. 345/956), for instance, talks
about *dar al-huram* and does not use the term *harīm* to refer spatially to
the women's quarters.[20] Al-Tanukhi's *Nishwar al-Muhadara* mentions the
women's quarters in an anecdote involving Ibn al-Jassass. He had been imprisoned in the caliphal palace. A eunuch accompanied him through various areas of the palace, guiding him to the caliph's mother's quarters (dar
al-Sayyida), so that she could be the one to release him, as she was the one
who interceded on his behalf.[21] Moreover, when al-Muqtadir decided to
have the vizier Ibn al-Furat imprisoned, the vizier's palace was pillaged.
The sources refer to the private areas of Ibn al-Furat's palace by using the
term *dur* (plural of dar): Al-Sabi' (d. 448/1056) talks about the dwellings
of his children and wives (*dur awladihi wa ahlihi*); 'Arib (d. ca. 370/980) also
refers to the dur; and Miskawayh states that his huram were disgraced and
his dwellings (*durahu*) pillaged.[22] Other references which occur in *Nishwar*
similarly refer to the women's quarters as *dur al-huram*.[23] Thus, in contemporary and near-contemporary sources, the term *harīm* generally does
not seem to have been used to specifically express women's spatial location
within a house, but rather to refer to a specific group of people.

THE HAREM OF AL-MUQTADIR

The death of the Abbasid caliph al-Muktafi in 295/908 led to a crisis, since
he had made no provisions for the succession. Ja'far [al-Muqtadir], the
thirteen-year-old brother of al-Muktafi, was proclaimed caliph despite ob-

jections raised on account of his age. His caliphate, a period of unstable government, started out with the appointment of a sort of regency council composed of Shaghab, his mother; Gharib, his maternal uncle; Mu'nis, the treasurer; General Mu'nis al-Muzaffar, leader of the Baghdad troops; Safi, the chief eunuch; and Sawsan, the chamberlain. This situation allowed members of the administration, servants in the palace, viziers, and women in the caliphal harem to negotiate the realities of political power among themselves. Although al-Muqtadir's caliphate differed from some others in having this regency council and thus may have allowed a greater degree of negotiation than was the case in other caliphal households, the composition of his household was probably similar to those of other caliphs.

In the early fourth/tenth century, the *dar al-khilafa*, or caliph's residence, was a large complex made up of a number of palaces. The configuration of these palaces as well as their internal organization remains unknown. Not only is the archaeological information insufficient, but so is the textual information, according to the noted art historian Oleg Grabar, for "nowhere do we read a description that can be translated into architectural forms."[24]

We do know that the dar al-khilafa functioned simultaneously as a stage set for the representation of caliphal power, as the administrative center of a vast empire, and as a residence for the caliphal family. Prominent women had their own apartments within this complex, and it is probably at this time that a separate women's quarter within the palace first emerged.[25] The Abbasid harem of the early fourth/tenth century included family members and the administrative, or service, hierarchy. The former included the caliph's mother, wives, concubines, and children, and his unmarried, widowed, or divorced sisters and aunts. The administrative hierarchy included the high-ranking administrative officers of the harem: eunuchs; stewardesses, whose role is discussed below; female servants, who performed the housekeeping tasks of the harem; and female slaves. Notes Hilal al-Sabi': "It is generally believed that in the days of al-Muqtadir bi-allah . . . the residence contained 11,000 eunuchs [*khadim*] — 7,000 blacks and 4,000 white Slavs . . . 4,000 free and slave girls and thousands of chamber servants."[26]

The caliphal harem consisted of diverse communities of varying ages that interacted with each other in different ways and at different levels. The harem space was the site of a web of female relationships, structured by its own internal hierarchies. Of course, the caliphal harem of the fourth/tenth century was polygamous. The caliph had not only the four legal wives but also a multiplicity of concubines who populated the caliphal harem. Once a concubine had borne a child, she became an *umm al-walad* and

enjoyed a legally and socially enhanced position.[27] The hope of attaining
the status of queen mother — as happened to al-Muqtadir's mother — must
have been entertained by every concubine taken into the harem. A Byzantine by birth, Umm al-Muqtadir, then called Naʿim, had been bought by
the caliph al-Muʿtadid (r. 279/892–289/902). In 282/895, Naʿim gave birth
to a son, Jaʿfar. At that point, the caliph changed her name to Shaghab.
Her producing a son was felt to be troublesome (*shaghab*) for the other
wives of the caliph — hence her name. As an *umm al-walad*, she was freed
on al-Muʿtadid's death, becoming the most influential person at the court.
Operating within the harem, Shaghab and her retinue were not able to
cross the threshold that separated the private from the public sphere. But
this restriction had little impact for, in reality, major politics was conducted
from the private rooms of the caliphal palace.

Access to the caliph's mother was particularly important during the
reign of al-Muqtadir. She figures prominently in the annals of this period
through her political interference, her financial contributions to the government, and her wide-ranging philanthropic activities. The sources highlight the closeness between the caliph and his mother, stating that the
caliph used to spend a lot of time at his mother's quarters in the harem.

One source states that upon hearing of his new appointment as vizier,
al-Khasibi "wished that he had not taken charge of the vizierate," realizing
that being a secretary (*katib*) for Umm al-Muqtadir was better for him than
being the caliph's vizier. Al-Khasibi's appointment as vizier was related to
his closeness to Umm al-Muqtadir. It was she who, together with her sister
Khatif, suggested that he be appointed vizier in 313/925. Previously, he had
been the katib of the stewardess Thumal.[28] Thus, his political career owed
a great deal to harem women.

Umm al-Muqtadir played an important part in the power struggle
within and between factions at the court. On various occasions, she re-
assessed the political situation for her son. One such incident happened in
311/923, when the vizier, Ibn al-Furat, hoping to arrest the chief chamberlain, Nasr, nearly won al-Muqtadir's acquiescence — but for the intervention of Umm al-Muqtadir. She not only saved Nasr but also, more importantly, redressed the balance of power among the caliph's courtiers. Umm
al-Muqtadir reminded her son that Ibn al-Furat had already removed General Muʿnis from his entourage. His current wish to ruin Nasr, she told her
son, was "in order to get you under his power." She then asked him: "On
whom, I should like to know, will you call for aid if he means mischief and

plots your dethronement?"[29] Umm al-Muqtadir successfully convinced the caliph that Nasr's contribution to his security was more important than his money, which the caliph would confiscate from Nasr upon his arrest. Nasr's connections with Umm al-Muqtadir were crucial for his survival.

In addition to providing sound political advice to her son, she supported the reign through her financial contributions and her philanthropic activities. When the Carmathians threatened Baghdad in 927 CE, Umm al-Muqtadir gave half a million dinars of her own money to the public treasury to be spent on the troops. Her act was momentous for, in the words of the vizier 'Ali b. 'Isa, "since the demise of the Blessed Prophet, no more serious disaster has befallen the Muslims than this."[30] Umm al-Muqtadir's generosity also focused on pilgrims. Ibn al-Jawzi states: "Shaghab is said to have devoted one million dinars each year from her private estates to the pilgrimage. She was devoted to the pilgrims' welfare, sending water tanks and doctors and ordering that the reservoirs be fixed."[31] Umm al-Muqtadir's economic power was based on her agricultural estates, which she had received as land grants. Her very wealth became a source of power, and this in turn allowed her to foster a series of subordinate patronage networks. She had her own retinue of secretaries and other officials.

Very few references are made to the harem section of the palatial complex in the literary sources. A rare description of the harem of al-Muqtadir is contained in *Kitab al-Faraj ba'da al-shidda*. A young cloth merchant, wishing to marry a harem stewardess (*qahramana*) of the caliph's mother, was sneaked into the palace for an interview with Umm al-Muqtadir. The merchant concealed himself inside a box among other boxes, in which the qahramana pretended to be bringing clothes and other effects to Umm al-Muqtadir. The qahramana had to pass through groups of eunuchs guarding the doors of various apartments in the harem; they all demanded to inspect the boxes. She yelled at some and cajoled others until she reached the chief eunuch, who insisted on inspecting the content of the boxes. Once again, her cunning saved her, and she managed to pass through. The young merchant managed to meet Umm al-Muqtadir the following day.[32]

This report contains information about the harem section of the palace, the hallways and gateways, and the meticulous security measures, all the responsibility of the eunuch guardians. Eunuchs were at the heart of the harem, monitoring access and partaking in all the informal politics that took place in it. Accepted as a functionally legitimate group, this distinctive gender group flourished in spite of the fact that Islamic law prohibited the making of eunuchs within the lands of Islam.[33] Caring for the women and guarding them required large numbers of slaves and eunuchs. Eunuchs played an important role as servants and guardians within the caliph's women's quarters.

However, the previous anecdote is particularly significant in that it accents the length in both spatial and temporal terms that was required to move within and between various parts of the palace complex. The distance that had to be traversed to reach the harem has important implications for movement between the harem and the public areas of the palace. Distances had the potential to affect frequency of communication and could constitute a limiting factor for quick access to the caliph and those close to him. Equally important, this description reveals a multilayered veiled space—using Apter's term—where barriers to access are concentrically enumerated, constituting an exploration of the "spatial sensation of claustration."[34] Nevertheless, the anecdote is primarily focused on the very transgression of the barriers.

Eunuchs acted as messengers because they could enter any gendered space forbidden to other men. Indeed, the eunuch servants were permitted to move freely in all parts of the caliphal complex. Their duties embraced the whole compound, for they served as intermediaries between their master and his wives, concubines, and female relatives. Their connections to women in the harem gave eunuchs opportunities to influence men in high positions. An episode concerning the black eunuch Muflih shows that this intimate access gave eunuchs considerable influence. Following his dismissal as vizier, Hamid, trying to have an audience with the caliph, came in 311/923 to the palace and met with Nasr, the chief chamberlain. But Nasr's need to rely on Muflih was inescapable, as Muflih was "the official who demanded admission to al-Muqtadir when the latter was in his private apartments." As the chief eunuch, Muflih controlled access to the caliph when the latter was in the harem. Because Nasr could not enter the harem, he had to call on Muflih. It was the latter's status as eunuch—in other words, his liminal gender ascription as an unsexed man—which gave Muflih precious access. The power of the eunuchs stemmed directly from this one factor: they had spatial access to the caliph in his private quarters, the harem, when no other men did.[35]

Perhaps the only category of harem women whose members did not have to abide by the spatial restrictions was the harem stewardess, the qahramana, who performed a number of executive and managerial functions in order to ensure the smooth running of the household. Everyone in the immense household had to be fed and clothed, and their other daily needs had to be provided for. In order to fulfill these duties, qahramanas had the unique privilege (for women) of going in and out of the palace: the other harem women, even the concubines, were not allowed to leave the palace. The qahramanas' mobility gave them numerous opportunities to exercise influence. One qahramana, Umm Musa, became the center of a major patronage network. There was, thus, a sequence of subsidiary courts that could act as rival focuses of politics and patronage. Female members of the household not only advanced themselves but promoted others as well — or kept them back.

Proximity to the caliph and his mother was one sure way of building a power base at court. And as everything going to the caliph had to pass through the filter of his entourage before it could reach him, the qahramanas were able to forge alliances with powerful and influential people through their intercessions with the caliph and his mother. Umm Musa acted as the principal intermediary between the caliph's mother and the caliph, as well as among other officials of the court. We read that during the caliphate of al-Muqtadir, "various knaves managed to write letters and convey them through Umm Musa to al-Muqtadir requesting posts and promising money."[36] The influence of the qahramanas was manifested in their role in successful plots against viziers and other high officials. Attempting to bring about the dismissal of Ibn al-Furat in 298–99/911–12, Muhammad b. Khaqan asked Umm Musa to relay a message to the caliph and his mother that implicated Ibn al-Furat in an Alid conspiracy against the caliph. They immediately imprisoned Ibn al-Furat, confiscated his wealth, and appointed Muhammad b. Khaqan as vizier.[37]

The activities of Zaydan, another qahramana, serve as an example of the qahramanas' political role. High-ranking prisoners of state were committed to Zaydan's custody for mild incarceration in the caliphal complex. Her role as jailer allowed Zaydan to come into contact with influential persons, individuals who had temporarily fallen out of favor but who had the potential to rise to power and influence once again. Her exclusive access to these important personalities, and her ability to act as a mediator between her prisoners and the caliph, provided her with important leverage and allowed her to develop a web of influence built on past favors.[38]

Palace politics — or perhaps more accurately, harem politics — required the formation of temporary alliances within court and harem circles in order to obtain certain advantages such as money, power, and appointments to high office. In addition to the examples above, we read that Nasr, as chief chamberlain, sought an alliance with Thumal, a qahramana, in order to create new connections inside the harem.[39]

The power, influence, and access to wealth of the harem's women and eunuchs are confirmed in a letter that General Mu'nis addressed to the caliph. Mu'nis stated that the army was complaining bitterly about the money and land given to the eunuchs and women of the court, and about their participation in the administration. He demanded that certain eunuchs and women be dismissed and removed from the palace, and their possessions seized.[40] In his reply to Mu'nis, al-Muqtadir came to the defense of the eunuchs and women:

> Now what our friends propose in the matter of the eunuchs and women, whom they would cast out of the Palace and remove far away . . . so that they should be precluded and deprived of their fortunes and kept at a distance from them until they deliver up the money and the estates which are in their hands, and restore them to their rightful owners— that is a proposal, which, if they properly considered and examined it, they would know to be an unjust proposal, and one whose iniquity is obvious to me. Still, so anxious am I to agree with them . . . that I am giving orders for the seizure of some of their fiefs, for the abolition of their privileges . . . and for the removal from the palace of all whom it is permissible to expel while those who remain shall not be permitted to interfere with my administration or counsels.[41]

The answer acknowledges the powerful women and eunuchs as fief holders and points to the privileges they have. Explicit reference is made to their interference in the administration. The caliph promised to curb their political influence, but only in order to appease Mu'nis. Thus, the harem was clearly demarcated, yet its boundaries were permeable. Women's confinement in the harem did not mean that their power was curtailed.

HOUSEHOLD HAREMS

The large caliphal harem, with many women and eunuchs, was very different from most people's households. Outside the court, strict seclusion of women was practiced only by a small proportion of well-to-do urban families in which women did not play an active economic role. Moreover, polygamy was an expensive urban practice that was mainly the preserve of the elite. We get glimpses of household harems in al-Tanukhi's *Nishwar al-muhadara wa akhbar al-mudhakara* and *Kitab al-Faraj ba'da al-shidda*. In both works, al-Tanukhi presents anecdotes rich in detail on various aspects of Abbasid society, including women's lives, and he vividly illustrates many practices and attitudes. A large number of anecdotes in both the *Nishwar* and *al-Faraj* include stories of a familiar literary type, which uses factual details for purposes of verisimilitude. Julia Bray points out that while some of the stories draw on fact, they are also part of a rags-to-riches romance.[42]

The anecdotes' framing follows the formal pattern of historical reports. In his introduction to the *Nishwar*, al-Tanukhi lists the sources from which his information is derived, suggesting that these reports present a rich variety of examples of social behavior pertaining to Iraqi Muslim life and society in his time. *Al-Faraj* is a more difficult compilation to use, including anecdotes of various epochs centered around the theme of relief after adversity. What is particularly important about this compilation is that the information included does not concentrate on actions but rather on situations, which explains its attention to detail. Francesco Gabrieli stresses the important historical value of literary compilations such as *al-Faraj*, which constitutes a mine for the reconstruction of, among other subjects, private and economic life, institutions, and costume.[43]

This brief introduction to the anthologies of al-Tanukhi is warranted because of the problematic and hence rare usage of such compilations by historians. Although the anthologies do not conform to the common definition of what constitutes history,[44] Dominique Sourdel made use of al-Tanukhi's works in writing his history of the Abbasid vizierate, stating that if one is to consult adab works, "the most significant mine of historical anecdotes is found in the works of al-Tanukhi." Sourdel pointed out that the accounts in the *Nishwar*, based on contemporary reports, have the value of authentic testimony, and that even if one does not accept these anecdotes literally, it is not difficult to extricate their historical significance.[45] Despite its repetitiveness, its transmission of universal values, and its idealistic character, adab readjusts and actualizes its images and metaphors, recording the modifications and changes in society, its mentalities, and its sensibilities. As Jean Claude Vadet puts it, adab forms around itself the unanimity of the *corps social*.[46] Adab is representative inasmuch as it would never include material that did not conform to the world values of the compiler and his audience. One scholar has also remarked that it is difficult to see why one would suppose that certain themes in belles-lettres "were simply literary exercises which reveal nothing about the mental and emotional world" of the poets, narrators, and their audiences.[47] It is not necessary to take the following anecdotal references in any strict historical sense. The particular incident may or may not have happened. The weight should be rather on the setting and gender roles, and the expectations represented therein as apparently unremarkable social practice.

One anecdote in *al-Faraj* includes a description of an elite harem. It involves Abu Ja'far, who had been a secretary of the caliph's cousin and later became minister under the Turkish commander Bajkam (a military commander under caliph al-Radi, who reigned 934–940 CE). Abu Ja'far, hiding from Bajkam, disguised himself in women's clothes and, with a number of elderly women, went to the dar of Khatif, an aunt of al-Muqtadir. He entered the vestibule between the door and the actual dwelling and had one of the elderly women talk with the eunuch in charge. Khatif appeared in the vestibule, dismissed the eunuch, discovered her guest's identity, and then led the party through rooms, vestibules, and subterranean vaults until they reached a secret room at the end of a set of stairs.[48]

While this elite household seems to replicate on a much smaller scale the spatial division of the elaborate caliphal harem, al-Tanukhi's anthologies also provide information about more modest households. In another anecdote, a man mentions his marriage to a woman he loved. They lived happily for a long time: "Then it went with us the way it goes with many couples. She got angry at me and closed the door to her room, forbidding me to enter it. She told me that I should divorce her. I tried to conciliate her, to no avail. I asked her female relatives to mediate on my behalf, but it did not work." The husband, overtaken by grief and distress, camped at the woman's door, weeping and crying, until she was finally appeased.[49] The man's behavior makes the presence of other wives highly unlikely, and co-wives or even concubines are completely absent from this description. The only other females mentioned in the anecdote are the wife's female relatives.

Al-Tanukhi presents other household scenes. Before he became vizier, Ibn al-Furat once knocked at someone's door. The head of the household, a tailor, invited him in. The text goes on to mention something that has practically nothing to do with the substance of the encounter between the two men: the host "gave the guest's clothes to his wife [*zawjatuhu*] to wash while he conversed with him." This story refers to a single wife, not to one of the host's wives or one of his concubines. Later on, in the same anecdote, the tailor visited Ibn al-Furat, now vizier. He reminded him of his visit, and Ibn al-Furat inquired about "him, his wife [in the singular], and his children."[50] There are other such anecdotes that concern men of relatively modest means who seem to have only one wife.[51] It is impossible to conclude with any confidence, from these limited references, whether the protagonists were engaged in monogamous or polygamous marriages. However, it is necessary to look into all kinds of evidence in order to discern the frequency of polygamous marriages, and we should consider the possibility that monogamous serial marriages were common.

Both the *Nishwar* and *al-Faraj* provide, moreover, evidence contradicting the image of harems as impenetrable and inaccessible spaces. We are told of a young man, Bishr b. 'Abdallah, who fell in love with a woman who was jealously guarded by her husband. To allow her to spend a night with Bishr, he got a male friend to masquerade as the woman by putting on her clothes when she had left her house and returning there in her stead.[52]

Another transgression of the harem boundaries involves daughters of important notables in Baghdad who were caught committing immoral acts. Al-Tanukhi mentions police reports, "each one relating the day's events. All the reports mentioned raids undertaken against women who were found fornicating. They were the daughters of viziers, military commanders, and notables who had died or who had lost their positions."[53]

The *Nishwar* also discusses the daughter of Ibn Abi 'Awf, a wealthy and very influential man: "It was mentioned that the news spread in Baghdad that Ibn Abi 'Awf entered his home to find his daughter with a man who is not her *mahram*," that is, the man was not within a degree of consanguinity precluding marriage.[54] These passages inform us of raids undertaken by the police and of free women of a certain standing engaging in activities defined by their society as immoral. What connection do these stories about fornication bear to reality? Do they indicate that debauchery among upper-class women was commonplace or usual? In particular, what do these anecdotes tell us about women's seclusion in their harems? We cannot fully answer these questions, but these anecdotes do suggest that the walls of upper-class harems were not impenetrable. Moreover, the anecdotes illustrate a certain moral freedom among the upper classes that legal and religious texts do not intimate, and that contradict standard notions about what harems are.

Normative texts and literary texts say much about what was expected of women and men. If adab texts do not give us information about how men and women actually behaved, they do give us insights into how people might have behaved and what social constraints they might have faced. While the reality is difficult to capture, works such as al-Tanukhi's compilations can give us the social context in which the textual edifice was constructed. These writings reflect long-standing official discourses which allow us to better understand the cultural construct of expectations for both men and women in adab during the Abbasid period.

CONCLUSION

This chapter has examined Abbasid harems in Baghdad during the fourth/tenth century, using a variety of well-known historical and literary texts. The aim was to survey the sources for relevant references to harems, in order to set them up in opposition to the atemporal fantasy that continues to dilute our understanding. The references to al-Muqtadir's harem do not present the idle Orientalist harem but rather a harem which is first and foremost a political arena, in which highly positioned women, as well as leading eunuchs, participated in major caliphal politics. This is clearly not the male-dominated harem of the traditional narrative. Such a vision is also at odds with the Western fixation on the harem as a brothel-like sexual prison. Moreover, the information supports the assertion that the lines among family, community, and the public sphere of politics and power were blurred in premodern societies.[55] Although women did not hold actual political positions, they were well placed to influence public affairs, even if inconspicuously. Operating within the harem, Umm al-Muqtadir and her qahramanas were able at times to cross the threshold that separated the private from the public sphere. The restrictions that existed did not keep women from conducting politics in the women's quarters of the caliphal complex.

Evidence from the reign of al-Muqtadir, moreover, subverts the private-public binary structure that undergirds popular perceptions of the harem. As Peirce has made clear, to map onto the harem a European notion of public and private is to ignore the fact that within the spatial relations of seclusion, it was proximity to the interior of the caliphal household that led to power and status.[56] Ruby Lal has also pointed to the "imbrication of the Mughal domestic world in the everyday life of courts and kings or, equally, the imbrication of courts and kings in the everyday life of the domestic world."[57] In line with these conclusions, the harem of al-Muqtadir puts into question the nature of political power and the location of political activity. The textual evidence invalidates the stereotype of passive, indolent harem women, and draws a picture of women actively involved in court politics and exercising a high degree of influence. The image of the harem as a place of sequestration collapses in light of the various anecdotes and historical information offered here. The walls of the harems were porous, allowing contact with the exterior via the qahramanas and eunuchs. Moreover, the historical and semihistorical anecdotes are populated with characters who succeed in transgressing the boundaries of the caliphal harem and elite households.

The anecdotes in al-Tanukhi's anthologies, moreover, do not uphold the myth of the ubiquitous polygamous harem. This should propel us to expand our inquiry into marriage patterns in Abbasid societies. While the caliphal harem was polygamous and contained numerous concubines, references to more modest households imply monogamy. It also appears that women of certain classes were able to transgress some of the seemingly strict rules and limitations. The difference among classes in the definition of what was both proper and moral behavior for a woman calls for increasing subtlety in analyzing the role of harems in structuring the class and gender configurations of given Muslim societies. It is important to get detailed information about free women of various classes, and about slave girls. Such knowledge is vital to appreciate the various spatial positions assigned to them at various historical moments, and the multiplicity of social and moral possibilities available to diverse categories of women. Only with that information can we bridge the discrepancy between theoretical and real restrictions on women and provide a better understanding of Abbasid "harems."

NOTES

An earlier version of this chapter appeared as "Revisiting the Abbasid Harems," *Journal of Middle East Women's Studies* 1, no. 3 (fall 2005): 1–19. All translations are mine, unless otherwise indicated.

1 DelPlato, *Multiple Wives, Multiple Pleasures*, preface.
2 Laroui, *The Crisis of the Arab Intellectual*, 156–58.
3 Arkoun, *The Unthought in Contemporary Islamic Thought*, 10.
4 Ibid., 15.
5 Bonebakker has stated that the current definitions of adab are "too broad to provide a workable analytic framework," suggesting a more restricted definition to be used instead ("Adab and the Concept of Belles-Lettres," 5).
6 Leder and Kilpatrick, "Classical Arabic Prose Literature." See, for further discussion, El Cheikh, "Women's History."

7   Behdad, "The Eroticized Orient," 110.

8   Mernissi, *Le harem et l'occident*, 18–21.

9   "Harīm," *EI²* 3:209.

10   Keddie, "Introduction," 11.

11   Ahmed, "Western Ethnocentrism and Perceptions of the Harem," 524.

12   Badran, Introduction, 7. Al-Sayyid-Marsot has pointed out in "The Revolutionary Gentlewoman in Egypt" that authors tend to describe harem life in terms of extremes: as a lascivious place or as a place of idleness.

13   Afsaruddin, "Introduction."

14   Peirce, *The Imperial Harem*, 5.

15   Lewis, *Rethinking Orientalism*, 4.

16   Babayan, "The 'Aqā'id al-nisā'."

17   Lewis, *Gendering Orientalism*, 154.

18   Apter, "Female Trouble in the Colonial Harem."

19   H. Kennedy, *The Court of the Caliphs*, 160. See also Schick's chapter in this volume.

20   Al-Mas'udi, *Muruj al-dhahab wa ma'adin al-jawhar*, 4:248, 5:215.

21   Al-Tanukhi, *Nishwar al-muhadara wa akhbar al-mudhakara*, 7:233.

22   Al-Sabi', *Kitab tuhfat al-umara' fi tarikh al-wuzara',* 37; 'Arib, *Silat tarikh al-Tabari*, 29; Miskawayh, *Tajarib al-umam*, 1:20.

23   Al-Tanukhi, *Nishwar al-muhadara wa akhbar al-mudhakara*, 1:287, 3:101.

24   Grabar, *The Formation of Islamic Art*, 158.

25   H. Kennedy, *The Court of the Caliphs*, 164.

26   Al-Sabi', *Rusum dar al-khilafa*, 8.

27   A concubine who bore her master a child achieved the status of *umm al-walad* (mother of the child) and could no longer be sold, pawned, or given away. Most jurists agreed that the *umm al-walad* automatically became free on her master's death.

28   'Arib, *Silat tarikh al-Tabari*, 128.

29   Miskawayh, *Tajarib al-umam*, 1:117; see also al-Sabi', *Kitab tuhfat al-umara' fi tarikh al-wuzara',* 47.

30   Miskawayh, *Tajarib al-umam*, 1:180.

31   Ibn al-Jawzi, *al-Muntazam fi tarikh al-umam wa al-muluk*, 13:321.

32   Al-Tanukhi, *Kitab al-faraj ba'da al-shidda*, 4:362–68.

33   See De la Puente, "Sin linaje, sin alcurnia, sin hogar."

34   Apter, "Female Trouble in the Colonial Harem." It is interesting to note that Orientalist stereotypes dramatized the harem's inaccessibility. There is no ease of movement in the heart of the harem, but rather a boxing in of courtyards and rooms, each almost hermetically closed. See Grosrichard, *The Sultan's Court*, 126. On the scrupulous concerns about separation and partitioning in the architecture of the Ottoman harem, see Lad's chapter in this volume.

35   Miskawayh, *Tajarib al-umam*, 1:87; and *The Eclipse of the Abbasid Caliphate*, 1:96.

36   Miskawayh, *Tajarib al-umam*, 1:27.

37   Al-Sabi', *Kitab tuhfat al-umara' fi tarikh al-wuzara',* 272–73.

38   See for instance, ibid., 91.

39 Al-Suli, *Ma lam yunshar min awraq al-Suli*, 149.
40 Miskawayh, *Tajarib al-umam*, 1:189; and *The Eclipse of the Abbasid Caliphate*, 1:213.
41 Miskawayh, *Tajarib al-umam*, 1:189–90; and *The Eclipse of the Abbasid Caliphate*, 1:213–14.
42 Bray, "A Caliph and His Public Relations."
43 Gabrieli, "Il valore letterario e storico del farag ba'da s-sidda di Tanūhi."
44 Khalidi, *Arabic Historical Thought in the Classical Period*, 113.
45 Sourdel, *Le vizirat Abbaside de 749 à 936*, 1:35–36.
46 Vadet, "Les grands themes de l'adab dans le Rabi' al-abrar d'al-Zamakhshari."
47 El-Rouayheb, *Before Homosexuality in the Arab-Islamic World, 1500–1800*, 79.
48 Al-Tanukhi, *Kitab al-faraj ba'da al-shidda*, 4:37–38.
49 Ibid., 4:426.
50 Al-Tanukhi, *Nishwar al-muhadara wa akhbar al-mudhakara*, 4:66–67.
51 Ibid., 7:237. See Schick's chapter in this volume, where he states that the data on common people in Ottoman Istanbul do not support the view that most men were polygamous.
52 Al-Tanukhi, *Kitab al-faraj ba'da al-shidda*, 4:354–56.
53 Ibid., 4:5–6.
54 Al-Tanukhi, *Nishwar al-muhadara wa akhbar al-mudhakara*, 2:117.
55 Meriwether and Tucker, eds., introduction, *Social History of Women and Gender in the Modern Middle East*, 6.
56 Peirce, *The Imperial Harem*, 9.
57 Lal, "Historicizing the Harem," 603.

5 ✦ DOMESTICATING SEXUALITY

Harem Culture in Ottoman Imperial Law

Leslie Peirce

 When the Moroccan world traveler Ibn Battuta toured the Turkish principalities of western Anatolia in the 1330s, he was surprised to see so many women in public. And when he visited the nascent Ottoman polity, in his opinion the richest of these principalities, the traveler was received by the wife of Orhan (the second Ottoman ruler). Describing her as "a pious and excellent woman," Ibn Battuta noted that she "treated me honorably [and] gave me hospitality."[1] But by the mid-sixteenth century, when the German traveler Hans Dernschwam visited Istanbul, he remarked how few women were visible on the streets.[2] As for the royal family, always a trendsetter for the elites, women of the dynasty no longer received foreign dignitaries. Their infrequent forays outside the royal palace were carefully staged and increasingly limited to female elders.

Should female subjects of the empire aspire to emulate these shifting models of conduct, and if so, which females? People wanted and needed to sort out matters of status, and one way they did so was by looking to women's conduct as an indicator of social rank. Around the time of Dernschwam's visit, the chief mufti of the Ottoman Empire, Ebu

Suud, was busy issuing fatwas clarifying which women might be honored with the epithet *muhaddere*—a term perhaps best translated as "respectable" that, in sixteenth-century thinking, connoted a reputation for chaste behavior and its corollary, observation of the protocols of veiling and seclusion. A muhaddere woman was not confined to the house, declared the mufti, but when she went out—for example, to the baths or a wedding or for a visit in another neighborhood—she should be accompanied "by servants and attendants."[3]

The very number of Ebu Suud's fatwas on the subject suggests that his petitioners were anxious for answers regarding what constituted respectable conduct and what did not. Peasants as well as city dwellers tested the limits of muhaddere status: to the query, "Can [a woman] be muhaddere if she handles her own affairs with the people of the village and brings water from the well?" Ebu Suud summarily answered "No." In his most expansive answer on this measure of female respectability, the mufti made clear that he did not regard it as intrinsically Islamic: "It is not conformity to the prescriptions of the noble Sharia that is the essential element in being muhaddere," he wrote, "that is why non-Muslim women can also be muhaddere. A woman is muhaddere if she does not let herself be seen by persons other than members of her household and does not set about taking care of her affairs in person."[4] The muhaddere woman was following a social, not a religious, injunction, the mufti seemed to be saying. If the lines she drew were not sectarian, they were lines that established social class, since only a household of some means could afford to purchase slaves or hire servants to take on the duties of female domestic labor.

Neither Ebu Suud nor the petitioners who presented him with queries about women's social conduct used the term *harem* to refer to female seclusion in the home. In the sixteenth century, *harem* was a term used by Ottomans to refer to spaces more exalted than a domestic interior. It referred to the sacrosanct nature of such spaces—the interior of a mosque, or the inner quarters of the imperial palace (occupied by the sultan and his privileged servants). Being muhaddere was less about domestic confinement than it was about personal conduct and reputation. Nonetheless, as we see, reputation depended on carefully restricted appearance in public, thereby rendering domestic space the normative space for women—at least for those who could afford it. While technically anachronistic, this chapter will use the notion of "harem culture" as shorthand to refer to the complex of social practices that established the status of the muhaddere woman.

Was Ebu Suud in his fatwas merely endorsing social standards that were generated by the subjects of the Ottoman Empire, or was he making so-cial policy? The answer is probably both: by clarifying definitions, the chief mufti, because of his towering stature, was inevitably articulating norma-tive standards. However, Ebu Suud was not the only Ottoman authority concerned with the behavior of the empire's subjects and their social and sexual comportment. Ottoman ideology and practice granted a large legis-lative role directly to the sultans. They issued edicts and statutes known as *kanun*, and these kanuns were periodically compiled in statute collections known as *kanunnames* (books of statutes). The *Kanunname-i Osmanî*—the imperial Ottoman book of laws—was the most important and comprehen-sive of such compilations. It was in this document that the sultans publi-cized rules of sociosexual conduct, as well as penalties for their infraction.

This chapter examines the evolution of the *Kanunname-i Osmanî* (hence-forth referred to as the Kanunname) from the later fifteenth century to the mid-sixteenth. Its purpose is to explore questions of social change as re-flected in legal culture. It asks when and how the social culture of the harem was written into imperial law and thus became a normative element in Ottoman legal culture. Because the Kanunname was continually amended, its evolving text reveals shifting social standards as well as the Ottoman regime's growing stake in regulating sexual behavior. For example, the stat-utes on sexual conduct in the earliest version of the Kanunname (c. 1480) were largely limited to punishment of voluntary extramarital sex. Within less than a century, its provisions had multiplied to cover a broad range of social as well as specifically sexual conduct, forced as well as voluntary, in public spaces and in the confines of the home. Understanding how and why a spare legal scaffolding was transformed into an elaborate architecture of prescriptive and proscriptive behavior is the principal project of this essay.

Two intertwining themes structure the chapter. The first explores the world of domestic space, sex, and gender as it was imagined from the Otto-man imperial center; it does so by tracing the emergence of harem culture in successive redactions of the Kanunname. Here it is critical to discard the venerable Western stereotype of the harem, whose creatures are assumed to be female and hardly noteworthy for their chaste demeanor or economic enterprise. As Ebu Suud's fatwas reveal, the secluded woman might be a woman of affairs. Moreover, while illicit contact between adult females and males were its principal concern, the Kanunname gradually advanced a notion of the protected domicile that encompassed sons and slaves as well as wives and daughters.

The second theme considers what the Kanunname was meant to accomplish, both practically and ideologically, and what drove the habit of its continual redaction. It is important to situate the Kanunname's evolving vision of a well-ordered sociosexual universe in the context of an expanding and increasingly complex imperial territory that demanded regulation not only of economic and political life but also of public social life. Like the fatwas of the chief mufti, the Kanunname inevitably gave normative status to a variety of practices and prohibitions because it inscribed individual edicts in a collective document intended for empire-wide application. A question visited throughout this essay is the degree to which the sultan and his legal advisors were responding to grass-roots trends and conflicts as they edited and amended the Kanunname.

THE OTTOMAN KANUNNAME

It is the legislative activity of the four sultans who gave basic shape to the Ottoman Empire with which we are concerned. The reigns of Mehmed II, Bayezid II, Selim I, and Süleyman I spanned the long century of imperial consolidation from 1451 (the beginning of Mehmed's long reign) to 1566 (the death of Süleyman). The Kanunname was a significant product of the political aftermath of Mehmed's momentous conquest of Constantinople in 1453. This victory put an end to the millennium-old empire of the Byzantines and established a Muslim sovereign for the first time in the venerable queen of cities. One of the conspicuous acts that signaled the new imperial status of the Ottoman sultanate was the promulgation of laws. Mehmed II was the first Ottoman sovereign to publicly issue a comprehensive kanunname, which he did near the end of his reign.[5]

Because the Kanunname was not a fixed collation of statutes, I have hesitated to describe Mehmed's action in formulating and promulgating the initial version of the Kanunname as codifying imperial law. The Kanunname was a living, evolving document, and one could easily speak of multiple imperial kanunnames. Each of Mehmed's three successors elaborated upon the work of the previous sultan (his father) by periodically issuing amended versions of the Kanunname, dropping or revising some statutes and adding new ones. Even within a single sultan's reign, several versions of different date and different length might be circulating simultaneously.[6] The Kanunname was a royal blueprint for managing what was becoming an increasingly diverse and complex population as the empire continued to expand. Through the ongoing process of amendment by successive sultans, it adapted to the shifting circumstances and composition of the empire's subject populations.

There is a long history of sovereigns and lawmaking in the eastern Mediterranean and the ancient Near East. Islamic kanun (regulations; Arabic *qânûn*, pl. *qawânîn*) originated as royal edicts regulating taxation.[7] This emphasis persisted, and it is not surprising that the bulk of the Ottoman Kanunname was devoted to setting taxes and legislating relations between taxing authorities and taxpayers. But by the eleventh century CE, royal kanun had come to encompass public law more broadly, as a supplement to Islamic law (sharia), which was notoriously weak in the domain of criminal prosecution and in legal implementation in general. It came to be accepted, at least in the lands that were to comprise the Ottoman Empire, that it was the sovereign's duty and prerogative to prosecute "crimes against God." These were criminal acts deemed disruptive of public order, whose penalties were initially laid out in the Qur'an: adultery and fornication, sexual slander, theft, consumption of intoxicants, and highway robbery (the latter category would be broken down in the Ottoman Kanunname into the separate crimes of assault, robbery, and murder). By opening his Kanunname with criminal statutes that dealt principally with these crimes and variations on them, Mehmed II asserted several principles: his empire was based on the rule of law, the sovereign was the rightful chief architect of Ottoman justice, and a fundamental duty of the sovereign was the defense of God's law.

It is in sections of the Kanunname devoted to the definition of criminal acts and their punishments that the sociosexual world of Ottoman subjects as visualized by their sovereigns comes into view. These sections permit a reading of domestic life from the ground up as viewed from the top down. Let us take a moment to look at the structure of the Kanunname, the most extended discursive portrayal of the Ottoman sovereign's legal authority and responsibility. Criminal acts and the penalties they incur are the subject of the opening chapter(s) of all editions of the Kanunname. (The remaining chapters—the bulk of the Kanunname—deal primarily with taxes, the status of taxpayers, and their relations with tax collectors; the logic of combining God's law with taxation had partly to do with the prominence of money fines in Ottoman criminal management, giving the latter a distinctly fiscal cast.) The import of opening the Kanunname with this "penal code," as it has been called, was to suggest that the Ottoman sovereign's first legal responsibility was to preserve public order by prosecuting crimes against God. Within the penal code itself, the first topic, invariably, is sexual crime, treated under the general rubric of "*zina* [illicit sexual intercourse] and related acts."[8] In other words, the most important legal document of early modern Ottoman government—the empire's foundational legal blueprint—begins by mapping normative social and sexual relations.

Consistent with classical Islamic jurisprudence, *zina* in the Kanunname is defined primarily as adultery and fornication—that is, consensual heterosexual sex outside the permitted relationships of husband and wife or master and female slave. Statutes dealing with the separate crime of sexual slander (*kazf*)—incorrectly or maliciously accusing someone of *zina*—were usually included in the zina section as well. Over time, successive iterations of the Kanunname incorporated other forms of sexual congress, including nonconsensual sex and sex between males, as well as related matters such as abduction, physical and verbal harassment, molestation in public spaces, and even sex within the family. While Mehmed II's Kanunname contained twelve statutes in its zina section, the longest versions of Süleyman's Kanunname contained some three dozen or more. Thus it is primarily, although not exclusively, the zina section of the Kanunname that is the stage for the legal exposition of harem culture. In its sexualizing and policing of space, speech, and body, the Kanunname increasingly evoked the ideal of the harem (although never using the word)—a domestic regime that forbade visual and verbal as well as physical contact between strangers and dependents of the male head of household, and that put responsibility for the collective honor of the family on his shoulders and in his hands.

The Kanunname reveals more than a strictly imperial vision of a properly ordered domestic universe. Kanun as a legal genre and a legal practice included a heavy dose of customary law—that is, local practice that over time acquired the force of law.[9] Indeed, the term *kanun* carried overlapping meanings, ranging from traditional custom or rule of procedure (as in the standard phrase *kanun-ı kadim üzere*—"according to traditional practice") to an edict or regulatory code issued by the sovereign power. It was the gradual incorporation—or explicit rejection—of customary norms that accounts in large part for the Kanunname's increasing length in the period studied here.

These normative customary practices, some of ancient provenance in the legally minded Near East, might be in conflict with the principles of Islamic law. Indeed, kanun was, and had traditionally been, a bridge of compromise between Islamic sharia and customary practice. It is often alleged that kanun is secular while sharia is religious, but the Kanunname's conspicuous attention to the Qur'anic crimes underlines its role as a mediator between religious and customary sources of the law. Kanun was the art of the possible. As an example, let us consider the problem of adultery. Prosecution under strict Islamic law was virtually impossible because conviction required four witnesses of the act of penetration or confession of guilt by the adulterer, before the judge, on four separate occasions. Customary law, on the other hand, could be brutal in its sanctioning of what has come to be called honor killing, or the right of a husband to kill his adulterous wife and her lover (and sometimes the right of a father to kill his daughter). We will see that the Kanunname attempted to mediate between the inadequacy of sharia and the vigilante excess of customary practice.

The act of balancing Islamic and customary law was fraught with tension, despite the fact that Muslim sovereigns had pursued this task for centuries. One of the underlying themes of this essay is the shifting stance of the sultans toward the legal bases of their legitimacy and power. Take Selim I's Kanunname, for example: compared to his father's and grandfather's versions, it made few explicit concessions to the Islamic bases of sovereign authority. Rather, it justified imperial legal policy as *raison d'état*—*siyaset* in Ottoman parlance, the absolute legislative cum executive authority of the sultan that included the power to inflict punishment without trial by a judge. Selim's toughness was not without its context: his rapid conquests between 1514 and 1517 doubled the size of the empire and brought in populations, some of whom were unreconciled to Ottoman hegemony. It is critical to keep in mind that the century during which the Kanunname evolved was one of continued territorial expansion and the resultant challenge of pacifying and integrating new peoples into an Ottoman civil subjecthood. One resulting challenge was to make the Kanunname a workable rubric for administering the whole subject population—Christian and Jew as well as Muslim, slave as well as free, peasant and nomad as well as urban resident. Another challenge to the regime was to subordinate local power brokers as well as its own officials to sultanic authority. Documentary and literary sources abound with stories of abuse by local feudal lords and Ottoman officials, and over and over again the rhetoric of Ottoman justice celebrated the sultan's protection of the little person, in particular the peasant taxpayer, from exploitation.[10]

Let us now proceed to a review of the Kanunnames of the four authors of this major document of early modern Ottoman statecraft and adminis-tration: Mehmed II (r. 1451–81), Bayezid II (r. 1481–1512), Selim I (r. 1512–20), and Süleyman I (r. 1520–66). Our review proceeds chronologically be-cause our goal is to see when, how, and perhaps why harem culture came increasingly to represent an ideal sociosexual landscape in the eyes of the Ottoman regime.

THE KANUNNAME OF MEHMED II

In comparison with later versions of the Kanunname, that of Mehmed II displays little vision of a domestic harem. Its section "on zina and inten-tions [to commit zina]"[11] is spare, containing only twelve statutes. With one or possibly two exceptions, the statutes are confined to adult heterosexual acts that assume consent. Nearly half the zina section is taken up by the prescription of fines for adultery and fornication, a feature that is standard in all subsequent versions. The structure of fines comprises several stat-utes because it calculates penalties using two factors: first, civil status—married free persons, single free persons, and married and single slaves, all presumed to be Muslim; and second, degree of wealth—well-off, middling, poor, and destitute individuals. For example, well-off Muslim adulterers, male and female, pay the highest fine—300 akçes (the standard Ottoman silver coin), while their slave counterparts pay half that amount; a destitute Muslim male or female adulterer is fined 40 akçes, and the destitute slave half that amount. Parallel rates for fornicators (unmarried persons) ranged from 100 to 30 akçes. (Note that slaves, like free persons, were fined accord-ing to their personal wealth.)

In Mehmed's Kanunname, the spatial dynamics of potential sexual dis-order are rudimentary. In the geography of sexual crime, domestic space is regulated in a single statute: breaking into a dwelling by a person intent on zina merits the zina penalties, whether or not the perpetrator accomplishes his intent. As for public space, grabbing an adult woman, kissing her, or otherwise embracing her is punished by a beating (the bastinado) as well as a fine. The number of bastinado strokes is determined at the judge's dis-cretion (ta'zir), and the fine is one akçe for every two strokes. Nor is there much of a conceptual harem in this early book of laws—that is, a hierarchy of control whereby the male head of household is responsible for the con-duct of dependent family members. Married and unmarried women mirror their male counterparts in punishment: they pay the same fines for zina.

They also enjoy the same impunity from sexually slanderous accusations ("If a man says to a woman, 'I had sex with you,' and the woman denies this, the woman shall take an oath [of innocence], and the judge shall punish the man"; likewise, "If a woman or a girl says to a man, 'You had sex with me,' and the man denies this . . ."). Women and men are also subject to the same punishment for unsubstantiated slanderous accusations (a beating plus a fine).

Women are conspicuous sexual actors in the public sphere of Mehmed's Kanunname, intentionally committing crimes. Female pimps (*pezevenk*) receive the ta'zir punishment of a beating whose severity is, as usual, decided by the judge, plus a fine of one akçe per stroke. Only one statute exhibits deference to the authority of the male head of household, and this statute is also the only one that inscribes a customary practice in the Kanunname: a man who fails to divorce an adulterous wife must pay a fine (100 akçes for a rich man) for cuckoldry (*köftehorluk*). Here, finally, is a hint of the stereotypical harem dynamic: a man is dishonored, even guilty, if he fails to control his wife and is moreover willing to live with the dishonor she brings upon him. There is, however, a condition to this cuckold tax: the husband pays it only if his wife is a woman of independent means (*avret'in malı olsa*), presumably so that a woman unable to support herself is not cast out, lest she resort to further zina in the form of prostitution.

In sum, Mehmed's zina edicts are skeletal in comparison with what was to come. What they are is a minimal statement of the sovereign's responsibility to enforce Qur'anic penalties for illicit sex and sexual slander. The absence of non-Muslims in the criminal social body is noteworthy, for they will appear in every subsequent version of the Kanunname, where they incur half the fines of their Muslim counterparts. The majority of the subject population in Mehmed's time was Christian and surely harbored its own adulterers; hence, this absence confirms that the sultan's purpose was less the actual regulation of society than a proclamation that the Ottoman sovereign had now attained the stature to formulate an imperial law and, moreover, to assert his authority to prescribe exact penalties for the violation of God's law.

As a statement of the ruler's duty to implement Islamic law, the zina section of Mehmed's Kanunname reflects what we might call the sharia principle of gender symmetry in zina: men and women are partners in crime, equal sufferers in punishment. This symmetry is unbalanced only by the male's right to divorce a sexually compromised wife—a privilege, dating from biblical times, that is denied the betrayed woman. Beyond adultery and fornication, Mehmed's Kanunname is comparatively laissez-faire with regard to the monitoring of morals. While it punishes criminal intent as well as actual acts of zina, penalized acts of intent are only three: pimping, breaking into dwellings with sex in mind, and public molestation of mature women. Mehmed's edicts are aimed overwhelmingly at heterosexual perpetrators. The only collateral victims are women harassed on the street. Finally, customary law plays little role in this comparatively bare-bones treatment of sexual crime. Mehmed's Kanunname is not much of a window onto actual social practices and abuses, except that it acknowledges that there *were* adulterers, pimps, and sexual molesters.

THE KANUNNAME OF BAYEZID II

Every sultan put his own—and his legal advisers'—imprint on the amended version(s) of the Kanunname issued during his reign. Each updating also responded to the effects of a still-expanding empire—to ideological shifts and the repercussions of internal consolidation. Moreover, each incarnation of the Kanunname bore a generational stamp, as sultans reacted to the events and character of their fathers' reigns. Bayezid II, known as "the saint" (Veli), was more religious than his father Mehmed II, who is known even today as "the conqueror" (Fatih). Although he built up an Ottoman navy and pursued territorial expansion, Bayezid spent considerably less time than his father in the saddle.[12] Rather, Bayezid spent much of his long reign advancing the administrative consolidation of his ancestors' conquests.

Bayezid's administrative work is immediately evident in his Kanunname—with some 250 statutes, three times as long as Mehmed's.[13] It is structured in a more elaborate manner, with three chapters (bâb), each containing between four and seven sections (fasıl). Chapter 1, comprising four sections dealing with crime, opens with the zina section; continues with physical injury and murder; goes on to consumption of intoxicants, theft, and slander; and concludes with matters of siyaset. The first three sections, but not the fourth, were present in Mehmed's Kanunname, albeit in shorter form.

Among the conceptual advances made by Bayezid's Kanunname is the enlargement of what we might call the "legal nation"—that is, the complex population subject to imperial legislation. The inclusion of Christians and

Jews as criminal perpetrators signaled that kanun was now viewed by its formulators as the "law of the land"[14] rather than a law to be applied only to Muslims; in other words, the crimes of all subjects, regardless of religion, could be disruptive of social order and hence were subject to imperial oversight. The large number of provincial kanunnames issued by Bayezid confirms this point about the spreading grass-roots legal control exerted by the Ottoman regime. Furthermore, the incorporation of more customary-law statutes signaled that "society" in all its unruly cultural variety was coming under the scrutiny of imperial authorities, who were no longer willing to leave the definition of crime in the hands of local authorities.

The zina section of Bayezid's Kanunname is largely identical to that of Mehmed, even in the wording of its statutes. Its major innovation is the statute applying penalties for adultery and fornication to non-Muslims, who are fined at half the rate of their rich and poor, married and single, Muslim counterparts. Otherwise, Bayezid's Kanunname differs only in adding widows to the ranks of the guilty (they pay the fine assigned to single persons) and omitting young, unmarried females (daughters). Rather, it is in the new fourth section of chapter 1 (titled "Which Exclusively Declares Siyaset") that Bayezid and his advisers multiply statutes on illegal association between the sexes.[15]

These new statutes are fierce. The first prescribes castration for a man who abducts a girl or boy, enters a dwelling with "subversive intent" (*hiyanet*), or "comes" [on a raid] to abduct a woman or girl. The second statute, dealing with the aftermath of abduction, forces the person who marries an abducted female to her abductor to dissolve the marriage; it also punishes the marriage maker by cutting off his beard (a lesser form of emasculation). The final statute appears to preempt the dread act of honor killing. It prescribes execution by state authorities of any man caught in the sexual act with a married woman not his wife. This elliptically brief but powerful rule moves the right of execution—at least of the male lover and in the context of abduction—from the hands of a woman's husband to the hands of state officials. The option of punishing the woman, it would seem, remains a prerogative of her male relatives.

What these new items do is to amplify the zina statute on entering dwellings with sexual intent. They do so by grappling with the actual performance of that intent, left relatively untreated in Mehmed's Kanunname. The statute on abduction addresses an intractable practice, particularly common in tribal societies, that has persisted into modern times (disparate parts of the Ottoman Empire bore the influence of tribal cultures despite the regime's pressure on tribal groups to sedentarize). Abduction as a social practice might take place with the female's complicity, since it could be a route around obstacles to marriage—for example, parental resistance or the presence of older siblings whose marriages needed to come first. It is noteworthy that neither Mehmed II's nor Bayezid II's Kanunnames acknowledged the possibility of female compliance in abduction. This silence stands in contrast to the criminal agency and liability assumed by women in the zina section. This conundrum—why does the socially aseptic treatment of sexual crime in the zina section, but not the socially animated treatment in the siyaset section, include women in the criminal social body?—is an issue to which we will return. It points to the gap between the sharia principle of gender symmetry in sexual crime and the gender asymmetry of customary law.

To get a better sense of the place of siyaset in Bayezid's Kanunname, let us look at the types of penality it prescribed.[16] Ta'zir, the judge's discretionary imposition of beatings and occasionally imprisonment, was a common sharia punishment. Monetary fines (cürm), on the other hand, were not a classical sharia penalty, but rather a practice of ancient provenance in the region. As we have seen, these two types of penalty—ta'zir and cürm, beating and fine—were routine and often combined in the Kanunname, as if to symbolize the intertwining of religious and customary authority in the prosecution of everyday crime. Siyaset penalties, on the other hand, were harsher and connoted the full and deliberate weight of the political regime's punitive justice. They tended to be spectacular, in the Foucauldian sense of a physical display intended for public consumption: penalties in Bayezid's siyaset section included hanging for arsonists, slave rustlers, and habitual thieves; castration for sexual offenders; branding the forehead for male pimps; cutting off the limbs for highway robbers; and severing the hand of a habitual cutpurse, while a first-time offender was paraded around with a knife in his arm.

Now, let us comment briefly on what Bayezid's Kanunname suggests about the evolution of imperial legal ideology and practice. That Bayezid isolated these harsh new statutes in a section devoted to siyaset—here meaning the ruler's power to define and punish crime—suggests that he was making an explicit distinction between the religious and the political sources of legislative authority. It would be a mistake to think that this religiously minded sultan was squeamish about castration and other harsh customary-law practices and therefore isolated them from "pure," sharia-derived, zina legislation. Rather, Bayezid was reiterating the role of imperial authority in prosecution of justice. His delineation of siyaset in some twenty statutes (most of them unrelated to sexual crime) confirms the point about Mehmed's criminal edicts — that they announced the legal maturity of the Ottoman sultan, who now embraced the duty of enforcing God's law. Bayezid's contribution was to acknowledge in explicit detail that the latter alone was not sufficient to ensure sociosexual order in the polity.

THE KANUNNAME OF SELIM I

In the Kanunname versions attributed to Bayezid II's energetic and militant son Selim I, the arena of sexual crime is both more threatening and more rigorously prosecuted. It is a tougher world for the sexually undisciplined. The fines for adultery have gone up, at least for the rich Muslim male, who is now fined 400 rather than 300 akçes. Moreover, the harem has acquired a diverse population. Men have more to protect — not only wives, but also sons, daughters, and female slaves. Victims of street harassment are no longer merely "a person's wife" but also "a person's daughter," "a person's son," or "a person's slave."

Women — at least married women — have receded from the public sphere: they do not appear as unfettered or autonomous sexual actors. While obviously partners in some crimes, they are more salient as victims. In Selim's laws, neither widow nor female pimp are among the sexually criminal. Moreover, married women's responsibility for their misdeeds has passed to their husbands: when a wife commits adultery, it is the husband who is culpable — it is he who now pays the fine for zina. Since he is charged with the cuckold fine if he keeps his wife (that is, does not divorce her), the Kanunname implies that he may be liable for a double fine. To sum up, the husband has been put in charge of his wife.

This same man is also charged with keeping his minor sons from sexual liaisons wherein they "play the role of the slave girl" (keñizlik — here, the nondominant role in a homoerotic encounter). It is the father who takes the beating (but pays no fine) if such a liaison occurs because "the father must guard his son." Note, however, that the adolescent son who has reached legal majority incurs his own punishment in this matter (a severe ta'zir beating and a fine of one akçe per stroke). He is publicly responsible for his conduct, in contrast to his errant mother. Unmarried daughters, absent in Bayezid's Kanunname, now reappear as potential fornicators accountable for their transgressions.

Some versions of Selim's Kanunname even penetrate the domain of the household in order to monitor sexual activity within it. A man is now penalized for having sex with his wife's or his mother's female slave, or with his former wife from whom he is definitively divorced. His sexual hegemony within the household is not entirely circumscribed, however, for he is not to be penalized for the same infraction with his son's slave or with his own female slave who enjoys the privilege of a contract of future freedom.

In some areas of sexual crime, Selim's amendments are of a more minor nature. The point about abduction having already been made strongly by his father, Selim merely adds a heavy beating to the beard-cutting penalty inflicted on the person who marries an abducted female to her abductor. With regard to physical and verbal harassment on the street, Selim's major innovation is the additional classes of victims noted above; in addition, his Kanunname also permits the judge to imprison the harasser in a location he believes to be in the best interest of the community. Finally, Selim's Kanunname criminalizes bestiality with an animal owned by another; the penalty is a beating prescribed by the judge and a fine of one akçe per stroke.

Three major trends are evident in Selim's Kanunname. First, it extends the regime's prosecutorial reach by concentrating almost as much on victims as on perpetrators, detailing larger numbers and introducing new classes (slaves, children) of the casualties of crime. Linked to this issue of the victim is female accountability in sexual crime. The sexual world of Selim's law book is a man's world. Men have sex with both sexes, and men band together in gang abductions. All others — women, girls, boys, slaves — comprise the potential prey of the male aggressor and are therefore to be guarded by the male householder. The criminal autonomy of married women thus is erased, at least discursively (they seem to be committing sexual crime in the shadows).

Second, the Kanunname introduces homoerotic sex as a criminal act. This is the one major innovation of Selim's law book that is not foreshadowed in his father's or grandfather's Kanunname. However, homoerotic sex enters indirectly, as one variation in the repertoire of acts and preferences of sexual predators. In other words, it is not yet confronted in the Kanunname as a crime in and of itself, as it will be in Süleyman's Kanunname. It is documented but not labeled.

A third innovation of Selim's Kanunname is the definition and regulation of the household. Heretofore the Kanunname has been concerned primarily with individual actors; now the structured family emerges as a unit of legal vulnerability as well as accountability. The male head of household is now empowered over his dependents. On the other hand, as a corollary of his patriarchal authority, he is subject to more punitive actions: he pays fines for his wife's and his prepubescent son's indiscretions, thereby acquiring an enlarged burden of honor to defend. Moreover, his own sexual misconduct is more carefully scrutinized: he pays a higher fine for his own adultery, and his sexual relations with household members have come under the legal gaze of the regime. In sum, the success of Selim's design for social order in the empire appears to depend on the male householder's ability to maintain domestic order, including the management of his own libido.

A note on the contents of the various Kanunname versions attributed by scholars to Selim is in order at this point: there is considerable variation among them.[17] This is no doubt a measure of increasing legal activity at the center of government, as the production of and demand for kanun regulations multiplied and perhaps opened the door to unauthorized copies. Yet at the same time there is a cluster of persistent features—Selim's "signature statutes"—that help to identify the Kanunname manuscripts that belong to this sultan: the 400-akçe adultery fine, the requirement that a husband pay the fine of his adulteress wife, the inclusion of all household dependents in the street-harassment statute, and the statute criminalizing homoerotic acts by a boy or youth. From this perspective, Selim emerges even more sharply as the architect of the patriarchal household.

The terminology and the format employed in Selim's Kanunname render political legal authority—siyaset—a stronger force than religious legal authority, at least discursively. This characteristic of his Kanunname is consistent with several anecdotes about Selim's severity in imposing summary punishment, even on members of the governing class—for example, his order to execute 150 treasury officials, from which he was dissuaded with difficulty by the chief mufti.[18] In several statutes, the Kanunname calls for severe ta'zir, seemingly instructing judges to impose the maximum level of beating. Selim also moves the abduction statutes in with all other zina statutes, thus collapsing the distinction made by Bayezid II between the political and religious bases of imperial legal authority. It is as if Selim were impatient with the attention paid by his ancestors to this delicate balance.

Selim I is well known to posterity as *Yavuz* (the stern, even ferocious). But he was also accorded a lesser-known epithet: *Adil* (the just).[19] And his son Süleyman was *Kanunî* (the "kanunifier," the lawgiver), an epithet intended as a tribute. The development of imperial kanun, then, is not a simple story of an authoritarian regime's imposing more and more laws on the subject population for the purposes of social engineering and political control. Some of Selim's new statutes have the feel of a clarification issued to answer inquiries from the field about the fine points of a legal principle, just as Ebu Suud's several fatwas on the muhaddere woman responded to popular confusion about the practice of female seclusion. We can easily imagine a scenario in which judges attempting to apply the Kanunname were faced with silences or ambiguities in its text, and appealed from their metropolitan or provincial posts to imperial legal offices for answers. Accordingly, the drafters of the Kanunname appear to be open to grass-roots stimulus. In fact, Selim almost seems to be conversing with the empire's judges (examples of seemingly picayune details in his Kanunname are the statutes clarifying the degrees of guilt in a man's sexual relationships with household slaves and divorced wives, as well as a statute clarifying whether the penalty for sexual slander applied to a man who wrongly accused another of zina with a female of his household). Here it is important to bear in mind that the legal infrastructure of the empire had evolved considerably between the reigns of Mehmed II and Selim I: new cadres of judges, jurists, and legal scholars had been produced by the imperial *medreses* founded by Mehmed, Bayezid, and their leading statesmen, while newly conquered cities and towns required new courts and judges.

NEW TERRITORIES, NEW LEGAL REGIMES

The penal code of Mehmed's Kanunname contains almost no customary-law penalties; it is basic and "clean," so to speak, routinely applying ta'zir beatings and fines, envisioning a legal world ordered by judge and sultan. Bayezid's Kanunname, with its siyaset section, at first seems less modern, populated as it is by the cutpurse bearing a knife in his arm, the pimp with a branded forehead, and the castrated sexual predator. But it was not an antiquarian bent that impelled Bayezid to add such statutes, it was a politician's respect for the varied social and legal customs alive in his empire.[20] His Kanunname, in other words, gave executive force to a legal program many of whose particulars would have been familiar to the empire's subjects.

Accounting for this increasing responsiveness to social practice—for example, Bayezid's to the problem of abduction and Selim's to the sexual politics of the household—may seem a straightforward task. By the end of Selim's reign, the empire encompassed a more complex subject population, particularly after this sultan's momentous conquests in 1514 of eastern Anatolia and in 1516–17 of the Mamluk sultanate's domains in greater Syria, Egypt, and the Hijaz, home to the Muslim holy cities of Mecca and Medina. Customary-law influences and pressures proliferated as a result of these new conquests, as many new groups and cultures underwent the process of integration into imperial systems of administration.

The incorporation of the old Islamic lands, which had a longer experience of Islamic law than the original Ottoman heartlands, is often assumed to have introduced social and religious conservatism into Ottoman society. However, the impact of Selim's conquests on the social outlook of Ottoman legal culture is a matter of debate. For one thing, it is not at all clear that the habits of the Arab lands were any more conservative than those of Anatolia or the Balkans in the late fifteenth century.[21] And as we have seen, there were homegrown factors that can account for social change in the world of domestic space, sex, and gender, and the growing salience of harem culture. Bayezid's Kanunname had already magnified the place of household management as a critical feature of an ordered society. Moreover, Bayezid himself can be credited with setting a model for the patriarchal household: his numerous concubines, sons, daughters, and sons-in-law made the management of his large princely family a complex political task.[22] Last, but perhaps most important, the Ottoman regime had, by Selim's reign, produced its own formidable body of religious scholars and administrators who were ready to fill the legal vacuum created by the decline of administrative control in the later Mamluk decades.

Ottoman legal culture was affected by a number of legacies and influences, imperial (Islamic, Byzantine, and Turko-Mongol) as well as local and regional. I would like now to explore one regional influence predating Selim's conquests that was arguably of critical importance to Bayezid's and especially Selim's Kanunnames—the sociolegal world of the fifteenth-century Turkmen states of Anatolia. I want to suggest that the sociolegal culture of these states put a good deal of pressure on the Ottoman administration—pressure that at least partially accounts for the expanding legal architecture of the harem evident in the Kanunnames of these two sultans. Ömer Lûtfi Barkan, a scholar of Ottoman kanun, has repeatedly drawn attention to the influence on the Ottomans of the legal legacy of the two principal Turkmen states—the Akkoyunlu sultanate, which was based in western Iran but controlled eastern Anatolia, and the Dulkadir principality, whose territory stretched from central through southeastern Anatolia into northern Syria.[23] These two states challenged Mehmed II and Bayezid II, and it was not until Selim I's reign that their domains in greater Anatolia were finally conquered. Established in the fourteenth century, both regimes had a substantial impact on life in central and eastern Anatolia, northern Syria, and Iraq.

Turkmen rulers were legally observant Muslims, although their respect for God's law and its historical administration was tempered by a strong sense of tribal custom and the rights of chieftains. The several local kanun-names issued by Uzun Hasan, a renowned Akkoyunlu sultan who reigned from 1453 to 1478, dealt mainly with agricultural taxation. They were retained by the Ottoman administration until around 1518,[24] when Ottoman provincial kanunnames were introduced to the region, although the latter continued to cite various Akkoyunlu statutes. It is the Dulkadir legal regime that is of particular interest to us because of the criminal sections present in the Dulkadir Kanunname. This kanunname, which like its Ottoman counterpart existed in different redactions, remained in force under the Ottomans until as late as 1560 or so, when it was finally superseded by Ottoman provincial kanunnames.[25] Whether in its definition and regulation of crime it competed for grass-roots authority with the *Kanunname-i Osmani* is an unstudied question—and perhaps one that cannot be studied, given the paucity of court records or other local sources that might cast light on local legal life. However, that the Ottomans took so long to displace the Dulkadir Kanunname in the more densely tribal areas of the former Dulkadir domain is surely some measure of its tenacity on the ground.[26]

The Anatolian domains of the Akkoyunlu and Dulkadir were difficult areas for the Ottomans to control, both politically and socially. Selim I was famously watchful over these territories and fierce in his policies toward the empire's eastern frontier and the intractable populations that might threaten Ottoman control. In general, the challenge of controlling tribal groups—Bedouin Arab, Turkmen, and Kurd—was one that the empire never fully met. During the reigns of Bayezid, Selim, and Süleyman, the unruly and anti-Ottoman Turkmen tribes of Anatolia, northern Syria, and northern Iraq presented a particularly serious political crisis to the Ottoman regime because of their support of the increasingly militant and expansionist Safavid spiritual order, which in the early years of the sixteenth century spawned a new empire in Iran. In fact, it was these Turkmen, nominal subjects of the Ottoman sultan, who provided most of the military power for the astonishingly successful new state. Selim allegedly deposed his father in 1512 because of his failure to address the looming Safavid threat, and Selim's victory in battle over the new shah of Iran in 1514 brought Turkmen territory, if not Turkmen hearts, back into the Ottoman Empire. Let us turn now to the Dulkadir Kanunname to explore its character and possible relation to that of the Ottoman Kanunname.

THE DULKADIR KANUNNAME

Bertrandon de la Broquière, a late-fifteenth-century traveler in the East, told in his memoir of the female soldiers of Dulkadir.[27] Even Hans Dernschwam, who held the women of Istanbul to be of little account, noted that Dulkadir women handled horses well, riding astride like men. It may therefore seem paradoxical that the Dulkadir Kanunname was militant about gender relations.[28] It adamantly guards the domicile, sharing with the Ottoman Kanunname rulings on breaking into dwellings with sexual intent, abduction, and prevention of the marriage of an abducted female to her abductor. Like Selim's Kanunname, it depicts a starkly masculine world, where men are the instigators of sexual crime while women's and boys' sexual misconduct is portrayed as a product of men's assault. Yet at the same time, the Dulkadir Kanunname is more broadly cognizant of the potential complicity of these junior partners in crime: it reduces the severity of the instigator's punishment if his partner was a willing collaborator. On the fate of the female adulterer, however, it is utterly silent, unlike the Ottoman Kanunname; her punishment apparently rests in the hands of her male relatives.

Before looking at its statutes in detail, we should note that, like the Ottoman Kanunname, the Dulkadir Kanunname existed in variants. Or rather, two main variants have survived through their incorporation into Ottoman survey registers beginning in the 1520s.[29] One is the kanunname of Bozok, a largely tribal, central-Anatolian region that was part of the Dulkadir domain (and that would be notoriously resistant to Ottoman political control); the other is the kanunname of Ala ed-Devle, ruler of the Dulkadir principality from 1481 to 1515. The latter has somewhat more Arabic—that is, Islamic—terminology than the former, perhaps a reflection of the urban residence of Dulkadir princes and their patronage of Islamic institutions. It makes sense to assume that both variants reflected Dulkadir kanun practice of the early sixteenth century.

An outstanding feature of the Dulkadir Kanunname is that men are held responsible for the crimes committed by women. In the kanunname's zina section ("the regulations [ahkam] on zina and related matters"), only men are explicitly punished. The married adulterer is fined fifteen gold pieces, the single man guilty of fornication twelve or thirteen. (These fines were considerably higher than Ottoman fines for the same crimes.) A man who has sex with his fiancée suffers the zina penalty; however, if their amorous encounter stops short of sex, his fine is five gold pieces. In the case of abduction, while females (assumed to be unmarried) are recognized as potentially complicit, only the responsible males are punished: if the female is abducted willingly, her father or brother is fined twelve gold pieces; if unwillingly, her abductor pays the zina fine twice (regardless, it would seem, of whether sexual intercourse has actually taken place).

If Dulkadir females themselves paid reduced fines or none at all, they were not sexually reticent (perhaps the horsemanship lauded by European travelers figured in their ability to escape from their families). Factored into a number of statutes with which we are by now familiar, the "did she or didn't she" question determines the severity of the male's punishment. For example, if the female is complicit, a man guilty of breaking into a dwelling with intent to commit zina or of kissing or embracing her pays only five gold pieces instead of the usual zina fine. Moreover, in the Ala ed-Devle (but not the Bozok) Kanunname, her father or brother must pay the zina fine for her transgression. Both variants are adamant, however, that male relatives must compensate for female complicity in the case of abduction.

Abduction looms as more threatening and more complex in the Dulkadir than in the Ottoman Kanunname, perhaps not surprisingly in this largely tribal polity where intertribal raids were a common feature of life. Indeed, abduction by raiding parties is addressed in a statute that fines each member of the party eight gold pieces (Bozok) or fifteen (Ala ed-Devle, whose scenario includes breaking into a dwelling). Moreover, if someone should be injured while fighting off the raiders, the abductors are liable for compensation (diyet). On the problem of abduction as a subterfuge aimed at marriage, the Dulkadir Kanunname is more detailed and thus less arbitrary than the Ottoman Kanunname. It acknowledges the possibility that the female's male guardian may consent to the fait accompli of the couple's elopement. However, the guardian may insist on an annulment by appealing to the Islamic legal principle of küfüv (socioeconomic compatibility) — i.e., by claiming that his female relative is socially superior to her captor. These details suggest a longue durée persistence of strategies, explored in their modern manifestations in the work of the anthropologist Daniel Bates with nomads in the former Dulkadir domain, whereby young lovers use abduction to subvert barriers to marriage.[30] Perhaps the possibility of conspiratorial planning lay behind the kanunname statute that penalized mere conversation between an engaged couple.

As for the adulteress, the Dulkadir Kanunname displays none of the ambivalence regarding her legal accountability that its Ottoman counterpart does — that is, whether she or her cuckolded husband suffers the zina punishment. Rather, there is simply no mention of the adulteress, the reason apparently being that her punishment lies in the hands of her husband. The kanunname is adamant that the husband has the right to kill both his adulterous wife and her lover if he catches them in an amorous encounter. "Under sharia, he is guilty of homicide, but by customary law [*örfen*] he is not guilty," asserted the Bozok Kanunname. Ala ed-Devle's Kanunname is more adamant, acknowledging that honor killing was regarded by some as forbidden by customary law as well: "He is not guilty of homicide, nothing may be taken from him [as fine or compensation] on the pretext that he is guilty under customary law." It is hard to know how common honor killing actually was, but clearly it was common — or momentous — enough to generate debate about its legality.

In the light of this Dulkadir defense of honor killing, we can recall the opposite tack taken by Bayezid II in assigning the execution of a married woman's lover to state authorities ("a man who is caught with a [married] woman is punished by siyaset"). While it thus usurped the husband's right of execution, at least in the context of abduction, the Ottoman statute skipped over the issue of the wife's betrayal, perhaps hoping a cuckolded male would be satisfied with recouping his honor through divorcing his wife (recall the fine exacted from a man who failed to divorce an adulterous wife, a rule absent in the Dulkadir Kanunname). Under Süleyman I, however, the Ottoman Kanunname would sanction honor killing, apparently yielding to popular pressure, although with restrictive caveats.

Apart from honor killing, the most severely punished of zina-related crimes in the Dulkadir Kanunname was the abduction of boys (*oğlan*). The fierce penalty, which appears to apply to all members of an abducting party, is castration or a fine of twenty-four gold pieces. However, the scenario changes if the abductee is a catamite, presumably complicit in his capture: in this case, both parties are punished, either by the sharia penalty of a beating or by payment of the fine imposed on unmarried male fornicators (twelve gold pieces). Unlike the Ottoman policy, fathers are not expected to pay this fine if it is incurred by their minor sons. What should we make of this last ruling? Unlike the abduction of a daughter, the abduction of a boy is a capital crime, with which fathers have nothing to do—or *must not* have anything to do. The Dulkadir Kanunname may have been attempting to head off the same catastrophe of vigilante vengeance—a potential blood feud—that Bayezid tried to avoid by depriving a husband of the right to execute his adulterous wife.

The social world of the Dulkadir Kanunname is not a cosmopolitan one. No judges, no slaves, and no non-Muslims are present in its statutes. Consistent with a tribal ambience in which raiding was a way of life, the first crimes it details are highway robbery and theft. The world envisioned by the kanunname is not, however, a purely nomadic one, as there are also statutes regulating agricultural and commercial crimes. Nor does the kanunname ignore the expectations of sharia with regard to the ruler's cognizance of God's law. "God's crimes" are all present, and in its treatment of sexual slander (kazf), the kanunname is closer to the spirit of sharia than to parallel Ottoman statutes.[31] Indeed, the Dulkadir Kanunname pays attention—or at least gives lip service—to the canonical sharia penalties of stoning to death (for adulterers) and cutting off hands (for thieves), even though these penalties were for all practical purposes eschewed in favor of fines. For example, the statute on adultery states: "Whoever commits zina and it is proved in accordance with sharia [or] customary law, if he is not married *and the canonical punishment does not take place*, he is fined twelve gold pieces; if he is married *and stoning to death* [recm] *does not take place*, he is fined fifteen gold pieces." Not until Süleyman's reign does the Ottoman Kanunname contain such ritual nods to sharia penalties.

Let us now consider the relationship between the Dulkadir Kanunname and the evolution of the Ottoman Kanunname. We cannot settle for the simple premise that Ottoman rulers—who only gradually incorporated the kind of customary legislation present in the Dulkadir Kanunname, starting with Bayezid's statutes on abduction—were directly influenced by the Dulkadir practice of kanun. First, the Dulkadir Kanunname may well itself have been influenced by developments in Ottoman kanun, given that the Dulkadir rulers were at first neighbors—friendly, for the most part—of the Ottoman sultans, then their vassals, and only finally eliminated, in a brutal denouement, in 1522. Since we cannot be sure how representative the surviving texts of the Dulkadir Kanunname are of the legal regime of the principality in its heyday, it is difficult to say what influences the two Kanunname traditions exchanged and when. Second, it may very well be that the practices criminalized and penalized by the Dulkadir rulers were widespread and likewise prosecuted in Ottoman lands before they were canonized in the Ottoman Kanunnames. After all, the origins of the Ottoman dynastic house and its original followers were both Turkmen and Anatolian. And third, some legal sanctions incorporated in both kanunnames — for example, honor killing and the predominance of fines as criminal penalties — might be said to be embedded in the land itself; they had a long history in the region, being present, for example, in the legal codes of Anatolian Hittite rulers of the second millennium BCE.[32] All that said, the emphases shared by Selim's and the Dulkadir Kanunnames — the harsher fines for zina, the responsibility of male relatives for the crimes of their women, the abhorrence of sons taken as sexual objects of men — suggest that Selim was particularly attentive to Dulkadir law, not the least because it was he who brought the principality into the empire. In the end, however, whatever the vectors of influence, the affinities and undeniable influences generated by the evolution of kanun in the two polities had the outcome of expanding the role of the state in elaborating a legal architecture of harem culture.

THE KANUNNAME OF SÜLEYMAN I

The Kanunname of Süleyman I, the sultan who dominated the sixteenth century and whose reign was later viewed as the apogee of the Ottoman Empire, is a *summa* — a comprehensive treatment of imperial kanun that incorporates the work of his ancestors and adds new provisions as well as clarifying details.[33] Süleyman and his advisors also finished the work of assimilating the legal legacies of states conquered by his father — the Akkoyunlu, the Mamluk, and the Dulkadir. Dispensing with the deference that had been shown in earlier Ottoman provincial law to rulers of the late fifteenth century such as the Mamluk Qaytbay and the Akkoyunlu Hasan — Ala ed-Devle, not the peer of these sultans, remained uncited as the author of kanun — the rhetoric of Süleyman's edicts and provincial law codes unambiguously announced the full maturity of Ottoman kanun. Thus completed, probably sometime around 1540, the *Kanunname-i Osmani* stood essentially unrevised until the second half of the seventeenth century (and then it was the taxation sections that were the focus of amendment).

Like Bayezid's, Süleyman's Kanunname treats sexual crime in both the
zina section and a siyaset section. It restores statutes from his grandfather's
Kanunname that were ignored or superseded in his father's redactions,
while it continues the practice observable in the latter of elaborating the
fine points of existing statutes. The number of zina statutes in its many variants differs considerably, the largest totaling over forty.[34] Sometimes there
are multiple and contradictory rulings on a specific crime—for example, the
three rules on pimping (one under the rubric of zina and two under siyaset). Indeed, Süleyman's Kanunname is considerably more unabashed than
its predecessors about including conflicting rules, reminding us forcefully
that the Ottoman Kanunname was not a fixed code but rather a collection
of statutes that permitted latitude in their application.

The Ottoman encounter with customary law is advanced in two new
statutes in Süleyman's Kanunname, adding parallels with the Dulkadir Kanunname. Women's potential complicity in abduction is finally acknowledged. The guilty female is punished directly: her genitals are branded, a
seeming complement to the castration of her abductor. Now also penalized
are accomplices to an abduction: two punitive options are castration or a
ta'zir beating plus a fine no greater than 100 akçes (these penalties equal or
exceed the highest zina fines for fornication). Another new statute makes
a concession to the apparently tenacious habit of honor killing. The Kanunname now aims not at heading it off but rather at circumscribing it: the
husband's execution of his wife and her lover (in some versions, also the
father's execution of his daughter) is permissible provided that he immediately summons "the community" (cemaat) to witness the adulterers. If he
does so, the heirs of the murdered individuals cannot claim compensation
(i.e., his act is not homicide). As a kind of corollary, a man who wounds a
stranger he catches in his home is not to be prosecuted, as long as he immediately summons witnesses.

With Süleyman's reign, we can perhaps hazard a closer linkage between
the Ottoman and Dulkadir kanun traditions. The office of the chancel-
lery (nişancı), which was responsible for drafting new versions of the Ottoman Kanunname, presumably had a direct hand in the reinscription of the
Bozok and Ala ed-Devle Kanunnames in the cadastral survey registers disseminated during Süleyman's reign. In other words, imperial legal special-
ists were now actively working with both kanunname corpuses.

A final innovation of Süleyman's Kanunname is its criminalization of
sodomy as an act in and of itself, not merely as a byproduct of abduction.

Selim had already written the sodomized into the Kanunname by inflicting punishment on a son who had reached majority (*baliğ*) for "playing the role of the slave girl," and on the father if the boy were still immature. Now the sodomizer himself—assuming he has reached majority and is not feeble-minded—is punished with the zina fines (300 akçes for a rich married man, 100 for a rich single man, and so on). Thus the assimilation of homoerotic sex to the crime of zina has been completed. Sodomy is framed in the Kanunname in the Arabic language of jurisprudence, *livata*; indeed, the zina section of some versions of Süleyman's Kanunname is titled "on zina and livata."[35] In a logical extension of the premise that it is the sodomizer who is guilty, some versions of Süleyman's Kanunname punish a man who has anal intercourse with his wife, prescribing a heavy ta'zir beating and a fine of one akçe per stroke. But the Kanunname is silent on the adult male of sound mind (no longer "a person's son") who chooses the passive role.

Süleyman's Kanunname also reconciles some divergent tendencies in his ancestors' work. It reduces the zina fines stipulated by Selim, returning them to the levels set by Mehmed and Bayezid. Women's accountability for their criminal acts is reinstated: married and widowed women pay fines for adultery, fornication, and pimping. The provision insisted on by Selim—that a husband pay his adulterous wife's fine—is absent from a majority of manuscripts attributed to Süleyman.[36] Instead, the cuckold penalty appears to have taken its place by rising to the level of the adultery fines: the Kanunname adds a rider to the standard cuckold penalty of 100 akçes for a rich man—"but it has become the practice to take 300 akçes." Indeed, records of local courts suggest that "cuckold divorce" was a common practice,[37] and the wording of this rider suggests the pressure of popular practice on the Kanunname.

What has become of the harem in this last of the imperial law books from this long legal century? In contrast to the man's world of Selim's and the Dulkadir Kanunnames, Süleyman's law book gives the impression of women constantly engaging in forbidden sexual dalliance. The result is that the starkness of harem culture is diluted by the very variety of statutes that portray miscreant females. But we should not be deceived: the dynamics of the harem are just as present, and they have been reinforced by new restrictions on the public association of males and females. The burden of defending household honor still falls to the male, whose wife may compromise him in a multiplying variety of acts. The corollary of his duty to protect his son from sexual molestation is that his own sexual options have been further reduced through the criminalization of sodomy. To be sure, women

have been restored as criminal agents, but this probably has less to do with
a recuperation of their personal accountability—their own honor—than
with the realignment of the Kanunname with the sharia principle of gender symmetry in zina. This realignment appears as a corrective to Selim's
overemphasis on siyaset.

The impression of women out and about in Süleyman's Kanunname results from the sheer number of statutes that impose restrictions on their
public appearance. For instance, women now appear as public brawlers,
but only to be penalized: they receive severe ta'zir and a fine of one akçe per
stroke—unless they are "honorable" women (muhaddere), in which case
the husband is upbraided and fined twenty akçes (the humiliation of the
honorable man presumably being worth many blows and akçes). New statutes impose severe restrictions on male-female association. For a woman to
be merely seen with a man in a secluded place (halvet) is enough to bring
down ta'zir or the zina fines on both parties. The subterfuges of lovers married to others are targeted by a statute forbidding the authorities to marry a
woman who has been divorced for her morally loose reputation to the man
rumor has linked her with. In the effort to preserve morals, surveillance by
the local community is more regularly enjoined in this Kanunname.[38] Gossip is testimony, with many statutes using phrases like "if a woman is spoken of," "if people see a couple," and "if they can confirm the guilt of parties
killed or wounded by a male relative." The street has become virtually off-
limits as a zone where a woman can retain personal dignity and honor—
unless, as Ebu Suud suggested, she has a protective cordon of attendants
that provides her with a kind of portable harem.

CONCLUSION

The Kanunname studied in this chapter has evolved from a handful of basic
rules setting out the penalties for voluntary acts of adultery and fornication to a complex set of interrelated sanctions that impose a high degree of
sociosexual discipline on the subjects of the Ottoman Empire. The ideal of
the well-disciplined society portrayed in Süleyman's Kanunname is highly
restrictive and increasingly policed, with subjects themselves among the en-
forcers. Conversely, the Kanunname mirrors the tensions in a culture of arranged marriage where young couples as well as married men and women
angle to get free for love, so to speak. It also reflects a society struggling to
combat constructions of masculinity that admire the sexual adventurer.

In the light of successive editions of the Kanunname, the patriarchal household appears less an axiomatic oriental social formation than an evolving phenomenon that was, to a degree, consolidated by legal action. Especially in the kanunnames of the Dulkadir and Selim I, the male head of household emerges as the key to public discipline and order. But his authority is not absolute, and this is not only a matter of his own reduced sexual options. The ambiguity regarding his dependents' degree of responsibility for their own crimes is allowed to stand in the Kanunname. Provisions fluctuate regarding his older children and their guilt in fornication, as if imperial legislators were trying to make up their minds as to the optimum formula. More persistent is the ambiguous fate of his adulteress wife, that greatest threat to family honor. Most versions of the Kanunname portray her as an autonomously guilty party (hewing to the sharia principle of gender symmetry in sexual crime). Simultaneously, however, they assign accountability for her zina to her husband, giving him the choice of judging (divorcing her) or being judged (paying the penalty for humiliation if he keeps her). The framers of the Kanunname have thus conceded a good deal of legal leeway to local practice. This is most notable in the matter of honor killing, finally acknowledged in Süleyman's Kanunname as a practice over which enforcement of the regime's right of siyaset was no doubt deemed too costly. In other words, by tolerating legal ambiguity—for example, by sanctioning four options regarding the adulteress's punishment—the Kanuuname generates a negotiable model of sexual control.

Harem culture did not originate with Ottoman society of the fifteenth and sixteenth centuries. Regional precedents for the seclusion of elite women existed among the ancient Assyrians, the Persians, and the Byzantines before Muslims assimilated them. That Ibn Battuta, several years into his travels through Muslim-dominated North Africa and the Middle East, was sufficiently surprised by the absence of seclusion practices in the Turkish principalities of Anatolia to remark upon it implies that this region was unusual for the times. Clearly, the greater salience of harem culture by the sixteenth century was the effect of changing social mores—in part, no doubt, the displacement of Ottoman frontier values by the more sedate habits of urban culture. Emblematic of this change was the gradual transformation of the royal family from a military into a palace establishment. But the process was not smoothly linear. While Bayezid II's household was already an elaborate courtly one, his grandson Süleyman's martial aptitude was still being measured well into his reign by whether he would succeed in abducting the wife or son of his enemy, the Iranian shah.[39] Likewise, social change at the grass-roots level was not always clear in its meaning or direction, as Ebu Suud's muhaddere fatwas imply.

But do the successive redactions of the Kanunname accurately reflect the actual pace of social change? Is the Kanunname in fact a good source for measuring the advance of harem culture in Ottoman society? When Mehmed II's Kanunname was introduced toward the end of his reign, there was obviously already some form of legal apparatus in the Ottoman domains. The Dulkadir Kanunname, with its two regional versions surviving through the mid-sixteenth century, gives us a clue that there may have been a variety of regional legal programs and of local authorities left in place by the early Ottoman regime and loosely overseen. Late-fifteenth-century tales of Bayezid I (d. 1402) and his unruly, corrupt judges lend credence to such a scenario. In his move to standardize legal administrative practices, Mehmed's purpose in waiting until later in his reign may have been to enlarge loyal cadres of jurists, muftis, and judges available to draft as well as to disseminate and apply the Kanunname. Building upon his father's initial formulation, Bayezid II began in earnest the process of expanding the Kanunname's coverage. The point here is that harem culture was probably more widespread in the empire's domains than Mehmed's skeletal treatment of zina suggests, and the timeline of harem culture in the texts of the Kanunname may not precisely match the pace of social change on the ground. That is, the sultans may have been following as much as leading.

The multiplication of zina-related statutes between Mehmed and Süleyman's Kanunnames, then, reflects a reciprocal process — the interaction of social patterns on the ground with the dynamics of imperial consolidation. This essay has highlighted three intertwined legal processes at work in the Kanunname. The first is the growth of the legal nation envisioned by the framers of the Kanunname as subject to imperial law. The second is the intensified encounter with customary law — that is, with local legal practices and local legal regimes. Third, but not least, is the broadened definition of zina that moves beyond the sharia focus on the illicit sex act itself as a consensual, heterosexual affair to engagement with intent and consequence and with a variety of sexual behaviors and preferences.

No matter what historical precedents they absorbed, the Ottomans made the legal architecture of harem culture their own. The significance of working out a sociolegal program in the principal administrative document of the early modern empire can hardly be overestimated. The Kanunname, at least in its penal code, formulated a standardized middle road as reference for legal administrators throughout the empire. A product of its effort to be comprehensive was that the geography of sexual crime was ever more intimately mapped, with increasing numbers of behaviors flagged as criminal. As to the impact of the Kanunname's penal code in shaping social conduct on the ground, we do not yet have sufficient evidence to evaluate it. However, it is clear that the interpretive flexibility of the Kanunname was exploited by local governors and judges, as well as by local communities that found some of its norms uncongenial—for example, by men and women of modest circumstances who used their local court to resist muhaddere standards of moral judgment.[40] But the hard reality that the Kanunname set out criminal fines as well as taxes gave its statutes an immediate reality in the cities, towns, and villages of the empire.

NOTES

I am indebted to the scholarly work on kanun by Ömer Lûtfi Barkan, Halil İnalcık, Uriel Heyd, Ahmet Akgündüz, and Colin Imber, and to that on kanun in the context of the Ottoman courts by Ronald Jennings and Haim Gerber (among others). An earlier version of this essay appeared in Kermeli and Özel, *The Ottoman Empire*. All translations are mine, unless otherwise indicated.

1   Ibn Battuta, *The Travels of Ibn Battuta*, 2:454.
2   On Dernschwam's observations, see Seng, "Standing at the Gates of Justice," 187–89.
3   Düzdağ, *Şeyhülislam Ebussuûd Efendi Fetvaları Işığında 16: Asır Türk Hayatı*, 56.
4   Ibid.
5   On Ottoman Kanunnames, see Barkan, "Kânûn-nâme"; İnalcık, "kânûnnâme," in *EI²*. The fact that Mehmed's Kanunname survives in manuscript form from the early years of Bayezid II's reign has led to claims—by now largely dismissed—that it should be viewed, at least in part, as Bayezid's work.
6   Compare Uriel Heyd's longer version of Süleyman's Kanunname (*Studies in Old Ottoman Criminal Law*, 30–31 and 36–37) to the two shorter versions published by Ahmet Akgündüz (*Osmanlı Kanunnâmeleri ve Hukukî Tahlilleri*, vol. 4). Heyd groups thirty-eight manuscripts of Süleyman's Kanunname into four families—longer, shorter, shorter with additional sections, and incomplete; the manuscripts published by Akgündüz both belong to the "shorter" family.
7   On kanun, see "Ḳānûn" in *EI²* part i, "Law," by Y. Linant de Bellefonds and especially part iii, "Financial and Public Administration," by H. İnalcık.
8   Following sexual crime, the criminal-law section generally takes up the following categories of crime: (1) brawling/assault, (non-sexual) slander, and murder; and (2) drinking intoxicants, theft, and robbery.
9   On the role of customary law in Islamic jurisprudence, see Udovitch, "Islamic Law and the Social Context of Exchange in the Medieval Middle East," 445.

10 On this subject, see Peirce, *Morality Tales*, chap. 8.

11 *Fi'l-zina ve devâ'ihi*. For Mehmed II's Kanunname, see Akgündüz, *Osmanlı Kanun-nâmeleri ve Hukukî Tahlilleri*, vol. 1.

12 The primary reason why Bayezid avoided military campaigning was that European monarchs threatened a new anti-Ottoman crusade with the sultan's renegade brother, Cem, at its head.

13 Mehmed Arif, "Kanunname-i Al-i Osman," supplement (note that this kanunname was erroneously ascribed by Arif to Süleyman); Akgündüz, *Osmanlı Kanun-nâmeleri ve Hukukî Tahlilleri*, vol. 2.

14 On this point, see Al-Qattan, "Dhimmis in the Muslim Court," 433.

15 Akgündüz, *Osmanlı Kanunnâmeleri ve Hukukî Tahlilleri*, 2:42–43.

16 On the subject of penalties, Islamic law, and the Ottomans, see Schacht, *An Introduction to Islamic Law*, 89–92, 175 ff. Schacht's work is particularly useful because much of it is based on a mid-sixteenth-century Hanafi legal work by Ibrahim al-Halabi, which was commissioned by Selim I.

17 Different manuscripts of Selim's Kanunname, mostly undated, have been published. I have consulted the two versions published by Pulaha and Yücel in 1. *Selim Kânûnnâmeleri*, the first of which is a composite of two manuscripts located in Tirana, Albania, and the second a version dated 1520, whose provenance Yücel does not reveal; the version published by Akgündüz (*Osmanlı Kanunnâmeleri ve Hukukî Tahlilleri*, vol. 3); and the "Leningrad" manuscript published by Tveritinova (*Sultan I. Selim'in Kanun-namesi*), a facsimile of which appears in her own book (in Russian) and in Pulaha and Yücel's as well. On the basis of internal consistencies (e.g., the higher zina fines), it would seem that Akgündüz may be wrong in alleging that the first version in Pulaha and Yücel's work should be attributed to Süleyman; however, the 1520 version published by Yücel resembles Süleyman's Kanunname more than it does the early Selim (see note 34 below for further comment).

18 The story is recounted in Repp, *The Müfti of Istanbul*, 211.

19 Akgündüz, *Osmanlı Kanunnâmeleri ve Hukukî Tahlilleri*, 2:85.

20 Note the overall title of his Kanunname, *Kitab-ı Kavanin-i Örfiyye-i Osmanî*, which emphasizes plural regulations. Because of the multiple if interrelated connotations of *örf* (meaning customary practice, but also a synonym of kanun in its meaning of the extra-sharia legislative authority of the ruler), the title is difficult to render in English; "The Ottoman Book of Customary/Imperial Regulations" is an approximation. A similar difficulty is presented by chapter 1, titled "Which Itemizes and Clarifies [*zikreder ve beyan kılur*] the Fines and Siyaset Penalties Corresponding to Crimes."

21 On the habits of Cairene women, see Lutfi, "Manners and Customs of Fourteenth-Century Cairene Women."

22 Uluçay, "II. Bayezid'in Ailesi" and *Padişahların Kadınları ve Kızları*. See also Peirce, *The Imperial Harem*, chap. 3 and passim.

23 See Barkan's "Osmanlı Devrinde Akkoyunlu Hükümdarı Uzun Hasan Beye Ait Kanunlar" and his *XV ve XVIinci Asırlarda Osmanlı İmparatorluğunda Ziraî Ekonominin Hukukî ve Malî Esaslar: Kanunlar*, 119–20, 130.

24 Barkan, *XV ve XVIinci Asırlarda Osmanlı İmparatorluğunda Ziraî Ekonominin Hukukî ve Malî Esaslar: Kanunlar*, 145.

25 Ibid., 128, note 1; Peirce, *Morality Tales*, 321.

26 Unstudied at this point is the question of Akkoyunlu influence on the Dulkadir Kanunname.

27 De la Broquière, *Le Voyage d'Outremer*.

28 For the Dulkadir Kanunname, see Barkan, *Kanunlar*, 119–29, which gives both the Bozok and the Ala ed-Devle variants; and Heyd, *Old Ottoman Criminal Law*, 132–47, which relies primarily on the Bozok Kanunname but includes variations between it and the Ala ed-Devle Kanunname.

29 Both variants can be found in the massive survey of southeastern Anatolia, northern Iraq, and greater Syria that is dated 1526 (the survey register, "Tapu Tahrir Defteri" 998, is part of the cadastral survey collection housed in the Ottoman Prime Ministry Archives in Istanbul).

30 Bates, *Nomads and Farmers*, 72–79.

31 The Dulkadir Kanunname's treatment of slander (*buhtan*) distinguishes between the accused who have good moral reputations and those who have bad, and thus incorporates the legal concept of *muhsan/muhsana*, which the Ottoman Kanunname does not (although Ottoman fatwa literature and local court practice did).

32 Hoffner, "Legal and Social Institutions of Hittite Anatolia." Hoffner notes commonalities among Hittite, Babylonian, and Israelite laws.

33 On Süleyman's legal work, see İnalcık, "Suleiman the Lawgiver and Ottoman Law."

34 See Heyd, *Old Ottoman Criminal Law*, 29–30, on the different "families" of the Kanunname of Süleyman; the version published by Heyd is comprehensive, while the version published by Akgündüz (*Osmanlı Kanunnâmeleri ve Hukukî Tahlilleri*, vol. 4) is one of the shorter variants. There are clear affinities between Süleyman's Kanunname and what is claimed to be a late version of Selim's Kanunname (1520) by Yaşar Yücel, who has published it (without citing its provenance or archival location) in *1. Selim Kânûnnâmeleri*. It is therefore possible that some of the changes introduced by Süleyman were in fact introduced by his father; however, this "late Selim" variant lacks some of Selim's "signature statutes," so its attribution to Selim rather than Süleyman seems questionable.

35 E.g., the version published by Akgündüz, cited in the previous note.

36 Heyd, *Old Ottoman Criminal Law*, 96, note 6. It is worth noting that the Leningrad manuscript of Selim's Kanunname (see note 17 above) contains both the Mehmed/Bayezid rule that an adulteress pay her own zina fine and the Selim rule that her husband pay the fine (apparently as well as the cuckold penalty).

37 This is confirmed in my own work on Aintab in 1540–41, where in the space of thirteen months there were five cuckold divorces registered at the court, four by Muslim men and one by an Armenian Christian man (Peirce, *Morality Tales*, passim).

38 On the community's role in enforcing the precepts of sharia, see Cook, *Commanding Right and Forbidding Wrong in Islamic Thought*.

39 A letter from Süleyman's wife Hurrem to the sultan, then on military campaign, informed him that the Istanbul public was restlessly awaiting some positive news from the front: "neither the son of the heretic nor his wife has been captured, nothing has been happening" (Topkapı Palace Museum Archives, Istanbul, Evrak 5038).

40 See Peirce, *Morality Tales*, passim.

6 ✦ PANOPTIC BODIES

Black Eunuchs as Guardians of the Topkapı Harem

Jateen Lad

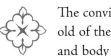 The conviction that the closely guarded threshold of the harem is synonymous with the space and body of the black eunuch finds perhaps its most candid expression in Jean-Léon Gérôme's painting *Le Garde du Serail* (1859) (fig. 1). In an act of direct confrontation, the eunuch stares back at the viewer, his luminous golden robes further drawing our gaze to him and away from that which he guards. The loose folds of his sleeve and a red sash purposefully reveal a cluster of weapons ready to dispense a severe punishment to any potential transgressor. The eunuch's faint shadow is cast onto a stout wooden gate crowned by a simple *muqarnas* arch and geometric relief. The sparse yet graceful lines decorating the surface of the door contrast with its only other detail—a bulky wooden lock which only the eunuch is entrusted to open or close.[1]

Gérôme's representation of the black eunuch is symptomatic of the tainted lens through which European artists and writers historically imagined and represented the Oriental harem. The anonymous figure of the black eunuch came to stand as a dark reminder of the eroticism and despotism inflaming the fictitious seraglio;[2] his body pur-

1 Jean-Léon Gérôme,
   Le Garde du Serail,
   1859, oil on panel,
   © and by kind
   permission of the
   Trustees of the
   Wallace Collection,
   London.

posefully "clipped" or "completely sheared"[3] in order to grant the absolute
ruler—what Orlando Patterson has named so well—"the ultimate slave."[4]
In the enormous corpus of European harem literature and paintings, sharp-
eyed eunuchs became a mandatory topos, their presence at the margins
bringing to light the perversity of the scenario which they helped frame:
the perfect, fair-skinned, and beautiful being entrusted to the incomplete,
dark, and mutilated.[5] But such is the interdependency of the black eunuch
with the harem, particularly with its outermost threshold, that Gérôme is
able to evoke the presence of the latter by merely depicting the figure whose
existence was considered to be identified by it. Any further detail would be

deemed extraneous. Without the locked gate behind him, the figure would simply be a guard; without the presence of the glaring eunuch, the wooden gate could be opened, and the space beyond would no longer be forbidden—or indeed considered a harem.

This essay is a consideration of the black eunuch and his guardianship of the harem inside the Topkapı Palace, in Istanbul—arguably the quintessential example of the harem.[6] To the Ottoman subject, however, the term *harem* did not allude to a space defined exclusively by gender or sexuality. Rather, the range of meanings is far more nuanced and heavily invested with moral, legal, and spatial implications. The word *harem* (transliterated as *harīm* in Arabic) stems from the Arabic root *h-r-m*, which, through all its derivations, conveys one or both of two interrelated meanings: to be forbidden or unlawful, and to declare inviolable or sacred. For example, *muhtaram* is one who is honored and venerated; *ihtiram* or hurma is the aspect that inspires respect and honor. At the same time, the worst transgressions and forbidden acts are referred to as *harām* (as in unclean food) as opposed to *halal*, meaning that which is permissible. The thief, who has broken one of God's laws, is termed *harami*. Thus, when considered spatially, a harem is an exclusive sanctuary to which general access is forbidden, and within which certain individuals and modes of behavior are deemed unlawful. The two most revered and venerated sites in the Ottoman world were the sacred precincts of Mecca and Medina, which were together referred to in Turkish as *ul-haremeyn*, with each individual harem strictly forbidden to non-Muslims. The Muslim religious precinct in Jerusalem, Islam's third most holy city, was referred to as *harem-i şerif* (the noble sanctuary). In the residential and palatial context, the *harem* referred to those quarters forbidden to all except the rightful owner, including but not limited to the deeply private apartments of the household's women. Indeed, according to certain classical Arabic lexicons, "the *harīm* of a house is what is contained within it once its door has been shut"—there being no specific reference to either women or any sacred qualities.[7]

In light of this broad range of meanings, this essay will confine the use of the term *harem* to a space that is considered forbidden, guarded, and inviolable—including, in this sense, the deeply private and exclusive quarters of the imperial family, but not with reference to its women (who will be referred to instead by their household titles). Although the term *harem* also referred to the women of the family, in the vocabulary of the Ottomans, it is important to note that the elaborate imperial household within the Topkapı precludes this for a number of reasons, each of which will be explained during the course of the essay. First, the Topkapı harem was not inhabited by women alone; large sections of the harem were designated for men—young boys and pages, princes, eunuchs, and, most important, the sultan himself. Second, this innermost precinct of the palace was termed the *harem-i hümayûn* (the imperial harem) and acquired an aura of inviolability because of the presence not of women, but of the sultan. Third, the women of the imperial family, and by extension their space, could not be considered a monolithic block. As in any wealthy household, the women were organized into a hierarchical and generational structure based upon blood relationships to the head of household, ties of concubinage and marriage, and level of sexual maturity—whether the woman was a young virgin or a sexually mature adult, a mother or beyond the age of childbearing.[8] Symptomatic of such family structures, the disposition of space was entirely asymmetric. Given this, the space of a single harem could offer multiple and often conflicting readings and interpretations. For example, the heavily guarded and secluded space of the *valide sultan* (the mother of the sultan) was indicative of her power and esteemed status as the family matriarch, whose authority was a consequence of her son's occupation of the throne. The same arrangement of walls and enclosing boundaries, in contrast, would be suggestive of incarceration for the several hundred lower ranking *cariye* (female slave girls), who were trained as personal servants of the wives, concubines, and the valide sultan. Given that the harem is a site of multiple readings, the broad aim of this essay is to attempt to understand the space of the harem from within, by examining some key architectural spaces belonging to one group of residents who were able to access all its parts: the black eunuchs.

Surprisingly, given the significant historical contributions of many senior harem eunuchs and the influential positions they occupied individually and collectively within the Topkapı Palace, there is only a small body of scholarship devoted to them. Ottoman historiography does offer biographies of selected chief harem eunuchs in the form of two compendiums,[9] and there have been recent studies focusing on arguably the most powerful occupant of that office, el-Hajj Beshir Agha (1717–46), whose intellectual and religious pursuits contributed to the Ottoman brand of Hanafi Islam and Sunni orthodoxy in general.[10] But voices from within the harem have escaped the historian's net thus far, and the black eunuchs as a body remain largely anonymous; considerable research needs to be undertaken to bring to light their roles within the imperial harem.

There is, however, one major source that has remained largely untapped, offering a rich quantity of material on the black eunuchs: the walls of the Topkapı Palace harem itself. Although the palace has been studied by architectural historians, the space of its harem has been described more than interpreted and has yet to receive the same level of analysis granted to the outer, ceremonial courtyards and chambers.[11] This essay seeks to redress this imbalance by bringing to the fore the highly articulated spaces of the most marginalized and yet most heavily populated section of the imperial palace. And it is within the fabric of this realm that the corps of black eunuchs most clearly impressed their presence and identity.

Using the well-preserved architecture of the harem as the principal document, this chapter explores the guardianship of the harem by the black eunuchs through a study of their most significant spaces. Of the many ceremonial, political, and household functions filled by the black eunuchs, their position as the trusted guardians of the sultan and his extensive household is the most familiar. But how was this important role translated architecturally? How did their designated spaces protect and guard the imperial family and preserve the forbidden and inviolable qualities of the harem — a condition deemed crucial not only to the integrity of the palace but, by extension, to the empire as a whole? By presenting interpretations of the principal thresholds, courtyards, and passages where the black eunuchs operated, the intention is not to distill a social history of their lives but to better understand the spatial qualities of the harem and the eunuchs' role as its guardians.

The first section discusses the play of the harem's most visible gates upon the public realm, arguing that their contrasting expressions were complicit in establishing an architecture built to remain unseen. Contrary to Gérôme's painting, the black eunuchs were not simply stationed at the margins of the harem but, as elaborated upon in the second section, served an extensive network of spaces — not all of which can be explored within the limitations of a single chapter. For the purposes of this study, the spaces under consideration are not the highly ornamental chambers characteristic of many portions of the harem, but more inconspicuous and liminal spaces, such as the network of critical thresholds, courtyards, and passages which extend from the outer margins of the harem to deep inside its core. By leading the reader through the confines of the harem, this section will show how the spaces occupied by the black eunuchs are representative of the mechanics or inner workings of the harem, instrumental in preserving it as a forbidden, inviolate, and protected sanctuary. The third section concerns the key mechanisms of control deep inside the harem. While the harem was closely guarded against any transgression from outside its boundaries, the precision of its internal spaces suggests that the black eunuchs were more engaged in preserving established hierarchies of power by maintaining segregation and controlling movement *within* the imperial family. At the same time, the deepest seclusion and strictest boundaries were drawn not around women but rather around men — namely, the sultan and princes. Throughout, the strategic placement of thresholds and windows and the routing of passages are representative of the control wielded by the black eunuchs over the various parts of the imperial family. Using the centralized position of the chief harem eunuch as a point of reference, this section begins to draw out many of the underlying complexities structuring this most asymmetric of spaces: its multiple and segregated layers, closely guarded hierarchies of power, and the surveillance to which the entire imperial family appears to have been subjected. The final section notes that while the authority of the chief harem eunuch was impressed upon the inner palace, the wealth and power of the eunuchs displayed inside their residential quarters concealed a profound sense of fragility and isolation.

A TALE OF TWO GATES

During the latter half of the sixteenth century, a series of unprecedented developments within the Topkapı Palace came to transform the *harem-i hümayûn* (the imperial harem) into a coherent and highly articulated imperial residence. During several successive reigns, the Ottoman sultans had become increasingly sedentary rulers, spending most of their time in their palaces; with the consolidation of their empire, an absolute image of sovereignty was cultivated, further distancing the ruler from his subjects. New imperial protocol demanded that the sultan remain secluded deep inside his palace; he would no longer appear in public (except for two annual religious holidays), and he would grant private audience to only a select few. At the same time, under the celebrated reign of Süleyman I (r. 1520–66), all members of the imperial family were gathered and consolidated into a single household at the Topkapı. Princes who had been dispersed for duty across the provinces were recalled, and—at the behest of Süleyman's influential wife, Hürrem—the extensive female household of royal mothers, wives, princesses, concubines, and their servants was moved to the Topkapı harem from the *saray-ı atik* (the Old Palace).[12]

This transformation of the harem remained concealed from the public, hidden as it was behind multiple layers and guarded thresholds within the Topkapı Palace. However, the palace was now both the imperial residence and the seat of power, and it thus had to balance courtly display with guarded privacy, hospitality with calculated closure. As a consequence, its layout was conceived of not only as a stage dramatizing the rare and heavily codified appearances of the sultan,[13] but also as a way to preserve the seclusion of the harem. In this regard, the Topkapı, despite its trappings of power and elaborate scale, may be likened to a traditional dwelling—with its outer countenance oriented toward the reception of guests, while the innermost quarters housed the family harem. The large, outermost courtyard was shaped as an expansive garden accessible to all. Indeed, the Qur'anic inscription over the outermost gateway, the Bab-i-Humayun, extended a warm welcome: "Enter you then, in peace and security!"[14] The second courtyard was the semipublic arena of government, where ordinary subjects petitioned the sultan's council (the Divan) and visiting dignitaries were received. But having been welcomed thus far, the outsider found his journey toward the heart of the palace at an abrupt end. From here on, the architectural imperative was to ensure that the harem remained elusive, a forbidden and inaccessible realm revealing no more than a distant silhouette. As the heart of the empire, the imperial harem existed beyond the bounds of permitted space, a defiant blind spot concealed by stark, windowless walls. It was essential that the harem embody an architecture that was built to remain unseen.

Spurred by these developments and the soaring numbers of inhabitants now residing at the heart of the palace, the numbers of palace eunuchs—both black and white—rose sharply. Court records suggest a sudden increase from a mere forty eunuchs serving under Selim I (r. 1512–20) in 1517 to between 600 and 800 during the succeeding reign of Süleyman I.[15] This number was to peak under the reign of Murad III (r. 1574–95), under whom the population of the Topkapı Palace was at its largest, including over 1,000 eunuchs. Yet, within these expanded ranks, a significant but still little understood shift in the balance of power arose, a change affirmed by an unprecedented appointment within the Topkapı harem.

Court registers record that in 1574, Murad III appointed a eunuch of Ethiopian origin named Mehmed Agha as the first black chief harem eunuch.[16] Known by the official title of *kızlar ağası* (the officer of the girls), the chief harem eunuch—a position assumed as the pinnacle of a long palace career—was to become not only the most powerful of the eunuchs but also, by the mid-seventeenth century, second only to the sultan within the empire. As chief eunuch, he was responsible not only for managing the organization and administration of the imperial residence but also for the selection, education, and training of the harem women.[17] During the earlier expansion of the empire, this and other senior offices had been the exclusive preserve of the white eunuchs, who until the reign of Süleyman I were far more numerous.[18] Acquired principally from the Orthodox Christian heartlands of the Balkans and later the Caucasus, many white eunuchs (or *saqaliba*, as they were commonly known to Ottomans) had lucrative and respected careers in the high offices of state and as military officers. For example, Suleiman Pasha, a eunuch of Hungarian origin, was a celebrated admiral of the Ottoman fleet; he conquered Yemen in 1538 and became grand vizier in 1541. However, under Murad III, principal control of the new, extensive imperial harem passed from the white eunuchs to the enormous corps of black eunuchs. By 1592, senior eunuchs of African origin had come to dominate the position of chief harem eunuch, and the transfer and creation of important posts brought to light a racial division of duties and quarters within the harem: white eunuchs attended the male pages, while the black African eunuchs served the more prestigious wing that housed the sultan and the female harem. Although the precise organization of their ranks is little known at present, it is clear that the majority of eunuchs served as functionaries across the imperial residence. Under the tutelage of the kızlar ağası, the younger eunuchs—such as the freshly recruited *en asağı* (the lowest) and the *acemi ağa* (the untrained)—underwent their own regimented cycle of training before being assigned the rank of *nevbet kalfa* (substitutes in the watch) and then more senior posts guarding the harem, such as *yeni saray bas kapı gulamı* (head doorkeeper). The senior members of the ranks of fully trained eunuchs, known as *hasıllı* (from the Arabic word meaning product), were charged with managing the complex financial affairs of the sultan and the senior royal women.[19]

A convincing answer to the question "Why African eunuchs?" remains elusive and may not be entirely understandable in terms of modern racial attitudes. In any case, the transfer of power from white to black eunuchs and their respective spatial alignments within the harem imply two things. First, a distinction based upon race clearly arose or became increasingly apparent. Second, a changing perception of black and white eunuchs placed an increased value upon the former at the expense of the latter, who appear less and less often over time in historical narratives. By the close of the sixteenth century, the dominance of black African eunuchs was secured, possibly because stronger notions of servitude had become culturally constructed and imposed upon their bodies, more specifically upon their blackness, at a moment when the availability of white eunuchs from the Caucasus region may have drastically diminished and access to the Sudanese and Abyssinian slave markets vastly increased.[20] Whatever the reasons may be, the changing demographics inside the Topkapı suggest that by the close of the sixteenth century, black eunuchs had become the preferred guardians of the royal household and the imperial harem.

This racial division of duties between the two groups of eunuchs acquired visibility at the harem's outermost margins. Here, each corps of eunuchs was assigned the guardianship of a highly sensitive threshold with vastly contrasting architectural expressions — one ceremonial and opulently adorned, the other relatively unassuming and more domestic in scale. In spite of any perceived polarization between the black and white eunuchs, both corps and gates combined effectively in a conscious program of deception to guard the harem from unlawful eyes. The first and most conspicuous was the Bab'üs-Saade (commonly known as the Gate of Felicity) (fig. 2a), a large, canopied, and highly decorative gateway, which remained under the official guard of the white chief threshold eunuch, known officially as the *kapı ağa*. The Bab'üs-Saade was the celebrated *porta regia* whose promise of fabulous and limitless possibilities had captivated outsiders for centuries. Yet its magnificence served to deceive. Rather than yield opportune glimpses into the harem courtyard beyond, its rare staged openings served to reveal, in a moment of high drama, the enthroned figure of the sultan alone within a private audience hall that was purposefully positioned to obstruct any meaningful views into the harem. Thus, the intertwining of architecture and ceremony at the threshold helped preserve the harem as a forbidden and inviolate inner sanctuary, withheld from the public gaze.

The seductive pull of the Bab'üs-Saade proved enduring for many centuries, providing as it did a tangible and suitably lavish symbol of a harem whose precise whereabouts remained obscure. Undoubtedly, this threshold granted the palace a ceremonial focus, but in the context of the harem, it may be considered no more than a foil, holding what Alain Grosrichard has termed "the monopoly of the gaze" from the true entrance to the harem, which remained inconspicuous.[21] In a shaded corner of the second courtyard, two unassuming iron gates might escape attention (fig. 2b). They ap-

2a and 2b
Strategic thresholds:
the fabled Gate of
Felicity (top) diverted
the gaze from the
true entrance to the
harem, the Carriage
Gate (bottom).
A door seemingly
identical to the latter
is located close by.
Photographs by the
author, 2006.

pear identical except in small details; however, one may be considered a
decoy.[22] The other, now known as the Arabalar Kapısı (or the Carriage
Gate), was actually constructed under the auspices of Mehmed Agha in
1587–88 and announced itself through gilt inscriptions as the actual entrance into the harem, or more precisely as the symbolic *harīm-i cennet-i
ʿalīde bāb-i sultānī* (the Sultanic Gate in the Harem of the Sublime Paradise).[23] This guarded treatment of the harem's thresholds successfully deceived many European visitors to the palace. For example, the influential
pictorial albums of Lambert Wyts and Ignace Mouradgea d'Ohsson's *Tableau général de l'empire othoman* remain oblivious of the Arabalar Kapısı as
they continue the long tradition of lauding the Bab'üs-Saade as the metaphoric highest threshold.[24]

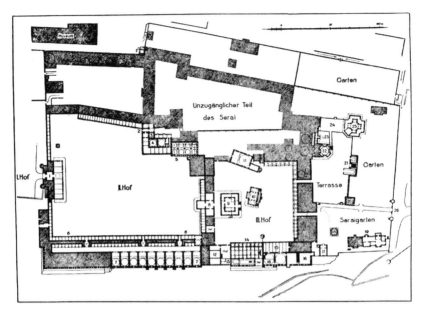

3   Cornelius Gurlitt's plan of the Topkapı Palace, showing the blank, uncharted section of the harem. Note the location of the Gate of Felicity between the two courtyards. (Gurlitt, *Die Baukunst Konstantinopels*, plate 12e).

Centuries later, long after the palace had been vacated, the play of these two gates continued to preserve the exclusivity of the harem and thwart curious outsiders.[25] In 1910, almost sixty years after the imperial household had been relocated, the German architectural historian Cornelius Gurlitt was granted unprecedented permission to produce a plan of the palace as part of his grand portfolio, *Die Baukunst Konstantinopels* (fig. 3). But having meticulously charted the two outermost courtyards, he was denied access into the harem, despite its long-deserted state. The details of his drawings suggest that the Bab'üs-Saade was opened, but he was forbidden to step inside, having to contend with limited, oblique views on either side of the audience hall. However, unlike those before him, Gurlitt did observe and record the Arabalar Kapısı—which he labels as "Tore ins Frauenhaus" (Gate into the House of Ladies)—and he was probably granted a fleeting glimpse beyond its iron doors. As a consequence, the large area of the harem remained blank in his published drawings, the incomplete nature of the plan explained by a label simply stating "Unzugänglicher Teil des Serai" (inaccessible part of the palace).[26] Thus, until the last decade of the empire, it

appeared an essential component of imperial power for the harem to exhibit an architecture built to remain unseen, disallowing even a voyeuristic
glimpse into an uninhabited space.

This astute and considered treatment of the principal thresholds provides an introduction to the sensitivities surrounding the harem and its
outermost boundaries. To the Ottoman subject, this inscribed a moral,
legal, and spatial boundary redolent of respect, family honor, and social
propriety. As discussed earlier, the harem was a family sanctuary, a place
to be revered and kept inviolate. It was one's duty to honor and protect
the harem, just as it was unlawful for outsiders to enter or even gaze upon
it. This range of meanings, loaded with a deep sense of taboo and shame,
would have existed in the cultural vocabulary of the Ottomans who cautiously averted their gaze from the harem rather than steal a glimpse inside.
Such sensitivities are evident in the architectonic miniatures produced by
the Ottoman court, such as Lokmān bin Seyyid Hüseyn's illustrations in
the "Hünernāme," which acknowledged both the Arabalar Kapısı and its
decoy gates but ensured that both remained graphically anonymous at the
margins of the ceremonial court.[27] The harem beyond was respectfully left
a void, unknown to the artist and too inviolate to be imagined, let alone
depicted. Similar discretion was observed in other contemporary fields of
expression, such as literature. For example, Mustafa 'Ali's famed treatise
on lifestyle and taste gave for each rank of the Ottoman male a detailed
list of possessions considered necessary accouterments of his social status.
An appropriately sized house was of great importance, with major bureau-
crats expected to occupy extensive mansions. The author leads the reader
through each ideal house, following sequential spaces of hospitality, service,
and audience, until "finally, there would be the Paradise-like chamber referred to as the innermost refuge, the abode of chastity dutifully hidden."[28]
Thus, having revealed the entire rest of the house, the author stops at the
threshold of the harem. To glance into the harem of another gentleman,
even in an idealized literary setting, was a forbidden act. A simple allusion
to its proximity was sufficient notice to stop.

Thus, the strategic placement of both the Bab'üs-Saade and the Arabalar
Kapısı projected the entire inner palace as a forbidden realm, a protected
and guarded sanctuary for the sultan and the imperial family. As in any
household of means, movement across the thresholds into or out of the
harem was strictly regulated by the visible ranks of eunuch guards. However, the outward expressions of both gates, perhaps deliberately, failed to

correspond with the importance of their respective eunuch corps within the harem — exaggerating the role of one, while downplaying that of the other. With their diminished numbers and importance, the corps of white eunuchs had become limited to the ceremonial opening and closing of the Bab'üs-Saade. In contrast, the outwardly simple Arabalar Kapısı was actually the outermost threshold of a complex sequence of spaces that extended the presence of the black eunuchs deep into the harem. By crossing into the harem and tracing the path extending from the Arabalar Kapısı, it will be shown that in addition to guarding the harem's outer margins, the spaces occupied by the black eunuchs were deeply engaged in the supervision and regulation of boundaries within the imperial family.

THE BOUNDARY OF EUNUCHS

Even a momentary glance at the plan of the Topkapı harem evokes the labyrinth alluded to with such compulsion in the European fantasies of the seraglio (figs. 4 and 5). Two very distinct sections are visible. The first, laid out axially behind the Bab'üs-Saade, was an expansive courtyard, which at first appears consistent with the outer public courts. To one side of this and behind the black eunuchs' Arabalar Kapısı lay the second, more distinct section of the harem. By contrast, this grew as a tangled, claustrophobic knot comprising over 300 chambers perched over miserly courtyards and a web of narrow twisting passages, all compressed within the corner of the palace grounds originally assigned to it.[29] Its cryptic plan charts no more than a moment in time — namely, its final state of rest when abandoned and finally opened to the gaze of strangers. This was a site in perpetual flux, as the needs of successive sultans and their families were fulfilled. Centuries of incremental alterations, rebuilding, extensions, and new decorative skins (either to suit functional requirements or mere whims of taste) ensured a palimpsest-like layering upon the one foundation. Yet this crowded ar-

4 Plan of the ground floor of the Topkapı harem, showing the arrangement of key spaces and thresholds together with the boundary of eunuchs: (1) Second or Divan Court; (2) Bab'üs-Saade (Gate of Felicity); (3) Arabalar Kapısı (Carriage Gate); (4) Court of the Male Pages; (5) Valide Taşlığı (courtyard of the sultan's mother); (6) Favorites' Courtyard; (7) Courtyard of the Girls (Cariyeler Taşlığı); (8) Courtyard of the Black Eunuchs (Karaağalar Taşlığı); (9) Main Gate (Cümle Kapısı); (10) Quarters of the White Eunuchs; (11) the sultan's chambers. Survey drawing by the author (after Eldem and Akozan, *Topkapı Sarayı*).

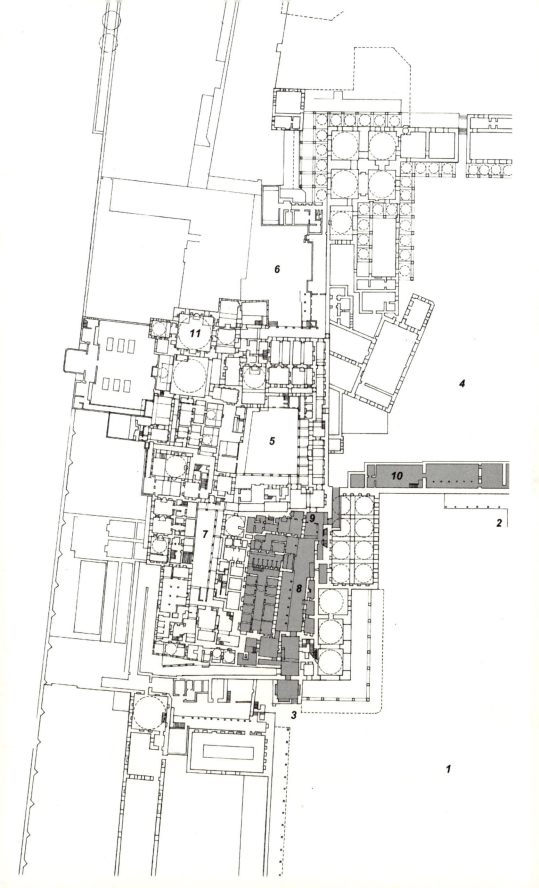

rangement of rooms and passages was not arbitrary. Rather, it constituted a precisely configured map of the imperial household, all held together by a network of spaces guarded by the black eunuchs.

Upon closer examination, the harem is seen to be composed of five tightly arranged courtyards of varying size. Aside from certain ceremonial spaces, the rooms enclosing each courtyard were predominantly residential and domestic in scale, housing several hundred occupants altogether. Archives of the Privy Purse Register, for example, indicate a harem population of 275 at the end of the sixteenth century—a number that rose above four hundred during the following century.[30] The most spacious of these courtyards, situated behind the Bab'üs-Saade, housed the large corps of male pages. The Valide Taşlığı, or courtyard of the valide sultan, was the most centrally located, indicating her position at the top of the harem hierarchy. The partially enclosed terrace immediately to its north was set aside for the sultan and his *ikbals*, selected young women who were being groomed for concubinage. Between the court of the valide sultan and the Arabalar Kapısı lay the two smallest and most cramped courtyards, each offering only a narrow sliver of sky to the most populous sections of the harem. The first of these, Cariyeler Taşlığı, or the Courtyard of the Girls, housed the *haseki*, or royal wives, and the remainder of the household women—including a large number of slave girls known collectively as cariye, who performed more

routine household duties and attended to the more senior women of the family.[31] Adjacent and strategically positioned at the margins of the semi-public Divan Court was the Karaağalar Taşlığı, or the Courtyard of the Black Eunuchs, an ingeniously laid out space that was instrumental in preserving the entire harem as a forbidden, inviolate sanctuary.

Despite its diminutive scale, the Karaağalar Taşlığı was arguably the most significant of the palace's inner courtyards. Situated at the margins of the second court, it defined the boundary of the harem, preserving the remainder of the inner palace as a forbidden and inviolate sanctuary. No more than five meters wide, the space is less a traditional courtyard than a broad cobbled passage, facing as it does the towering blank wall enclosing the Divan chambers. At one end, the courtyard extends back to the Arabalar Kapısı. When considered from inside, this gate is merely the outermost threshold of a complex sequence of spaces passing through light and dark courtyards, symbolic thresholds, twisting passages, and staggered openings which had to be negotiated in order to enter or leave the harem (fig. 6). For those select visitors, doctors, peddlers, and delivery boys who were allowed to step inside, the Arabalar Kapısı opened onto the Dolaplı Kubbe, a dark and somber antechamber, a place of waiting, preparation, and hearing in-

5 Looking down on the harem from the Tower of Justice. Photograph by the author, 2006.

6 The layered sequence
of spaces and thresh-
olds as the dimly lit
Şadırvanlı Taşlığı, or
Court of the Fountain,
opens into the long,
narrow Courtyard of
the Black Eunuchs.
Photograph by the
author, 2006.

structions.[32] There followed a small covered court, the Şadırvanlı Taşlığı (or the Court of the Fountain), where further stone portals and sentry points remained to be crossed, in front of the small eunuchs' mosque situated to one side.

Emerging into the daylight of the black eunuchs' courtyard presented a dazzling introduction to the inner palace. In contrast with the stark stone surfaces of the Divan Court, the high walls of this narrow court were richly embellished with decorative tiles flowering with cypresses, hyacinths, and tulips. Intricate arabesque designs framing evocative medallions surmounted jewel-encrusted doors, and bands of Qur'anic inscriptions capped a row of grilled windows. The grandeur of the single marble portico — necessitated by the chasm-like space of the court — was further heightened by the fine bronze lanterns hanging overhead. Amid this surface display, it was an ornamental gateway standing at the opposite end of the court, the Cümle Kapısı (fig. 7), or Main Gate, that was most significant in developing

7 The inscription above the ornate Cümle Kapısı, or Main Gate, identifies it as the main entrance to the harem. The apartments of the *kızlar ağası*, or chief eunuch, are to one side. Photograph by the author, 2006.

an architectural understanding of the harem as an actual space. In an echo of the Arabalar Kapısı, a framed gilt inscription identifies this threshold specifically as "the true entrance of the imperial harem," followed by the apt Qur'anic verse: "Do not enter the house of the Prophet except when you are allowed."[33]

The placement of the Cümle Kapısı and its inscription implies that the Courtyard of the Black Eunuchs was considered to lie outside the harem, a space of mediation between the sultan and the imperial household and the outer Divan Court and its appointed officials. Representative of a transitional zone at the beginning of the inner palace, it was here that permission to enter or leave the harem could be granted or denied. In this regard, the Topkapı Palace shows further parallels to a traditional Ottoman residence, with a plain exterior giving way to an ornate and decorative vestibule that displays the status of the household beyond.[34] In addition, the Courtyard of the Black Eunuchs, when taken together with the stations of the white eunuchs (on either side of the Bab'üs-Saade), set out a clear architectural boundary defining the precise limits of the imperial harem (fig. 4). And here the Topkapı harem presents a significant point to note: the harem was not defined exclusively by the place of the imperial women; the multilayered space of the eunuchs suggests that the entire inner palace, irrespective of the gender of its occupants, projected the qualities of a harem in its sense as a forbidden and guarded sanctuary.

Crucial to understanding the harem in nongendered terms was the large inner courtyard centered upon the Bab'üs-Saade and guarded by the white eunuchs. Housed within were a large number of male pages, young boys of Christian origin who were regularly collected under the *devşirme* system.[35] In the context of the imperial household, they may all be considered the symbolic sons of the sultan, raised as they were for imperial service across the provinces. Their modest, barrack-like dormitories and classrooms, where they were given instruction by eunuchs, lined sections of the court. However, a number of ornate pavilions and clusters of domed chambers conveyed a sense of grandeur and opulence.[36] After all, this court housed the sultan's private apartments until Süleyman I moved them to the more secluded half of the harem. The glimpse of impressive, airy porticoes facing onto the spacious garden courtyard led the sixteenth-century chronicler Kıvamı to exclaim: "Whoever stepped inside it would immediately think he was entering paradise."[37]

However, on account of its exclusively male population, generous scale, and location behind the Bab'üs-Saade, this courtyard is often referred to as the selâmlık—a term denoting the traditional male reception space of the Turkish home. Such a reading is largely the consequence of interpreting the harem as an exclusively female space. But, as this essay argues, the harem was defined not by gender but by notions of forbiddenness and inviolability constructed around the sultan and his family. Indeed, even before the sixteenth-century integration of the female household into the palace, this courtyard was referred to as the harem-i hümayûn on account of the sultan's presence there. Few people were privileged to go through the Bab'üs-Saade. All male guests entering the palace—be they ambassadors or petitioning subjects—were received in the outer Divan Court, and only by the sultan's appointed delegates. At the same time, the male pages residing within were, like the female members of his household, prevented from leaving the harem, at least until they were dispatched to their provincial posts upon graduating. Thus, all of the inner realm of the Topkapı constituted a harem, an exclusive sanctuary protecting the persons and property forbidden to others. It is for this reason that the buildings of the Imperial Treasury, the sacred relics of the Prophet, and the rich collections of the sultan's private library, among other highly prized assets, were also housed within the harem.

But the black eunuchs' courtyard, the Arabalar Kapısı, and the Cümle Kapısı—together with its words of warning—served an entirely different purpose when the perspective of the imperial household is taken into consideration. A harem was not defined against the eyes of the intruder alone. As a forbidden and inviolate sanctuary, its preservation also depended upon ensuring that those inside also remained inviolate. Any member of the imperial household seeking to leave the harem, including the male pages cloistered behind the ceremonial Bab'üs-Saade, was required to negotiate the same sequence of multiple, guarded thresholds and to undergo the same verification and preparation before entering the outside world, usually under the symbolic veil of the eunuchs, through the aptly named Arabalar Kapısı.

No doubt such organized outings were occasionally permitted for members of the imperial household. Yet for the most part, they remained within the confines of the harem. Bounded by walls on all four sides, no harem courtyard afforded the slightest visual connection with the outer public realm. The introversion and sense of confinement were most acute in the narrow Cariyeler Taşlığı, where the tempting sliver of sky above might only exacerbate an inhabitant's sense of isolation from the world. Only those chambers built atop the outer retaining walls of the palace were granted a view out across the Golden Horn and the Bosporus. The few latticed windows yielded stunning glimpses of a distant and inaccessible world. Even the valide sultan, for all her authority and status, could not fail to be reminded of her seclusion. Painted onto several walls of her private apartments were not only false windows but also numerous fanciful views of garden landscapes and distant island scenes. The upper walls of her bedchamber, for example, depicted a European-style palace in its landscaped setting, complete with flowing fountains, a bridge, and a lake shimmering on the horizon—a perspective she would have rarely if ever have been permitted to enjoy in reality. While the appeal of such décor is evidently an adoption of baroque and rococo tastes, the views may well contain a reminiscence of a short-lived excursion beyond the confines of the harem.

At the same time, historical developments suggest that occasions for entering the harem were equally rare. Under normal circumstances, the harem would be accessible to immediate male kin, who were permitted to visit mothers, wives, sisters, aunts, and daughters. In this regard, adult men and women would be permitted to share the same moral and physical space if they were what is referred to as *mahram*—that is, forbidden to marry each other by virtue of consanguinity.[38] But in the unique case of the Ottoman imperial family, such visits would have occurred with far less frequency due to the consolidation of the entire household—both male and female—into the same harem. This anomaly brings to light a pertinent question: with so few people entering the harem, and even fewer leaving it, what precisely is the purpose of the spaces occupied by the black eunuchs?

INSIDE THE HAREM: MECHANISMS OF CONTROL

From their recognized position at the margins of the harem, it is not at first apparent that the black eunuchs extended their influence deep inside. Through the Cümle Kapısı, their narrow, multilayered courtyard branched into a number of passages cutting across the inner palace, arteries stretching into the very heart of the palace (fig. 8). But these were not merely faceless corridors of access and circulation. Architecturally, these passages, gateways, and stations provided a definite framework around which individual chambers and quarters within the harem continued to evolve. Yet the precise shaping of each route, together with the opening and closing of their guarded doors, suggest that concerns for segregation, concealment, and surveillance were not the preserve of the harem's outer margins alone. Indeed, such sensitivities permeated its guarded outer boundaries to dictate the twist, turn, and thickness of every inner wall. Tracing specific sections of these innermost spaces brings to light how the black eunuchs may have controlled access to key sources of power within the harem—namely to the

8 Plan of the harem showing the convergence of all passages before the latticed window of the kızlar ağası: (1) Courtyard of the Black Eunuchs (Karaağalar Taşlığı); (2) the Golden Way (Altın Yol); (3) Imperial Council Hall and Sultan's Secret Window; (4) Shrine of the Sacred Relics of the Prophet (Hırka-i Saadet Dairesi); (5) the sultan's chambers; (6) Favorites' Courtyard; (7) Quarters of the Imprisoned Princes (Kafes); (8) Valide Taşlığı (courtyard of the sultan's mother); (9) Courtyard of the Girls (Cariyeler Taşlığı); (10) apartment of the Kızlar Ağası; (11) Kuşhane Kapısı (the Aviary Gate); (12) the mirrored vestibule; (13) the black eunuchs' residential barracks. Survey drawing by the author (after Eldem and Akozan, *Topkapı Sarayı*).

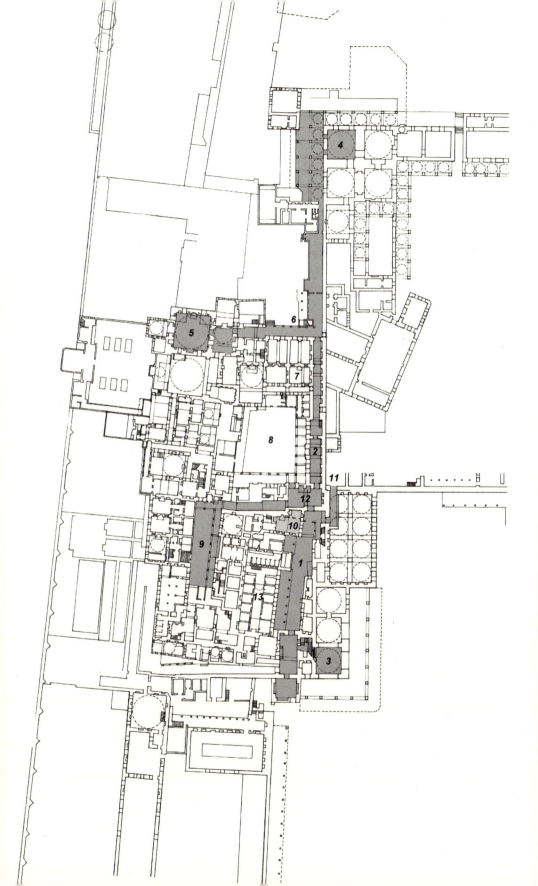

9   The Golden Way
(Altın Yol), with its
succession of thresholds
headed with Qur'anic
invocations. Photograph
by the author, 2006.

sultan, the princes, and certain invaluable assets — and also preserved the
hierarchy of power within the imperial household by segregating its different groups and ensuring that no movement into, out of, or, crucially, across
the harem could go unnoticed.

The most conspicuous of the passages controlled by the black eunuchs
was the Altın Yol, otherwise known as the fabled Golden Way (figs. 8
and 9). Its straight path can be traced from the eunuchs' courtyard through
the entire depth of the harem, before it opens onto an ornate portico at the
edge of the palace's most secluded gardens. The many dividing gates, decorative styles, and dark and illuminated spaces encountered along Altın Yol
may be regarded as an extension of the Courtyard of the Black Eunuchs.
On account of their control of the path and its high, blank masonry wall
facing the Courtyard of the Male Pages, the Altın Yol has long been considered the central spine dividing the inner palace along lines of gender. To a
certain extent, this is correct. The wall does indeed shield the mass of harem
women from the gaze of the male pages. The lack of any openings and the
blocked-up windows along its otherwise blank length does reinforce the

interpretation based upon gender. However, its divisive potential is not as simple as this might suggest.

In the context of the black eunuchs and their guardianship over key spaces and figures within the imperial household, the path of the Altın Yol presents another layer of meaning far removed from notions of gender. Upon closer examination, the Altın Yol, with the opening and closing of select gates along its length, becomes a clear extension of the Courtyard of the Black Eunuchs, as its path stretches from behind the imperial council chamber to the complex of domed chambers known as the Hırka-i Saadet Dairesi, or the Shrine of the Sacred Relics of the Prophet (fig. 8). At midpoint along the Altın Yol, a highly ornate passage branches off and leads to the private chambers of the sultan (fig. 8). As the source of power, the sultan, as mentioned at the beginning of this essay, was obliged to remain sequestered within the harem in accordance with Ottoman codes of sovereignty. His rare, highly dramatized public appearances projected his personal space as harem—inviolable, forbidden, and tinged with an aura of sanctity—an image the architecture suggests held true even within the sanctuary of the Topkapı. That his private chambers were in the least accessible corner of the inner palace established his remoteness from the public realm. Furthermore, to access his space from within the harem required negotiating the greatest number of guarded thresholds. By controlling the Altın Yol, the eunuchs guarded access to the sultan, segregating him from other members of his household and, in the process, consolidating their power as his exclusive mediators. Indeed, a corps of senior black eunuchs, collectively known as *müsahibs* (from the Arabic word meaning companion), guarded his presence both inside and outside the palace. In the *Book of Festivals* (1720) produced under Ahmed III, for example, the celebrated court painter Levni has depicted the müsahibs flanking the enthroned sultan in over twenty of his illustrations.[39] Inside the harem, the müsahibs segregated the sultan from other members of his family by maintaining their close attendance on his person within the imperial bedchamber and by standing guard in the ornate antechamber, an immediacy often allowing them to assert a direct influence upon the sovereign. Indeed, by the eighteenth century, the müsahibs acted as a means of communication between the sultan and other members of the family.[40] This extreme seclusion cast the sultan's space as *the* harem within a harem, the most inviolable and forbidden site in the empire, a quality reinforced by the conspicuously thick walls enclosing his ornate, domed bedchamber.[41]

Tales of the sultan's seclusion within his heavily guarded private chambers may appear exaggerated, but they certainly contributed to his aura during rare ceremonial appearances. Surrounded by his intimate circle of müsahibs, the sultan had guarded and exclusive access through the Altın Yol to three chambers which served to enhance the inviolable, forbidden, and sacred qualities of his presence to his subjects. First, on occasions of imperial ceremony, he could access the Courtyard of the Male Pages for his rare appearances enthroned in the Chamber of Petitions. Second, each Friday and on feast days, he would visit the Hırka-i Saadet Dairesi and seek blessings from the sacred relics preserved there. It was, after all, the Ottomans' possession of the mantle and sacred standard of the Prophet that conferred upon the Ottoman sultans the proud title *hadım ul-haremeyn ül-şerifeyn* (the servant of the two noble sanctuaries) and the legitimacy to assume the Topkapı Palace as the seat of the caliphate.[42] Third, the sultan could go, unobserved except by his closest eunuchs, to his royal window to secretly overlook the proceedings of his vizier and ministers in the imperial council hall. In this regard, the Altın Yol may be interpreted as a guarded and exclusive passage permitting the eunuchs to segregate the sultan, and the spaces most symbolic of his power and legitimacy, from the remainder of the imperial household.

Such concerns for the preservation and consolidation of the sultan's power also enforced spatial divisions within the imperial family which cut across lines of gender. Firstly, the ikbals, those select young women being groomed for bearing sons to the sultan (and so future heirs to the dynasty) were kept apart from the remainder of the female household. They were granted a row of six seemingly identical suites in the northernmost courtyard (fig. 8). However, their elegant two-room apartments were easily missed, being intentionally sited above the portico of the Altın Yol and accessible only by a secret stair, again under the guard of the black eunuchs. As the princes grew up, they guaranteed the perpetuation of the dynasty. However, they were also victims of the most intense levels of seclusion with the harem.

Until the end of the sixteenth century, the Ottoman struggles over succession followed a particularly bloody pattern, with the one victorious prince ordering the simultaneous execution of all his rival stepbrothers, regardless of their age, on the day he ascended the throne. Under Mehmed III (r. 1595–1603), who incidentally gained the throne without opposition, the practice of royal fratricide was abandoned, and the princes were condemned to a life of imprisonment deep inside the harem, under the constant guard of the black eunuchs.[43] Unlike the household women, who were occasionally permitted outside the harem on organized and heavily chaperoned outings, the princes were never allowed to emerge and remained largely unknown. Their lowly family status condemned them to be forbidden both spatially and sexually, prevented as they were from growing beards or fathering children—even though, it is believed, they were permitted concubines. As a consequence of their incarceration, their dedicated cells became known, somewhat appropriately, as Kafes (the cage; also called the Courtyard of the Imprisoned Princes). These cells occupied the most internalized section of the harem, in one corner of the valide sultan's courtyard, and were accessible only from the Altın Yol (fig. 8).[44] Here, numerous tightly packed apartments were kept isolated within an already closed domain, a place of exile cleverly woven within the harem. Though several chambers maintain the elegant domed ceilings and fireplaces discernible elsewhere in the harem, many rooms were cramped and entirely devoid of windows. Views into adjacent courtyards were blocked, not only to preserve gender boundaries but also to enforce the sense of total confinement. Bounded by these walls and under the guard of the black eunuchs, the princes spent their lives out of touch with both the outer world and their extended family. The harem was, after all, an ideal setting for a prison.

Thus, by guarding and controlling access to the Altın Yol from within the palace, the black eunuchs established a harem within a harem, drawing a boundary around those figures, spaces, and assets considered the most forbidden and inviolable within the imperial household. The political and dynastic demands which shaped the Altın Yol and its selective chambers are representative of how seemingly unassuming and marginal spaces controlled by the black eunuchs divided the harem internally. The courtyards, passages, and thresholds under the eunuchs' watchful gaze ensured that each distinct family group—cariye, ikbals, wives, valide sultan, male pages, and princes—remained, for the most part, within their own courtyards and chambers. An architecture of calculated and staggered openings, changes in level, sentries and gateways, impermeable walls, and discreetly placed windows drew boundaries within the household, guarding against any touch or gaze that might be deemed unlawful. Each wall stood as a prohibition, the structure of the space corresponding to the status of those within. Ironically, the voyeuristic frustration (as Grosrichard puts it: "each time a threshold is crossed, a new and uncertain fate is embarked upon always leading from one prison to another")[45] is misplaced, being considerably more apt within the harem than from beyond its enclosing walls. Indeed, the trepidation surrounding all movement was made more palatable by the Qur'anic invocation inscribed over many of the internal gates: "God Almighty who opens the doors! Open us a fortunate door!"

Though the younger male and female members of the imperial family were strictly kept apart, the precisely routed spaces of the black eunuchs bring to light more complex familial boundaries that cut across lines of gender. For example, the sultan as head of household was segregated from his imprisoned stepbrothers and the young male pages, while the valide sultan was removed from the ikbal, haseki, and cariye ranks (fig. 8), suggesting that notions of sexual maturity and purity of royal blood were equally divisive. Also discernible is the separation of the one from the multiple—the cramped plurality of the anonymous male and female slaves at the peripheries of the harem enhancing the power and singularity of the valide sultan and her son, the sultan, at the center. Thus, if we view the harem as a diagram of power, then the eunuchs were its principal upholders, ensuring that the Ottoman obsession with status and hierarchy emanated from its core. The seat of power, after all, had to present an ideal model.

By virtue of the scrupulous concerns for segregation and the close control of movement represented by the spaces of the black eunuchs, the architecture of the harem comes to resemble the institutions of corrective training and discipline examined by Michel Foucault in his *Discipline and Punish*. This seems logical. Aside from political preoccupations with dynastic reproduction, the imperative of the harem lay in meticulously training the young male and female slaves for imperial service to sustain the balance of power across the provinces. A household spatially and hierarchically divided within itself serves to differentiate, train, and instill among family members an allegiance to moral and spatial boundaries using the black eunuchs as the instruments of disciplinary power. With the sound of the beating drum at dawn, the mechanics of the harem were set in motion: gates were opened, orders conveyed, instruction received, visitors chaperoned, deliveries taken, and food distributed before the gates were locked again. If we conceive of the harem as a "mechanism for training," then in Foucault's terms the functions of pedagogy and surveillance become one.[46] Hence, within the harem, the eunuchs were at once the guardians and the tutors, the mediators and the supervisors.

Guarding the harem's visibility from outsiders and inhabitants alike, the site's complex geometries, hierarchies, and inequalities of space ex-

10   The latticed window
      of the Kızlar Ağası.
      Photograph by the
      author, 2006.

hibit an ingenious mechanism of control. Within the labyrinthine layout of
the harem, all paths deliberately converged before the station of the kızlar
ağası, the chief eunuch, the most senior official among the guardians of the
harem. His quarters, at the head of the Karaağalar Taşlığı and adjacent to
the Cümle Kapısı, were strategically stationed to endow him with the gaze
denied to others. Under his latticed window, no movement into, out of,
or across the harem was meant to go unnoticed (figs. 8 and 10). Any interaction between the different members and ranks of the imperial family required passing this central point. For this reason, those gates opening into
the innermost courts and chambers of the harem were positioned under his
watchful gaze. Immediately opposite, for example, a short, angled passage
shielded the Kuşhane Kapısı,[47] which provided the only connection between the male and predominantly female sections of the household (fig. 8).

11   The mirrored vestibule, a sentry point where iron gates opened onto different sections of the harem. The large, gilt-framed mirrors were strategically placed to aid surveillance across these thresholds. Photograph by the author, 2006.

By contrast to the ceremonially charged Bab'üs-Saade, this narrow door served as the day-to-day entrance leading into and out of the Courtyard of the Male Pages.

In addition, the latticed window of the kızlar ağası overlooked a small vestibule, which was mostly empty, except for the large mirrors hung on its walls (figs. 8 and 11). It was a central sentry point, and all movement and communications across the harem were channeled through its three seemingly identical iron gates guarding the courtyards of the concubines and the valide sultan as well as the Altın Yol. Indeed, this unassuming and generally overlooked space was central to the mechanics of the harem. The opening and closing of its gates controlled the visibility of the harem from within, concealing and revealing, expanding and contracting the extent of the inner palace that was considered accessible, both morally and spatially, to the person passing through. Thresholds, courtyards, and passages open one moment were closed the next, considered harem, forbidden and withheld from view. With the gates locked, the harem was reduced to a maze of indeterminate passages leading nowhere, its courtyards and residents segregated from one another. Once the gates were opened, the careful and regulated passage from one courtyard to another, and between one household group and another, was permitted, with the eunuchs, as ever, the watchful guardians.

Thus, despite the black eunuchs' position at the margins, the architecture suggests that they were central to all communication within the harem. With all movement and interaction within the imperial household radiating from their quarters, they could access the chambers of others, acting alternately as crucial mediators and formidable barriers when the need arose.[48] Whether a group of male pages was being led toward a ceremony in the Hünkâr Sofası, the harem's one room for large gatherings, or the valide sultan and a retinue of harem ladies were being chaperoned toward the Arabalar Kapısı for a rare outing, or the sultan himself was crossing from one side of the palace to the other, all movement was monitored by the eunuchs. In their hands lay the keys to each internal gate, the actions of locking and unlocking changing the extent of the harem to be revealed with each movement. The one exception was, of course, the valide sultan, who—as a measure of her political and familial authority—was permitted direct access to the private chambers of her son, the sultan, from her own apartments. In light of her generational seniority, a steady stream of family members would daily pass the station of the kızlar ağası as they sought her counsel. At the same time, it is not difficult to imagine—particularly given the political influence of the mothers of the sultans during the sixteenth and seventeenth centuries—the vigilance of eunuchs opening, closing, and guarding gates as dignitaries, as well as women from other aristocratic households, were permitted on occasion to step inside the harem to seek an audience with her.

Such mechanics defined the spaces of the black eunuchs within the Topkapı Palace and shaped the multilayered space of the imperial harem. In contrast to the architecture at its margins, segregation and surveillance inside the harem were enforced less through stark, windowless walls than by means of "the calculation of openings, of filled and empty spaces, passages and transparencies . . . to allow a better observation."[49] Control radiated from the central position of the kızlar ağası, making it possible to take the instrument of surveillance and the close control of movement into the heart of the household. Indeed, his all-seeing latticed window is parallel to the sultan's own celebrated window—overlooking the governance of the grand vizier and the imperial council in the Divan chamber—a symbol of power and control which—as Foucault puts it so aptly—was "always visible and unverifiable."[50] Thus, the architectural imperative within the harem was to exert a strict surveillance upon all members of the imperial family, to ensure that the hierarchy of power was preserved and nobody violated his or her assigned boundaries.

Thus, the black eunuchs, and the kızlar ağası in particular, occupied strategic positions of authority and access. At a site defined by internal segregation and divisions of space, they were favorably placed, being largely free of the boundaries they imposed upon others. Where the architectural imperative was to conceal and separate, true power was the preserve of those who had the freedom of both sight and movement—a potency, no matter how attenuated at times, that could significantly affect the affairs of state. On numerous occasions, senior black eunuchs, either acting alone or in league with senior harem women, exerted palpable influence upon imperial affairs. In the early seventeenth century, for example, Mustafa Agha, then chief eunuch, succeeded in installing Mustafa I on the throne following the death of his brother, Ahmed I (r. 1603–17), breaking the traditional pattern of succession from father to son. Thirty years later, the bitter struggle between rival women for regency over the boy sultan Mehmed IV (r. 1648–87) ended in the murder of the redoubtable valide sultan Kösem by a corps of black eunuchs, headed by Suleiman Agha, who remained loyal to her ambitious daughter-in-law, Turhan.

CONCLUSION: EXPRESSIONS OF POWER AND FRAGILITY

Given the black eunuchs' guardianship of the inner palace from both within and without, the architectural layout of the Topkapı harem may be considered a representation of their power. But what exactly was the nature of their authority? This essay now returns to the space where the inner palace was first entered, to read contrasting expressions of power and fragility. As the centralized point through which all paths were threaded, the Karaağalar Taşlığı, or Courtyard of the Black Eunuchs, sought to display the authority and wealth of the kızlar ağası and his followers to the other harem residents. As previously mentioned, for those permitted to enter the inner palace, this courtyard may be considered a suitably ornamental vestibule mediating between the Divan Court and the private apartments of the imperial family. However, from the internal context of the harem, another interpretation is possible. That the eunuchs' courtyard is adorned externally is an immediate contrast with the more modest facades evident elsewhere in the harem. Though numerous chambers and quarters were decorated internally with characteristic tiles, their more visible external surfaces recall, instead, vernacular expressions from the Ottoman regions: for instance, a glimpse into the Favorites' Courtyard evokes the timber-framed houses of Safranbolu. The domestic scale and flat material qualities of the Cariyeler Taşlığı, or the Courtyard of the Girls, was indicative of its fate as a space denied any external spectatorship. In contrast, anyone glancing into the Courtyard of the Black Eunuchs could not fail to notice the fine marble portico and the decorative tiled and inscribed surfaces embellishing its high walls. This was an architecture intent on display.

In addition to showing the black eunuchs' wealth and authority to members of the imperial household and guests, the decor was aimed at the eunuchs themselves. This was, after all, where they lived. Easily overlooked amid the floral tile work were framed architectural depictions of the sacred mosques at Mecca and Medina, whose depth of detail and accuracy suggest a familiarity transcending universal Muslim reverence (fig. 12).

As was an established practice with eunuchs from the Mamluk courts before them, the Ottomans granted many black eunuchs retiring from imperial service in the palace appointments as the ritual guardians of the Kaaba in Mecca and the tomb of the Prophet in Medina.[51] Thus, in the context of the sacred, the palatial, and the household, the body of the eunuch came to define, guard, and mediate across critical thresholds and boundaries. Consequently, popular adoration, a profusion of charitable endowments, and imperial stipends enriched the eunuchs' coffers. Inevitably, some individuals squandered their wealth—senior eunuchs were prone to their own displays of status, maintaining extensive households and large retinues—but the eunuchs dispensed substantial amounts on charity. Much of their revenue endowed pious *waqfs*, foundations in perpetuity to benefit less privileged eunuchs, with each act of benevolence recorded not in closed bureaucratic files but inscribed in gilt upon the exterior walls of their barracks (fig. 13). One waqf inscription, for example, records the fact that Ḥāfiz 'Isā, the kızlar ağası in 1819–20, gave a considerable sum to provide candles, oils, and medications for the sick eunuchs of the harem. Other inscriptions list how revenues of waqfs founded by other members of the palace—be it royal women or janissaries—should be distributed annually to the various ranks of eunuchs. For example, the revenues of the endowments founded by the janissaries of the Eighteenth Regiment during the reign of Mahmud II (r. 1808–39) describe how the kızlar ağası was to re-

12   The seventeenth-century tiled panel of the sacred mosque at Mecca inside the black eunuchs' small mosque. Photograph by the author, 2006.

ceive 2,000 kurus,[52] the treasurer 1,000, the harem guard at the Old Palace 750, and the head doorkeeper at the Topkapı 600.[53] Indeed, by the end of the seventeenth century, the kızlar ağası himself supervised the imperial waqfs established to benefit the holy cities of Mecca and Medina, the details of which were inscribed upon the walls.[54] These inscriptions shimmered from afar, accentuating the display of material wealth lining the courtyard, but remained legible up close to the eunuchs alone, not only projecting an existence beyond the confines of the palace but also celebrating their collective identity and the fraternal bonds which sought to embrace all eunuchs.[55]

However, the architecture suggests that the wealth and authority displayed by the rich ornamentation may only have been skin deep. Furthermore, the very hierarchies and inequalities of space upheld by the eunuchs' guardianship over the imperial household are in evidence inside their own residential quarters. A glance behind the highly ornamental facade reveals an impoverished interior, hardly befitting the residence of those appointed as the sultan's delegates. While the kızlar ağası may have occupied a spacious suite of chambers on the ground floor, hundreds of his subordinates were crammed into tiny, unadorned, windowless cells on the upper three floors according to rank (figs. 8 and 14). Given the severe constraints on

13 A tall, gilt panel headed with the *tughra*, or official calligraphic seal, of Mustafa IV and inscribed with the names of waqf foundations, set between the windows of the Courtyard of the Black Eunuchs. Photograph by the author, 2006.

space, as elsewhere inside the harem, much of the original ground floor portico was subsequently filled in with residential quarters in an effort to house everyone (fig. 10). But conditions were little improved; the barracks remained overcrowded and cold, heated by a single fire, while the row of latrines was too close and inadequately separated from the living quarters. Such living conditions seem monastic or even squalid and suggest the modest power enjoyed by the rank-and-file eunuchs.

And it was within such conditions that the majority of the several hundred black eunuchs serving inside the Topkapı Palace lived out their days. Endowed with the privilege of sight and movement within the blind spot that was the harem, the black eunuchs became the surrogate eyes of the sultan—yet, in a cruel twist of fate, they fell victims of their own power. Exerting control over a household of slaves, they disciplined, educated, and trained others, preparing them to leave the palace while they themselves remained behind, forever the sultan's abject slaves. The acquisition of power may have helped to heal their wounds metaphorically, but the condition of

14 Interior of the black
    eunuchs' barracks.
    The atrium serves
    as the only source of
    light for four stories of
    cells and dormitories.
    Photograph by the
    author, 2006.

their bodies was irreversible, and the absence marked violently upon their flesh irrevocably identified them. The physical ambiguity of their bodies defined the spaces they occupied and controlled: at once a formidable barrier and yet permeable, segregating yet mediating, marvelous yet squalid.

NOTES

An earlier version of this chapter was presented at the conference on "The Harem in History and Imagination," sponsored by the Aga Khan Program for Islamic Architecture at the Massachusetts Institute of Technology, May 7–8, 2004. All translations are mine, unless otherwise indicated.

1 In popular nineteenth-century ethnographic accounts and artistic representations of the Muslim house published in the West, the wooden lock fixed to the front door became a key detail through which the technological efficiency and rationality of the colonized was questioned. For example, Lane depicts and describes the form and mechanism of the lock, concluding that "it is not difficult to pick this kind of lock" (*An Account of the Manners and Customs of the Modern Egyptians*, 21). This same comment was later repeated in Lane-Poole, *The Story of Cairo*, 15.

2   Within the context of Orientalist representations of the harem, the terms *seraglio* and *serail* were derived from *sarāy*, meaning palace in Turkish. Yet there was a widespread belief that the etymological root for both terms was the Italian verb *serrare*, meaning to lock or close.

3   The methods of castration and the varieties of eunuchs reportedly available often form a lengthy and somewhat perverse digression in the enormous corpus of European harem literature. The surgical and physiological aspects prove to be predictably repetitious but add to the image of violence, irrationality, and cultural inferiority of the East. The most accessible, though not altogether enlightened, account—gleaned from seventeenth- and eighteenth-century texts—is provided in Penzer, *The Harēm*, 125–51.

    Unsurprisingly, the European accounts from this period had little use for the writings of Islamic jurists who had historically composed a range of opinions and treatises upon the body of the eunuch. While the various surgical categories of eunuchs were also discussed, such legal and theological based deliberations were placed within the broader discourses concerning sexual morality and social ethics—reflecting the eunuch as an integral presence in Islamic societies over the centuries and not as the peripheral anomaly who induced such profound unease in European writers. Very few of these Islamic opinions have been studied but the perspective of a fourteenth-century Mamluk jurist, 'Abd al-Wahhab al-Subki, is briefly related in Shaun Marmon's excellent *Eunuchs and Sacred Boundaries in Islamic Society*, 61–63.

4   Patterson posits that eunuchs, like many types of slaves, were alienated from their natal group, but it was their inability to build kinship ties which guaranteed "no basis of existence in their new societies except their masters [and they] were likely to be totally loyal to him" (*Slavery and Social Death*, 311). While these peculiar qualities of eunuchs are well understood, another angle of inquiry may ask why throughout history cultures have sought to control the sexually active by manufacturing and selecting people who had no place in the reproductive cycle of society.

    Though the fundamental question "Why eunuchs?" is beyond the scope of this essay and remains unanswered, some possible responses have remained constant over time. That their heightened loyalty and devotion toward their master was a consequence of their absence of any competing familial ties was first articulated by Xenophon in his *Cyropaedia*—translated by Wayne Ambler as *The Education of Cyrus*—when Cyrus, having captured Babylon and wary of assassination, contemplates the competing loyalties of his married guards before identifying eunuchs, "deprived of all these ties," to serve "near his own body [*sōma*]" (book 7, chap. 5, 59, 65). In response to doubts about their strength, Xenophon draws a comparison with horses, dogs, and bulls that "when castrated give up their . . . disobedience, but are not deprived of their strength and energy."

5   The harem fantasies referred to in this essay are those that largely existed in the European imagination as constructed under the Orientalist agenda. The extent to which Muslim societies produced their own fantasies, fictional representations, and popular myths about the harem and its black eunuchs, and how these may have been inspired by or partially derived from European representations, are addressed

in the chapters by Orit Bashkin, A. Holly Shissler, and Marilyn Booth in the third part of this volume.

6   The harem at the Topkapı Palace was the site that perhaps more than any other fuelled and perpetuated European fantasies of the harem as the Grand Seraglio. For a Lacanian analysis of the *fantasme* of the black eunuch in the seraglio as represented in the seventeenth- and eighteenth-century European imagination, see Grosrichard, *The Sultan's Court*, 147–65 (Liz Heron's translation of the seminal *Structure du sérail: La fiction du despotisme Asiatique dans l'Occident classique*).

7   Ibn Manzur, *Lisan al-ʿarab*, vol. 1, 615. From the outset, it must be stated that there exist innumerable interpretations and variations of the term *harem* (or *harīm*) throughout different regions and under various schools of jurisprudence. Each interpretation may exhibit its own subtle nuances, and each manifestation may have been shaped by its own distinct history and context. Mamluk Arabic lexicographers, such as Ibn Manzur, elaborate for several pages upon the multitude of derivations of the *h-r-m* root. Similarly, the Qur'an contains many derivatives of the *h-r-m* root but never uses any to make a direct reference to women or their assigned domestic space. Instead, the derivatives refer to dietary laws, prohibitions during the pilgrimage, the holy months, and the sacred precincts of Mecca, in which it is forbidden to kill.

8   The complexities underlying the hierarchical structure within the Ottoman imperial family are discussed at length in Peirce, *The Imperial Harem*.

9   A biographical listing of the *kızlar ağası*—the title of the chief harem eunuchs— of the Topkapı was compiled by the Ottoman historian Ahmed Resmi Efendi (c. 1694–1783) in his *Hamilet ül-kübera'* (the ostrich plumes of the great). Reading like an Ottoman who's who, this book notes the origins and professional careers of thirty-eight eunuchs, beginning with Mehmed Agha, who served as chief eunuch between 1574 and 1590, and ending with Moralı Beşir Agha (1746–52). The downfall and execution of the latter is of particular interest. Shorter biographies of select harem eunuchs are also contained in Mehmed Süreyya Bey's (1845–1909) *Sicill-i Osmani*. Later Ottoman historiography, however, does provide some information on the structure and hierarchy of the institution, in compendiums such as the *Tārīh-i ʿAtā* compiled by the nineteenth-century historian, Tayyārzāde Ahmed ʿAtā.

10   Hathaway, *Beshir Agha*.

11   For a thorough architectural history and analysis of the Topkapı Palace as an arena constructed for the ceremonial display of imperial power, see Necipoğlu, *Architecture, Ceremonial, and Power*. A tour through the principal harem buildings with accompanying photographs is provided in Rogers, *The Topkapı Saray Museum*.

12   For a concise study of the shifting images of Ottoman sovereignty from the frontier warrior to the sedentary sultan, and the politics behind the relocation of the female household, see Peirce, *The Imperial Harem*, 119–218.

13   Necipoğlu, "Framing the Gaze in Ottoman, Safavid and Mughal Palaces."

14   For a collection of the inscriptions throughout the palace buildings, see Şeref, "Topkapu Sarāy-i Hümāyūnı," no. 5 (1910), 274.

15 Köseoğlu provides numbers regarding the harem eunuchs from archival records ("A Tour of the Harem Apartments of the Topkapı Saray," 29).

16 The precise meaning of the title Agha has been the subject of much debate and remains somewhat unclear. In the Ottoman Empire, it was considered a flexible title granted to officers of high rank and was not a title granted exclusively to senior eunuchs.

17 For a concise summary of the principal duties of the *kızlar ağası*, see Uzuncarşılı, *Osman Devletinin Saray Teşkilâti*, 173 ff.

18 To date, history has paid the white eunuchs even less attention than the blacks. It is generally accepted that white eunuchs in the Ottoman court were chosen from Slavic, Hungarian, Caucasian, and Armenian slaves. Batur very briefly lists some senior white eunuchs who were appointed to high offices of state, including grand vizier, during the fifteenth and sixteenth centuries ("The Harem as an Institution in Ottoman Life," 24). Unfortunately, the archival references are not noted.

19 Given the succession of changes in the Topkapı harem over the centuries, it can be assumed that the institution of black eunuchs also changed, with each rank having its own history as positions were introduced and superseded, lost precedence, or were abolished. The precise organization of black eunuchs during the period of change under Murad III is little known at present. Later Ottoman historiography, however, does provide some information on the structure and hierarchy of the institution, in compendiums such as the *Tārīh-i 'Atā* compiled by the nineteenth-century historian Tayyārzāde Ahmed 'Atā, a brief summary of which is given in Batur, "The Harem as an Institution in Ottoman Life," 23–24.

20 The fundamental questions concerning the long-standing and deep-rooted preference for black eunuchs, their rivalry with white eunuchs, and the reasons for the decline and ultimate disappearance of the latter need to be resolved at some point through historical research. The answers may well lie in a combination of interrelated factors, including the changing Ottoman perceptions of different races. Equally relevant may be market forces, especially supply: eunuchs were, after all, products of a flourishing international slave trade. The Ottoman conquest of the Mamluk sultanate during the reign of Selim I certainly made the thriving slave route through the Sudan and Abyssinia more accessible. Of all the slaves openly traded, black eunuchs came to be regarded as the most prized and possibly only the households of wealthy governors and officials in the new Ottoman province could afford them. During their early service in those households, black eunuchs presumably learned the rudiments of court protocol before being presented as gifts to the sultan.

21 Grosrichard uses this phrase in defining the despotic prerogative to control or deny the sight of others (*The Sultan's Court*, 56–63). This chapter argues that the architectural stage for such ceremonies is implicated in this act of control.

22 This adjacent gate leads to the barracks of the famed imperial guards known as the Halberdiers. An inscribed panel records the date of construction as 1586–87, showing that this area of the inner palace was expanded around the same time as the Arabalar Kapısı.

23 See Peirce, *The Imperial Harem*, 119–218.

24 Wyts, "Voyages de Lambert Wyts en Turquie, 1574," Codex Vindob, Manuscript 3325. Nationalbibliothek, Vienna; Mouradgea d'Ohsson, *Tableau général de l'empire othoman*.

25 In the wake of the Tanzimat reforms during the mid-nineteenth century, reformist sultans such as Mahmud II (r. 1808–39) and Abdul-Mejid I (r. 1839–61) recognized the anachronistic image of sovereignty expressed by the Topkapı Palace. With their widespread reorganization of the empire along prevailing European models, the Topkapı was abandoned in 1853 in favor of the grandiose Dolmabahçe Palace, the first in a series of waterfront palaces based upon monumental European models. In contrast to that of the Topkapı, the new harem remained indistinguishable amid the symmetrical wings and neobaroque ornamentation of such display-oriented palaces. Meanwhile, the abandoned Topkapı was preserved as a monument to the Ottoman dynasty, remaining the site of imperial accession and religious rituals until the final collapse of the empire, in 1923.

26 The plans and photographic plates of the Topkapı Palace produced by Gurlitt composed one of thirty-nine sections of his grand 1912 portfolio, *Die Baukunst Konstantinopels*. Despite its large blanks, Gurlitt's plan was considered at the time the most accurate architectural representation of the Topkapı, superseding generations of plans based upon brief glimpses, hearsay, and pure imagination. Such was the continuing fascination with the palace that simplified versions of the new plan appeared in contemporary tourist guidebooks, including Baedeker's (*Baedekers Konstantinopel*, 156).

    Almost seven decades after Gurlitt, a comprehensive and extremely detailed survey of the entire palace, including the harem quarters, was conducted by the architects Sedad Eldem and Feridun Akozan. The catalog of plans, photographs, and hypothetical reconstructions was published as Eldem and Akozan, *Topkapı Sarayı*.

27 Lokmān bin Seyyid Hüseyn, *Hünernāme*, 2 vols. (1584–88). Istanbul: Topkapı Sarayı. Hazine, 1523–24, fol. 18b, 19a.

28 Quoted in Tietze, "Mustafa 'Ali on Luxury and the Status Symbols of Ottoman Gentlemen," 586.

29 Like all densely populated quarters, the Topkapı harem had humble beginnings. According to the prevailing consensus based upon a few sources in the palace archives, the Topkapı originally housed only a select number of concubines in a small appendage, probably on the site of the present harem. The full imperial household of the sultan's mother, aunts, wives, children, sisters, and slaves were housed in the Old Palace (saray-ı atik), which once stood on the site of the present Istanbul University. Following the move of the entire imperial household into the Topkapı harem during the reign of Süleyman I, the Old Palace is understood to have succumbed to a more mournful fate, being used to house the harems of deceased sultans.

30 A tabulated summary of the Privy Purse Registers from 1552 to 1652 is provided in Peirce, *The Imperial Harem*, 122.

31 A peculiar anomaly in the Topkapı harem was the less favorable status of the sultan's official wives, who for reasons of dynastic policies, were forbidden from bearing children.

32 Here the ladies of the harem are understood to have assembled before being conducted, fully veiled and under the guard of black eunuchs, into waiting carriages outside (hence, the name attributed to its external door, the Carriage Gate).

33 Qur'an 33:53.

34 The spatial relationship between eunuchs and the vestibule of a dwelling are discussed, in a Mamluk literary context, in Marmon, *Eunuchs and Sacred Boundaries in Islamic Society*, 3–9.

35 This system was a form of human taxation of non-Muslims which helped secure a supply of servants loyal only to the sultan. References to the system can be readily found in numerous works on the social and political history of the Ottoman Empire.

36 For detailed descriptions of the royal structures in the Court of the Male Pages — or, as it is now commonly known, the Third Court — see Necipoğlu, *Architecture, Ceremonial, and Power*, 111–58.

37 Quoted in ibid., 91.

38 Who may share moral and physical space is explicitly stated in Qur'an 4:23.

39 The *Book of Festivals*, produced by Ahmed III's court chronicler, Vehbi, and illustrated by Levni, has been published in an English edition (*Levni and the Sûrnâme: The Story of an Eighteenth-Century Ottoman Festival*, edited by Esin Atil).

40 The sultan's companions were originally drawn from different palace functionaries. However, by the eighteenth century, this privileged position had become the exclusive preserve of the black eunuchs.

41 The sultan's domed bedchamber was constructed under Murad III. Descriptions of this space are provided in Necipoğlu, *Architecture, Ceremonial, and Power*, 165–72; Köseoğlu, "A Tour of the Harem Apartments of the Topkapı Saray," 32–33.

42 These holy relics were brought to Istanbul and installed inside the Topkapı harem after the 1517 conquest of the Mamluk sultanate. Following this, the Ottomans conferred upon themselves the title of hadım ul-haremeyn ül-şerifeyn.

43 The end of royal fratricide is discussed in Peirce, *The Imperial Harem*, 101–3.

44 In many descriptions of the Topkapı Palace, the princes' area was identified with the highly ornate twin pavilions close to the sultan's bedchamber. But upon reflection, this seems unlikely. Aside from the issue of numbers, the confinement of princes overlooking the Favorites' Courtyard would have compromised the harem of those young women who were being groomed especially for the sultan.

45 Grosrichard, *The Sultan's Court*, 126.

46 Foucault, *Discipline and Punish*, 172.

47 The precise meaning of this gate's name remains open to debate. Kuşhane Kapısı can be interpreted as Aviary Gate, and a small aviary may have been located close by. But another meaning of kuşhane is "saucepan," according to Redhouse's *Turkish and English Lexicon*, which has led to the suggestion that the gate was named after a small kitchen. Indeed, it is believed that food prepared in the vast royal kitchens

(located off the Divan Court) was carried through here for distribution across the harem.

48 At this point, it must be mentioned that another type of occupant could move freely within the harem. Like the eunuch, the prepubescent child was also deemed "incomplete" in his or her sexuality and so could access different spaces and cross critical boundaries segregating men and women without unsettling the moral harmony of the household.

49 Foucault, *Discipline and Punish*, 172.

50 Ibid., 201. The sultan's "unverifiable" presence overlooking the imperial council chamber has been famously depicted in an engraving included in Mouradgea d'Ohsson, *Tableau général de l'Empire ottoman*. The comparisons with the latticed window of the *kızlar ağası* are striking.

51 For a study of the practice under the Mamluk sultans, see Marmon, *Eunuchs and Sacred Boundaries in Islamic Society*.

52 The kuru was the standard unit of currency in the Ottoman Empire.

53 Brief translations of a few waqf inscriptions, including the revenues due to particular ranks of eunuchs, are provided in Köseoğlu, "A Tour of the Harem Apartments of the Topkapı Saray," 28–29.

54 Although the imperial waqfs have been little studied, several articles address the pious endowments and economic activities of various Ottoman harem eunuchs exiled to Cairo. For example, 'Abd al-'Aziz and Crecelius studied the transcription for Beshir Agha's *sabil-kuttab*, a commonly endowed charitable building that combined a drinking water fountain with a classroom above, in Cairo ("The *Awqāf* of al-Hajj Bashir Agha in Cairo"). Hathaway describes the estate of Abbas Agha, chief eunuch in 1667–71 ("The Wealth and Influence of an Exiled Ottoman Eunuch in Egypt").

55 Marmon expands upon the strong sense of solidarity enveloping eunuchs during the Mamluk period, by which they constructed their own collective sacred and imperial identity (*Eunuchs and Sacred Boundaries in Islamic Society*). The architecture of the black eunuchs' courtyard and the inscriptions point to a similar sense of fraternity among the Ottoman eunuchs. However, as each senior member of the harem had his or her own staff of eunuchs, understanding to what extent, if any, factions and competing loyalties compromised the fraternity and solidarity of black eunuchs requires further research.

What a joy it would be to the Prince of Wales to have one
[a harem].

—PRINCESS CAROLINE, 1816[1]

7 ◆ WHERE ELITES MEET

Harem Visits, Sea Bathing, and Sociabilities in
Precolonial Tunisia, c. 1800–1881

Julia Clancy-Smith

 Strolling along the Corniche in La Marsa, a
community twelve miles from Tunis, one immediately notices a curious structure half sub-
merged in the water. Topped by a whitewashed dome,
with balconies and verandas facing the Mediterranean, it
is linked to the beach by a small walkway. To the right, another identical, if smaller, edifice sits abandoned and half
in ruins; fishermen use it to store nets. The larger building, however, is a tony three-star restaurant named Qubbat
al-Hawa, which serves alcohol until the wee hours of the
morning and attracts a mainly European tourist clientele.

In the nineteenth century, gracious neo-Moorish buildings such as these, known as *bayt al-bahr* (sea houses), lined
the shore from La Marsa to the hot springs of Hammam
Lif. They served as bathing pavilions for the elite families
of Tunis, especially the princesses of the Husaynid dynasty
(1705–1957). While elevated rank brought them various
kinds of seclusion for most of their adult lives, the women
for whom these pavilions were constructed enjoyed sea
bathing for its social and health-conferring benefits. Not far
from the shore stood elegant palaces that housed the capi-

tal's great families — along with their extended kin, clients, and servants — during the hottest months of the year. These charming, if dilapidated, structures are the architectural remains of a seaside culture of sociability that combined politics and leisure, harem visits and diplomacy, business and water therapy. Included in this culture, often in surprisingly intimate ways, were European notables who participated in the same social forms and seasonal rhythms as their Muslim peers, which brought them into the heart of Tunisian family life — the household or dar, including the harem.

This chapter salvages a social universe buried under a series of binaries: Muslim versus Christian, premodern versus modern, household versus the state, and colonial versus precolonial. In addition, the triumphant nationalism after the fall of the dynasty destroyed much of the physical evidence and archives for this seaside culture. Nevertheless, an ethnographic recreation of the forms, spaces, and meanings of this nearly vanished sociability is possible through an approach that is primarily household-based. As Bahloul and others have argued, in house-centered societies, like Tunisia, "the house and the domestic group are social units that define community organization, the forms of social exchange, the inheritance system, and the transmission of knowledge."[2]

Households were not only economic and procreative units: they also managed leisure, health-seeking activities, and social communication in ways that involved their members in alliances beyond kin-defined networks. Women's quarters were also important spaces of materiality and display, where gifts from foreign diplomats or monarchs might be on view. And households moved about according to the season — from the Tunis *madina* (historic city) to La Marsa, Carthage, or Hammam Lif — and thus were neither immobile, nor were their members "caged," as European writings from the period invariably portrayed them. Viewed from this perspective, the household emerges as a critical site of sociability in this particular cultural and historical context, although conventional wisdom has held otherwise.

Since the French scholar Maurice Agulhon first elaborated the notion of *sociabilité* in the 1960s, historians have probed the significance of diverse associational forms — from Masonic lodges and clubs to cafes and confraternities — that allegedly lay outside of family structures and thus operated as midwives of modernity.[3] Juxtaposed, often implicitly, against these expressions of extrafamilial modernities was the southern sociability that the literature assumed to be a distinguishing feature of kin-based Mediterranean societies, where the ascendancy of the clan inhibited associational life—a defining feature of modernity itself. A second related assumption specific to Muslim societies held that households with harems (separate women's quarters) were inaccessible to the outside world and thus excluded from wider social, and particularly political, networks transcending the boundaries of kinship.[4] In Orientalist discourse, the word *harem* conjured up an imagined border encircling elite households and their members that severely limited or even impeded social traffic.[5]

This chapter will argue that specific kinds of sociabilities involving Tunisian and allied European notables were characteristic of Husaynid political culture, and that the women of elite households, together with their kin, friends, and clients, were critical to the system's smooth functioning.[6] Not focusing solely upon harems moves the discussion forward—away from its current fixation on foreign, mainly European, representations of Muslim women—and toward an appreciation of the myriad ways that elite households shaped, and were shaped by, various kinds of exchanges and circuits. This approach invites us to see the range of social practices that implicated Europeans in the palace-harem complex and therefore in the capital city's elite society. Thus, harem visits—highly ritualized social calls excluding most, but not all, men due to norms of sexual segregation—can be recast as critical for diplomacy, gift giving, and friendships. The ties of amity forged by these rituals resulted in handsome bonuses—not least, in the long-term loans of princely seaside villas to select European families.

Visits between households, whether in Tunis or at the beach, represented one strand in larger webs of social behaviors that structured the precolonial order.[7] Moreover, the Mediterranean villa, dismissed by earlier historians as merely a space of frivolous entertainment, emerges as a site of sociopolitical negotiation. For our purposes, sociability is loosely defined as networks, both homogeneous and heterogeneous in nature, generated by the great households as their members entertained clients, negotiated marriages, acted as patrons, conducted business, celebrated festivals, and indulged in therapeutic activities, such as hydrotherapy.[8] The core issue of whether household-based sociabilities belonged within the charmed circle of emerging forms of modernity is taken up in the last section of the chapter.

The major questions are: how were social visits, leisure, and health-seeking mediated by households connected to the exercise of power? How did harems and households manage political and social relationships, in-

cluding distaff diplomacy? How did landlord politics, patronage, and seaside diplomacy implicate long-term resident foreigners, mainly Europeans,
in the harem-palace complex of the capital city? And in what ways did
non-Tunisians, mainly European residents, participate in local cultural and
social forms attached to the sea?

A CULTURE FROM THE SEA

Some of the most ubiquitous symbols employed in Tunisian folk art are
linked to the sea. Taxicab drivers hang fish medallions on their windshields
to ward off the evil eye and prevent car accidents. The small wooden vessels that ply the waters at night in search of fish are decorated with brightly
colored evil-eye and fish motifs. Shopkeepers in the madina used to do
a good business selling Mediterranean talismans—in the shape of fish—
for home use. Tunisian Arabic is replete with references to the sea; one of
the country's most notable families is the Bahri clan, whose name means
"of the sea." Finally, the greatest culinary honor that one can bestow upon
dinner guests is to serve up the choicest dish of all: an extravagant seafood
couscous. Fast disappearing under the onslaught of globalization, with its
attendant cultural and economic maladies, this culture struggles to survive
in today's Tunisia. It is most clearly perceived in the dramatic annual shift
from the social life of the cold, wet winters to the tempo of late June, when
families gather at the beach and the denizens of coastal villages, such as La
Marsa, ask neighbors if they have taken their first sea bath of the season.

In the early nineteenth century, the ruling dynasty occupied the principal palace complex, the Bardo, located outside of Tunis. Smaller palaces
were scattered around, mainly along the Mediterranean coast. The Bardo
resembled a small city since each prince—and they were legion—boasted
his own palace and household containing hundreds of people. Originally
modeled after the Ottoman harem, but on a less sumptuous scale, Husaynid harems in the nineteenth century were still guarded by black and white
eunuchs. Personal physicians, attendants, nurses, cooks, servants, and so
forth were numerous and subject to an intricate hierarchy.[9]

The women's section of the palace was vast, containing hundreds of
people who were surprisingly diverse; its members were not only of different racial or ethnic backgrounds but also of different social stations and, at
times, of different religions. People came and went freely. Thus, the households' edges were not fixed but porous in terms of who was a member and

who was not. Depending upon their personal dispositions, some rulers
took relatively few wives and concubines, while others, such as Muhammad
Bey (r. 1855–59), were enthusiastically polygamous. And they were eclectic
in their choices: wives of Italian Catholic origin were quite numerous by the
late eighteenth century.[10] In contrast, the Maliki urban notables or a'yan of
Tunis were generally monogamous, and often refused to give their daughters in marriage to the ruling family, although they maintained close social
and political relations with the Husaynids. Their households, less luxurious
in nature and smaller in scale, were located on certain streets in the madina.

During the torrid summer months, the palace and *haute bourgeoisie* performed tightly choreographed rites that entailed packing up entire households and relocating to residences at the seaside—moving scores, if not
hundreds, of people. The families returned to the capital only after the
harvests, when they undertook elaborate preparations of foodstuffs in an-
ticipation of winter. To staff summer villas, wealthy families transported
enormous cohorts of relatives, retainers, hangers-on, and servants (as well
as slaves, in the period before abolition). But it was not only the ruling
family or court elite who fled to the beach during the summer. Powerful
'ulama families, both Maliki and Hanafi, spent the winter in palaces clus-
tered in identifiable neighborhoods or *hawmat* in the madina; the areas
around Nahj al-Basha (Street of the Pasha) or Nahj al-Hukkam (Street of
the Judges) boasted high concentrations of religious notables.

But in summer this all changed. When the first scorching winds burst
upon Tunis, families such as the Bayrams or Ben Achour (or Ibn 'Ashur)
fled to villas situated on or near the shore. (Today many of these residences, formerly occupied only in summer months, are year-round family
dwellings, as in the case of the Ben 'Achour clan's lovely compound in La
Marsa.)[11] Relocation to the coast allowed these families to forge or preserve bonds, including the all-important matter of marriage alliances, with
other households in ways different from customary sociability in the capital. This summer princely progress so key to elite identity was reflected
in local Islamic marriage contracts and prenuptial agreements designating
where the bride would reside during specific seasons of the year. The contract for one bride from Tunis wed to a Qayrawani (a man from the city of
al-Qayrawan in the interior) "stipulated that the husband consent to bring
his wife to Tunis every six months and rent a vacation house for her in one
of the beach suburbs of the capital."[12]

In short, "going to the beach" constituted one of the most visible signs of high social rank, a tradition that persisted well into the colonial period. Baron Ernst von Hesse-Wartegg, an Austrian traveler who spent a considerable amount of time in Tunis, noted around 1880: "In spring, when the hot days begin, I have often seen long rows of hermetically-closed carriages with armed eunuchs on the boxes and guards on horseback, leave town (Tunis) to go to the watering-places or country seats of the neighborhood—these were the harems of the rich, changing domicile for some months."[13] The court's seasonal mobility might be conceptualized as one symbolic performance of authority taken from a larger repertoire. Two major manifestations of power in motion existed in Tunisia. First was the *mahalla*, which tied people of the mountains, steppes, and oases to the dynasty and capital city through justice, taxation, and expropriation. The second displacement was the movement of the Husaynid family; the government, including scribes and ministers; and urban notables to seaside palaces where they resided between June and late September. Well before the French protectorate, the summer relocation drew in its wake increasing numbers of Europeans and other foreign residents. While women never accompanied the mahalla (as far as we know), they were intimately involved in the royal progress of the summer holiday.

Upper-class Muslim women eagerly welcomed the Mediterranean season since it conferred on them more liberty of movement.[14] These months were marked by celebrations of joyful events in the life cycle of the family—births, circumcisions, betrothals, and marriages—that were often accompanied by performances of Andalusian music. The term *khala'a*, a Tunisian Arabic glossing of a word that in classical Arabic usage has libertine associations, meant summertime festivities or recreation near the sea that frequently resounded with music.[15] In addition to family gatherings often lasting into the night and visits to saints' shrines, sea bathing was a favorite pastime for women. Although it is uncertain when this architectural genre first developed, the bayt al-bahr translated gendered leisure and healing practices into concrete form. Simple shelters—or, in the case of the aristocratic or princely families, splendid marble and stone structures—set into the water with trap doors in the middle, over the sea, permitted elite women to bathe unseen. The family of Mustafa Agha, whose summer house was constructed around 1829 in the neighborhood of Carthage known as al-Kram, had two wooden sea houses with walkways connected to the shore; women, men, and children from the large extended family retreated to these bathing pavilions to spend the day together taking the waters.[16]

The French artist Charles Lallemand painted a lovely, colored image in 1890 of the bathing house in La Marsa now converted into a tourist restaurant. Lallemand tells us: "The women of La Marsa and Sidi Bou Said take sea baths here far from inquiring eyes. They arrive in carriages with the shades pulled down. In the middle of the building is a swimming pool through which the sea water enters freely. The princesses of the bey's family have a similar bathing house not far away from this one."[17]

Ordinary Tunisians, both Muslim and Jewish, also practiced sea bathing and hydrotherapy or, in the desert oases, visited hot springs to cure a variety of conditions, including infertility. In many cases, they frequented the same hot springs as the Romans had. At the port of Halq al-Wad, women who could not afford seaside pavilions went at night to the sandy beach and bathed fully dressed, in light summer apparel. The Tunisian state decreed certain spa towns, such as Kelibia, tax-free zones where the *mahsulat*, onerous impositions on exchanges of goods and services, did not apply — which attracted sellers and buyers from all over.[18] Therefore local and regional trade were linked to the big business that hydrotherapy represented.

The three most popular hot springs in the Tunis region were Hammam Lif (or Hammam al-Nif), ten miles from the capital; Korbous, thirty-three miles away by winding trails; and Nabeul, on the eastern flank of the Cap Bon. However, distance measured by roads or miles was relatively unimportant because most cure-seekers sailed or rowed skiffs from summer residences in Kram, Carthage, or La Goulette to reach hydrotherapy spots across the Bay of Tunis. Hammam Lif is situated at the foot of the mountain known as Bu Qarnayn, or the two-horned mountain. Frequented since Punic times, the small village of Naro, as the Carthaginians called it, was renamed Aquae Persianae by the Romans. In the eighteenth century, 'Ali Pasha, then bey of Tunis, constructed a bath pavilion at Hammam Lif which subsequently boasted a bathing pool and a caravansary for merchants and caravans traveling across the Maghreb; once again, trade was combined with hydrotherapy. In 1756, a member of the Bayram family, Muhammad ibn Hassin, undertook a scientific study of Tunisia's different hot springs, classifying them according to their efficacy in healing.[19]

Beginning in 1826, Husayn Bey expanded the Hammam Lif palace and facilities in order to take extended cures with the court in attendance. Completed several years later, the new palace included an ensemble of two-story buildings, a monumental entrance, and gardens with a kiosk.[20] Husayn Bey paid dearly for his thermal treatment: early in 1244/1829, while he was in

Hammam Lif, some of his courtiers in Tunis robbed the state treasury, and later that same year, a cabal attempted to overthrow the ruler.[21] By the mid-nineteenth century, Hammam Lif boasted the beys' palace, an array of outbuildings, and "a grand bathing establishment situated near the Roman baths."[22] Both Tunisian and European cure-seekers from the capital city brought along servants as well as provisions and rented small houses or rooms in the neighborhood from the locals, often for extended periods of time.[23] After his first stroke, Ahmad Bey spent much of his time either residing in the Hammam Lif palace belonging to a court favorite, Mustafa Sahib al-Tabi', or in his own palace in La Goulette, presumably taking the waters to speed his recovery.[24]

Located on the western edge of the Cap Bon, Korbous, or Aquae Calidae Carpitanae, had been the spa of choice for wealthy Romans from Carthage because its hot sulphur springs were believed highly efficacious. By the early nineteenth century, Korbous was a place of no great importance since it could be reached only with great difficulty by land. Local people served as guides along the trails leading to the hot springs and made a living by renting out rooms in their homes to visitors. Then Ahmad Bey built a palace bathing complex that led to a moderate boom in the village's fortunes, as the ruler's presence brought improvements in the roads—making the springs more accessible. Tunisians and resident Europeans used the waters of Korbous to treat rheumatism, arthritis, dermatitis, and digestive problems, among other ailments. While documentation on cure-seekers in Korbous in the precolonial period is scarce, a well-known poet from Tunis, al-Baji al-Mas'udi (1810–80), sought a cure there, apparently staying for an extended period of time. The experience moved him to compose nostalgic verses lauding the capital city, which he must have missed terribly while he was in exile some miles away.[25]

But the sacred was never far removed from health-seeking behavior and social praxis. As was true of most springs in North Africa, the waters of Korbous enjoyed the protection of a renowned saint, Sidi Abu 'Ammara, whose *zawiya* (or tomb shrine) was the object of veneration and pilgrimage; women in particular sought the saint's blessings as a remedy for infertility. While the saint's tomb remains in Korbous, today the village serves a very restricted clientele of local cure-seekers, and the beys' palace is in sad disarray. Set on a hill overlooking the town, with a splendid view of the Gulf of Tunis, the zawiya's present dilapidated condition hints at a serious erosion in spiritual reputation.

The third main hydrotherapy station is Nabeul, the most distant from the capital. While documentation on precolonial bathing practices is not abundant, evidence from the early protectorate demonstrates the persistence of older patterns of sociability, leisure, and health-seeking behavior. In his 1892 report to Justin Massicault, the French resident-general from 1886 to 1892, Louis Créput, a colonial official in Nabeul noted: "The climate of Nabeul is so temperate and so mild that the town serves as a summer resort for Jewish and Muslim families from elsewhere who come to take the waters. The trip between the town and the sea is done via a taxi service which has discount prices of 15 centimes per person. Several outdoor public establishments—both Jewish and Muslim—serve drinks and confer upon the beach an animated atmosphere that frequently lasts into the night."[26]

In contrast to the sociospatial organization that colonial officials and re-sort promoters later imposed upon thermal spas like Korbous or Nabeul, *hammam* and *shati'* (beach) signified a number of interrelated things in the cultural vocabulary of the time. The word *hammam* could mean a steam bath, a bathing pool, a thermal spa, or simply a watering place. Weekly visits to public baths constituted religious duties tied to Islamic and Jewish purity and pollution taboos closely linked to bodily health, spiritual well-being, and morality. But visiting urban bath houses was also a social ritual, as were sea bathing and taking thermal waters. Thus the religious and so-cial—and the purified and political—were enmeshed in complex ways. In addition, the fact that Europeans and others rented rooms or cottages from the local inhabitants of thermal sites, such as Hammam Lif and Korbous, indicates that a form of health tourism existed in Tunisia well before colo-nialism. The rentals of simple abodes near springs or the sea paralleled the exchanges of sumptuous palace properties among elites, suggesting that hot springs were places where differences in religion and social class did not prevent seasonal mixing, as demonstrated by Créput's 1892 report on Nabeul.

ELITE AMUSEMENTS, SEASIDE DIPLOMACY, AND HAREM VISITS

To appreciate the role played by seasonality and space in relations between the Husaynid family and court and foreign notables, we need to return to the three most important spatial coordinates in the capital city region: first, Tunis proper; second, the nearby Mediterranean villages; and third, the Bardo, a small town with a palace complex.[27] At the Bardo, European consuls paid formal visits in the rulers' audience chambers, but the presence there of the *mahkama* (hall of justice) attracted throngs of subjects from across the country to importune those in power—which meant that getting the bey's ear for very long was difficult.[28] In addition, the Bardo was not close to Tunis, where most Europeans resided. Thus, a topographical element that heightened the political importance of summer socializing was the fact that it was easier to gain access to, and thus wring favors from, rulers or palace retainers in the cozy atmosphere of the suburbs during summer months than during the winter court season.

What emerges from this mapping exercise are the residential strategies pursued by Europeans, who duplicated the summer rituals of the court and a'yan by clustering in close proximity to, and frequently in, villas owned by the palace. In 1831, Sir Thomas Reade, the British consul general, wrote: "The house which I reside in at present is in the country, in the midst of those occupied in the hot months and in some instances even in the winter by the other consuls, and is only one hour and one half from the Bey's palace, and not more than half the distance that Tunis is from the anchorage, which is certainly a great advantage."[29] Other European consuls voiced identical sentiments about the desirability of lodging close to the Husaynids since this meant, among other things, that they were strategically placed so as to get concessions from the ruler or his ministers.

The Husaynid family owned much of the beachfront real estate graced by magnificent palaces, villas, and pavilions ornamented with fountains, patios, and luxuriant gardens of bougainvillea, jasmine, and palm trees. The assortment of available palaces resulted in part from a widely held local belief that, if a ruler died in a particular residence, it would bring misfortune upon his successor to inhabit that same space, which had become *mshuma* (dishonored).[30] With palaces continually under construction, there were lots to spare, so the beys or princes leased or, more often, loaned for extended periods the most elegant of these palaces to the most powerful Europeans. The practice had apparently begun in the eighteenth century, when rulers attempted to persuade French diplomats and military officers expert in the arts of warfare to remain in the country by offering them inducements such as accommodations. In 1793, Hammuda Pasha (r. 1782–1814) proposed to the current French consul, Devioze, who had resided in Tunis for some twenty years, to take him under "my special protection [*garde*] and offer to you a residence either in my palace or in one of my seaside villas [*maisons de plaisance*]."[31]

This was a shrewd move, since it created ties of indebtedness and social obligation through the gift of housing; the beys were, in effect, the Europeans' landlords. Indeed, even today, the most magnificent ambassadorial accommodation by far is the French residence, called La Camilla—a former bey's palace in La Marsa with a superb sea view that was "loaned" to France before 1881. British consuls and their families were also lodged in villas provided by the beys. In 1845, James Richardson, a member of the British and Foreign Anti-Slavery Society who spent much time in Tunisia, noted that when "Hussain Bey died 1835, he loved the English and heaped privileges upon them. The royal palace of the Abdellia [sic], situated in La Marsa, in the neighborhood of Carthage, was ceded to Sir Thomas Reade as a country residence, for a moderate rent . . . once the bey honored Reade by dining with him at the Abdellia, an honor never before nor since accorded any European consul."[32]

Short-term loans of palatial residences greased the wheels of diplomacy and, in at least one instance, may have helped to avert military hostilities. In 1816, just after Caroline, Princess of Wales, and her Italian tutor (and alleged lover) arrived in Tunisia during their tour of classical sites, a menacing naval expedition appeared at La Goulette, under the command of Lord Exmouth. In what can only be characterized as hospitality under fire, Muhammad Bey "feted [the Princess] in accordance with her rank . . . even appointing his son to accompany her on visits around the country."[33] The ruler housed the princess and her retinue at the Dar al-Bey in the heart of Tunis, where a beautiful palace reserved for the most distinguished visitors had been lavishly decorated specifically for the royal visitors. While concessions forced upon the bey by the British admiral played a major role in the expedition's peaceful denouement, the majestic welcome afforded Princess Caroline by the Husaynids dampened Exmouth's ardor to bombard the city. Dignitaries such as the duc de Montpensier, the prince de Joinville, and the duc d'Aumale, all of whom visited Tunis between 1845 and 1846, were housed in the same palace as the Princess of Wales.[34] In 1881, as the protectorate was being imposed, Hesse-Wartegg, a reliable source, observed: "Besides the above-named palaces, there are in Tunis and its environs several others of colossal dimensions and great beauty. But on inquiry they turn out to be the palaces of former Beys, given by their successors to the foreign Consuls or to Tunisian favourites."[35] In fact, the practice of landlord diplomacy and the bestowal of high-end housing, an established Husaynid strategy for managing bigger, more aggressive foreign states and statesmen, persisted even after 1881.

The Husaynids employed an identical strategy with Catholic missionaries from the 1840s on, providing them with preexisting buildings, such as barracks no longer in use, to convert into schools and clinics. And, as was true for diplomats and diplomacy, the summer months in Mediterranean villages afforded opportunities to carry on theological debates, or interfaith dialogues. During his many years in Tunis during the 1840s and 1850s, Abbé François Bourgade "maintained constant and amicable relations with the 'ulama and highly placed officials from the bey's court at their villages in La Marsa and Sidi Bou Said," where he "took part in theological discussions of which educated Muslims are so fond."[36] However, the hospitality was not one-sided. From the time of Ahmad Bey on, rulers and members of their entourage sometimes participated in balls and other grand occasions organized by their European associates. When the new French consulate, located outside the city gates of Tunis near the Bab al-Bahr (the building is now the former French embassy on Avenue Bourguiba), was inaugurated with great pomp in December 1861, Muhammad al-Sadiq Bey and the heir apparent took part in the festivities hosted by the French consul, Léon Roches.[37]

After improvements in the roads linking the capital with the coastal suburbs, more and more Europeans acquired seaside residences. Far from the heat and hubbub of Tunis proper, consular families, members of court, and government officials routinely met each other. Combining diplomacy with socializing in a manner reminiscent of fashionable European spas like Vichy, these gatherings functioned as informal salons.[38] In her letters, Christina Wood, the wife of the British consul, Richard Wood, portrays the summer season during the 1860s as a time for intense socializing with members of the Tunisian court and consular corps, which resulted in the circulation of critical information. In July 1861, she "dined at Marsa with the Raffos on Sunday," obtaining confidential information from Countess Raffo, whose husband was among the highest officials in the government. The latest political gossip from Europe and the Mediterranean, diplomatic postings, and the intimate doings of Tunis elites were reported over dinner in La Marsa.[39] Balls, costume parties, and musical evenings served as antidotes to the ennui of daily life.[40]

As might be expected in a semi-enclosed social universe, personal rivalries, petty bickering, and scandalous behavior—or accusations of such—marked relationships and influenced diplomacy as well. The best documented case in the genre of *liaisons dangereuses* took place in the salon overseen during the 1860s and 1870s by Luigia Traverso Mussalli—the wife of Elias Mussalli and the alleged mistress of two French consuls, Léon Roches (who held the post 1855–63) and Théodore Roustan (1874–82). Elias Mussalli served as a valued interpreter to Ahmad Bey from 1847 on; this position catapulted him into the ministry of foreign affairs, where he embezzled state funds until his dismissal in 1871–72. His post was restored to him in 1879 after Luigia intervened on her cuckolded husband's behalf with her lover, Roustan, who in turn importuned Muhammad al-Sadiq Bey's chief physician, Francisco Mascaro, who had the ruler's ear—and so the lines of patronage and lobbying went.[41]

Regarded as a great beauty even at the age of forty, Luigia used her household as a political club for one of two principal factions in Tunisia, the French party—which included a number of Italian residents loyal to France. She presided over meetings, discussions, and soirees and appeared in public with Roustan at official diplomatic functions, apparently with her husband's consent, or at least indifference.[42] Unfortunately, Luigia never wrote her side of the affair, but in July 1861, Christina Wood sent a letter to her husband, then in Syria, with the latest summertime gossip concerning the Mussallis: "Madame Elias has arrived at Goletta, it is officially announced that she is in an interesting state, a most interesting fact for us, also Madame Mascaro (don't laugh)."[43] France's designs upon Tunisia as well as anti-Italian strategies were worked out in Luigia's salon, as were a number of Catholic missionary projects dear to the heart of Cardinal Lavigerie—which also aimed at keeping out Italian missionaries, who were seen as a threat to French missions.

In addition to gossipy dinners, Tunisia held other attractions, although the pursuit of leisure was deeply gendered as well as subject to class. Men from consular or mercantile families went on shooting parties with those of similar rank in the marshes near the shore, which were rich in fowl and other game. John Gibson, the British consul who caught malaria on one such hunting expedition and died in 1833, provides a perfect example of how upper-class males spent their leisure time: "No person entered more completely into all the Enjoyments or amusements this country affords than he did during the seven years that he lived here; he kept a large stud of horses, three carriages, innumerable dogs, and followed all the field sports with peculiar ardor."[44] At times, European women rode horseback in the countryside around Tunis; Princess Caroline, who might be considered the first modern female tourist in North Africa, apparently did so during her

1816 visit. Frequenting cafes and taverns was another gendered pastime, mainly for men of modest social rank, until more respectable establishments, such as Parisian-type hotels and dining rooms, sprang up in later decades and became meeting places for the well-heeled.

GENDER AND VISITING

How did gender shape social venues and amusements for women, whether Tunisian or European? High-status European women called upon the wives and female relatives of the beys, either at the Bardo or the summer palaces. The narratives of these visits provide a restricted glimpse into a universe that is, regrettably, not well documented. However, entertaining European visitors and friends constituted one social duty among a constellation of obligations of Husaynid women. Among the most essential public and religious functions were charity and patronage.[45] When Husayn Bey's favorite wife, Lalla Fatima, died tragically in 1827 after childbirth, she was mourned by the bey's subjects as well as resident Europeans and particularly by the poor of Tunis to whom she had shown great benevolence. A second eulogy for her, written by Ahmad Ibn Abi Diyaf, reveals that women from the great households mastered the art of protocol so important to state functions. In addition to devoting herself to benevolent work, Lalla Fatima knew the intricate ranking system for the city's notables and involved herself directly in the socially critical matter of *walima* (banquets).[46] Wealthy women invested personal or family wealth in land, real estate, or commercial enterprises, such as urban coffeehouses, so entrepreneurial pursuits occupied their time.

In contrast to the abundant literature on harem visits in Egypt or Turkey, nineteenth-century accounts written by women who were received at the beys' palace are surprisingly scarce; nor is there evidence of European governesses serving the great families of Tunis as was the case in Istanbul and Cairo, where educated women from Europe found ready employment.[47] As was true elsewhere in the Ottoman Empire, Husaynid harems were highly diverse because they housed women and men of different ethnic or racial groups, social classes, and religious affiliations. Members of the resident European or diplomatic community resided in or near palace compounds, such as the Bardo, where the Raffo family occupied a palace—in addition to their seaside palace in La Marsa. In sum, little is known about the inner workings of the beys' palaces, especially about the lives or even the names of harem women. Episodic panegyric commentary on Husaynid women is scattered throughout Ibn Abi Diyaf's chronicle; Ahmad Bey's sister is briefly described as "the chaste, revered Lady Fatuma," but there is nothing more about her.[48]

Given the nature of the evidence, a narrative from circa 1835 by Madame Berner, the widow of a Danish consul, is particularly valuable — all the more so since she had resided in Tunis for years prior to her husband's accidental death by drowning and knew the country quite well.[49] In 1835 Berner and a bevy of female friends called upon the princesses at the Bardo palace; they were greeted by one of the bey's chief ministers, who conducted the ladies as far as the harem's second interior court, where he took leave of them. In Berner's words: "The wife of the Bey, richly but not tastefully dressed, sat opposite to us on the Ottoman, but rose on our entrance and requested us to take places near her, with the words, 'May your entrance be blessed and may you remain as long as it pleases you.'"[50] The marriage of the bey's second daughter to a high-ranking court official was then being celebrated, and the European ladies were invited to attend some of the week-long festivities. According to Madame Berner:

> The constant entertainment consisted again only of sweetmeats and pastry, coffee, chocolate, lemonade but the Bey was this time far more talkative, and played the host in the most affable manner — saying frequently that we were here in our own house, and might do whatever we pleased. He himself took the light, to show us the bridal bed, which was of white satin, tastefully embroidered with gold.[51]

Of note in this account is what Berner mentions in passing about the ruler — that he was "this time far more talkative," which suggests that she had conversed with him in the same setting during an earlier visit. Lady Mary Temple — the wife of Sir Grenville Temple, who was then on a diplomatic mission to Tunis — also visited the Bardo in 1833, where she was presented to "her Highness the Lillah Kabira [the ruler's first wife] in a patio, adorned in the usual oriental style with fountains." Lady Temple reported:

> The Lillah herself, though much larger than we should in Europe consider becoming, was however amongst the least of the set. She was not pretty, but the expression of her face was most agreeable and good-humoured, and I felt quite sorry for her when I heard shortly afterward that she had been put aside by the Bey to make way for a young girl of thirteen. The Lillah asked if I had no children, when hearing that I had

a little boy, inquired why I had not brought him and seemed really sorry. When we had finished our luscious repast, she ordered all the remaining cakes to be put into a basket and desired that I would take them for my child. She had her own little boy of about two years old in her arms.[52]

These two visits were followed by another social call sometime in 1844 by the women and children of Sir Thomas Reade's family, including a Miss Smith, who was probably the Reades' governess and who provided another account. It was more than a casual social event since, as Miss Smith noted, "we promised to give them [English consular officials] a faithful report of all that we saw and heard." This time the European ladies went to a summer palace in La Marsa belonging to the heir apparent, Sidi Muhammad:

> The [princesses] generally reside at the Bardo, except two or three months in the summer when Sidi Mohammed takes his family to his country-house, situated near the sea at Marsa, from whence they have beautiful views of the sea, the coast, Cape Bon, the isle of Zembra, etc., for although the ladies' windows or jalousies are so constructed, that it is impossible for them to be seen by people outside, yet they can themselves see from within very tolerably all that passes . . . It was at this marine villa that we saw the Lillah . . . We entered by a great arched door . . . into a square courtyard, in which we were pleased with the sight of peacocks, turkeys, Barbary doves and other birds . . . we entered a marble patio . . . in which played refreshingly two or three marble fountains, the noise of the falling water gracefully enchanting the ear, and the scattered spray diffusing a delightful coolness through the place. When the heat is very great this place is covered with an awning of silk and other stuff. From an apartment opposite to this window, at the door of which hung a curtain, the Lillah met us, and, kissing us on each cheek, ushered us into the room, where we found several ladies, relatives and visitors sitting in the Oriental fashion, on a couch or divan, placed around the room, and its only furniture . . . All the Lillahs behaved in a quite lady-like manner, a sister of Sidi Mohammed particularly so, although of course they were very inquisitive, examining our dresses and asking us a thousand questions — more particularly on the article of marriage.[53]

On this occasion, the European and Tunisian women ventured together outside the palace, where tents were pitched near the beach so that the women could promenade in the company of their visitors while they took the air, "passing through the olive groves and vineyards to the sea-side."[54]

This scene evokes Qajar and Ottoman miniatures depicting groups of women socializing in the gardens of Istanbul or other imperial cities, although this genre of representational art did not exist in North Africa.[55] Moreover, the theme of the caged or imprisoned harem inmates is present in the accounts collected by Richardson, which represents a trope that occurs throughout the European travel and harem literature of the period, whether about North Africa or the Ottoman capital. Another leitmotif is the corpulence of upper-class Tunisian women, a cultural commentary also found in French accounts of Egyptian women during the 1798 occupation and in much other Orientalist literature. Many more social calls must have been paid by resident European women to the city's great households, but records of those visits have not yet surfaced.[56]

Reports of harem socializing offer rich, ethnographic evidence about the physicality of daily life within upper-class residential compounds. Details of clothing, dress, food, furniture, and furnishings—in addition to female body mass—in turn supply clues about taste, aesthetics, and the critical matter of gifts that greatly influenced the politics of sociability. Here is Miss Smith's description of the chief wife's private apartment:

> The Lillah . . . then arose inviting us to go up stairs into her gallery, which we found was a very long narrow room paved with marble and splendidly furnished. One side was formed of a continuation of latticed windows with a divan, or ottoman, running the whole length of the apartment, on the other side was a recess; the walls were partly covered with a few pictures, mirrors and several clocks, for the Moors are fond of having a great number of clocks and watches hanging up together; there were also marble tables, on which were thickly strewn rich ornaments and other fantastic nicknackery; besides there were European sofas and chairs, chandeliers and lamps, for at most of the respectable Moorish houses as also at the Bardo, European furniture is now fashionable, and will undoubtedly continue so.[57]

Thus, by the mid-nineteenth century, the ruling family and state elites furnished parts of their palaces in Louis XVI style—much to the disappointment of first-time callers, who naturally looked forward eagerly to seeing exotic or outlandish sights. Lavish presents from European monarchs—gilt mirrors, oil paintings, gold watches, bejeweled clocks, and rich textiles—graced interior apartments, including the women's quarters.[58] These costly items were not mere decoration, since their display denoted the strength of diplomatic relations between the Husaynids and various European powers.

In 1825 a French frigate arrived in Tunis from Marseilles, bearing presents from Paris sent back with Sidi Mahmud Kahia's delegation to France on the occasion of Charles X's accession to the throne: "The French king sent gifts to the Bey, consisting of French manufactures in silk, brocade, broad clothes, cashmere, cambric, porcelain, besides some vases and plateaux in silver gilt and eight superb lace dresses for the ladies of the Harem."[59] Richardson noted regarding Ahmad Bey's private apartments:

> In the new suites of rooms added to the Bardo, particularly those belonging to his highness, the Bey has followed as much as possible European taste and imitated the Royal apartments of European sovereigns. One spacious hall, commonly called the <u>Saloon</u>, is especially deserving of notice being superbly garnished with sofas, chairs, tables, curtains, looking-glasses, and pictures, oil-paintings and prints in immense profusion . . . A number of the portraits of foreign princes hang up in these state-rooms. There is also a very good likeness of the Bey himself drawn by Mr. Ferriere, British vice-consul. The Bey's bedroom—in which there is a regular European bed and bedstand—is also adorned with various portraits, and amongst the rest there is a portrait of Sir Thomas Reade, one of the Bey's principal supporters and counselor in any difficulties with foreign governments which arise in the Begum.[60]

But the flow of rare and costly presents went both ways across the Mediterranean. When Sidi Mahmud Kahia arrived in Paris in 1825, he brought as gifts from Husayn Bey the following, as well as many other offerings: horses, lions, ostriches, gazelles, racing camels, perfumes, tiger and lion skins, silk textiles, and a saddle richly ornamented in gold. Included in these diplomatic exchanges of material objects was female attire, some intended for the Husaynid princesses—the lace dresses referred to above—and others for the queen of France. Among the gifts sent in 1825 was "a Moorish costume," made from silk and gold material, worn only by elite Tunisian women. The recipients in Paris were charmed but observed that "it is difficult to imagine the august Marie-Thérèse-Charlotte of France . . . dressed in pants ornamented with silk and gold."[61] The pants (*culottes*) referred to were the *sirwal* worn under tunics.

But the important dimension here is that gift giving was gendered and reinforced ties of friendship between heads of state. The bey relied on the gendered politics of gift giving to defuse a mounting diplomatic crisis in 1828 over the use of four-wheeled carriages. Traditionally, only the ruler enjoyed the right to travel in a four-wheeled carriage, which constituted a public sign of paramount sovereignty. When Sir Thomas Reade imported such a carriage in a deliberate challenge to older diplomatic protocol, the stage was set for a confrontation over the ruler's claim to privilege. However, Husayn Bey saved face and avoided a showdown by bestowing his own carriage upon Lady Reade as an act of munificence. Because his rival had obtained a mark of favor, the French consul, Mathieu de Lesseps, immediately demanded the same right to this kind of conveyance. Husayn Bey soothingly informed him that as soon as Lady de Lesseps arrived in Tunisia, he would give her a four-wheeled carriage as well.[62]

While seaside socializing was part of the normal summer routine for Tunisian women and their long-term European friends, the Husaynid court also offered a well-oiled and orchestrated performance of harem tours to important foreign visitors. In the 1840s, the court at the Bardo palace employed an Italian woman as guide and interpreter for female visitors. Lady Mary Elizabeth Herbert, Baroness Herbert of Lea, made a tour in 1871 that constituted a form of palace- or harem-hopping as she visited princesses of the Husaynid family and other notables, such as the Bin 'Ayyad, at their residences—five or six palaces and households, from the Bardo to La Marsa. At each stop, hospitality was lavished upon Herbert and the British consul's wife, Christina Wood, who conducted the tour since she was a close friend of the bey's female relatives and spoke Tunisian Arabic. Letters exchanged between the wives of consuls and the princesses demonstrate true affection. A letter sent in 1860 by Camille Roches to one of the Husaynid princesses (unnamed but referred to as *mar'at al-wazir*; perhaps the wife of Mustafa Khaznadar) reveals the existence of very strong emotional attachments between the two women.[63]

Being male did not necessarily exclude the curious visitor from the harem's sacrosanct space. When Hesse-Wartegg was received at the Bardo in the summer of 1881, he too was ushered into the private women's quarters to admire the beautifully wrought decor—all of the ladies were then absent, probably in residence at one of the Mediterranean palaces. Allowing foreign dignitaries into the women's apartments may have been a way of bestowing particular favor.[64] After all, the Tunisian delegation to France, headed by Ahmad Bey in 1846, had marveled at the wonders of the Versailles palace and been admitted into the king's family apartments—why wouldn't the Husaynids return the compliment and display the luxuries of their private dwellings, observing, of course, the dictates of gender segregation?[65]

Yet there was an explicitly political dimension to this system of ritualized visiting. As C. A. Bayly has shown in *Empire and Information*, harems — with their multitude of kin, servants, and retainers, all of whom belonged to widespread social networks — represented critical funds of inside information and political gossip, as was the case in European courts. In 1835 the British consul alleged that several Mamluks "in the bey's seraglio" were being secretly paid by the French government to pass along classified information about what transpired in the heart of the palace.[66] In addition, since the ruling bey's mother was the most powerful female figure in the Husaynid household, establishing friendships with her could result in social, or even political, advantage. For example, Ahmad Bey consulted with his mother prior to undertaking his state trip to France in 1846. As mentioned above, social calls by European women also permitted covert intelligence gathering — as Miss Smith acknowledged in the concluding sentence of her narrative: "I am sorry that my account of the harem of Sidi Mohammed is so uninteresting, but I have made the best I could of the few incidents."[67]

Hesse-Wartegg admitted that he collected information on the beys' harems by interrogating resident European women: "Though I cannot boast of having penetrated during my stay in Tunis into a harem while it was inhabited by its tenants, I was fortunate enough to hear everything worth knowing from European ladies who, by a long residence in Tunis, as well as through their intimate relations with the established feminine world, were better entitled than anybody else to give me the necessary particulars."[68] But intelligence gathering, like gift giving, flowed in both directions. If the beys opened up their harems to visitors who subsequently passed along what they had seen and heard to others in Tunis, the fact that the beys' families lodged Europeans in high-end seaside housing rewarded the Tunisian ruling class with information about what their tenants were up to. After all, many Europeans had Tunisian subjects or Maltese expatriates as domestic servants, and they must have relished their position as gossip brokers.

As tourism to French Algeria greatly expanded, precolonial Tunisia was added to the list of attractions on the circuit for European travelers. Lady Herbert, who arrived in Tunis after a tour of Algeria in 1871, had come for relief from rheumatism: "Being anxious to judge for myself as to this country and especially to test the efficacy of certain warm springs, which had been strongly recommended to me by a Paris doctor for rheumatism, I started last January [1871] with my eldest daughter [for North Africa]."[69]

That Lady Herbert had ventured overseas to take the waters on the recommendation of a French physician indicates that health tourism was taking off in this period. Moreover, she inventoried the rental housing market in Algiers and Tunis for invalids back in London who were considering "taking houses there for the winter," since she enjoyed uncommon access to the private rooms of domestic residences. Well-traveled and well-heeled, Lady Herbert knew a prime tourist spot when she saw it:

> Between this spot [Carthage] and Goletta were a number of villas and country houses, or rather sea-side watering-places of the Bey's family or his ministers; and I can conceive no more enjoyable spot in the summertime than this sea-shore with its big shady rocks, beautiful sands, lovely shells, and glorious blue sky . . . Mrs. Wood told me that it was her children's greatest delight to come here for the day from their country house at Marsa which is only a few miles off, and I did not wonder at their taste.[70]

In short, the beys, their wives, and female relatives employed seaside villa diplomacy as an astute stratagem for maintaining alliances and political ties with resident or visiting European notables—a delicate exercise in managing relations between states.

WHERE ELITES MEET: THE SEA AND THE BATH

The cult of seaside holidays, a largely English social and cultural invention, appears to have merged with the growing awareness of the health benefits of salt or spa mineral waters by the European—particularly German—scientific world in the very late eighteenth century.[71] As beach resorts and bathing caught on among European middle classes during the nineteenth century, regulations governing behavior spread across the Mediterranean world and Europe. For example, the British-controlled Greek Ionian islands enacted statutes in 1836 regulating hours and places of public bathing. Some provisions were inspired by safety concerns, but the final clause was aimed at public morality—"bathing by men is forbidden anytime that women are present"—although in Great Britain, bathing was not always sexually segregated.[72] In France, sea bathing had become the rage by the 1860s, driven by the social imperative of summer holidays away from Paris that turned quiet villages on the Normandy coast, such as Deauville and Trouville, into elegant watering spots.

In Tunisia, sea bathing was a well-established practice among resident Europeans quite early in the century. In 1834, the English vice-consul, William Carleton, stated that he frequently went to the beach at La Marsa to bathe and had been so doing for years.[73] Expanded immigrant settlement after the 1830s transformed small, sleepy Mediterranean suburbs into bustling towns. When the founder of the Order of the Sisters of Saint-Joseph, Emilie de Vialar, returned to Tunisia in 1843, she went to La Marsa to visit one of the order's houses. The sisters discovered that during the season, many town inhabitants indulged in sea baths, scandalizing some nuns. Other sisters, however, desired to experience for themselves the benefits of salt water, which raised the delicate issue of modesty. Vialar resolved the problem by declaring that bathing could take place only in "a completely enclosed tent in the form of a pavilion that reached all the way to the water's edge which [the sisters] should only use when La Marsa's bathers were absent."[74] This solution resembles the princesses' bathing houses set right in the water, although they were on a much more glorious scale.

In July 1858, Charles Cubisol, whose vice-consular office was in La Goulette, investigated disagreements over proper beach behavior in a report titled "Établissement des bains de mer sur la plage." Important here is that the port, whose population included thousands of "Europeans, Moors, Maltese or Jews, of which many were fishermen or boatmen," was rapidly being peopled by indigent Mediterranean islanders.[75] Immigration had partially transformed the older system of aligning residential neighborhoods with religious affiliation or legal jurisdiction. And newer spaces of leisure and sociability were the most contested, since codes of conduct had yet to be worked out. After mid-century, disagreements about the appropriate use of these spaces increasingly led to conflict—in one case over different ways of behaving at the beach while sea bathing.

In this case, called the La Goulette affair, some bathers had placed tents—the precursor to the bathing machine—on the sand in such a way as to deny others direct access to the water, provoking alarm over privacy while in a state of undress. Since Muhammad Bey had bequeathed this beach property to La Goulette's mainly foreign inhabitants, the port's governor, Khayr al-Din, was called upon to mediate between warring bathing factions. In his letter to the feuding Europeans, Khayr al-Din stipulated that individuals could not encroach upon a space designated as "public" in accordance with the recognized principle of "communal rights of access." What is fascinating about this seemingly trivial matter is that, while Tunisians also bathed there, it appears that none of them were involved in this particular dispute. In effect, the Husaynid state, through Khayr al-Din's decision, spelled out beach-use regulations for Europeans, who held widely varying ideas about decency as well as about what constituted public and private spaces.[76]

As was true in Europe at the time, those at the top of the social pyramid sought water therapies in more exclusive circumstances than La Goulette's public beach—from the privacy of villas adjacent to the water. Christina Wood's 1861 letters to her husband, Richard, while he was on mission in Syria, demonstrate the extent to which Tunisians and Europeans of the same class socialized together, naturally maintaining gender segregation. In the summer, Mrs. Wood wrote: "We have been all as well as possible . . . profiting by the baths." A bit later she states: "We are all quite flourishing since we are installed here. The children are very much improved and live in the open air . . . Baby is quite well and lively again, she takes her salt water baths . . . I go every morning [to the beach] but have only taken a few baths."[77] Wood provided details on dinner parties and visits back and forth between the consular class and their Tunisian neighbors, which included female-only visits to the Husaynid princesses. The seaside residence that the Woods occupied in the summer months belonged to the ruling family but had been loaned to them.

Christina Wood commented to her absent husband upon the kinds of intimate social exchanges possible during the summer months: "Our neighbors, the Caid's [qa'id] family are too kind and good-natured and very quite good people . . . Si Hussein called to see me today and left me a letter to enclose for you. He really is a great friend of yours and a first-rate fellow worked to death in his new office, he complains that he has not a moment for exercise."[78] Wood reported that she had "made great friends with the ladies [of the qa'id's family] and am making great progress in Arabic," which the "ladies" were teaching her. This represents a nice reversal of conventional nineteenth-century narratives of foreign governesses' teaching European languages to women or children in Ottoman households.

Despite its relative distance and difficulty of access, Korbous too became increasingly attractive for hydrotherapy. From at least the 1820s, members of the diplomatic and resident foreign community utilized its hot mineral waters for medical purposes; Tunisians had always looked to the site for physical and spiritual healing. Cubisol's predecessor as French vice-consul in La Goulette, Louis Gaspary, noted in April of 1824: "My mother-in-law

is counting on going to Korbous at the beginning of May and she would be
very happy if Madame Guys [the French consul's wife] would honor her
by going there with her." They were to travel by small boat since that was
considerably quicker and safer than going by land, but bad sailing weather
in April and May delayed the trip. However, by 26 May, he reported: "I just
arrived back from Korbous where I left Mme. Guys in very good health.
Our trip there was short and happy; she is with her daughter; they went by
a little boat."[79] Two months later, in June 1824, the ladies were still at the
Korbous, whose waters had very much improved Mme. Guys's health. The
women were provided for by Gaspary's brother, who went back and forth
by skiff from La Goulette carrying messages, food, and provisions.

This early, rather rare account raises a number of questions. One wonders where Mesdames Gaspary and Guys resided, as they were absent from
home for two months, and their visit occurred prior to Ahmad Bey's building program at Korbous. While the sources do not say so explicitly, the
women must have lived in Tunisian houses, since at the time there were
neither hotels nor other amenities; leasing domestic space to cure-seekers
was a major source of livelihood for the inhabitants of the small village, as
it is today. Whether the French took their baths with Tunisian women remains uncertain, although it is very likely; in any case, they must have been
treated by local female healers.

Decrees by beys from 1787 on periodically reconfirmed the rights exercised by the saintly descendants of Sidi 'Ammara over the baths, springs,
and bathing pool at Korbous; the decrees specifically mention female members of the lineage. In 1835, Mustapha Bey's decree lists the shaykh's sister,
Mas'uda, as part of the family "responsible for the administration and surveillance of the zawiya at Hammam Korbous as well as the buildings and
baths." Another woman, Khadija, is mentioned in 1840 as a part of the clan.
What precise role women from the lineage played in the management of
the springs or in water treatments—intimately linked to spiritual healing
and the sacred—remains uncertain, but their presence in the documents is
suggestive. A decree from 1875 mentions a cafe at the site for the first time.[80]

As ever greater numbers of Europeans sought out Tunisian or Algerian hot springs for their healing benefits, another current of health-seeking
tourists moved in the opposite direction across the sea. High-ranking Tunisian officials and even religious notables began frequenting European spas.
The religious scholar Muhammad Bayram V, who suffered from a serious
"nervous affliction," consulted physicians in Paris and sought cures in pres-

tigious European centers.[81] However, the political and therapeutic were never far apart. After Khayr al-Din's fall from grace in 1876, he received the ruler's permission to go to France in 1877 and 1878—even though he was theoretically under palace arrest in Tunis—for cures at Vichy and Saint-Nectaire.[82] Thus health seeking offered a convenient rationale for leaving the country—only a few years before French troops invaded Tunisia in 1881, and colonial officials forced Muhammad al-Sadiq Bey to sign away his kingdom at the seaside palace, in the 1883 La Marsa convention.

COLONIAL POSTSCRIPTS

In 1905 the protectorate compelled the Tunisian state to cede the springs at Korbous to a French company, the Compagnie des Eaux Thermales, which eventually acquired full ownership of the bathing pools as well as huge shares of the villagers' houses, land, and water. But the takeover was delayed for a time by a bitter, protracted struggle waged by the family of Sidi 'Ammara and other property holders. Significantly enough, even as pressures mounted on the bey and the *idarat al-ahbas* (Muslim pious foundations) to hand over land titles to the Compagnie, officials at the Direction de Santé held that "indigent Muslims at Korbous should be able to get care for free because Korbous is important to all of the country's Muslims"— a statement that hinted that the Compagnie's fight for control of the hot springs would not be an easy one to win.[83]

Over a decade ago, Dane Kennedy demonstrated that after the 1857 mutiny in India, hill stations became increasingly critical to the practices of the British Empire and as such suffered profound cultural permutations. Originally mountains sacred to both Muslims and Hindus, then playgrounds for Britons on tour, these whimsical, high-altitude outposts were ultimately transformed into the administrative and political heart of the empire: there officials, soldiers, and their families enjoyed hygienic isolation and cultural quarantine from the "natives" below.[84] Following the British lead, scholars like Eric Jennings are now tracing the processes whereby indigenous healing practices throughout the French empire were appropriated to promote health tourism, which drew sociospatial boundaries grounded in racial hygienics between science and superstition, the colonizer and the colonized. Yet the colonial situation can be fully intelligible only if earlier social arrangements are recovered and reconstructed, however arduous this might be due to problems of documentation.[85]

The origins of spatially segregated colonial hydrotherapy by "race"—
usually conflated with religion—and class envisioned by colonial spa promoters lie not in 1881 or 1883, but rather in this slightly later colonial period
after 1900. While the Compagnie des Eaux Thermales in Korbous attempted to insulate middle-class Europeans patients from local spa users
by employing the scare tactic of rumors that the locals had syphilis, the promoters were unable to completely banish Muslims or Jews—or even indigent Europeans—from the spa's small confines. In part this was because
both Tunisians and foreigners had frequented local beaches and thermal
springs more or less together for nearly a century prior to the creation of
what Jennings so aptly terms "recompression chambers" for ailing French
nationals returning home from the empire's tropical reaches.[86] Moreover,
in the colonial period, upper- and middle-class Tunisians continued to seek
cures in Korbous, even if they "kept their distance from Europeans."[87] And
until 1905, when French laws separating the Catholic Church and the state
were enacted in Tunisia, missionaries were allowed entry to spas free of
charge. Colonial spas did, however, effectively sever the sacral dimensions
of thermal cures from the purely therapeutic, while also partially erasing the
contributions of age-old Tunisian healing arts associated with water.

Mary Lynn Stewart and other historians have demonstrated that bathing regularly for hygienic purposes only caught on in France in the late
nineteenth century and the early twentieth, although hydrotherapy had
been prescribed for nervous disorders for over a hundred years.[88] While this
was rarely, if ever, acknowledged, colonial spas drew inspiration from older
North African practices and beliefs tied to the sea and its health-conferring
benefits for body, spirit, and society. One wonders if the Europeans who
frequented Tunisia—with its ancient culture of weekly hammam visits, sea
baths, and thermal cures—introduced more modern notions of hygiene
when they returned to Europe, or at least eased the acceptance of novel
ideas regarding water and the body.[89]

The increasing numbers of European female tourists and travelers to
North Africa, who often sought out relationships with local elite families
and households, brought significant changes to travel and travel guides;
as part of this process, a blurring of genres occurred as older literary conventions governing travel accounts gave way to tourist guidebooks. Lady
Herbert's narrative of adventures and cures in Algeria and Tunisia, while
emblematic of the earlier genre of travel writing, anticipated the more modern, popular guidebook since it contained practical suggestions for the trav-

eler — notably, how to rent suitable houses for the season from local families. And as Kenneth Perkins's work demonstrates for nineteenth-century Algiers, British ladies on tour were offered sightseeing options not available to men: visiting "native" women and Muslim families in the intimate setting of the household. Was the growth of gendered travel packages a variation on the harem visit?[90]

What impact did women travelers such as Lady Herbert exert upon local gender ideologies and praxis? Not too long after her excursion, the women of the harem began traveling to Europe. *Le Petit Tunisien Indépendent* reported in 1886 that the harem of Mustafa ibn Isma'il, a high-ranking notable in the Tunisian court, had returned from an extended stay in Paris. The traveling household included several princesses and "six Mauresques" who had also been part of the harem in Paris. The ladies wore "French clothes" — at least while boarding the ship in Marseille for La Goulette — and were under the close guard of a eunuch.[91] What is irrefutable is that the persistence of precolonial practices governing bathing and hydrotherapy to no small degree shaped — and undermined — the colonial project of spas for an exclusively bourgeois European clientele.

THE HOTEL ZEPHYR, LA MARSA

The bathing pavilions and summer palaces that once adorned coastal villages bear witness to the significance of the sea for elite sociabilities. The Husaynid dynasty employed beach diplomacy, harem visits, and other expressions of hospitality to assimilate, at least partially, resident Europeans and visitors into the prevailing culture — one ultimately grounded in Islamic norms regarding purity and pollution taboos. How has viewing the palace-harem complex and households as interlocking webs of sociability and communication changed understandings of the precolonial era? The older literature on the Tunisian governing class tended to characterize it as passive and thus ineffective when confronted with increasingly aggressive demands by European states and statesmen prior to 1881.[92]

Yet, as disseminators of favors and information, elite households were critical to the conduct of foreign and domestic politics. The palace adroitly handled interactions with local Europeans through seaside diplomacy, including the loan of Mediterranean villas and a dramatic repertoire of well-rehearsed harem visits. Moreover, by revisiting harem visits from a comparative perspective, it becomes clear that a lack of historicization obscures considerable differences in the practice's local social expressions and meanings. The members of the large Reade household resided in Tunis for nearly twenty-five years, from 1825 to 1849. Thus, the periodic social calls paid by women of that family to the Husaynid princesses did not have the same valence as the harem encounters studied by Mary Roberts and other scholars, which fall into the category of short-term tours. In addition, the Reades' summer house was a gift from the bey, and thus the English family resided in spaces identical to those called home by the Tunisian elite. One needs to speculate, however, on the significance of the court's extended stays in seaside villages from the mid-1850s on, separated from Tunis and the Bardo. Did the fact that the beys were surrounded by—indeed, beleaguered by—Europeans in that particular space mean that the Mediterranean palaces had become a sort of gilded cage?

Our approach also raises questions about the older historiography on Muslim households which held, without adequate evidence, that the existence of harems impeded wider social contacts with the outside world, and thus participated in modernity. One of the major issues addressed here has been periodicity and the assumed rupture between the precolonial and colonial periods. Scholars arguing for the durability of "the precolonial" after—even long after—the advent of full-scale imperial rule in Asia or Africa use political institutions or economic arrangements as evidence to buttress their positions. Forms of sociability such as visiting, leisure, and health offer a different point of entry to rethink these issues. In any case, the notion that the precolonial and the premodern were more or less equivalent—or that kin-based systems of sociability were hostile to modernity—seems inadmissible for nineteenth-century Tunisia.[93]

One unanticipated finding from our reconstruction of a largely vanished social world has been the importance of what I call the seasonality of sociability, meaning that the lives of both diplomats and state officials followed different rhythms in winter and summer, each of which was associated with gendered spaces and varying intensities of interaction and exchange—and of course, quarrels and back stabbing.

What were the long-term implications of household-regulated socializing that shaped the play of politics in both precolonial and early colonial Tunisia? We have already seen that schemes for the Korbous hot springs were thwarted because of the force of tradition, including the fact that Europeans of ordinary status and indeterminate nationality had long sought cures there. Most importantly, French Tunisia's large and politically autonomous Italian community—some of whose ancestors, like the Jewish

Finzi family originally from Leghorn, had arrived in the early nineteenth century—imposed practical limits on the more brutal forms of classic colonial oppression. Even after 1900, seaside socializing between the Tunisian aristocracy and European notables continued in the once-elegant Hotel Zephyr, in La Marsa, a stone's throw from the beach and situated so as to catch light breezes off the sea. My neighbor and friend, Naila Rostem—a member of the old Tunisian-Turkish aristocracy, whose family memory stretches back to the early twentieth century—informed me that elites used to gather regularly in the hotel on summer evenings. According to her, "during balls and soirees at the Zephyr, the champagne flowed." Fresh fish plucked from local waters and prepared for midnight suppers were "immense"—much bigger than they are now—or so social memory, probably infused with nostalgia, would have it.

The final demise of this princely seaside culture and society came in 1958, when Habib Bourguiba personally oversaw the destruction of many of La Marsa's palaces and women's bathing pavilions. The president of the newly independent state unleashed bulldozers and crews armed with dynamite upon ornate neo-Moorish structures and their lush gardens. According to the son of the last head gardener serving the Husaynid dynasty, Bourguiba "ran around like a happy child and said, 'Here! Destroy! Blow this up.'"[94] It is significant that Bourguiba did not also order the demolition of such blatantly colonial monuments as the Tunis train station or central post office. In effect, the palaces were visible reminders of the Husaynid dynasty, which had endured for two and a half centuries, and of the great families of Tunis, including Naila Rostem's lineage. Nationalist fervor as well as a personal vendetta conspired to bury a princely, seaside culture under its own ruins. In 2001, Tunisia's ruling family seized the Hotel Zephyr, had it demolished, and constructed an American-style shopping mall in its place.

NOTES

Special thanks to Dalenda Larguèche for taking me to Korbous when she wanted to go to Bizerte instead, and to my La Marsa family, the Rostems, for initiating me into the social practices of summer. Eric T. Jennings generously shared his in-progress research with me, now published as *Curing the Colonizers*. All translations are mine, unless otherwise indicated.

1 Quoted in Day, *At Home in Carthage*, 14.
2 A fuller version of this article is found in Julia Clancy-Smith, *Mediterraneans*; Bahloul, *The Architecture of Memory*, 51. See also Duben and Behar, *Istanbul Households*.
3 Carlier, "Le Café maure"; Boutier, "Un autre Midi."

4　The literature on Orientalist representations of North African, and particularly of Turkish or Egyptian, women is too abundant to cite here; for a discussion of some of the problems in that literature, see Burton's 1999 reviewed work(s): *Gendering Orientalism: Race, Femininity, and Representation* by Reina Lewis and *Colonial Fantasies: Towards a Feminist Reading of Orientalism* by Meyda Yeğenoğlu. Both Roberts, in *Intimate Outsiders*, and El Cheikh, in "Revisiting the Abbasid Harims," provide overviews of the evolution of scholarly thinking. I do not mean to imply that Western representations of women and gender are unimportant; rather, I seek to press scholars for more explicit links between rhetoric, representation, and praxis on the ground. See Clancy-Smith, "Le regard colonial," "The Intimate, the Familial, and the Local in Trans-National Histories of Gender," and "Exoticism, Erasures, and Absence: The Peopling of Algiers, 1830–1900," 19–61.

5　At worst, harems or Muslim households by their very nature were characterized as blocking the evolution of social institutions and progress and hindering art, literature, and science; in depictions of Algerian Muslim society, the household, family, and harem were all conflated for polemical purposes; see Clancy-Smith, "Le regard colonial," 27–30. The nineteenth-century discourse on modernity and the family was, not surprisingly, contradictory. On the one hand, the middle-class family was constructed as a refuge from the stresses and strains of the modern world. On the other hand, the family was regarded by Third Republic French liberals as the site par excellence for social engineering and thus as the potential crucible of modernity—or the major obstacle to it—if the kinship structure in question was non-European or nonbourgeois. The Muslim family was almost universally portrayed as the site of concealed female oppression.

6　I use the terms *harem* and *household* almost interchangeably, although strictly speaking the harem was one section of a larger domestic compound.

7　The Tunis elite and European residents or travelers generated what little documentation exists. As with so many other questions, the record for sociabilities is sparse and fragmented; lack of evidence allows only cursory treatment of important topics. Moreover, the triumphant nationalism of the postcolonial state resulted in the demolition of much of the physical evidence for this seaside culture. For the same reason, the history of the Husaynid family was taboo until very recently. Regrettably, Tunisian women in this period did not write about themselves, nor produce anything akin to *Harem Years*, the memoirs of Huda Shaarawi, the Egyptian feminist.

8　On leisure, a concept not yet analyzed for nineteenth-century Tunisian society, see Larguèche, "Loisirs, sociabilité et mutations culturelles dans la régence de Tunis à l'époque Ottomane."

9　Bey in this context means roughly prince or regent because the Husaynid dynasty maintained the partial fiction of being politically subordinate to the Ottoman sultans.

10　Moalla, *The Regency of Tunis and the Ottoman Porte*, 79–80; Ben Achour, *Catégories de la Société Tunisoise dans la deuxième moitié du XIXème siècle*, 226–27.

11　Green, *The Tunisian Ulama, 1873–1915*, 50. On the Husaynid family, whose history awaits its historian, see F. Bey, *La Dernière Odalisque*; E. Bey, *Les Beys de Tunis (1705–1957)*; Ben Achour, *La Cour du Bey de Tunis*.

12 Blili, *Histoire de familles*, 86–87.

13 Hesse-Wartegg, *Tunis*, 85–86. Hesse-Wartegg (1854–1918) was one of the nineteenth century's foremost travelers and travel writers; he published over twenty works on his journeys from America to the Amazon to North Africa and East Asia. In Tunis he was received with honors by the ruling family, due to his reputation.

14 In Egypt, under the khedive Tawfiq (r. 1879–92), the suburb of Helwan became a winter retreat for palace and urban elites. A theater, casino, and gardens graced the town; but more important, its location outside the capital allowed upper-class women more freedom, according to Shaarawi, *Harem Years*. The Ottoman family also moved about in summer, when they took up residence along the Bosporus. The Ottoman-Egyptian elite often maintained palaces on the Bosporus as well; see Roberts, *Intimate Outsiders*, 7.

15 Abdesselem, *Les historiens Tunisiens*, 93.

16 Interview with Madame Hasiba Agha, Carthage, Tunisia, November 2007.

17 Lallemand, *Tunis au XIXe siècle*, 149.

18 Bachrouch, *Le Saint et le Prince en Tunisie*, 387.

19 Bergaoui, *Tourisme et Voyages en Tunisie*, 76. Malinas claims that Muhammad ibn Hassan Bayram's manuscript was in fact a translation that he had done in 1171/1756 from Latin to Arabic of a study written by Yusuf al-Guir, a Christian physician converted to Islam who resided in Tunis (*Notice sur le groupe hydro-minéral de Korbous*, 3).

20 Raymond, *Chronique des rois de Tunis*, 2:92.

21 Ibn Abi al-Diyaf, *Ithaf ahl al-zaman bi akhbar muluk tunis wa 'ahd al-aman*, 4:207.

22 Raymond, *Chronique des rois de Tunis*, 2:57.

23 Dunant, *Notice sur la Régence de Tunis*, 122–23.

24 Sabaï, *Mustapha Saheb Ettabaa*, 23; Ibn Abi al-Diyaf, *Ithaf ahl al-zaman bi akhbar muluk Tunis wa 'ahd al-aman*, 4:156–59.

25 Ben Achour, *Catégories de la Société Tunisoise dans la deuxième moitié du XIXème siècle*, 31, 37; Bin Hamida, *Al-Baji al-Mas'udi*.

26 Louis Créput, "Notice sur le Contrôle Civile de Nabeul," recueil 5, bobine 5, Institut de Recherche sur le Maghreb Contemporain, Tunis.

27 Corbin, *The Lure of the Sea*, particularly 187–281.

28 Ben Achour, *La Cour du Bey de Tunis*, xxi.

29 Sir Thomas Reade to foreign secretary, Henry Temple, the Viscount Palmerston, December 23, 1831, Foreign Office series, Tunisia (hereafter FO) 77/22, National Archives of the United Kingdom, London (hereafter NAUK).

30 A number of resident Europeans commented upon this, including Count Filippi, the Sardinian consul in Tunis, quoted in Monchicourt, *Relations inédites de Nyssen, Filippi et Calligaris*, 86.

31 Debbasch, *La nation française en Tunisie*, quote 243. The fact that Europeans were confined to residential compounds in the madina explains offers of high-end housing because lodgings were scarce.

32 James Richardson, "An Account of the Present State of Tunis," with appended "Addendum on the Tunisian Harem," 1845, p. 20, FO 102/29, NAUK.

33 Ibn Abi Diyaf, *Ithaf* 3:147.

34 British consulate logbook, July 1828, FO 77/21, NAUK; Monchicourt, *Relations*, 86, note 4.

35 Hesse-Wartegg, *Tunis*, 46.

36 Pons, *La nouvelle église d'Afrique*, 228.

37 Henri Hugon, "Une ambassade tunisienne à Paris en 1825 (Mission de Si Mahmoud Kahia)," 111.

38 Blackbourn, "'Taking the Waters.'"

39 Christina Wood to Richard Wood, July 5, 1861, box 1, personal correspondence, 1855–99, papers of Sir Richard Wood, St. Antony's College, Oxford (hereinafter Wood to Wood).

40 Ibid. For the Mardi Gras costume party thrown at the British consulate in Tunis, Vicomte Alfred de Caston composed a long, exceedingly bad French poem dedicated to Christina Wood, which he had printed for the guests—which gives us an idea of how the diplomatic corps spent their leisure time.

41 Ganiage, *Les Origines du Protectorat Français en Tunisie*, 447–61; Cambon, "Lettres de Tunisie."

42 Martel, *Luis-Arnold et Joseph Allegro*, 128–30.

43 Wood to Wood; and O'Donnell, *Lavigerie in Tunisia*, 61–62.

44 Sir Thomas Reade to Palmerston, December 5, 1834, FO 77/25, NAUK.

45 The Ottoman princess 'Aziza 'Uthmana funded a large number of public and private charities in Tunis during the seventeenth century, including hospitals and shelters for the poor; see Larguèche, "Femme et don pour la ville."

46 Ibn Abi Diyaf, *Ithaf* 3:202–3.

47 On the importance of governesses in the Ottoman Empire, see Petzen, "'Matmazels' nell'harem."

48 Ibn Abi Diyaf, *Ithaf ahl al-zaman bi akhbar muluk tunis wa 'ahd al-aman*, edited by Ahmed 'Abd al-Salam (Tunis: al-Jami'a al-Tunisiya, 1971), 212. For example, the physician's account of palace service in anonymous mss, c. 1830s, F 80 1697, CAOM. Aisen-Elouafi, "Being Ottoman," makes a considerable contribution to our understanding of the palace women.

49 James Richardson's stated purpose in collecting firsthand harem accounts was "to present a proper idea of Tunisian female aristocracy to the reader" ("An Account of the Present State of Tunis," with appended "Addendum on the Tunisian Harem," 1845, p. 53, FO 102/29, NAUK). As far as can be ascertained, his account was never published, although it was reproduced in 1847 in confidential documents for use by the English foreign office as "Confidential Print No. 137" (London: T. R. Harrison, 1847). As far as we know, Berner's account has survived only in an abbreviated form inserted into Richardson's report; see Clancy-Smith, "A Visit to a Tunisian Harem."

50 Berner, quoted in Richardson, "Addendum on the Tunisian Harem," 60.

51 Berner, quoted in ibid., 62.

52 Major Sir Grenville T. Temple, *Excursions in the Mediterranean. Algiers and Tunis*, 1: 196.

53 Smith, quoted in Richardson, 53–54.

54 Smith, quoted in ibid. 59.

55 And, *Turkish Miniature Painting*. That book draws upon the eighteenth-century work by Enderunlu Fazil, *Zenaname* (book of women).

56 Stockdale, *Colonial Encounters among English and Palestinian Women*, 66; Roberts, *Intimate Outsiders*.

57 Smith, quoted in Richardson, "Addendum on the Tunisian Harem," 56–57.

58 Roberts discusses the materiality of Istanbul harems. Comparatively speaking, the interiors of the Husaynid residences seem to have been furnished in European style slightly earlier than was the case in Istanbul (*Intimate Outsiders*, 59–79). Was this the influence of the resident Europeans serving the palace class in Tunis, or of the Sardinian and Sicilian Mamluk connection? Windler discusses the political and cultural significance of gift giving (*La diplomatie comme expérience de l'autre*, 485–535). A detailed list of the astonishing quantity of valuable gifts sent to Tunis from Paris is found in Hugon, "Une ambassade tunisienne à Paris en 1825."

59 Sir Thomas Reade to Earl Bathurst, August 18, 1825, FO 77/16, NAUK.

60 Richardson, "Addendum on the Tunisian Harem," 64.

61 Hugon, "Une ambassade tunisienne à Paris en 1825," 111.

62 Windler, *La diplomatie comme expérience de l'autre*, 268–69.

63 Camille Roches, January 8, 1860, box 207, folder 96, Archives Nationales de Tunisie (hereafter ANT). See also Herbert, *A Search after Sunshine*, 248–63.

64 Hesse-Wartegg, *Tunis*, 82–83.

65 F. Bey, "Le 1er décembre 1846," *Histoire*. Ahmad Bey was received in the French king's family salon, where he was presented to the queen and princesses.

66 Sir Thomas Reade to Palmerston, April 29, 1835, FO 77/26, NAUK.

67 Smith, quoted in Richardson, "Addendum on the Tunisian Harem," 59. See also Bayly, *Empire and Information*, 18–19, 38–39; Clancy-Smith, "A Visit to a Tunisian Harem," 46, 49.

68 Hesse-Wartegg, *Tunis*, 82–83.

69 Herbert, *A Search after Sunshine*, 3. See also 242–64.

70 Ibid., quote, 258–59.

71 Gerbod, "Une forme de sociabilité bourgeoise."

72 Gallant, *Experiencing Dominion*, 67. See also Corbin, *The Lure of the Sea*, 254–57.

73 "Affidavit of Mr. William Carleton, British vice-consul, of the Aldelia in the Regency of Tunis," July 21, 1834, FO 77/25, NAUK.

74 Quoted in Cavasino, *Emilie de Vialar Fondatrice*, 123, letter from Emilie de Vialar to François Bourgade, August 21, 1843.

75 Dunant, *Notice sur la Régence de Tunis*, 99.

76 Charles Cubisol to Adolphe Rousseau, July 29, 1858, and letter in Arabic by Khayr al-Din, box 413, Centre d'Archives Diplomatiques, Nantes, France (hereafter CADN). Khayr al-Din appears to have been relying upon Islamic law regarding the use of public spaces.

77 Wood to Wood.

78 Ibid.

79 Louis Gaspary to Pierre Gaspary April 24, 1824, box 407, CADN.

80 "Beylical decrees relating to Hammam Korbous," 1787–1885, series E, box 377, folder 3, ANT.

81 Muhammad Bayram V began traveling to France and Italy in 1875 for treatment for a serious nervous disorder, including an experimental treatment with electricity by a well-known French physician in Paris; see Abdesselem, *Les historiens Tunisiens des XVIIe, XVIIIe et XIXe siècles*, 392; Bayram, *Safwat al-'itibar* 1:96–103.

82 Khayr al-Din, "Mémoires," 42.

83 The folder containing the "Beylical decrees relating to Hammam Korbous," 1787–1885, series E, box 377, folder 3, ANT, contains numerous, heart-wrenching petitions in Arabic from the villagers and Sidi 'Ammara lineage opposing the takeover by appeals to social justice; for example, March 30, 1906, "the sheik of the Sidi 'Ammara complains that their lands were expropriated."

84 D. Kennedy, *The Magic Mountains*. It can be argued that precolonial Tunisia could more usefully be compared to eighteenth-century India than to the Raj. However, post-1830 Tunisia was very different from eighteenth-century India in terms of the sheer numbers of expatriate Europeans residing there, and the larger Mediterranean political context that Tunisian ruling elites had to negotiate.

85 Conklin and Clancy-Smith, Introduction.

86 Jennings, *Curing the Colonizers*, 166–67.

87 Arnaud, *Les eaux thermales*, 6.

88 M. Stewart, *For Health and Beauty*, 56–74.

89 On the intersections between French colonial identification with, and glorification of, things Roman in North Africa, see Lorcin, "Rome and France in Africa."

90 Perkins, "So Near and Yet So Far."

91 *Le Petit Tunisien Indépendant*, March 12, 1886, p. 1.

92 See, for example, Chater, *Dépendance et mutations précoloniales*.

93 Bayly, *The Birth of the Modern World*; Scott and Hirschkind, *Powers of the Secular Modern*. On the difficulties of defining modernity, see Saler, "Modernity and Enchantment."

94 Thanks to James A. Miller and to Laurence O. Michalak for sharing important material on Bourguiba's personal, visceral hatred for the Husaynid family. As soon as Tunisia was declared a republic, President Bourguiba alerted the press to the fact that he was going to evict Amin Bey—the last ruler—from his Carthage palace early in the morning so as to humiliate the seventy-three-year-old man. Bourguiba's intent was to have photographers ready to shoot pictures of him in an undignified state. In his speeches, Bourguiba frequently claimed that the Husaynids were not really Tunisians.

8 ◆ THE HAREM AS BIOGRAPHY

Domestic Architecture, Gender, and Nostalgia in Modern Syria

Heghnar Zeitlian Watenpaugh

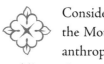 Consider an 1873 photograph of the regents of the Mount Vernon Ladies' Association, a philanthropic organization (fig. 1). Well-dressed, middle-aged women are seated in the portico of the recently restored Mount Vernon, the home of George Washington, the first president of the United States.[1] They surround a marble bust of the patriarch himself. The wealthy, educated, and patriotic mothers of the republic thus depict themselves as the custodians of the estate and the legacy of the father of their country.

This image is emblematic of the early period of historic preservation in the United States and dramatically highlights its gendered dimension: the respectable mothers of today preserve the legacy of the great man of the past by restoring his property. They also ensure that the property is accessible to the general public, for the sake of instructing it in national history as well as civic virtues. The patriotic mothers thus construct the founding father as an exemplar, enshrining his political and cultural authority through historic preservation and the agency of display.[2] This image summarizes the relationship between the construction of

1   The regents of the Mount Vernon Ladies' Association, surrounding a bust of George
Washington. Photograph by Leet Brothers, 1873. Courtesy of Mount Vernon Ladies'
Association, BW-4928-B.

gender and cultural authority in a society and that society's relationship
with its patrimony, as embodied in practices of preservation.

Preservation or conservation, the modern practice of restoring buildings from the past for new uses and meanings in the present, originated
in late-eighteenth-century Europe. Today, conservation is a modern professional practice based on rules and regulations that arose in Western
Europe through the nineteenth century and into the twentieth.[3] The modern modular concept of conservation has been implemented in a standardized form throughout the world.

Heritage means the set of tangible and intangible objects and attributes
that a society inherits from the past and maintains for the future. Like
conservation, heritage is a modern, institutionalized, and professionalized
set of practices that manages a society's relationship to its past. Barbara
Kirshenblatt-Gimblett defines heritage as "a mode of cultural production
that has recourse to the past and produces something new. Heritage as a
mode of cultural production adds value to the outmoded by making it into
an exhibition of itself . . . heritage is created through metacultural operations
that extend museological values and methods (collection, documentation,
preservation, presentation, evaluation, and interpretation) to living persons,
their knowledge, practices, artifacts, social worlds, and life spaces."[4]

Now consider another image, this time one in writing: a woman sits in the reception room of an old Aleppine home, hostess to a group of literati. The image of the home is familiar to the text's readers, invoking nostalgia for a local past. In this chapter, I critique the practices and discourses of preservation in a contemporary society through the prism of gender — more specifically, through representations of women in houses — and the messages these convey about women's places and houses as places for women. If the harem is a thing of the past, represented through the figures of the women who inhabited it, in such representations, I argue, the domestic space itself has come to stand in for the woman. Representational work on behalf of preservation in the present may also do gender work, offering a certain interpretation of women's public and private personae in past and present. The setting of the chapter is 1990s Syria, particularly the northern city of Aleppo, and the ubiquitous courtyard house, the physical setting that housed the family life of the harem before it was progressively supplanted by newer types of domestic architecture, beginning in the late nineteenth century.

Since the early 1990s, Syrian popular culture has witnessed a renewed interest in the visible past. Under the rubric of what is called al-'awda ila al-tarikh (the return to history), cultural forms such as television serials focusing on the recent past, filmed in historical settings, are eagerly consumed. Old and new novels set in historical periods and memoirs are widely read and commented upon in intellectual and popular circles. This phenomenon has also included the commercialization and commodification of historical architecture. One of the most intriguing focuses of this "return" is the old courtyard house — often called a bayt 'arabi (Arab-style house) — a typology of elite urban domestic architecture. Anthropologists and historians of contemporary Syria have noted the peculiar trajectories of this specific element of the past from museum displays to reproduction and recontextualization as settings for restaurants, festivals, or nightclubs. These constructions of the past, imbued with nostalgia, often foreground traditional gender roles.

This chapter initiates a critique of literary constructions of the old courtyard house and of its physical preservation by focusing on the question of how biographies of a prominent woman, and the spatial hierarchies that they stage, operate to further or foreclose particular representations of social and gendered experience. I employ nineteenth- and twentieth-century biographies of Aleppo's first modern poetess, Mariyana Marrash, who lived and wrote in the second half of the nineteenth century. Marrash was one of this city's first female figures to have a public persona. Yet her biographies spatialize her less as a published poet in the public sphere and more as a hostess presiding over gatherings in the old courtyard house. Thus, the description of the architecture of the home is made to stand in for her biography. This occultation[5] of the person of the female subject of the biography and its replacement by the house—its architecture and the social mores that inhabit it—are both outcomes and shapers of the nostalgic "return" to a Syrian past.

But before we meet Marrash, we must enter the imagined domestic space in which these biographies house her.

THE COURTYARD HOUSE AS AN OBJECT OF HERITAGE

Syria's rich ancient urban heritage boasts at least one city that competes for the title of longest continuously inhabited city in history: Aleppo.[6] An ancient citadel, rebuilt many times, dominates the city. There is a classic 1930s photograph of Aleppo's skyline, showing a parade of minarets that surmount monuments dating from the earliest to more recent periods of Islamic history (fig. 2). For the pedestrian strolling down a street at the time the photograph was taken, all the minarets were, in a real sense, contemporary—to one another and to the pedestrian. Built at various times, they formed then, as they do today, the visible, experienced fabric of the city.

Beginning in the second half of the nineteenth century, in Aleppo as elsewhere in the Ottoman Empire, governors and local elites initiated extensive urban modernization projects. They created suburbs laid out according to modern principles of urban planning, which contrasted visibly with the old urban fabric.[7] The elite families moved out of their courtyard houses and into convenient, modern villas or apartment buildings (fig. 3). At the time they were laid out and settled, the new neighborhoods were admired by Aleppines for combining the best of the old and new styles. People appreciated such modern urban features as wide streets, multistory villas, and amenities like the new railway station that well suited their modernizing, bourgeois lifestyle. The Aleppine historian and jurist Kamil al-Ghazzi (1853?–1933) described the suburb of 'Aziziyya (begun in the 1870s) this way: "It is considered one of the greatest neighborhoods of Aleppo and the one with the largest streets and most magnificent houses . . . [the houses] combine the old style and the new style . . . you see houses there [that] are like great palaces on wide streets."[8]

2   View of Aleppo, looking west. The skyline of the city is defined by a row of minarets that surmount monuments. From Sauvaget, *Alep*, vol. 2, plate XL.

Through the twentieth century, as urban populations expanded, families continued to settle in modern apartment buildings in outlying suburbs away from the old urban core. From the 1950s through the 1970s, many Syrian writers and politicians saw the adoption of modern types of housing as an indication of social and economic progress. In such an understanding, the old courtyard house was not an object of nostalgic longing, but rather the setting of a traditional and backward existence. For example, Bashir al-'Azma (1910–92), a physician and politician who served as health minister of Syria, excoriated the courtyard houses as unhygienic.[9] He condemned them in comparison to healthful, modern apartments with indoor plumbing, the type of housing occupied by increasingly larger numbers of urban Syrians. The homes left behind in the old city remained unoccupied, were sold or rented to poorer immigrants from the countryside, or were converted to less prestigious uses, such as schools and orphanages. As domestic architecture, they became devalued and dilapidated.

It is only recently that the historical layers of the old city of Aleppo, not only its celebrated monuments, have been the object of particular attention, praise, and pride, and that efforts at conserving, upgrading, and displaying the city's architectural treasures have been made. In the past century, along with tremendous urban growth and a population explosion, Aleppo has seen several campaigns of urban renewal and preservation of the city's historic core, with varying degrees of success.

3   The European-style villa of a notable family in the modern suburb of 'Aziziyya, Aleppo
    (built around 1930; architect, Paul Micaëlli). Photograph by the author, 1997.

The transformation of the urban fabric has been accompanied by vigorous debates involving international and local experts, planners, architects,
historians, and local leaders.[10] During the French mandate (1920–46), and
after Syria gained its independence from France in 1946, master plans were
drawn up to regulate the expansion of the new republic's major cities. From
the 1950s to the 1970s, a succession of urban planners envisaged piercing the
old city with large thoroughfares suitable for vehicular traffic. The city implemented these recommendations piecemeal over the years, resulting in a
significant loss of the urban fabric in the historic core. Modern high rises
went up on either side of these thoroughfares, creating up-to-date commercial corridors. Some well-known monuments, such as the Great Mosque,
were preserved and acquired a new urban context of wide streets, traffic
lights, and spatial isolation.

In the early 1980s, an alliance between local architects and Western experts and urbanists lobbied to have Aleppo declared a UNESCO World
Heritage Site. Following its listing in 1986, the aggressive campaigns of
urban transformation stopped. While city officials had previously worked

to transform an aging urban environment for contemporary economic uses, they now had to protect and preserve the same environment as patrimony, an object of cultural value. In other words, as Omar Abdulaziz Hallaj has observed, the Syrian state went from being the instigator of the destruction of the old city in the name of modernization, to becoming the preserver of the city in the name of heritage.[11]

But this is not just a question of local recognition. Since it was declared a World Heritage Site, Aleppo has attracted the attention of experts and tourists, from North America and Western Europe and from around the Middle East. Various local institutions and entrepreneurs, as well as international development and conservation organizations, have undertaken projects to rehabilitate the old city and to address its severe infrastructural and preservation problems. The directorate of religious endowments (*awqaf*) focuses on the restoration of religious structures under its jurisdiction. In the mid-1990s, the German Technical Cooperation Corporation (GTZ), initiated a program to improve infrastructure in select parts of the city, as well as offering small loans and architectural expertise to inhabitants to help them repair the historic structures in which they live and work.[12] Since 1999, the Historic Cities Support Programme of the Aga Khan Trust for Culture has been restoring the Citadel of Aleppo, as part of an effort to restore several historic castles throughout Syria. The trust espouses an approach that privileges the historic and aesthetic qualities of selected monuments and seeks to place them within self-sustaining, socially responsible development programs.[13] The city of Aleppo — headed by its young mayor, Ma'an Shibli — was awarded the Veronica Rudge Green Prize in Urban Design for these efforts by Harvard University's Graduate School of Design in 2005.[14]

Alongside institutions, individual property owners and entrepreneurs have also seized upon the renewed interest in the old city's architectural fabric. While organizations tend to focus on infrastructure, neighborhoods, historical monuments, or urban archaeology, the efforts of individual entrepreneurs unsurprisingly focus on individual buildings — specifically in this case, courtyard houses — and their commercial potential.[15] The real estate market for courtyard houses has been reinvigorated. A great many old homes are being renovated in Aleppo and Damascus, some by their owners for their own use, and others, more visibly, as commercial establishments. An architecture that had been relegated to low-prestige uses is now being converted to profitable enterprises that derive their appeal from their newly revalued setting. Aleppo's Judayda neighborhood, particularly the area around al-Hatab Square and Sissi Street, has become quite gentrified since 1995, with restaurants, bed-and-breakfasts, souvenir shops, and bars operating in refurbished courtyard houses. Judayda has become a favorite destination for fashionable Syrians and tourists alike, and in this sense it is a vibrant and successful urban area.

Some Aleppine architects and critics, however, have declined to celebrate this development. They point out that the majority of the old city remains underprivileged, and that the rehabilitation efforts have produced a new type of real estate speculation that benefits some but not most urban dwell-ers.[16] The majority of the 150,000 inhabitants of the old city are members of large, poor families that live in substandard and overcrowded conditions. Not far beyond the itineraries of monuments and businesses patronized by middle-class Syrians and tourists, poverty is often visible, and underground economies flourish.[17] In such areas of the old city, particularly the eastern neighborhoods, the old courtyard house is not an object of aesthetic de-light. Rather, it is often simply the abject reality of a dilapidated dwelling, where repeated attempts at repairs are constantly defeated by an obsolete architecture that seems to stifle rather than shelter.[18]

Analyzing the transformation of the urban character and use of the courtyard house in Aleppo allows me to consider how the idea of heri-tage in Syria has coalesced around domestic architecture. I address not the process of preservation itself—with its relative successes and failures—but rather the local understandings of the object of preservation, the courtyard house.

After independence in 1946, when the exodus of elite and middle-class urban Syrians to modern neighborhoods had become comprehensive and irreversible, the courtyard house began to emerge in state cultural institu-tions as an object of heritage. The Directorate of Antiquities and Museums created two major Museums of Popular Traditions (*matahif al-taqalid al-sha'biyya*), both located in magnificent examples of early modern do-mestic urban architecture: the museum in Damascus (established in 1954) in Qasr al-'Azm, the eighteenth-century home of As'ad Pasha al-'Azm,[19] and the museum in Aleppo (established in 1967) in the eighteenth-century Bayt Ajiqbash (as of 1979).[20] As I have argued elsewhere, at these museums, both the architectural setting and the objects on display were abstracted from their original contexts and presented together as a simulacrum of an authentic old Syrian house, not as objects of historical or artistic interest

4 Diorama of an eighteenth-
century women's reception
room, in the Damascus
Museum of Popular Tradi-
tions (Qasr al-'Azm). Photograph by Reha Günay, 1983.
Courtesy of the Aga Khan
Award for Architecture.

in their own right.[21] The collections at the two folklore museums consist of
objects and furnishings of everyday use from the late Ottoman period, arranged to suggest their original function in the home. Several rooms at Qasr
al-'Azm contain dioramas, such as the men's reception room, the women's
reception room, and the bathhouse, showing mannequins dressed in period
costume and engaged in quotidian activities with appropriate props (fig. 4).
The two stately homes where the museums are housed, particularly Bayt
Ajiqbash, are examples of the modernizing and Westernizing taste of the
Ottoman eighteenth century; they were built by members of the elite who
adopted Istanbul's newest trends. The displays, however, have no preten-
sion to be historically accurate to the eighteenth-century moment. They
do not document a development—stylistic or historical—but rather reconstruct a timeless moment of premodernity. Unlike the national art museums in Damascus and Aleppo, where masterpieces are displayed in the
strictly chronological order of their creation and carefully labeled, at the

folklore museum, the displays are not objects of art, nor are they arranged by date. Consequently the displays at the Museums of Popular Traditions give the impression not of a specific time and place, but rather of a timeless folkloric past.

The timeless presentation elaborated in these state institutions in the 1950s and 1960s echoes the manner in which the old courtyard house is envisioned and depicted today. There is, however, a critical difference: the audience. While today's reimaginings of the courtyard house are immensely popular among Syrians, the Museums of Popular Traditions do not have a loyal or enthusiastic following. Museums in Syria are often deserted, apart from tourists and schoolchildren who arrive on their respective buses. As in many countries of the global South, the museums are state institutions, props of national identity, but they have not necessarily become vital or even relevant settings for the local community.[22] In contrast, Syrians— especially the young—throng to the newly restored commercial venues of the courtyard houses: the restaurants, cafes, and nightclubs. The restored courtyard houses have succeeded where the museums have failed, in attracting a young audience to a patrimonial setting.

As noted previously, Syrian popular culture in the 1990s witnessed a renewed interest in the visible past and the commercialization and commodification of historic form in the shape of historical television serials. Filmed in historical settings and presented under the rubric of the return to history, as noted above, these not only find an eager popular audience but also have attracted scholarly attention.[23] Every other year, Damascus hosts the immensely popular Ma'rad al-Tawthiq (festival of documentation), in which various government agencies exhibit historic documents. Also popular, as noted above, are recent and older historical novels and memoirs recounting life in the old courtyard house. A favorite is the bittersweet memoir by Siham Turjuman, *Ya mal al-Sham*, whose author, not coincidentally, is an activist for the preservation of Damascus's old city.[24] Even novels that are far from tenderly nostalgic about the past focus tightly on the spatial setting of the home and associate it with female characters.[25] This is the case in Samar 'Attar's *al-Bayt fi sahat 'Arnus*, a novel that places the house at the center of the life of three women, even as it denounces the suffocating drudgery of the futile, repetitive housekeeping chores that structure the women's daily lives and mirror their repression by Syrian society.

What makes this phenomenon especially noteworthy is the fact that in Syria—unlike many other locales, where Westerners rather than local citizens, and the old rather than the young, seek out the historical and the patrimonial—the popular appeal of history is felt by people from all walks of life, even those who are urban and young. In her perceptive *A New Old Damascus*, the anthropologist Christa Salamandra tracked the reproduction and recontextualization of certain forms and images of the past, ranging from the old Damascene house to traditional foods and their social meaning and use in contemporary Damascus. Building on the question, "Who benefits from the prestige of 'tradition'?" she noted that certain groups in Damascus touted their real or imagined connection to the city's past for the sake of creating and enforcing social distinctions and group identities: "Old-city themed art exhibits and other events of reimagining provide narratives of social identity that run counter to the nominally inclusive constructions of the state . . . nostalgic constructs, and the reaction to them by excluded groups, serve as modes of social distinction, as various social actors vie over prestige and recognition in a context of shifting values. Old Damascus, as both physical space and imagined ideal, forms a significant fault line between the different groups sharing the city. Selective consumption and rejection of old Damascus is the stuff of boundary construction and reconstruction."[26]

The discourse surrounding the courtyard house in Aleppo is similar to that outlined above for Damascus. However, while the construction of social distinction is politically charged in the capital, its political claims are somewhat muted in the northern provincial city, which has its own distinctive, heterogeneous social landscape—defined by the presence of significant Christian communities and of bilingual groups (Armenians and Kurds).

What is the distinctive physical configuration of the courtyard homes of Syrian cities (fig. 5)? Dating from the sixteenth through the eighteenth centuries, the houses have a well-defined spatial order based on sociological, cultural, and climatic concerns.[27] From the exterior, they are characterized by a discreet presence on the street, with a modest door and few if any windows. Once one crosses the threshold, one enters an interior courtyard, usually rectangular and always open to the sky. The courtyard is surrounded by multiple stories of domestic areas. Two of the courtyard's sides often feature privileged spaces. A richly decorated facade on the courtyard signals the winter reception room, or *qaʻa*. Often cruciform and domed in plan, the qaʻa features an ornate interior, with walls and ceilings lined with painted wooden panels and floors covered in marble mosaic. Summer receptions are held in the courtyard, centered around a pool, an enclosed

5 *Iwan* and courtyard, Bayt
Dallal (today the Cilicia
Elementary School), Aleppo.
Various sections date to the
sixteenth through the eigh-
teenth centuries. G. Eric and
Edith Matson Photograph
Collection, 1936. Courtesy
of the Library of Congress,
Prints and Photographs Di-
vision, LC-DIG-matpc-03558.

planter containing fragrant citrus trees, or a built-in stage for entertainers,
anchored by an elevated *iwan* (a three-sided, vaulted room; locally pro-
nounced "liwan") open to the courtyard. In Aleppo iwans always face north
for climatic reasons.[28] Apart from these focal spaces, the courtyard house
features rooms that communicate with the courtyard rather than laterally
with each other, as well as amenities such as kitchens, latrines, and underground storage areas.

The physical refurbishment of the courtyard houses in contemporary
Syria has been highly uneven, ranging from thoughtful restorations by
trained architects to hasty remodelings burdened with Orientalizing details. Adaptive reuse has sometimes mandated the alteration of specific elements. Sometimes the feel of the new use of a space is quite distinct from
that of its early modern use—as in the case of courtyards now covered and
heated in the winter. This is not unexpected: while a hotel set in a courtyard house claims to offer an authentic historical architectural experience, it
must of course be a modern hotel with modern amenities to attract guests.

6   Reception room of the Martini house, Aleppo (1978; architect, Omar Wasfi Martini). Fragments of decoration from an eighteenth-century courtyard house are recontextualized as part of a modern interior design. Photograph by Martini, 1978–83. Courtesy of the Aga Khan Award for Architecture.

In terms of physical rather than discursive recreations of the old courtyard house experience, one must also note another phenomenon: the recreation of selective fragments of the courtyard house in new contexts. In addition to the renovation of homes in the old city, an "Old Aleppo" feel is often evoked in modern homes and businesses through the selective deployment of premodern decorative schemes. Apartments in the new suburbs with modern floor plans sometimes feature reception rooms adorned with contemporary recreations of painted wooden panels featuring calligraphy and floral and geometric ornamentation, glass lamps, gilt mirrors, low tables topped with brass trays, and other decorative elements associated with traditional homes. An Ottoman-period ornate wooden ceiling surmounts the reception room of the Martini house (fig. 6)[29] in the new neighborhood of al-Shahba'. The ceiling's edges are lined with modern mirrors that alternate with antique wooden floral panels. Additional floral and calligraphic panels decorate the walls and have been mounted on modern doors. The salon's décor combines low, Oriental tables and furnishings in the so-called Louis Farouk style—a local version of highly ornate, early modern European-type furniture, featuring gilt details, heavy frames, and crystal chandeliers. The Ottoman ceiling and panels used at the Martini house, dated 1747, were salvaged from the demolished courtyard house known as Bayt Hamawiyya in the neighborhood of Qarliq at the northeastern edge of the old city.[30]

The design of the Martini house was one of the earliest to intentionally incorporate historical fragments into the salon of a modern elite home, pre-dating Aleppo's listing as a World Heritage Site. Such decorative schemes, sometimes even including a separate Oriental salon, are generally a fix-ture in the homes of families that consider themselves upper class or have upper-class aspirations. The use of elements of old décor in modern interior design in the Middle East, while new in and of itself, indexes a refined taste as opposed to the nouveau-riche gluttony for all things new and imported. Its emphasis on authentic or recreated heirlooms is meant to indicate and reinforce the family's status as an old family—possibly, though not neces-sarily, including its membership in the ranks of the a'yan (notables), the traditional Sunni Muslim elite with inherited wealth, land ownership, and social prestige, and with deep historical roots in Aleppo. Many such fami-lies proudly display their (male) ancestors' biographies in such venerated books as Raghib al-Tabbakh's 1920s compendium of the notable citizens of Aleppo.[31] As Salamandra shows in the case of similar families in Damas-cus,[32] this process of achieving distinction acquires urgency in a social con-text where the political, economic, and social dominance of the traditional elite can no longer be taken for granted and is often obsolete, as a result of Syria's social upheavals since independence.

Businesses also combine new and old fragments: the Sheraton hotel in Damascus features an Oriental cafe that offers water pipes and tradi-tional beverages, essentially recreating a traditional coffeehouse such as al-Nawfara in the old city within the confines of an expensive hotel that caters to middle-class Syrians and foreigners.[33] At work is the process whereby a historic form or practice, divorced from its original social and historical context, becomes a commodity that can be recontextualized and reproduced anywhere. I do not demean this process of commodification and recontextualization in and of itself: it certainly can be a creative act of reformulating the past for new uses and meanings in the present. Yet it is important to observe that while the fabric of the old city of Aleppo, with its long history, is what lends these forms their cultural capital; it is their selective reproduction away from the city that is being consumed.[34]

This divorce of a valued form from its context should not escape us. In modern Syria, the taste for Ottoman-period domestic architecture is in a sense a selective remembrance of the local visual past. The courtyard house

and its parts are commodified and consumed without any interest in the social context that produced them. There is little sense of the historical setting
in which these houses were built: the provinces of the Ottoman Empire,
where fashions emanated from the imperial center, and in which provincial
cities vied with each other. There is also no full discussion of the type of
familial and household relationships that the courtyard house fostered: the
seclusion of high-status women, the exploitation of servants or slaves, and
polygamy. Since it has become an object of nostalgic longing, the courtyard
house in contemporary imagination is not approached critically.

One way to demonstrate this is through a critique of the literary constructions of the old courtyard house and of its physical preservation
through the prism of gender, by focusing on the biographies of a prominent woman and the spatial hierarchies that they stage.

THE COURTYARD HOUSE AS A LITERARY CONSTRUCTION

Mariyana Marrash (1848–1919) lived in Aleppo her entire life (fig. 7).
Knowledge about her life comes from a handful of Arabic-language biographies written throughout the twentieth century.[35] Filib di Tarazi stated in
Tarikh al-sihafa al-'arabiyya (history of Arabic journalism) that she was the
first Arab woman to have ever published an article in a newspaper.[36] Early
biographies (including Tarazi's) attributed the flowering of her literary tal-
ent to the influence of both her parents, who were intellectuals in their own
right, and to her two brothers, Fransis and 'Abdallah Marrash, important
literary figures in Aleppo and in the Arabic-speaking diaspora.[37] In encouraging their daughter to be educated, her parents challenged the widely held
belief that it was unseemly to educate a girl, "so she would not sit in the
men's reception room."[38] This formulation reflects a clear awareness of the
spatial dimension of gender roles: a traditional respectable woman does not
sit in the men's reception room; an educated modern woman might claim
the right to occupy that space, disrupting its norms. We will return to this
idea below.

Mariyana Marrash lived at the time of the *nahda* (awakening), the term
used to describe the flowering of modern intellectual life in the Arabic-
speaking provinces of the Ottoman Empire in the nineteenth century.
Although the cities associated with this movement are Beirut, Cairo, and
Damascus, Aleppo was also a crucial site. Aleppines are always quick to
remind one that the nahda originated in their city, because it had the first

7   Mariyana Marrash. From
Filib di Tarazi, *Tarikh
al-sihafa al-'arabiyya*, vol. 1,
part 2, p. 241.

printing press in the Middle East to publish Arabic books.[39] Thus modern
Arabic literature was promoted in Aleppo, even though the city's literary
communities were essentially polyglot: books and newspapers were published in Ottoman Turkish, Arabic, Armenian, Hebrew, and French.

Some of the modern men and women of letters who made up the active
intellectual community of Aleppo lived in new suburbs such as 'Aziziyya,
discussed above and shown in figure 3, while others lived in the premodern
neighborhoods of Judayda.[40] While Christians from a variety of Uniate and
Eastern sects were prominent in this literary movement, its members came
from all the communities of the city. Many, like the Marrash brothers, had
strong connections to Arabophone communities in the diaspora and were
transnational actors. Some of the prominent figures of Aleppo's nineteenth
century are still well remembered, including the newspaper editor Rizqallah Hassun and the Islamic modernist 'Abd al-Rahman al-Kawakibi.[41]

Biographies of Mariyana Marrash from the early twentieth century inform us that she excelled in her knowledge of Arabic and French, as well as
in mathematics; appreciated music; and played the *qanun* (a Middle Eastern stringed instrument) beautifully. Al-Tabbakh observed that she was
unique in Aleppo, and "people looked at her with a different eye."[42] Her

exceptional status prompted many prominent young men to seek her hand in marriage. She initially wished to remain single, but after her mother's death she was persuaded to marry and chose Habib Ghadban,[43] a scion of a respectable local Christian family; they had three children. The early-twentieth-century biographies emphasize Marrash's unusual agency in her decision to marry and in her choice of spouse.[44] The biographies all place this information ahead of an account of her writing, emphasizing that Marrash realized herself procreatively as well as aesthetically. Another biography emphasizes Marrash's qualities as an exemplary mother: "they [her children] had [in Marrash] a good trainer of children [murabbiyya], a tender mother, a paragon in polite behavior and home management."[45] The biographers moved on to Marrash's writing career, informing their readers that her first article was published in a newspaper in 1870. Many of her poems and articles were collected in a volume entitled *Bint Fikr* (daughter of intellect), published in 1893.[46] The subjects of her poems ranged from the education of women to praise of the mother of Sultan 'Abd al-Hamid, a eulogy of Jamil Pasha (the modernizing governor of Aleppo), and an elegy on the occasion of the death of her brother Fransis. The biographies from the early twentieth century include excerpts from her poems.[47]

We are also given some personal information. Marrash traveled to Europe once. She was famous for her gentle nature, her beautiful singing voice, and—most important—her salon, which she made into an unofficial club (*nadi*) for refined people (*ahl al-fadl*).[48] The refined people included intellectuals of both sexes, who conversed on the topics of science and letters.

Marrash's biographers emphasized her positive role as an exemplar for women's behavior and as an educator of women. Her writing aimed at "inciting women to attain true cultural refinement [*tamaddun*]," wrote 'Isa Iskandar al-Ma'luf in 1919.[49] Raghib al-Tabbakh observed in 1925 that Marrash's writing asked women to give up the traditionally feminine qualities of cowardice and avarice, and to strive instead for resolve and courage.[50]

Marrash's intellectual life was exceptional, but it was in line with the behavior of other exceptional women of the period who were educated, published their views in journals, and hosted literary salons where intellectuals of both sexes mingled: one can think of Princess Nazli Fazil (c. 1840–1913), a niece of the Khedive Isma'il, in Cairo,[51] and Mayy Ziyada (1886–1941), a Palestinian-Lebanese resident in Cairo. These women intellectuals were among the first to have a public persona. They achieved this not necessarily through their physical presence outside the domestic realm, but rather through their writing published in the public sphere, and by turning their domestic settings into semipublic spaces for intellectuals. Entrance to the salons, however, was presumably tightly controlled.

What is unusual about the case of Mariyana Marrash is the development of her image as constructed in her biographies. While her earliest biographies (by Tarazi, al-Himsi, al-Ma'luf, and al-Tabbakh) foreground her identity as a poet and quote excerpts from her poetry, her most recent biography, published in 1995 by the local intellectual Antwan Sha'rawi, deviates from this pattern.[52] The biography appeared in *Majallat al-Dad*, one of the oldest privately owned journals in Syria. This general-interest publication, widely read in Aleppo, is strongly associated with the city's bourgeoisie and features articles on a variety of subjects by local intellectuals such as Sha'rawi, Mahmud Hiraytani, and 'Abdallah Yurki Hallaq. It can thus be considered a good barometer of local debates and reflections.

In the 1995 biography, we get a brief, basic narrative of Marrash's life, preceded by detailed narratives of the lives and work of her two brothers. This section repeats the main points of previous biographies, apparently reflecting al-Tabbakh's most closely. The bulk of the 1995 biography, however, is original, and is a detailed description of Marrash's salon. The description is presumably apocryphal: we do not know exactly where her home was located. More important, perhaps, we can only guess, based on historical information, who attended her salon and what they discussed. In contrast, Qustaki al-Himsi, who was a frequent guest at what he called *mujulis al-adab wa al-ahbab* (assemblies of literatures and loved ones), provided very few concrete details about them in his biography of Marrash, choosing instead to share excerpts from her poetry.[53] Thus it appears that al-Himsi considered Marrash's domestic salon evenings as part of her public persona, or at the very least he gave more space to Marrash's poetry than to her salon.

Sha'rawi does not quote the poetry of Marrash. The poetry quoted in his biography is that found on the calligraphic panels that decorated Ottoman-period domestic interiors: he cites some anonymous poetic couplets as he describes the calligraphic panel's formal qualities as a material object.[54] Sha'rawi's imagination of Marrash's literary evenings extends to a list of the guests, which reads like a lively portrait of the intellectual life of Aleppo in the late nineteenth century and the early twentieth. Among those who attended were "Jibra'il al-Dallal and his wife Markarit [Marguerite] 'Ajuri, who was so beautiful that when she frequented the Opera in Paris the

French newspapers called her the 'Star of the East.' Qustaki al-Himsi with his silver-handled ebony cane, the young poet Fiktur [Victor] Khayyat . . . Shaykh'Abd al-Rahman al-Kawakibi, Shaykh'Abd al-Salam al-Tarmanini, Fransis Marrash, Rizqallah Hassun, Shaykh Kamil al-Ghazzi, the poet Antwan al-Saqqal with his son Mikha'il, the merchant Antun Sha'rawi [an ancestor of the author] with a gold watch-chain on his chest, and his wife Hilin [Helen] Shahiyat."[55] Thus Marrash hosted the brightest minds of the city at her gatherings. At first reading, it would seem that the traditional anxiety presented in the 1919 biography, that an educated woman would dare to sit in the men's reception room, had come to pass: Marrash not only sat in the reception room, but she presided over a gathering that included men and women, and members of various religious communities. However, in Sha'rawi's presentation, admission to the men's reception room does not empower the poetess. Rather, as Sha'rawi crafts his description, he relegates Marrash to the role of silent hostess, multiplying discussions of her appearance, food, and house, and displacing any discussions of her achievements or her contributions to the intellectual conversation.

Indeed, Sha'rawi tells us that when "Sitt Mariyana" hosted her salon, she always wore the latest European fashions, dressed either all in black or all in white, with lace around her collar.[56] Sha'rawi's text features a long and poetic discussion of the physical, sensual characteristics of the courtyard house, including a disquisition on the sensual pleasures afforded by sitting in the shadow of the citrus trees in the summer and by the scent of jasmine in the evening. He lovingly describes the courtyard house's reception room (qa'a).[57] The literary salon featured discussions of topics agreed upon one week in advance, such as Abbasid poetry. Guests recited poems, including Marrash's favorite, ancient passages in which the legendary poet-hero 'Antara addresses his beloved 'Abla.[58] As they smoked the water pipe, Marrash's guests engaged in poetic competitions and games. One competition forced each player to begin a new line of poetry with the last word of the previous player's line.[59] We are also given detailed descriptions of what was eaten, in a veritable catalog of Aleppine culinary delicacies, arranged by season: rose-petal jam in May and, at other times of year, *kibbe labaniyye* (meatballs in yogurt sauce), candied eggplant, and bitter orange syrup. As Sha'rawi reminds us, a popular proverb holds that the Aleppine values food: *al-Halabi bihibb batnuh* (the Aleppine loves his stomach).[60] Local wines and arrack, an anise-flavored alcoholic beverage, were consumed, and discussions went on until dawn, when breakfast was served.

Sha'rawi's imagined depiction of Marrash's literary salon focuses on a few select interior areas of the home: the reception spaces, especially the qa'a, iwan, and the courtyard; their decorative elements and furnishings; and the social activities they housed. This particular imagining of the space of the courtyard house as a literary salon does not cast it as a female-only space—this is not a harem in that sense. Rather, the courtyard house as literary salon is a place where a select group of middle-class intellectuals of both sexes congregate. Sha'rawi describes individuals through small yet significant details that reveal their middle-class status: Mrs. 'Ajuri attends the opera in Paris, al-Himsi carries an elegant cane, Marrash wears lace collars, and his own ancestor sports a gold watch and chain. Thus the description of Mariyana Marrash as a hostess also presents her class and a particular kind of bourgeois sociability. The literary salon portrayed here does not resemble the traditional social gatherings at the courtyard house as reconstructed in the dioramas of Qasr al-'Azm, where social life is segregated by gender. Even so, Sha'rawi's depiction endorses conservative gender roles in that it minimizes the intellectual achievement of its ostensible subject, Marrash, and emphasizes instead her role as hostess (as imagined by him): a more feminine domestic role, inflected by modern middle-class values. This is markedly less progressive than the stress on Marrash's literary legacy in earlier biographies.

What has happened between the beginning and the end of the twentieth century in the construction of the image of the first published poetess in the Arabic language? Rather than excerpting her poetry, Sha'rawi offers us a description of an idealized courtyard house inhabited by a well-to-do, hospitable family. The poetess is now spatialized less as an intellectual and a cultural producer in the public sphere, and more as a hostess presiding over gatherings of mostly male intellectuals in the old courtyard house. Thus the description of the architecture of the home and the social activities within it are made to stand in for her biography. How can we account for this occultation of the self? It is certain that this interest in the courtyard house occurs only in the discussion of a female intellectual. Sha'rawi's 1995 biography of Fransis Marrash emphasizes his poetic career and describes his behavior at the Paris Opera, a public space in a foreign land. Fransis's life is told through his travels and his poetry, while Mariyana's is told through a description of her house and her guests. Unlike the early twentieth century, then, the late twentieth century reverted to some well-established gendered tropes, key among them the indissoluble link between female and domestic space.

The emphasis of the 1995 biography on a nostalgic depiction of the delights of the courtyard house is firmly located in the 1990s Syrian interest in the historical, and in the privileging of the courtyard house as a nostalgic object. Nostalgia (*hanin*) is a mode that is well known in Arabic letters, particularly in the twentieth century: nostalgia for lost Palestine, nostalgia for the 1960s, *ayyam al-'izz* (the glory days), nostalgia for the greatness of the Arabs in the medieval period. All are common, as are personal remembrances of idyllic village childhoods and youths spent under now-deposed monarchs. Nostalgia harkens back to both past times and lost places. It relies on the past and on memories, but this is a past that is idealized and fantasized, a past that might never have existed. As Michael Kammen asserts, "nostalgia . . . is essentially history without guilt. Heritage is something that suffuses us with pride rather than shame."[61] Nostalgia is seductive and contagious, and not only in the Arab world; its commercial exploitation is pervasive, for example, in Western popular culture. Nostalgia has many detractors: it is easily devalued as a naive, effusive, romantic feeling—regressive, refusing to see things as they really were.[62] Nostalgia exercises an enduring seduction, providing a bittersweet pleasure. Yet the nostalgic past is not altogether fictitious. The philosopher Edward Casey has countered the devalorization of nostalgia in contemporary theory by suggesting that it is a mode of memory. He has argued that nostalgia is a unique form of remembering, despite its affinity with the imagination—one that is distinct from the faithful recollection of past events, places, and facts—and that it provides a special insight onto the past: "Nostalgia takes us forcefully out of our accustomed ways of thinking about memory and the past. By leading us into a past that was never given in a present, it liberates us from a preoccupation with the rigors of recollection . . . [nostalgia provides] the possibility of retrieving the past in ways other than via an explicitly recollective modality."[63]

While nostalgia can be deeply personal, it can also be collective. Moreover, it can be institutionalized, as in national museums and memorials, where a given, authoritative version of the past is transformed into heritage.[64] Nostalgic discourse becomes public through rehearsal, repetition, reproduction, and dissemination. This publicness moves nostalgia out of the realm of the individual and into the realm of the community, and endows it with an authority that purely personal modes of nostalgia may not possess. The anthropologist Jane Hill emphasizes the political dimension of nostalgic discourse, nostalgia as an act of power.[65] In this sense, nostalgia performs a certain political work. It casts the present always as inferior to the past. As Salamandra has observed in the case of Damascus, the nostalgic discourse of old Damascus supported its proponents' claims to cultural capital based on their depiction of their place in a past social hierarchy. Nostalgic discourse can also displace other imaginings—counterdiscourses. Perhaps most worrisome, nostalgia can even displace the crafting of history, or historical investigation. In this sense, nostalgia interferes with and prevents a critical recollective approach to the past.

In discussions throughout the Islamic world today, historical narratives are frequently imbued with nostalgia, and objects of heritage such as the old courtyard house are viewed through the lens of nostalgia. Far from being simply a harmless indulgence in longing for the good old days, this mode also performs an essential political work in the present. It preempts and prevents a critical engagement with the past, among other things, and encourages a regressive retreat into comforting memories of an imaginary past. What is needed is not to demean and dismiss the nostalgic mode, but rather to take it seriously, to approach it critically, and to understand its psychological and philosophical underpinnings. One must ask why this nostalgic mode is so urgently endorsed: why has it become so authoritative?

The evolving construction of the biography of Mariyana Marrash reveals the gendered underpinnings of this nostalgic turn. Sha'rawi's text substitutes a tender and nostalgic view of the courtyard house for a critical study of a female intellectual figure. The nostalgic discourse of the old courtyard house that dominates discourses of heritage in Syria today presents a very clearly gendered vision of the past. It casts men and women in distinct hierarchical roles within the home and without, roles which are presumably comforting. Concerning as it does the late nineteenth century, a time of intense social change in gender roles and domestic architecture, the creation of this timeless "before time" when the family lived in a courtyard house rather than a modern apartment, and where every member of the family kept to his or her proper place, appears strikingly regressive. The biographies of Marrash written in the early twentieth century evince the anxiety produced by changing gender roles. They show how her upbringing challenged widely held beliefs about a woman's place; and their insistence that Marrash engaged in intellectual activity without shortchanging her traditional domestic duties as household manager, wife, and mother seems to preempt their readers' possible objections to a woman's intrusion into the public sphere.[66] In 1995, this tension does not appear. Rather, the nostalgic invocation of the old courtyard house works to mask both the intense social change of Marrash's time and the cultural transformations of Sha'rawi's lifetime. Nostalgia creates an illusion of timelessness that contributes to numbing the critical aspect of writing.

The case of Mariyana Marrash starkly shows how nostalgia for the old courtyard house overwhelms the person of the female subject of the biography; in fact, the description of the house displaces the description of the human subject. By being cast as a hostess, Marrash is written out of the narrative, to be replaced by the house and the list of guests who themselves become key actors, and to be overwhelmed by descriptions of poetic competitions and culinary delights. In the context of postindependence Syria — particularly since the establishment of a socialist, aggressively secular Baathist regime that advocates the limited emancipation of women — the status of women produces anxiety.[67] In this context, to put a woman in her place, as the 1995 biography does, is all the more urgent in the case of the first woman to venture into the public sphere and intellectual activity. The courtyard house, restored and made into an object of heritage or a commodity in its physical dimension, imagined and described as a represented space, thus is instrumentalized to reorder society's gender roles, which derive their legitimacy from their purported connection to the past. The last paragraph of the 1995 biography finally abandons Marrash to introduce another host altogether: a *kararji*, or old-fashioned master of ceremonies who presides over the party late into the night. By the time the reader gets to the end of the biography, the person of Mariyana Marrash is already forgotten, replaced by the image of the courtyard house and an idealized bourgeois domestic sociability, where, we are no doubt to conclude, a woman finds her true place.

NOTES

All translations are my own, unless otherwise noted. I thank Nasser Rabbat, Susan Slyomovics, Marilyn Booth, and the anonymous referees of Duke University Press for their valuable comments and suggestions.

1 For the context of this photograph, see Bluestone, "Academics in Tennis Shoes."

2 The expression *agency of display* comes from Kirshenblatt-Gimblett, *Destination Culture*.

3 For an introduction to the history of preservation, see Jokilehto, *A History of Architectural Conservation*; Choay, *The Invention of the Historic Monument*; Lowenthal, *The Past Is a Foreign Country*.

4 Kirshenblatt-Gimblett, "From Ethnology to Heritage."

5 I use the term *occultation* to mean the instance when one object is hidden by another

object that passes between it and the observer, emphasizing a dynamic spatial relationship between the observer and multiple objects in movement.

6 For an overview of the urban history of Aleppo, see Sauvaget, *Alep*. For the recent history of the city, see Gaube and Wirth, *Aleppo*; Bianca, *Urban Form in the Arab World*, chap. 13.

7 David, "Nouvelles architectures domestiques à Alep au XIXe siècle"; David and Baker, "Élaboration de la nouveauté en architecture en Syrie"; David and Hubert, "Maisons et immeubles du début du XXe siècle à Alep"; Kurdi, "Al-Tatawwur al-'umrani li-Halab fi muwajaha al-ta'thirat al-Urubbiyya."

8 Al-Ghazzi, *Kitab nahr al-dhahab fi tarikh Halab*, 2:397.

9 I thank Nasser Rabbat for alerting me to Bashir al-'Azma's comments on the courtyard house in his autobiography (al-'Azma, *Jil al-hazima*). That autobiography is discussed in Schumann, *Radikalnationalismus in Syrien und Libanon* and "The Generation of Broad Expectations."

10 Friès, "Les plans d'Alep et de Damas"; Qudsi, "Aleppo"; David, "Politique et urbanisme à Alep, le projet de Bab al-Faradj"; Bianca et al., *The Conservation of the Old City of Aleppo*.

11 Hallaj, "The Process of Valuation of Urban Heritage," 200–201.

12 Khechen, "Spatial Patterns in Transformation."

13 Bianca, *Syria*; archives of the Historic Cities Support Program, Aga Khan Trust for Culture, Geneva, especially file 90272; conversations with Stephen Battle, project manager for the program in Syria, Geneva, June 22 and 26, 2007. For a critique of the haste with which the trust's work on the citadel has been conducted, see Gonnella, "The Citadel of Aleppo."

14 Busquets, ed. *Aleppo*.

15 Watenpaugh, "Knowledge, Heritage, Representation."

16 On the recent developments in the rehabilitation of the old city of Aleppo, Hallaj observes: "State intervention leads to accelerated land speculation (with a visible side effect of increased investment in restoration of heritage assets); yet it contributes to the breaking down of social networks" ("Process of Valuation of Urban Heritage," 2:204).

17 Hivernel, "Bab al-Nayrab, un faubourg d'Alep, hors de la ville et dans la cité."

18 See Khechen, "Spatial Patterns in Transformation," for interviews with city dwellers and information on site visits.

19 The 'Azm Palace was restored extensively after being damaged during the 1925 French bombardment of Damascus; see Archives of the Aga Khan Award for Architecture, Geneva (henceforth AKAA), 444.SYR.

20 Al-Mudiriyya al-'amma lil-athar wa al-matahif, *Dalil al-matahif wa al-mawaqi' al-athariyya fi Suriyya*.

21 Watenpaugh, "Museums and the Construction of National History in Syria and Lebanon."

22 Qasr al-'Azm often hosts musical evenings sponsored by the ministry of culture. A similar problem of the audiences of museums in India is discussed in Guha-Thakurta, *Monuments, Objects, Histories*, especially chap. 6.

23 Blecher, "When Television Is Mandatory"; Kawakibi, "Le rôle de la télévision dans la relecture de l'histoire"; Early, "Syrian Television Drama"; Salamandra, "Moustache Hairs Lost" and *A New Old Damascus*, especially chap. 4.

24 Turjuman, *Ya Mal al-Sham*. There have been numerous reprints, and the English translation is *Daughter of Damascus*, giving the author's name as Siham Tergeman. On Turjuman's preservationist work, see Salamandra, *A New Old Damascus*.

25 'Attar, *al-Bayt fi sahat 'Arnus*, translated as *The House on Arnus Square*. I thank Nasser Rabbat for bringing this author to my attention.

26 Salamandra, *A New Old Damascus*, 89.

27 David, "La cour-jardin des maisons d'Alep à l'époque ottomane" and "Une grande maison de la fin du XVIe siècle à Alep"; Gonnella, *Ein christlich-orientalisches Wohnhaus des 17. Jahrhunderts aus Aleppo (Syrien)*; Duda, *Innenarchitektur syruscher Stadthäuser des 16.-18. Jh. Die Sammlung Henri Pharaon in Beirut*; Cerasi, "The Formation of Ottoman House Types."

28 Abdulac, "Traditional Housing Design in Arab Countries."

29 The 1978 Martini house is documented in AKAA, 377.SYR. This house is distinct from the courtyard house of the same name near Judayda, restored in the 1990s.

30 Architect's statement, AKAA, 377.SYR. On the Qarliq neighborhood, see al-Ghazzi, *Kitab nahr al-dhahab fi tarikh Halab*, 2:248–49.

31 Al-Tabbakh, *I'lam al-nubala' bi-tarikh Halab al-shahba.'*

32 Salamandra, *A New Old Damascus*, 79–89.

33 Ibid., 75–76.

34 Watenpaugh, "Knowledge, Heritage, Representation."

35 On modern biographies of women in the Arab world, see Booth, *May Her Likes Be Multiplied*.

36 Tarazi, *Tarikh*, vol. 1, part 2, p. 241.

37 'Isa Iskandar al-Ma'luf, "Shahirat al-Nisa': Mariyana Marrash al-Halabiyya," *Fatat al-sharq* 13:9 (June 15, 1919): 345–51, as quoted and analyzed in Booth, *May Her Likes Be Multiplied*, 75, 125.

38 'Isa Iskander al-Ma'luf, "Mariyana Marrash," quoted in ibid., 125.

39 The publisher was the Matba'a Maruniyya, and the first book printed, in 1706, was an Arabic translation of the Bible.

40 It is rarely possible to know with certainty where an individual lived, but Qustaki al-Himsi's palatial modern home in 'Aziziyya is still extant.

41 Al-Himsi, *Udaba' Halab*; Juha, *Al-hayat al-fikriyya fi Halab fi al-qarn al-tasi' 'ashar*.

42 Al-Tabbakh, *I'lam al-nubala'*, 7:567.

43 Al-Himsi, *Udaba' Halab*, 92; al-Tabbakh, *I'lam al-nubala'*, 7:568.

44 In this, Marrash's biographies seem consistent with other early-twentieth-century biographies that often highlighted women's agency in their choice of spouse and in the marital relationship. See Booth, *May Her Likes Be Multiplied*, 206–19.

45 Rizqallah Afandi Khawwam, "Shahirat al-Nisa': al-Sayyida Mariyana Marrash," *Fatat al-sharq* 5:10 (July 15, 1911): 362, translated and discussed in Booth, *May Her Likes Be Multiplied*, 221.

46 I have been unable to locate a copy of this publication.

47 Al-Himsi, *Udaba' Halab*, 91–94; al-Tabbakh, *I'lam al-nubala'*, 7:567–71; Tarazi, *Tarikh*, vol. 1, part 2, p. 241–45.

48 Al-Tabbakh, *I'lam al-nubala'*, 7:571.

49 Quoted in Booth, *May Her Likes Be Multiplied*, 75.

50 Al-Tabbakh, *I'lam al-nubala'*, 7:568.

51 Badran, *Feminists, Islam, and Nation*, 7, 257, 258; R. Allen, "Writings of Members of the Nazli Circle."

52 Sha'rawi, "Al al-Marrash."

53 Al-Himsi, *Udaba' Halab*, 92.

54 Sha'rawi, "Al al-Marrash," 43–45.

55 Ibid., 46–47.

56 Ibid., 47.

57 Ibid., 43–45.

58 Ibid., 49.

59 Ibid., 51.

60 Ibid., 60.

61 Kammen, *Mystic Chords of Memory*, 688.

62 Simmel, "The Ruin"; Boym, *The Future of Nostalgia*; K. Stewart, "Nostalgia: A Polemic."

63 Casey, "The World of Nostalgia," 366.

64 See Lowenthal, *The Past Is a Foreign Country* and *Possessed by the Past*.

65 Hill, "'Today There Is No Respect.'"

66 On the place of motherhood in the biographies of exemplary Arab women, see Booth, *May Her Likes Be Multiplied*, 219–25.

67 Altoma, "The Emancipation of Women in Contemporary Syrian Literature"; Salamandra, *A New Old Damascus*, chap. 2.

PART III · HAREMS ENVISIONED

Spaces are characterized—defined—by socially inscribed bodies. The space is a place because the presence of specifically described bodies makes it so. In the descriptions of harems by European artists—whether in paintings, photographs, or written texts—clothing (or the lack of it) is a marked part of the picture, as Joan DelPlato shows us in chapter 10. Furthermore, the representation implies—constructs—sexual desires imposed on the bodies of the represented, but coded within the worlds of the implied observer or reader: a fantasy of what might be possible in that other world. In chapter 9, Nancy Micklewright notes the "shift between the imagined and the real" in photographs taken of and then by Ottomans. European photographers working in Istanbul had to be responsive to tourists' increasing firsthand acquaintance with the sights on which photographers focused, and also to local elites' knowledge of—and probably their critical attitudes toward—conventions

of harem art. Poses and props that would have been familiar to viewers of
the paintings DelPlato analyzes are present in this later art of photography,
yet they are also used playfully and critically. Increasingly, photography became a local pursuit. Micklewright shares with us photographs of Ottoman
domestic interiors suggestive of local elite consumption patterns that might
have disappointed European seekers of a "genuine" harem experience.

Thus, if nineteenth-century art and travel literature of European provenance was saturated with harem images, intellectuals and artists from and
in the Middle East were no less intent on imaginatively sketching the interiors of social life. Whether they drew on historical scenes or on their own
contemporary worlds, Turkish and Arab visual and literary artists often
turned a critical and activist eye on the scenarios they imagined.

When domestic spaces were described by the men and women who inhabited them—and who perhaps wanted to change patterns of daily life,
moving away from the practices of seclusion or semiseclusion practiced by
elites in Arab and Turkish cities—the harem as a middle-class home could
be imagined as a space for learning new modes of conduct and relationship,
as A. Holly Shissler shows us in chapter 12. Reformist writers such as the
Ottoman Ahmet Midhat Efendi, whose novels Shissler opens for us, and
the Arab Jurji Zaydan, whose historical fiction Orit Bashkin explores in
chapter 11, critiqued old ways and pointed the way toward the new, calibrat-
ing a local modernity that might borrow from but would not fully mimic
the ways of the West. Their fiction created modern heroes and heroines—
sometimes in historical garb—who had the potential as role models to rival
the Prophet's female contemporaries. Into the twentieth century, domestic
fiction took a lead in imagining home spaces: in chapter 13, Marilyn Booth
considers the critical potential of cheaply printed, "ventriloquized" memoirs that portrayed young women escaping elite households, where seclusion meant subjection to the father's dictates on schooling, comportment,
and marriage. The harem is turned inside out, as no longer a space of protection, but rather one of peril.

9 ✦ HAREM/HOUSE/SET

Domestic Interiors in Photography from the Late Ottoman World

Nancy Micklewright

 The harem of the nineteenth-century Middle East was an Orientalist construction, but it was also an actual place where real people lived out their lives. The harem, as well as all of its attendant associations, occupies an unstable place in our discourse, shifting between versions of the real and the imagined. The harem shares this instability, this shifting between the real and the imagined, with the photograph. Itself a creation of the nineteenth century, the photograph was valued above all for its truthfulness—even as consumers and practitioners of the new art knew firsthand the constructed nature of the photographic image. Perhaps not surprisingly given the characteristics they share, in the nineteenth century the harem and the photograph came together as a site where complex and often competing visions of the harem could be negotiated. In the pages that follow, I will examine a number of different harems, constructed by photographers and their subjects for a variety of purposes.

The harem whose illustrations are examined here embodies the duality of definition that characterizes the manner in which the word *harem* is used throughout this book.

On the one hand, it is a powerful and evocative construction, primarily by European artists and authors, of an imagined lifestyle, only loosely connected to an actual domestic space or social institution. On the other hand, it is the physical room or rooms of an Ottoman house where the women and young children of the family spent their time, where female visitors were welcomed, and where, under specific circumstances, male family members could also be present. While the harem as imaginary construction existed only in the literature, paintings, and photographs of its creators, we also encounter the physical, lived harem in literature as visitors to Ottoman homes described their visits to women's spaces in the books they wrote. And as we will see, actual domestic interiors, including the spaces defined as harems, also appear in the Ottoman photographic record. Thus the imagined and the actual harems share at least one characteristic: their (re)presentation in words and pictures.

Working with historical photographs as we are doing here can be a murky enterprise, so I will preface this analysis with a brief notation on how I understand photographs. I value historical photographs as objects which tell us about a range of artistic practice, about patronage on a scale which does not often get noticed in the study of other media, and about consumption, again among a wide section of the population. Looking carefully at the kinds of photographs that Ottoman subjects produced or purchased informs us about details of their lives, and also about larger issues involving changing social identities and shifts in cultural practices. In the context of this chapter, the word *Ottoman* refers to residents of the Ottoman Empire. If I am singling out a specific group within Ottoman society, I will make that clear. Finally, my focus here is on photographic production and consumption in Istanbul. We know something about what was going on in the other cities of the Ottoman Empire in terms of photography, and much less about what went on in smaller towns and remote areas. Some similarities but many more differences govern photography's reach into different parts of the Ottoman Empire and the Middle East more generally; analysis in this chapter depends specifically on Istanbul as a center of production and reception.

We will be working our way through a series of photographs taken between 1858 and 1913, primarily in Istanbul. As I noted above, the harem that appears in these photographs moves between the harem as constructed by European artists and writers in painting, photography, and travel literature, and the harem as an actual living space. While I am looking primarily

1 Roger Fenton, "Pasha and
   Bayadère," 1858. Department
   of Photographs, J. Paul Getty
   Museum, Los Angeles.

at the physical setting, in many cases people occupy that setting, so we will
also consider who or what these photographic subjects represent and what
they are communicating. It is the shift between the imagined and the real
(to the extent that it is possible to talk about "the real" in the context of a
photograph) in both setting and subject that is at the center of my project.
While the arrangement of images and ideas in this chapter is not strictly
chronological, there is an element of linear chronology in the way in which
photographic images of the harem developed, the contexts in which they
were produced, and who purchased them.

By the time that British photographer Roger Fenton produced the 1858
albumen print entitled "Pasha and Bayadère" (fig. 1), the genre of "harem
woman" was well established as a trope for Orientalist painters[1] and informed the work of the European photographers who traveled to the
Middle East in the first decades after photography's invention in 1839. Fenton visited the region as a war photographer and first came to widespread
public attention as a result of his pictures of the Crimean War in 1855, a
significant accomplishment both from a technical point of view and in the
history of photographic war reportage. With the exception of his time in

the Crimea, Fenton worked and lived primarily in England, where he produced the series of fifty-one Orientalist views to which this image belongs.[2]

Fenton created the harem setting in this image specifically for the series of photographs he made, and he used it with little variation for the other photographs in the series. Its defining elements are a lavish use of textiles of different colors, textures, and patterns to create the space, which is furnished with a low couch and cushions. Smaller decorative elements—the inlaid table, a tray bearing a coffee pot and cups, the two pipes, and the musical instruments (spike fiddle, tambourine, and drum) fill out the scene. The three harem inhabitants, whose poses were carefully orchestrated by Fenton, wear a hodgepodge of garments that cannot be identified as the dress of any one place but that are obviously intended to evoke the region generally. The skylights of Fenton's London studio are just visible in the image, as are the wires holding the dancer's arms in place for the exposure time of the photograph.

This photograph was exhibited in 1859 in London at the sixth annual exhibition of the Photographic Society, along with a few others from the series. They met with mixed reviews, some critics describing them as admirable illustrations of Eastern scenes of actual life, and others finding them unconvincing in their obvious artifice. As far as I know, they were not exhibited again and were not available for purchase. Most of the surviving examples of Fenton's Orientalist series survived in three albums that were sold in London auctions between 1978 and 1982.[3]

As Fenton was working in London, other photographers were setting up shop in the cities of the Middle East, providing photographs to both tourists and local residents. They too produced harem photographs, but they were working in a different context and for a somewhat different audience, composed of those who had actually traveled to the region or who were living there for some period of time.[4] It is well known that tourists' expectations of what they would see in the Middle East would have been shaped by the extensive illustrated travel literature available to them. Less often discussed is the extent to which those expectations may have been challenged, or at least modified, by the barrage of sights and experiences tourists encountered as they moved from the pages of their books to the streets of an actual city. Once visitors were surrounded by actual buildings, markets, local inhabitants, and a plethora of souvenirs, they would have demanded a greater congruity between what they saw around them and what appeared in the tourist photographs created in distant London studios. Photogra-

2   Sebah & Joaillier. N.245.
Research Library. The Getty
Research Institute, Los
Angeles (96.R.14).

phers working for a local tourist audience would have catered to a patron
base requiring images that matched, at least to some extent, the diversity,
intensity, and detail of their experiences as visitors.

To get a sense of how the harem images of photographers working in
the region were related to Fenton's or others made in Europe, we can look
at a small sample of the numerous harem photographs that were produced
in the heyday of commercial tourist photography in the region, from about
1865 to 1890 (fig. 2). This is the time when tourists' guidebooks directed
them to photographers' shops, where they selected their photographs from
catalogues which contained hundreds of choices: they could order images
of monuments, street scenes, landscapes, and human types. Patrons could
also purchase ready-made albums. If they preferred to select images from
the catalogs, their photographs could have been assembled for them into
albums in the shop, or they could have made their own albums later.

The photograph shown in figure 2, by the Istanbul firm of Sebah and
Joaillier,[5] is remarkably similar to the Fenton image in terms of the elements used to evoke the harem. We see the same use of textiles to define a
space and a range of small decorative objects: inlaid table, water pipe, and

metal vessels of various kinds. Studio photographers were adept at creating a variety of settings within the confines of the same interior space, a fact clearly demonstrated by harem photographs. While some settings are more elaborate than others, the physical boundaries of the harem are defined either by textiles draped on wall and floor, or by a standard interior back-drop of the kind seen in numerous studio images of this period, combined with carpets or other floor coverings. The physical space of the studio often included a window (natural light being important from a technical point of view), but the view from the window was never included in the harem scene, thus reinforcing both the sense of interiority of the image itself and the confining nature of the stereotypical harem.

In figure 2, the central figure is of course the harem inhabitant, dressed in appropriately exotic clothes and sitting calmly, looking out of the pic-ture. When the dozens of variations of this subject that were produced by Sebah and Joaillier are compared, we get a sense of the typical vocabulary they employed. The harem is evoked through the costume and pose of the model, the ubiquitous small inlaid table and water pipe, and a range of other props. A couch, rug, and painted backdrop that often appear in the photographs are studio props that allow unsigned photographs to be iden-tified as the work of Sebah and Joaillier. The costume worn by the women in their harem photographs could be either a beautiful embroidered silk *entari* with matching şalvar, the kind of dress that would have been widely worn by wealthy women a few decades earlier, or the generic harem outfit of the model in figure 2.

In figure 3, we see a more elaborate harem construction by Sebah and Joaillier, employing three models. Although their signature does not ap-pear on the image, the backdrop and other props clearly identify this as their work. Music, one of the standard activities of harem women — as they were described by Orientalist artists and some travelers — is evoked by the two women holding instruments. In many of Sebah and Joaillier's harem images, the model at the center of the scene is presented for the exami-nation of the viewer, sitting or reclining on furniture or on the floor. This photograph, with a woman extended across the front of the picture frame, arm above her head and apparently relaxed by the tobacco and music, en-gages the sexual imagination of the viewer in a much more explicit and direct way than the others we have seen so far.[6]

Of course, Sebah and Joaillier were not the only commercial photog-raphers in the Middle East to produce harem scenes. Looking at an ex-

3   Sebah & Joaillier. N.655. Research Library. The Getty Research Institute, Los Angeles
    (96.R.14).

ample of a harem image by a different photographer is instructive, in terms
of identifying both individual variation and the common elements drawn
on by commercial photographers to signal a harem setting in this period
(fig. 4). Guillaume Berggren was a Swedish photographer with a studio in
Istanbul from about 1870 to 1910; he had a thriving business for most of that
time.[7] His photograph also incorporates what we may call iconic elements
used to signal a harem: small tables, water pipe, metal vessels, at least one
carpet, often a couch, and in this case a small fan, as well as, of course, the
model, dressed here in entari and şalvar.

Comparing Berggren's image with those of Sebah and Joaillier, it is easy
to see that the vocabulary is very similar, but a careful examination of the
photographs reveals that the exact objects used — for example, the small
table or water pipe — differ in their details. Similarly, larger elements of furniture, rugs, or backdrops used to create the harem setting reveal small but
visible differences. While the limited range of variation in these elements
indicates the relatively static nature of the harem setting as it was created
by commercial photographers, differences among individual elements allow

4   G. Berggren. N.265. Research Library. The Getty Research Institute, Los Angeles (96.R.14).

the identification of unsigned photographs based on the appearance of the same water pipe, the same carpet, the same octagonal table as can be found in signed images, as in the case of the Sebah and Joaillier photograph in figure 3.

Sebah and Joaillier, Berggren, and numerous others ran successful commercial studios over a long period in Istanbul.[8] Their clients included tourists, foreign residents, Ottomans, and the government, for whom they produced portraits, documentary photographs, and the full repertoire of tourist images. Harem scenes were a staple of the tourist catalogs, although as I have written elsewhere, I believe that these images were much less prevalent in the nineteenth century than we imagine.[9] In addition, we tend to assume a canonical version for them, which is what we have so far examined.

When we have the opportunity to look beyond the harem scenes most often published in photo histories—the canonical versions—we find some surprising images (fig. 5). This photograph by Sebah and Joaillier includes all the set elements of the harem—textiles, water pipe, table, and so on— but here they are turned on their head, just as the model is. Instead of a

5   Sebah & Joaillier. N.918. Research Library. The Getty Research Institute, Los Angeles (96.R.14).

sensuous presentation of a beautifully dressed, languorous woman, we are presented with a woman looking at us upside-down, a mischievous smile on her face. In this silly or even slightly ridiculous picture, the photographer and the model disrupt the standard version of the harem scene photograph. By playing with the stereotype itself, they reveal both their understanding of it and their willingness to engage it critically yet humorously.

Perhaps a more common variation of the canonical harem photograph is that represented by figure 6, in which the harem setting and indeed the costumes of the photographer's studio have remained intact, but the bodies inhabiting the clothing are those of European visitors rather than photographer's models. Dressing up was a pleasurable tourist pastime—we have countless examples of photographers, artists, and authors who disguised themselves so that they could go unnoticed among local residents—but it was also something that people did just to see what it felt like. Often, as in this example, their dressing up took place at the photographer's studio. Sometimes we can figure out what is going on by just looking; in other cases, we have documentation to help us.

Concerning this image, by Berggren, we know that these four Swedes—

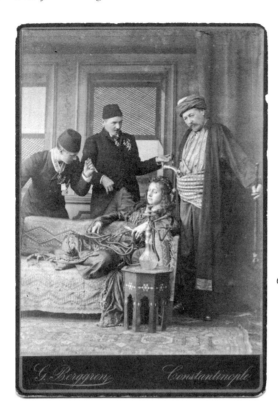

6 Guillaume Berggren.
Photograph of Axel Adel-
sköld, Anders Zorn, Claes
Adelsköld, and Emma Zorn,
Christmas Eve, 1885. Zorn
Museum, Mora, Sweden.
Courtesy Zornsamlingarna,
Mora, Sweden.

a well-known painter and his wife, and a Swedish politician and his son—
were newly arrived in Istanbul in December 1885. For amusement they
visited Berggren's studio, where they dressed up and acted out a tableau
involving a slave trader, a lovely slave, and two men who want to buy her.
The story of the photograph appears in the memoirs of the politician.[10]

The dress-up tableau created by Berggren and his Swedish visitors in
figure 6 is a slightly more elaborate version of the popular tourist souvenir
photograph in which the foreign visitor tries on the clothing, and temporarily the identity, of a local type. For foreign women, trying on harem costumes and posing in the "harem" setting of the photographer's studio must
have been almost irresistible, given the enormous fascination that the idea
of the harem exerted. Trying on costumes in the photographer's studio (or
at the Turkish homes that foreign women occasionally visited)[11] was a respectable means of trying on another identity, one that carried with it the
allure of sexual indulgence and sensuous luxury. Yet cultural cross-dressing
was also pleasurable because, in its very ephemerality, it underlined the true

7 Ali Sami. Family photograph, 1908. Private collection.

nonnative identity of the subject and thus reinforced the social boundaries the cross-dressing purported to blur.[12] However, while the cross-dressing itself was ephemeral, the photograph was not. As a permanent reminder of experimenting with a different and seductive identity, the dress-up photograph served as a kind of trophy that testified to a temptation that had been confronted and overcome.

Let us shift our attention, though, from the harem created by Istanbul photographers in their studios to the harems in which Ottomans in Istanbul actually lived—in other words, to the domestic interiors of Ottoman families in this period. How do those domestic interiors or harems compare with the photographic constructions created for the tourist? Although a fuller discussion of this topic is beyond what I can consider here, we know that in the second half of the nineteenth century, Ottoman domestic interiors began to change, along with many other aspects of Ottoman culture.[13]

Yet we can view a few of the extremely rare photographs which allow us a glimpse into houses in this period, beginning with a photograph by Ali Sami, an Ottoman military official, of his family, taken in 1908 (fig. 7). Ali Sami (1866–1936) was trained as an artillery officer but spent most of his career teaching art and photography at the Imperial School of Engineers, as well as working as a military photographer for Abdul Hamid. He also

8   Ali Sami. Hamide hanım
1905. Ali Sami. Private
collection.

took a great many photographs of his friends and family, some of which are
now in a private collection in Istanbul.[14] In this photograph, the family and
their four different newspapers are the focus of the image, not the room
itself, but we can see a few details: the marble-topped dresser and matching
mirror, the chair in which one woman is sitting, and the photographs on the
dresser. We should also note the ease with which this family presents itself
for the camera and collaborates with the photographer to create a particular image.

     As we have seen in the harem photographs of Sebah and Joaillier, and
in countless other examples of nineteenth-century photography from all
over the world, it was standard practice on the part of photographers to
use props to evoke a particular setting. What interests me in figure 8, a
1905 portrait of a young woman, Hamide hanım (in the Ottoman context, hanım is an honorific title, similar to madam or mademoiselle), are
the props that Ali Sami has selected to create, in a typical photographic
shorthand, an interior context for his subject, in this case a young woman
who was the daughter of a close family friend, the painter Hoca Ali Riza.

9   Photographer unknown. Family grouping outside of house. Research Library.
     The Getty Research Institute, Los Angeles (96.R.14).

Hamide hanım inhabits a photographic space that includes a floor lamp, a
side table, and a bentwood chair, all elements of a European-style parlor.
There is nothing of the harem of Sebah and Joaillier here, nor was there in
the interior depicted in the previous image.

Photographs made by the Ottomans of their own homes have only rarely
entered the published photographic record, which is one reason why Ali
Sami's work is of such great interest. An intriguing group of photographs,
a series of fifty-nine snapshot images[15] now in the Getty Research Institute Special Collections, provides a second example of Ottoman domestic
interiors (fig. 9). The acquisition notes for the collection say merely "Ottoman family, 1890, diverse images."[16] That date is corroborated by the clothing worn by some of the women in the images, which can be dated to the
1890s.[17]

The photographs were probably made using a simple box camera, the
kind that began to be generally available beginning in the 1880s. In this
context, it is important to remember the degree to which the appearance of
these new, simple cameras changed the ways in which photography could
be used.[18] Many more people now had access to making pictures and thus
to taking control of how they presented themselves and their lives photo-

graphically. As I looked through this group of snapshots, I wondered who among the family members pictured was the photographer—possibly it was the gentleman in the center of this group in a military uniform, since it was in the Imperial School of Engineers that photographic training was first widely available to Ottoman Muslims.

The snapshots are the work of an enthusiastic amateur photographer, and they were all taken within a short time of each other—the people in the photographs remain the same age and, in some cases, wear the same clothes. The range of subject matter is similar to the kinds of photos we take of our families today: parties, portraits, special events, what the house looks like, and so on. The same ten or so people are in all of the images, plus a few others who are obviously visitors. Looking through them over and over again, it is tempting to give all of the family members names and stories, but that is beyond the parameters of this chapter. The photographs we will examine here are a representative sample of the larger group of interior images. About half of the entire group was taken outdoors, mostly in the garden of the house. They are fascinating for a variety of reasons, but since our concern here is domestic interiors, these outdoor images are also beyond the scope of my present project.

In figure 9, the focus is on the family grouping with the house as a backdrop, so we see only a part of the facade. The group of nine people is tightly organized around the man who is seated in the middle, wearing a military uniform with a sword across one knee, flanked on his left by two small boys. The other six figures in this group are women of varying ages, including someone who is partly out of the picture frame, in the doorway. The two little boys, leaning against the man in the center, all three with their arms folded across their chests, seem closely connected to one another, as do the older and younger women sitting to our left. The two women and the central man form another closely connected cluster within the larger group, all of whom seem to be sitting on the front steps of their house. This photograph, and the relationships it reveals among its subjects, serves as a kind of introduction to many of the people who appear, in different groupings, in the other photographs in the series.

The photographs also take us inside the house, showing several room interiors. Empty of people, these seem to have been intended to document the state of the room, the furniture, and various decorations at the time of the photograph. These photographs, of which figure 10 is one example, provide rare and extremely valuable evidence of the consumption habits of

10 Photographer unknown. Room interior. Research Library. The Getty Research
    Institute, Los Angeles (96.R.14).

this class of Ottomans, and the ways in which they constructed their domestic interiors in this period. The room is crowded with objects. We are
looking at one wall, defined by floor-to-ceiling cupboards flanking a niche
at one end of the room. The cupboard doors are decorated with carved
wood objects and other items. With its carefully symmetrical arrangement
of portraits painted on fans, vases, figural sculptures, and decorative trays
grouped around the four center objects, the niche seems to be the focus of
the image.

As we examine the photograph carefully, we note two other pieces of
furniture whose sole function seems to be as display surfaces for decorative
objects, as well as a few more obviously utilitarian things like the fireplace
tools hanging on the wall to the right. In front of the niche is an asymmet-
rical, wooden upholstered couch or chaise, with a piece of decorative fabric draped over one arm. The center of the room seems to be taken up by
a large table and chairs, but it is partly cut out of the picture and hard to
read. This room, obviously a living space for the family pictured in front of
their house, is completely full, and nothing which appears in this room signals the harem of the tourist photograph. In other words, there is virtually
no overlap between the set of objects used by commercial photographers to

11   Photographer unknown. Family drinking tea. Research Library. The Getty Research
      Institute, Los Angeles (96.R.14).

signal "harem" and the objects which some Ottomans in the same period
chose for their own living spaces.[19]

A number of the images in this group of snapshots record specific social
moments in the life of this family. For example, in a carefully posed view of
a tea party (fig. 11), we recognize three people from the family scene from
the house exterior: the two women sitting on the couch and the young boy
standing between them. They are joined by another woman, seated to the
left, a young girl standing behind her, and a man looking at the camera,
seated on a low chair or on the floor. Everyone is nicely dressed in fashionable European clothes, which, at this time, would have been commonly
worn by many Istanbul residents in the elite and emerging middle classes.
Pouring tea is generally the prerogative of the hostess, which is helpful in
trying to figure out the family relationships here. The group is in a shallow
space, gathered on and around a couch against a wall between two windows.[20] Behind the couch, the wall is draped with fabric, on which is hung

12 Photographer unknown. Family dressed up. Research Library. The Getty Research Institute, Los Angeles (96.R.14).

a large framed image, difficult to make out. Below that, also framed, leaning against the couch is what seems to be a page of calligraphy.[21]

In figure 12, we see the family formally posed, with three people looking directly out at the camera and four looking off into space, in a parody of the stereotypical harem scene. We recognize the setting as that in the tea-drinking scene, and four of the same people, with everyone again arranged around the couch. However, this is neither a straightforward family scene, as was the previous photograph, nor is it a simple posed tableau in the ama-teur theatrical tradition of the period. Here, everyone is wearing bizarre clothes; the men have on turbans, robes, and some kind of draped cloth garment under the robes, with belts (not the sashes which would have been typical for traditional dress) holding their outfits together. The women are all swathed in what look like lightweight bedcovers or tablecloths.[22] The three older women have scarf-type arrangements on their hair, but not the actual *yaşmaks* they would have normally worn outside the house. The two younger women are in the guise of servants, one on either side of the group, offering plates—one with two coffee cups, the other with little pastries.

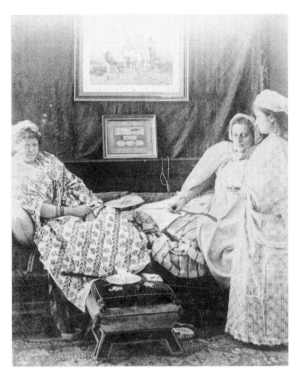

13 Photographer unknown. Harem women. Research Library. The Getty Research Institute, Los Angeles (96.R.14).

There is a glass water pipe on the carpet in front of them, and one of the men is holding onto a long pipe stem.

The next image presents another in what I think of as the harem series,[23] with two women from the previous photograph reclining on the couch, attended by one of the young servants (fig. 13). We see the same setting and similar props: beads, a fan, and the plates of refreshments. These photographs remind us again of the way in which different visions, different constructions of the same subjects, coexisted and collided in the studios of commercial photographers in Istanbul and elsewhere. When Ottoman residents of Istanbul visited the shops of commercial photographers in order to have their portraits made, they would have been able to examine at their leisure the repertoire of imagery available for sale to tourists, including harem scenes. Here is one response to those commercial tourist photographs, produced by people who were clearly completely familiar with the standard harem scene and its individual components.

In an essay from 2000, Zeynep Çelik includes a brief passage describing a fictional exchange between the Turkish author Fatma Aliye Hanım (1862–

1936) and three Parisian women visitors to her home, in which Fatma Aliye Hanım "brings an album that includes a photograph of a woman dressed according to the image in the minds of the guests . . . She then deconstructs the exotic 'Turkish' scene in the photograph: the head scarf is the Arabian kaffiyeh, the vest and the pants are Albanian."[24] Although Fatma Aliye Hanım's account in this case is a fictional one, it points up the Ottoman woman's familiarity with both the stereotype and its constructed nature, a familiarity which was no doubt shared by many visually literate Ottomans.

The Ottoman snapshots, playing with the harem stereotype, reveal not only an understanding of the stereotype but also a complex sense of parody. By inhabiting the stereotype themselves and intentionally constructing a defective version, the photographer and his subjects are claiming their own agency in addressing (and mocking) Western constructions of their society. As Mary Roberts has written about a similar sort of photograph, "What better demonstration of mastery of another culture than to parody that culture's stereotypes of one's own? To joke in a foreign tongue displays a sophisticated grasp of that language."[25] The fact that several examples of such photographic parodies have surfaced in the relatively small corpus of published Ottoman photographs is indicative of the sophistication with which Ottomans approached both photography and cultural critique in the late years of the empire.[26]

The particular collection of photographs illustrated in this chapter—assembled, it is essential to point out, from many hundreds of possible choices—presents us with evidence of cultural interaction in overlapping and contradictory contexts. First and most obviously, they tell us about the creation of imaginary harems by photographers, either for their own purposes, in the case of Fenton, or for a specific market, in the case of Sebah and Joaillier and many others. These imaginary harems were a significant part of a complex, unstable, multivalent Orientalism that shaped much of the cultural interaction in this period and region. We also see in the photographs that even harem scenes, for which such a clear canon of imagery had been developed, were sometimes unpredictable, even unruly. When we shift our attention to the photographs taken by Ottoman Turks of their own families, we see a sophisticated understanding of the potential of the camera to create certain constructions of home and family life: thus the Ali Sami family with its four newspapers, and the second family with its tea parties. If we look through those constructions, we find, in the furniture and other objects which frame the family members, evidence for the new uses of domestic space and new consumption patterns emerging in this period. Finally, in their evidence for a counternarrative around the Orientalist stereotype of the harem, a counternarrative not confined to the intellectual or artistic elite, the photographs are enormously useful for complicating and deepening our understanding of harem imagery and its various impacts in the Ottoman world.

NOTES

I would like to thank Nasser Rabbat for his invitation to participate in the 2004 MIT symposium, "The Harem in History and Imagination," where I presented an earlier version of this work, and to thank conference participants for their helpful comments. All translations are mine, unless otherwise indicated.

1 There is an extensive literature on Orientalist painting, including harem images. For a range of approaches to this complex topic, see Beaulieu and Roberts, *Orientalism's Interlocutors*; Lewis, *Gendering Orientalism*; MacKenzie, *Orientalism*; Nochlin, "The Imaginary Orient"; and Rosenthal, *Orientalism*.

2 These images were the subject of an excellent short book by Baldwin, *Roger Fenton*.

3 Ibid., 6, 102.

4 Ottomans would have patronized these same photographers, but it is my assumption that harem photographs and other types were not necessarily purchased by Ottomans themselves, although they would certainly have seen them when they visited the studios.

5 See Özendes, *Sébah & Joaillier'den Foto Sabah'a*. According to Özendes, Pascal Sébah, born c. 1823, was of Syrian Christian and Armenian descent and married an Armenian woman when he was forty-three. Although specific details vary according to the source, Pascal (or his son Jean, following Pascal's death, in 1886) joined forces with French photographer Policarpe Joaillier in the 1880s. They had a studio in Pera and perhaps another in Cairo, and theirs was a prolific and successful business.

6 In fact, this example is about as sexually explicit as harem photographs generally get, a clear indication that the sexuality of these images resides much more in the imagination of the viewer than in the actual photograph. This body of material is in sharp distinction to the material popularized by Alloula in his 1986 book, *The Colonial Harem*, in which he focuses exclusively on explicitly sexual and revealing postcards of women from the Algerian colonial context.

7 For Berggren, see Wigh, *Fotografiska Vyer Från Bosporen Och Konstantinopel*.

8 We know that there were large numbers of commercial photographers active in Istanbul in this period. See, for example, W. Allen, "Sixty-five Istanbul Photographers, 1887–1914"; Çizgen, *Photography in the Ottoman Empire*, reference section.

9 See Micklewright, *A Victorian Traveler in the Middle East*, especially 102–11.

10 Wigh, *Fotografiska Vyer Från Bosporen Och Konstantinopel*, 32.

11 For many female visitors to Istanbul, the opportunity to visit Ottoman women at

home and see a "real" harem firsthand was an essential aspect of their experience. However, language barriers were often impenetrable, and thus activities where speech was not essential—such as trying on each other's clothing—became central. See Lewis and Micklewright, *Gender, Modernity and Liberty*, for a discussion of these visits and extracts written by English and Ottoman women describing them.

12 Lewis, *Rethinking Orientalism*, and Roberts, "Cultural Crossings," both provide important insights into the practice of cultural cross-dressing as well as access to earlier work on the subject.

13 For an initial investigation of this subject, including an extensive bibliography, see Schechter, *Transitions in Domestic Consumption and Family Life in the Modern Middle East*.

14 Ali Sami's photographs were published in Çizgen, *Photographer/Fotografçi Ali Sami*.

15 The term *snapshot* was originally used to refer to the photographs taken with the Brownie cameras introduced by the Kodak company beginning in the 1880s. While it is not possible to know whether these photographs were actually taken using a Kodak box camera, it is clear from the informality of the posing of some of the subjects and the fact that multiple copies of the same image were printed in slightly different sizes, that this group of images is the work of an enthusiastic amateur photographer, not a professional, and thus are exactly the kind of images that the invention of the Brownie camera made possible.

16 These snapshots were acquired as part of the Gigord Collection, which was purchased by the Getty Research Institute from Pierre de Gigord in 1996.

17 In several of the photographs women are wearing jackets or dresses with huge sleeves, known as leg-of-mutton sleeves. These were popular in the 1890s, going out of favor in the early years of the twentieth century.

18 For a good introduction to the history of the snapshot see Coe and Gates, *The Snapshot Photograph*; Ford and Steinouth, *You Press the Button, We Do the Rest*.

19 We know that the decorating aesthetic of the Victorian period favored what looks to our contemporary eyes to be excesses of surface ornament and innumerable small knickknacks, but this room seems overdecorated even by Victorian standards. While the point of most photographs of uninhabited rooms is most likely to record a moment in the life of the house, this room could have been set up specifically for the photograph by bringing in favorite pieces from other areas of the house to intensify its decorated state and signal even more emphatically the au courant taste of this family.

20 While it is interesting that none of the photographs which show family groups take place in the empty rooms whose furnishings were so carefully documented, this is most likely a result of the technical limitations of the relatively unsophisticated snapshot camera and the lighting requirements for group scenes.

21 I am grateful to İrvin Schick for calling this detail to my attention, and for tentatively identifying the calligraphy as an *icazet*, a kind of calligraphic proficiency or graduation certificate, which serves to identify this family as Muslim.

22 The lavishly embroidered and beautifully sewn clothing that would have been worn by the mothers and grandmothers of the women in this photograph was often saved, which is how nineteenth-century examples of dress have ended up in museum collections and for sale in the bazaar. It seems likely that these people could have found suitable clothing, had they been interested in a faithful reconstruction of the Ottoman past—a fact which reinforces the conscious nature of their ironic reconstruction of a harem scene.

23 There are a total of seven photographs in the "harem" series, all set in the same space and involving different combinations of the same group of people, some with only women and some with only men. An assortment of the same props appears in all of the images.

24 This story from Fatma Aliye Hanım's *Nisvan-ı Islam* (women of Islam; 1891–92) is paraphrased by Çelik, "Speaking Back to Orientalist Discourse at the World's Columbian Exposition." I am grateful to her for bringing it to my attention.

25 See Roberts, "Cultural Crossings," 89.

26 In addition to the snapshots discussed here, and the pair of photographs of the Ottoman-Egyptian Princess Nazli Hanum in Roberts's "Cultural Crossings," Çizgen's *Photographer/Fotografçı Ali Sami* includes a photograph of Hamide hanım posing for the camera as a harem girl. It is obvious that other similar photographs may yet be found in collections still in private hands.

10 • DRESS AND UNDRESS

Clothing and Eroticism in Nineteenth-Century Visual Representations of the Harem

Joan DelPlato

 This study considers images of the dressed and undressed harem woman produced in nineteenth-century France and Britain. Visual representations of the harem often functioned to titillate, inform, and create identity for the Western Self and the Eastern Other, and clothing could be understood to support those ends. This investigation asks how the Orientalist construction of the eroticized Eastern female Other played out visually in select examples of art. More specifically, it seeks to articulate the nature of Western erotics in four representative harem pictures and understand how clothing contributed so fundamentally to envisioning its dynamics.

Clothed and nude bodies are coexisting subjects of art. Anne Hollander, the doyenne of the study of fashion in European fine art, contends that bodies of females depicted as nude or nearly nude have much in common with fully clothed females, and that the nude is definable by the absence of dress, while the heavily clad body signifies the absence of nudity.[1] I would like to build upon Hollander's observations and argue that pictures of harem nudes are definable in relationship to the drapery they wear, and that the erotic dynamic evolves out of their relationship to it. I go further than Hollander in exploring gender constructions within (and beyond) the pictures of undressed harem women. And in the cases of the two fully clothed women of the harem that I analyze, I am interested in some basic psychosexual principles at work in the construction of Western desire / visual mastery over images that seem to be purely aesthetic. I maintain that Orientalist attitudes surface in the erotics of art as a subtle arena of colonialist domination, making my viewpoint more politicized than Hollander's.

Whether the harem woman was shown clothed in elaborate garb or clothed in nudity, these images offer strikingly similar sets of scholarly issues across the national divide that separated Britain and France.[2] The two countries' histories and art were intertwined.[3] They shared innovations in industry and clothing production, an artistically informed intelligentsia, and a position of world dominance over colonies and spheres of influence. British and French commentators alike referred to the Ottoman Empire as the "sick man of Europe." Both countries' economic relationships with Turkey favored those dominant states. From the Anglo-Ottoman Treaty of 1838, which guaranteed free trade for England but broke up Ottoman commercial monopolies, through the end of the century, Turkey was increasingly disadvantaged.[4]

The dominant Western visual dynamic at play in the eroticism of the pictures I will discuss is premised on the economic dominance of England and France. Such an imbalance affected the very material products at issue in a study of harem clothing. The classic economic relationship between colonizer and colonized was established over the terrain of the manufacture of cloth and clothing. By 1905, when Turkey began to keep statistics on its imports and exports, it exported raw materials such as wool, cotton, valonia, cocoons, and silk waste, totaling £3.2 million, while it imported manufactured goods such as woolen goods, cotton prints (calico), American cloth, and cotton thread totaling £5.5 million.[5] The gap between Turkish exports and imports of goods related to clothing manufacture illustrates Ottoman Turkey's financial dependence on the West. Thus the actual clothing referenced in British and French pictorial representations unproblematically as Eastern might be considered Western as well.[6]

Maintaining a distinction between Eastern and Western femininity was essential to nineteenth-century artists' construction of the erotics of the harem. Male artists faced a dilemma: how to locate key features of the authentic harem and the women who inhabited it, when that sacred institution was inaccessible to them. By consulting printed books about the harem, artists could defer to authorities who presumably offered them the truth about the harem, which they could pass along as knowledge. In the process, the intertextual referencing of such authorities revealed artists' rarefied cultural aspirations as well as their struggle with crude popular stereotypes about the unbridled sexual activity of the harem. Indeed, the artist was compelled to call upon a variety of other texts not only to ensure the artwork's subject as an Eastern scene but also to construct the erotic dimensions of his harem picture, including the clothing portrayed.

Several of these interrelated questions about representing the harem— Who are its authorities? What is true about it? What is the nature of the representation's interdependence with other texts?—surface in other chapters in this volume, whether the scholarly subject is visual or verbal texts. Marilyn Booth notes the devices used by the narrator (presented as male) in A. 'Atiya's *Mudhakkirat 'amil fi biqa' al-'ahirat* (memoirs of a worker in whores' whereabouts) to assume authority in speaking for fallen women. That voice, like that of other characters in the book, claims that his are "true narratives, real stories."[7] Booth draws us into an "intertextual circuit" to help understand the 1920s' literary market as well as to construct meanings for the harem narratives she analyzes; similarly, Orit Bashkin points out that readers familiar with earlier texts would bring more levels of interpretation to their readings than would those with no prior experience of reading such texts. Nancy Micklewright raises the issue of the photograph, whose history, even more so than that of the painting, was thought to bear an indexical relationship to real life—though this is problematic on a deeper level when photographs of the harem are at stake. "Modern" nineteenth- and twentieth-century viewers and readers (rightly) suspected falsification, staging, and exaggeration of the innumerable harem texts they encountered. Claims to authenticity, authority, and consistency with other texts became a strategy of avowal or disavowal inherent in the harem representation.

INGRES'S *GRANDE ODALISQUE* (1814)

The *Grande Odalisque* (fig. 1) by Jean Auguste Dominique Ingres is one of the most frequently represented nudes in the history of Western art. Ingres titles his painting an "odalisque" (*odalik*), a word originally referring to a female slave concubine. By the mid-eighteenth century, however, the

1 Jean Auguste Dominique Ingres, *Grande Odalisque*, 1814, oil, Paris, Musée du Louvre.
©Photo RMN. Photo courtesy of Erich Lessing/Art Resource, NY.

term had found its way to the West where, tellingly, it referred to a genre
of paintings of the female nude who was only nominally Eastern. Despite
its status as the work of an Old Master and its recognizability in popular
culture, Ingres's painting has only rarely been considered as a depiction of
a harem inmate, and even more rarely has her clothing been the focus of
scholarly attention, though the work has served as a vehicle for other agendas in the nearly two centuries since it was painted.[8] And yet, as Aileen
Ribeiro reminds us: "One of the ways in which artists and writers entered
the world of oriental imagination was through costume and textiles, which
were so different from the clothing and accessories of the West."[9]

The picture occupies a place that is unrivaled in the history of French
academic art. However, our popular cultural and scholarly familiarity with
the work has blinded us to crucial aspects of it. Though we think we know
the painting, its eroticism has not yet been accorded sustained attention,
especially in tandem with its subject of the harem odalisque and her clothing. A close examination of this nude's discarded clothing and its intertextual referents defines the odalisque and differentiates her identity from the
French viewer's.[10] An analysis also reveals curious understandings of the
dynamics of harem erotics in the early and mid-nineteenth century.

The Middle Eastern referent of the work had been made timely by
Napoleon's expedition to Egypt in 1797 and the group of savants who re-

mained in the country afterward. In the period including the first showing of *Grande Odalisque* in 1819 and its later exhibitions in 1846 and 1855, the French presence in Algeria was solidified symbolically by the 1843 capture of the *smala* or traveling capital of Abd Al-Qadir, the Algerian resistance leader. Led by the Duke of Aumale, son of King Louis-Philippe, the French raid killed 300 Algerians, while 3,000 were taken prisoner, including members of Abd Al-Qadir's family within the sacrosanct harem.[11] Thus, the reception of Ingres's painting and the commentary on its eroticized presentation of a nominally Middle Eastern woman need to be understood within the context of unfolding historical events and the French parliament's advocacy of the total conquest of Algeria.

In the *Grande Odalisque*, a single nude woman, flank turned away, occupies the frontal space of the picture plane and exposes her elongated limbs and torso. She makes eye contact with the viewer over her right shoulder. In a flirtatious game, the body is exposed but concealed. To understand the central figure of a harem odalisque, we must focus on what are usually considered the painting's ancillary elements: her turban and jewelry, worn on the body; and discarded clothing around and under it. Collectively these objects can be named "dress" or "fashion," and they are actually primary in conveying meaning. Ulrich Lehmann notes: "Fashion's most absorbing fascination [is that] it challenges us to transpose transitoriness, also the hallmark of modernity, into a medium of high regard while maintaining its distinct characteristics."[12] The work's eroticism was so compelling that it prompted some critics to complain that Ingres had exceeded the standards of good taste necessary for high art. The woman's dress contributed to that perception.

Unlike many French nudes, Ingres's odalisque is not covered by a wisp of academic drapery, that formless white cloth traditionally placed over female genitalia as a means for Academy-trained artists to demonstrate their skill in reproducing fabric folds while serving as a nod toward propriety. Instead this uncorseted woman[13] lies upon at least two distinct garments: one thin, white, and semitransparent; the other a gold fabric of a heavier weight, probably intended to be read as satin, judging from its boxier folds. Between them lies an elaborate piece of jewelry. As for the white garment, Hollander describes in some detail the homely shift, or chemise, as "the one basic undergarment" for all European women and men for about fifteen centuries. Voluminous, simple, and white, it was knee-length and varied in sleeve length and height, though it displayed virtually no decoration, as be-

fitted its private function.[14] The same garment functioned as a nightdress
worn by both sexes and for three centuries in Europe, according to Philippe
Perrot.[15] The nightdress was a very intimate article of personal clothing.
Simple in style and cut and unadorned, it was not to be seen outside the
bedroom, nor was it to be mentioned in conversation.[16] But here it is presented in publicly visible high art at a time when the harem was understood
by its European apologists as the private, female section of the rich Eastern home.[17] Ingres's inclusion of the chemise helps eroticize the scene: this
was the garment closest to the pictured woman's skin, as it is the last object
the odalisque has taken off and placed atop the pile of her outer clothing.
Nonetheless, Ingres keeps the white chemise respectable by minimizing its
recognizability as underwear or nightwear. And this garment located next
to a satiny garment is called "a staple combination in the High Renaissance
female costume,"[18] a combination Ingres repeats in order to aestheticize his
odalisque.

Identifiable as Western, the clothing under the odalisque's body can also
be read as Eastern, as reported by a notable British woman writer and harem
visitor. The layers of clothing that Ingres paints bear a strong resemblance
to those described by Lady Mary Wortley Montagu in her *Letters*. Wife of
a British ambassador to Turkey, Lady Mary—a feminist woman of letters
and reputedly a beauty and a wit—advocated crosscultural respect for the
harem, despite its basis in polygyny and slavery (at least for elite households
and the Ottoman court). Montagu went so far as to have herself and her
son, Edward, painted in a harem around 1717 by Jean-Baptiste Vanmour.[19]
It has long been acknowledged in the Ingres literature that, while Ingres
was constructing his 1862 painting *Turkish Bath*, he copied into his personal
notebooks portions of Lady Mary's Letter 107, in which she claimed to have
opened the stays of her corset at a women's bath, much to the amazement of
the Turkish women there.[20] I want to argue that another letter of hers influenced Ingres's choices in making *Grande Odalisque*. In Letter 110—written
to her sister Lady Mar on April 18, 1717, from Adrianople—Lady Mary
provides a description of clothing worn by a haremite, an account that I believe provided specific details for Ingres's odalisque. Lady Mary had visited
two harems that night, defining them basically as the women's homes. In
her description of the clothing of the second harem's lady, there are dense
clusterings of description that resemble the dress Ingres paints. Note the
artist's differentiation of silver brocade and gauze fabrics and compare that
to Lady Mary's comment: "She was dress'd in a Caftan of Gold brocade

flowerd with Silver very well fited to her Shape and shewing to advantage
the beauty of her Bosom, only shaded by the Thin Gause of her shift."[21]

Where Ingres emphasizes the figure's arms and jewelry, especially the
distinctive belt, head jewels, and hair plaits, Lady Mary comments upon
"her lovely Arms adorn'd with bracelets of Diamonds, and her broad Girdle
set round with Diamonds; upon her Head a rich Turkish Handkercheif
[sic] of pink and Silver, her own fine black Hair hanging a great length in
various Tresses, and on one side of her Head some bodkins of Jewells."[22]
And Ingres includes an incense burner at the odalisque's feet, while Lady
Mary writes: "The dancing slaves entered the room with silver Censors in
their hands and perfum'd the air with Amber, Aloes wood and other rich
Scents."[23] The details of Ingres's painting are both eroticized and made
presumably Eastern by the artist's use of Lady Mary's authoritative letters,
first published posthumously in 1762. They were published multiple times
in English and French throughout the nineteenth century.[24] Ingres rather
inventively—but cautiously—piles these "authentic" clothes atop one another rather than risk draping them erroneously over a standing body.[25]
His prominent placement of the odalisque and her fur in the front center of
the picture plane recalls Lady Mary's comment: "In the innermost [room],
I found the Lady sitting on her Sofa in a Sable vest,"[26] a description that
might have influenced Ingres's overall vision of the woman.

The eroticism of the *Grande Odalisque* is further heightened by Ingres's
strategic placement of drapery over the bifurcation of her buttocks and
his obscuring the nipple of the right breast with her arm and her left eye
with shadow. The odalisque's modesty functions as clothing. The body parts
covered are precisely those whose presence is evoked.[27] Perrot's observations about the paradoxes of clothing are borne out: "Clothing . . . reveals
as it veils and showcases the sexually charged body parts it conceals . . .
The very modesty for which it vouches suggests the fascination of what it
covers."[28]

Similarly, drapery in art acts as a framing device which both displays the
subject and also contains the body, according to Lynda Nead, in her study
of nudity and obscenity. She observes that drapery "shores up the female
body—sealing orifices and preventing marginal matter from transgressing
the boundary dividing the inside of the body and the outside." Drapery
helps to separate "the self from the space of the other," thereby establishing identity.[29] Nead's feminine "other" can be conflated with Edward
Said's Middle Eastern "other" when considering this painting.[30] Eroticized

drapery functions to separate an eroticized female spectacle from a male spectator and further differentiates West from East.

At the painting's first exhibition in the 1819 Salon, it drew little commentary, but at the 1855 Exposition Universelle, when three intertwined trends had developed—public awareness of the East, international coverage of events there through the burgeoning press, and French academic Orientalism—it was featured in a room devoted to the work of Ingres. Nearly every one of the sixty-five critics who commented on the paintings at the exhibition commented on Ingres's *Grande Odalisque*, as Carol Ockman has noted. Nonetheless, few critics referred to the dynamics of Ingres's eroticism, and their discourse seems dominated by a focus on his use of line.[31] Not surprisingly, given the conventions of aesthetic commentary in nineteenth-century France, there was no explicit discussion of the *Grande Odalisque*'s relevance to contemporary colonial politics in Algeria.

However, Théophile Gautier wrote an unusual appreciation of *Grande Odalisque* germane to my argument that the painting's erotics are heightened by the relationship of the figure's body to her clothing, which also gives rise to her distinct identity as a harem inmate. Gautier was undoubtedly considered well positioned to write a review of the subject, as he had traveled to the Middle East in 1852 and published his *Constantinople* in 1853. In that work, his chapter titled "The Women" opens: "The first question invariably addressed to every traveler on his return from the East, is 'Well, and the women?' To which each responds by a smile, more or less mysterious according to his degree of fatuity, implying, however, a fair amount of romantic adventures."[32] Gautier suggests the trendiness of the question of harem sex for French audiences, but he denies any direct experience of Middle Eastern women. Claiming to have gotten his information from a well-connected Frenchwoman who did gain access to a harem, he describes in detail the room furnishings, the harem women's food, and their clothing and diamonds.

A close study of Gautier's language in his response to the showing of Ingres's *Grande Odalisque* reveals much. He writes that the odalisque has the "breasts of a Greek Venus, sculpted by Cleomenes for the temple of Cyprus and transported to the harem of the pasha."[33] On the one hand, Gautier's reference to the Greeks might be considered simply an expression of the esteem of the Academy for classicism. On the other hand, in describing this odalisque as a Greek who had become a harem inmate, Gautier reiterates the long-standing theme of the captured Greek woman forced into harem slavery by the cruel Turks — though his Greece is nominally the ancient one and not the nineteenth-century Christian one.[34] Prevalent in the politicized language of the Greek war of independence in the 1820s, the trope of the Greek harem slave had by the 1850s lost its radical-liberal flavor for Gautier, a critic of the Right, who retreats into the depoliticized aesthetic language of universality, perhaps considered the better backdrop for an exploration of erotics.

Gautier explicitly references the beholder when he writes that the odalisque is "turning her head toward the viewer," offering a sophisticated understanding of the conflation of the viewer as a stand-in for the pasha, and suggesting the processes of fantasy and projection so crucial for erotic art's dynamic interchange with the spectator. The fuller context for Gautier's phrase suggests that conveying erotic desire requires active agency: "Half-raised on her elbow buried in pillows, the odalisque, turning her head toward the viewer with a graceful movement, reveals shoulders of a golden whiteness, a back in whose supple flesh runs a delicious serpentine line."[35]

The odalisque is painted performing a simple, yet powerful movement in revealing her lovely shoulders and back to the viewer. An assertive movement is necessary in arriving at nakedness, according to Georges Bataille: "Stripping naked is [a] decisive action. Nakedness offers a contrast to self-possession." In response to that quote from Bataille, Mario Perniola comments on the close connections between desire and other drives, "the drive to undress oneself and others, [and] to transgress the taboo of nakedness."[36] But Gautier says that the odalisque "displays her chaste nudity," which is oxymoronic: she is the perpetrator in her act of displaying, but she is also passive in her chastity; we are again told that hers are "virgin breasts."[37] In short, the ideal eroticized female is untouched but actively gives herself — presumably for the first time — to the viewer, who is assumed to be male.[38] No reused prostitute,[39] the odalisque is available for the exclusive delectation of the viewer, and under his eyes only, does she comes alive and into her sexual potential. Therein lies the erotics of this woman for Gautier. Jacques Lacan articulates one of the basic presumptions (his term is "defects") of psychoanalytical understandings of Western bourgeois notions of sexual life: that "it is not enough to be subjects of need or objects of love — they must hold the place of the cause of desire."[40] Gautier's reading of the painting's erotic dimension seems grounded in this phallocentric assumption of the male (viewer) as the source for female desire, which, once aroused, in turn enflames the desire of the man. It is noteworthy that Gautier infers that this woman lavishes her virgin attention on the viewer, while the polygynous structure of the harem presumes that she is one of several women who share the master's affection. Likewise, Ingres's placement of a single woman in this picture plane heightens this moment of intimacy: there is no pictorial reference to other wives or concubines. The erotic dynamics of monogamy are enlivened by the tease of polygyny in both picture and commentary.

In writing of the clothing she has just discarded, Gautier implies that Ingres captures the transition from dress to undress, activating the pictorial surface by suggesting movement through time as well as space, without settling too quickly upon either state. This transition is of interest to Perniola, who describes the process by which the composed, self-assured, and clothed body moves toward self-abnegation and disarray; it is that very movement which lies at the heart of his concept of eroticism. "In the figurative arts," he writes, "eroticism appears as a relationship between clothing and nudity. Therefore, it is conditional on the possibility of movement—transit—from one state to the other."[41] Ingres's ruse to show the female odalisque in the process of undressing herself is thus highly charged.

Relatedly, Ingres shows clothing removed and cast around the odalisque. Gautier, too, notes this: discarded garments are "strewn here and there."[42] Eroticism is intensified in a painting, claims Hollander, when nudity is accompanied by "everyday objects."[43] Though she does not pursue why, we can extrapolate from Perniola: discarded clothing and other tangible objects around a nude body offer a heightened contrast between the clothed state, associated with the repressed and its release, and thus providing a visual map for the trajectory the viewer is invited to take as he or she moves from the quotidian to a heightened state of arousal.

In addition to reading Ingres's odalisque as a virgin who experiences a sexual awakening, caught in stop-action as she undresses herself, Gautier articulates the painting's erotic impact on him by fetishizing the figure's body parts. From head to shoulders to back to legs to feet, toes, arms, hips, breasts, mouth, cheeks, small of the back—even her nostril and blue-green pupil: his inventory of sites serves as urgent verbal foreplay. This fragmentation of the female body, a frequent strategy in the developing modernist aesthetic, evolves from a series he constructs, a process of naming and refining in litany form, which suggests its obsessive basis. Gautier's two paragraphs name female body parts in relationship to clothing and other exotica: an elbow falls into pillows; feet sink into rugs from Smyrna and brush against alabaster steps of harem pools; the turban fringe touches the nape of the neck; braids of hair are echoed in a pearl headdress. The desirous language that Gautier uses to describe the odalisque's lowering a fan further demonstrates that the erotic appeal of her body is enhanced by the objects that surround it: the fan is a fetishized frame for the emergence of the woman's body. He writes that she is "holding a feathered fan which slips, removing itself sufficiently from the body to allow virgin breasts of exquisite form to be seen."[44] Gautier's description, which moves from body parts to objects—pillows and fan—serves to supplement and amplify the enticing parts of her anatomy. Like desire which is never sated, Gautier is compelled to feverishly seek new sites; his obsessive language inevitably fails to capture the total effect of the odalisque's appeal.

Ingres's painting can be more deeply interpreted by borrowing some basic tools of psychoanalysis describing the operations of desire. Lacan reworks Freud's conception of displacement and condensation—dream processes in which the unconscious creates defense mechanisms—into the processes he names metonymy and metaphor. Metonymy, particularly relevant here, is the psychic defense in which the subject utilizes parts to stand for a whole. So for Gautier, the odalisque is apprehended through her body parts just as, in Lacan's example, a ship is understood by the subject's reference to a sail. Lacan writes that "desire *is* a metonymy,"[45] by which he suggests that this drive is serially attached to fragments of love objects. The objects of desire are in flux (consider Gautier's litany of things and body parts), "eternally extending toward the *desire for something else*."[46] Gautier's verbal recreation of the female odalisque is linguistically disjointed and fragmented.

Metonymic devices also appear in Ingres's painting. The female body he paints suffers from spatial disjunctures—of the attenuated torso and limbs, the knee that rises abruptly, the oddly placed feet. The *Grande Odalisque*'s body and spatial discontinuity keep the viewer's focus on the details of eye, back, feet, shoulder. Gautier's response indicates the flitting quality of the eye as it seeks to take in the whole figure at once. Each text—whether painting or critical commentary—is worked to reconstitute the presence of a desired but perpetually absent figure.

Gautier's mention of the odalisque's feathered fan invites a closer analysis of it in the painting. Ingres's placement of both feathered fan and fur garment at the very site of the dark shadow between the odalisque's legs doubly metaphorizes the unseen pubic hair, whose texture resembles both feather and fur. The elimination of body hair on a nude was a time-honored hallmark of fine art, and Ingres does not violate it. In nature, feathers, fur, and hair are analogous as cover for flesh, whether animal or human. Eastern women's custom of removing pubic hair was known in Ingres's time, as elaborate depilatory processes at the public baths had been documented in European travelers' accounts since the sixteenth century.[47] Thus I argue that Ingres's feathers and fur draw erotic appeal from referencing the specifically Eastern practice of denuding the pubes (then considered a rather outré custom in Europe, and known to only some viewers) all the while maintaining the line of French academic propriety. These exotic objects allow Ingres to coyly allude to female genitalia, and more precisely to the interior vaginal space, around which the entire pictorial composition revolves. This space itself is, of course, merely a void, a displacement of a Western male libidinous drive, which this painting celebrates — despite the gender of its patron, Queen Caroline Bonaparte Murat of Naples, the youngest sister of Napoleon.[48]

MAURIN'S *CONSTANTINOPLE* (1833)

Like thousands of popular prints produced on a great range of subjects during the July Monarchy, Nicolas Eustache Maurin's *Constantinople* (fig. 2) is indeterminate in historical context: we cannot document precisely who viewed this picture, or how it was read. Still, it is clear that the artist deftly manipulates harem clothing, jewelry, and furnishings in carving out the artwork's erotic dynamic, heightened by his use of intertextual references to Eastern (and Western) love stories. As a printed object, the work demonstrates a virtuoso treatment of the lithographic medium, suggesting that it may once have been an illustration to a luxury book. With a high degree of technical skill, Maurin has indicated a theatrical imagined space and a variety of textures: young flesh; silk sheet; patterned upholstery, fabric, and carpet; multicolored glass windowpane; peacock-feathered fan; fresh nosegay; the sheen of light on blond curls (readable as a clue to the subject's identity as a lighter-complected Circassian slave, reputedly more valuable than a darker-skinned slave).[49]

   In a room that is outfitted in a variety of fine fabrics, the dramatic narrative unfolds as we see an adulterous young couple, somnolent in their postcoital bliss, their clothing (such as it is) full of import. Her lovely young arms cradle his head; even in sleep he leans intensely toward her, his unbearded face and neck vulnerably exposed. At stage left, we glimpse a pasha, who pushes aside a curtain while backing into the room; close to his venge-

2 Nicolas Eustache Maurin, *Constantinople*, 1833, lithograph. Photo courtesy of the
Bibliothèque Nationale de France, Paris.

ful heart, he hides his lethal dagger in one hand. A decorated scimitar is
found in his other hand, and he has double murder in mind. The drama
is in our realization that the blissful couple is doomed before they learn
their fate. Her hands contrast strongly with those of her standing master:
her bejeweled fingers and wrists suggest that her circle of love will be van-
quished by a circle of death; the scimitar will replace her arms around the
lover's neck as the instrument of his beheading.

Several intertextual referents on the theme of illicit love and impending
doom can be found for Maurin's print. The first text has to do with Paolo
and Francesca of Rimini, an adulterous thirteenth-century Italian couple.
In this story, a woman and her brother-in-law fall in love and are discovered
by her husband, Gianciotto Malatesta, who kills them on the spot. They
are immortalized in Canto 5 of Dante's *Inferno*, where they are in limbo in
the second circle of hell, doomed to move like the winds, for all eternity
sensing each other's presence but never allowed to touch. When Dante the
traveler encounters them, Francesca tells the story of their love—the couple
read the story Lancelot together and fell into each other with a kiss—and
of their double murder in a heart-wrenching passage, including a curious

reversal of gender roles as Paolo simply weeps while Francesca talks. By Maurin's time, the story had been depicted by several French and British artists, including William Blake; Ary Scheffer, who exhibited one version of the subject at the Paris Salon in 1835; and Ingres in 1819 and again in 1855–60.

Another text about lethal love that may have affected Maurin's image is a scene from the *Arabian Nights* that appears in the first pages of the book's prologue. Though brief, the scene of marital infidelity sets in motion the theme of King Schahzenan's distrust of women, which is echoed in a second scene concerning his brother, Sultan Schahriar, who also murders his unfaithful wife. The two brothers' double deception lays the foundation for the major conceit of the entire work: the success of Scheherazad, the vizier's daughter, who tells Schahriar fanciful tales and in so doing spares her life and ultimately ensures his love for her. The king discovers his wife's affair with "one of the lowest officers of the household." Maurin's picture corresponds to this description of Schahzenan's deadly response, found in Edward Forster's English translation of Antoine Galland's first translation of the *Arabian Nights* to appear in the West: "The unfortunate monarch, yielding to his first fury, drew his scimitar, and, approaching the bed, with one stroke changed their sleep into death: then taking them up, one after the other, he threw them from the window into the foss, that surrounded the palace."[50]

If this is indeed an illustration from the *Arabian Nights*, Maurin is interested in the psychological drama, as the king's dark facial expression reveals that his incredulity has given way to anger in this, the climactic moment before the unsuspecting couple is killed.

Though produced after Maurin's print, the writing of (again) Théophile Gautier attests to the long-standing, mythic status of the trope of the harem penetrated by a male interloper, who can also be Western. In recounting his own journey to Constantinople in his 1853 book by the same name, Gautier writes tongue-in-cheek about such a story:

> Nothing is more charming in an Eastern tale, than to read, how an old woman, in a deserted street, made you a sign to follow her cautiously, and at a distance; and introduced you, by a secret door, into an apartment heaped with all the luxuries of the Orient, where, reclining upon a superb divan, a sultana gleaming with jewels, — which, however, paled beside her superb loveliness, — impatiently awaited your coming, and received you with smiles of tenderness and welcome. In due course, the

adventure should terminate by the sudden arrival of the master, who scarcely leaves you time to fly by the back-door; unless, indeed, a more tragical [sic] climax is attained, by a contest from which you barely escape with life, and the plunge into the Bosphorus, at dead of night, of a sack which bears some vague resemblance to the human form.[51]

That the Westerner who "penetrates" the harem is also endangered is part of the erotic *frisson* for both the protagonist and the reader in the canard's retelling. When he encounters the beautiful harem woman, she is inevitably dressed in elegant clothing and extravagant jewelry, emblematic at three levels. Most obviously, these luxurious objects indicate the luxurious institution in which she takes part. As frequent French rococo symbols, silks, furs, and jewelry could reference her genitalia. Expensive clothing and gems could also be read to express the depth of the pasha's passion for her. All three possible referents are themes in Maurin's print as well.

In the print, the woman's clothing recalls the sheer white chemise discussed above. Here it has been pushed down so low on her shoulders as to suggest a cross between a sheet and a fetching décolletage, highlighting the whiteness of her breast—the better to indicate the target for the imminent placement of the phallic dagger, a final declaration of ownership of the lawfully masculine placed within the flesh of the female. In the dynamics of viewing, the fabric through which the master moves forms a heavier and stiffer—a more "masculine"—counterpart to her delicate body covering. Indeed, the contrast of their clothing helps reiterate the central visual dynamic between the upright, dark-complexioned pasha and the reclining, blond odalisque. To emphasize that marital infidelity is at stake here, the very center of the pictorial composition (as in Ingres's *Grande Odalisque*) is the shadowed pocket of dark space that occurs at the juncture of the hem of the woman's chemise, located high on her thigh.

The interloper's clothing contrasts markedly with the pasha's. To suggest boyish flirtation, the lover is made effeminate for a French audience in his light skirt and velvet jacket heavily embroidered with gold braid. His short, dark curls form a counterpart to the woman's hair: they are topped by a cap that contrasts with the tradition and power symbolized by the pasha's intricate, heavy turban. The lover crosses both his arms and legs to more compactly fit into the woman's arms, giving a sense of his lower social station and perhaps even a childlike character to his body, a substitute love object for her childless body.

By virtue of the youth and attractiveness of the couple, qualities enhanced by their costuming and the dress of the room, the print sides with them and against the swarthy pasha, who embodies a tradition of marital fidelity that is tyrannical as well as violent. The picture implies that we are witnessing "overkill": the "little sin" of infidelity is punished by the "big sin" of murder. In the absence of a just legal system, the husband becomes the judge, jury, and executioner, even if the marriage may be faulty in the great age gap between its partners. Coupling for love's sake is untenable in the face of old-world traditions.

This print, subtle as it is in technique, is blatant in its stereotyping of Eastern gender demeanors: the female/wife is all body and love, the male/husband calculating and heartless. The artist implies that the harem, perceived as coercive and thought to harbor the practice of arranged marriages, prevents female choice in love partners, thus duping and denying nature, which leads to tragic results.

A long-standing anxiety about the harem expressed by both Europeans and reformist writers in the Ottoman Empire is that its old-style arranged marriage could not survive modernized shifts to what A. Holly Shissler in this volume calls "companionate marriage." Her summary of the Turkish Ahmet Midhat Efendi's views on the harem reiterates, nearly a century later, the point of Maurin's print: "Unions made without choice or between individuals who are not suitable for each other will be lacking in genuine affection and will result in misfortune." Similarly, Bashkin's description of older versus newer marriage practices, the former grounded in the "authoritarian control of the husband/master," is useful in considering the changes in the structure of marriage—whether in Western Europe or in the Ottoman Empire and its Arab provinces.

Jammed into the tight space of the physical area of the harem, Maurin's abundant décor serves as an expression of the profusion of passion. Fine clothing and other intricately textured fabrics provide evidence of the deadly sin of *luxuria*. Just as these characters are covered either in fine (or very little) clothing, the room is suffused with tactile and visual stimulants. The "sexual excesses" of the harem take place in "a universe of generalized perversion and the absolute limitlessness of pleasure," to borrow Malek Alloula's terms.[52] Ultimately, the wealthy, polygynous harem life of pleasure—understood as material and moral excess—is both enjoyed and condemned in this print.

3 John Frederick Lewis,
   In the Bey's Garden,
   Asia Minor, 1865, oil.
   Courtesy of Harris
   Museum and Art Gallery,
   Preston, Lancashire, UK/
   Bridgeman Art Library.

LEWIS'S *IN THE BEY'S GARDEN, ASIA MINOR* (1865)

The major painter of the harem in Victorian England was unquestionably John Frederick Lewis (1805–76), who was most active in the third quarter of the nineteenth century. His painting *In the Bey's Garden, Asia Minor* (fig. 3) reveals a sophisticated handling of harem clothing and female sensuality. Though dramatically different from the two French images of the harem nude discussed above, the clothing in this image also employs intertextuality, suggesting the artist's search for authenticity. Like the French images of harem women, *Bey's Garden* utilizes dress to eroticize and feminize the scene, and in so doing elicits multiple layers of meaning.

   The narrative is less a dramatic moment in a story that unfolds over time, as in Maurin's print, and more a phenomenological encounter with an elegant harem woman. It is less syntagmatic and more paradigmatic. The woman's prosaic action of cutting flowers in a garden and placing them in a vase is less significant than the fact that the whole scene is a burst of fabrics, colors, textures, and light. Her dress and headgear are thick and finely woven, as indicated by the boxy creases at her hemline and the way her veil falls at her back. Patterns woven into her garments, especially the paisley floral designs in her belt and the floral tapestry atop her head, blend with the poppies, lilies, roses, and fuchsia that surround her and tumble, cut and uncut, from the picture plane to suffuse the space. More painted flowers decorate the ceramic vessels — the tall vase and the pot and plate on the stairs. Indeed, the lines between flowers, fabric, and female are blurred as are those between nature and representation.

This very point was the source of elation for an art critic writing in the *Athenaeum* when the painting was exhibited in 1865, a reviewer who raves in language that indeed blurs the boundaries among beautiful woman, beautiful clothing, and beautiful flowers, as he describes the painting: "A Circassian damsel, fair after her fashion, a model of grace in action is cutting lilies to fill with them a beaker of rich china which stands at her feet. The whole picture is superbly bright and lovely in colour: see the lady's kirtle, and, as a still more exquisite piece of painting, the lush flowers that stand in the parterre and the jar."[53]

For this reviewer, the work is extremely successful overall, due largely to its exquisite handling of the detail and Lewis's status as a knowledgeable traveler to the East: "Mr. J. F. Lewis paints Oriental subjects with new force and solidity, the results of genuine knowledge and travel perfected . . . If we stand near this work its details are singularly rich and beautiful in treatment; when we are a little removed it appears as broad as it is brilliant."[54]

Besides the *Athenaeum* critic, another fan of Lewis's painting was, presumably, the work's patron, Richard Newsham — a rich, middle-class lawyer and philanthropist whose father had earned his wealth from banking and the cotton trade.[55] It is tempting to view Newsham's attraction to Lewis's picture — so attentive to clothing, down to the detail of its fabric and threads — in light of his own family's history as commercial textile traders.

Curiously, on this very point — the value of Lewis's excruciating detail of clothing and flowers — *The Times* of London is ambivalent. That paper's critic admires the painting technique in the dress ("the lady's dress is wonderfully painted, every separate tone and texture elaborated with almost painful minuteness"). In the same passage, the work is criticized as too mechanical, likening Lewis's technique to crowd-pleasing lighting effects popular in England and France: "The head that crowns this collection of microscopically imitated garments is doll-like, flat, and unreal in a most disappointing degree, looking like a face lighted, in the fashion of a transparency, by a light placed behind it. Indeed, the French painters have a phrase *peindre à la lanterne*, for just this style of work." The review deals an additional blow to Lewis by calling him a poor role model for young artists, one who relies on facile special effects. Lewis's "exquisite manipulation" "can [n]ever lead to large or noble results." The critic searches in vain for a higher meaning to Lewis's work, which fails to transcend its status of a visual record of fine clothing: "However wonderful and lovely in parts, his works as a whole, and except on a smaller scale, can never take rank but as miracles of handiwork."[56] Such a discrepancy between the critics suggests that Lewis's painting touched a nerve in art circles, where people were struggling to locate art in an era that saw obsessive interest in fashion as misguided, and painting's photographic reproduction of clothing as shallow.[57]

The clothing in Lewis's *Bey's Garden* suggests several intertextual references which I argue were necessary to lend accuracy to a subject steeped in centuries of mythology and exaggeration. One referent is the Qur'an, in its passages describing paradise. There, the earthly harem reflected the heavenly harem in which the (male) faithful were to be rewarded with houris — dark-eyed virgins offered to faithful believers in the afterlife. There is no reason to doubt that Lewis was familiar with the Qur'an. After his decade-long sojourn in Egypt, where William Makepeace Thackeray visited him and claimed that he looked and dressed like a native, Lewis's harem pictures included portions of Muslim scriptures; one harem painting from 1876 is even titled *Houri*.

In the descriptions of paradise offered by an edition of the Qur'an that Lewis was likely to have known, the clothing worn by the souls of the faithful and the couches on which they sit are made of green brocade and silk.[58] Islamic scholars and believers alike have considered the color green a celestial hue, as it represents the ultimate spiritual oasis in greatest contrast to the desiccation of death and the desert; moreover, it is the color of great spiritual experiences.[59] Green is the dominant color in Lewis's harem woman's jacket, and brocaded silk appears prominently in his picture.

The scene is outdoors, in a garden walled with trees. The garden, a rich cultural symbol in Islam, offers respite to the weary traveler on earth and in paradise. Indeed, paradise is a garden, as is mentioned more than 130 times

4 Edward William Lane,
   *A Lady in the Dress
   Worn in Private*, woodcut
   from *An Account of the
   Manners and Customs of
   the Modern Egyptians*,
   vol. 1, first published in
   1836.

in the Qur'an. Though it is very large (sometimes referred to as a double garden), it is enclosed by walls. It is filled with flowers, each of which has a holy meaning; collectively, they can be understood to praise Allah. Though Lewis titles this painting *In the Bey's Garden*, it may well be considered to represent God's garden. Thus the clothing in this painting supports a reading of this image as a scene in sacred paradise.

A second intertextual reference for the clothing Lewis paints is to be found in an illustration to the classic work by the great Egyptian scholar and traveler Edward William Lane, *An Account of the Manners and Customs of the Modern Egyptians*, titled *A Lady in the Dress Worn in Private*[60] (fig. 4). The similarities between Lewis's oil painting and the woodcut by his friend Lane are remarkable.[61] Lewis borrows from Lane's woodcut the cut of the lady's clothing, its striped skirt and sleeves, its multilayered fit close to the body, and especially the drape of the hem on the ground. Lane begins this section of his book by saying: "The dress of the women of the middle and higher orders is handsome and elegant."[62] First published in 1836, Lane's illustrated book, which had at least eleven English editions in the nineteenth century, was a major source for intellectuals and artists. Lewis, who also brought back samples of women's Egyptian clothing which were worn by Marian, his model and wife (an Englishwoman whom he met and married while in Egypt),[63] also stays true to some of the detail of Lane's verbal description of the dress that upper-class Egyptian women wore at home.

Lewis makes his woman's jacket shorter and forgoes the harem pants (which would be improper for a lady in Victorian England), but he does indicate the full-length vest that buttons at the midriff, which Lane names a *yel'-ek* "worn tight to the body and arms" and having long, wide sleeves.[64] Both Lane and Lewis make this a striped fabric and extend sleeves of the same material beyond the jacket in their pictures. Lane specifies, and Lewis has understood, that the yel'-ek "is open, likewise, on each side, from the height of the hip, downwards." Both pictures illustrate Lane's comment that the hem of the yel'-ek "should exceed that length by two or three inches, or more." Around the bosom, the yel'-ek is cut to allow a shirt to be visible. Lewis also indicates the "square shawl, or an embroidered kerchief, doubled diagonally, is put loosely round the waist as a girdle."[65] Lewis adds a cloth jacket, which Lane shows in a view from the back on another print, describing it as a *sal'tah* often made of velvet.[66] As for the headdress, Lewis paints more of the turban that is visible in Lane's second print, made of two or more kerchiefs "always wound in a high, flat shape, very different from that of the turban of the men"[67] and sometimes having a crowning headpiece.

Lane does not allude to a particular function of the clothing as a symbolic displacement for the feminine body. But the *Athenaeum* and *The Times* do suggest symbolic aspects of the flowers, fabrics, and female in presenting them as contiguous. The clothing on the woman in *Bey's Garden* does not merely cover the body, serving as a denial or an escape from it, but—like the nudity utilized in both Ingres's and Maurin's images—the clothing in Lewis's painting develops an intrigue about the unseen body, as basic to its eroticism. Echoing Michel Foucault's contention that the Victorians had an excess of discourse about sexuality rather than a repression of it,[68] I believe that the painting reiterates the harem woman's body through fabrics, flowers, and vessels. The relationship of clothing to body is more precisely that of metaphor, a form of disavowal in which whole objects are likened to the desired object on the basis of similar qualities. In Lewis's painting, pieces of the fashion ensemble become crucial markers of the feminine body. The headscarf covers lustrous dark hair, yet its rectangular, flat sections echo the hair's parting and texture. The light, gauzy linen undergarment at the neckline and wrists repeats the creamy skin color and alludes to the tactility of the flesh. The napped white edging of the sal'tah covers and announces the presence of breasts located several layers beneath. The bulky girdle calls the viewer's attention to the womb within, mimicking a uterine shape in its paisley motif. Similarly, the flowers in both pots and vases resemble this woman and her tall cylindrical form, topped by the beauteous bloom of the face.

CLOTHING AND THE ORIENTALIST WEB

Lewis's intellectual project in *Bey's Garden* approximates Lane's in his *Account of the Manners and Customs of the Modern Egyptians*. But we can widen our conceptual web to encompass all four producers of the visual cultural texts analyzed here. Three points need to be made about their connectedness. First of all, each person was given the rank of authority because of his social and cultural prestige. Lewis and Lane had extensive, firsthand encounters with the Middle East, while Ingres (who never traveled there) became one of the highest ranking members of the French Academy, and by his death was called a French master. Maurin's life is undocumented, but his outstanding artistic technique grants his work certain cultural mastery as well. Edward Said recognizes the power inherent in this European elevation of these men as cross-cultural experts, noting: "The role of the specially trained and equipped expert took on an added dimension: the Orientalist could be regarded as the special agent of Western power as it attempted policy *vis-à-vis* the Orient. Every learned (and not so learned) European traveler in the Orient felt himself to be a representative Westerner who had gotten beneath the films of obscurity."[69]

Second, each of these four cultural texts reveals the artist's desire to present fragments of dress as fragments of reality about the Eastern Other. The total complexity of the Eastern Other's life, it is presumed, can be captured by a thorough accumulation of details describing that life. Every thread within a fabric within a garment, every strand of hair, every flower in a garden, every jewel within a belt — these are the raw materials out of which a product thought to be valuable can be assembled, one that is valuable because it is presumed to be accurate and true. When the art critic of *The Times* quoted above writes that "the lady's dress is wonderfully painted, every separate tone and texture elaborated with almost painful minuteness," Lewis's painting, like Lane's writing, elicits an awe that is an appropriate response to the detail it gives clothing. Yet, as Said underlines, such an empirical assemblage of detail is neither truth nor "reality" but rather strands of invented truth, which these experts are then free to rework and editorialize upon: "The learned Orientalist's attitude was that of a scientist who surveyed a series of textual fragments, which he thereafter edited and arranged."[70]

These cultural authorities reference other cultural authorities on the topic of harem women's clothing. Lewis references Lane; Maurin references the *Arabian Nights*; Ingres references Lady Mary Wortley Montagu. Indeed, the preface by Edward Forster to the 1802 edition of *Arabian Nights* quoted above excerpted Lady Mary's Letter 110 that describes harem women's clothing and contains some of the most visual language,[71] while suggesting the density of the intertextual web at stake here. Said's critique of the impenetrable web of Orientalism implicates not only the scholar and artist Edward William Lane, whom he names throughout, but also the artists we have analyzed in this study. Said writes: "Amongst themselves Orientalists treat each other's work in the same citationary way."[72] Power is shifted from one intellectual to another, and a closed system of Orientalist thought is set in place. Harem texts, even pictorial ones, only refer to other texts and cannot directly reference an external reality.

Inescapably, the history of clothing's function within the harem picture is steeped in the tension between the pure and the forbidden, a dichotomy that operates on many levels. In French erotic harem pictures such as Ingres's and Maurin's this is more obvious, but in Lewis's and Lane's imagery as well, where decorum is seemingly upheld, representations of clothing serve to control the Oriental by upholding the construction of a Western masterful gaze. The Arabic harīm has connotations of both the forbidden and the sacred.[73] At its most fundamental, the Western erotics offered by the harem picture is both an acknowledgment and a violation of the sanctity of Muslim private life. Some would undoubtedly argue that each art object flouts the sacred,[74] a life force that is holy in Eastern and Western cultures alike. All four artworks to a greater or lesser extent derive their erotic frisson by dancing on the edge of deep impropriety at the same time that they are considered to be edifying, cross-cultural pictorial records. The tantalizing nature of the forbidden underpins all four pictures; only in the Maurin print do the lethal consequences of such a possession become expressed, as the interloper embodies the curious, presumptuous Western position. These harem images suggest that for nineteenth-century artists, thinkers, and their audiences, the eros of the harem was heightened by thanatos, the death drive. From the viewpoint of those in the Middle East, the Western pictorial rendering of the harem may well be "one of the forms of the aesthetic justification of colonial violence."[75]

NOTES

A portion of this chapter was first delivered at the Nineteenth-Century French Studies Association's annual conference at the University of Missouri in St. Louis, October 2004, as part of a panel called "The Legacy of the French Nude," chaired by Susan Waller, whose comments I appreciate. I am also grateful to the students in three of my art history courses — Imagining the Harem, Clothing in Art, and Lacan and Visual Pleasure — for their interest in this topic and their real contribution to stimulating my thinking about it. I would also like to thank Bryan Goodwin for his close reading and helpful suggestions. All translations are mine, unless otherwise indicated.

1   Hollander argues that nude bodies, rather than remaining static over time, are presented as if molded by the vicissitudes of fashion, and that the form and emphasis of particular body parts, even unclothed, suggest the effects of uplift, spread, nipping, undulation, trimming, and spillage that nineteenth-century fashion tried to achieve (*Fabric of Vision*, chap. 3). She also argues that images of the heavily clothed solitary and contemplative female dressed in a multitude of layers (two examples of which I analyze below), especially in later nineteenth-century European painting, are made to appear as if the woman *is* her clothes and is therefore freed from the need for nakedness (ibid., 165).

2   The particular mode of slavery in the Ottoman aristocratic and court harem figured prominently in shaping the rhetoric of international politics. In England and France, hysteria over the existence of polygyny and the making of eunuchs and slavery was readily melded with an anti-Ottoman agenda. But all of this also touched upon politics and policies at home, including debates in England and France over such incendiary topics as divorce, the corset and dress reform, prostitution, servanthood, and women's roles.

3   Comparing British and French imagery is unconventional in art history, where scholarship is still generally conceived of within national schools. After all, the two countries had different religions, histories, and social mores. And while France had a long-standing tradition of honoring the nude in art, Britain did not. The august critic John Ruskin wrote quite vehemently in 1872 against depicting the nude in art, on the ground that "even among the people where it was the most frank and pure, it unquestionably led to evil far greater than any good which demonstrably can

be traced to it" (*Works of John Ruskin*, 22:235). Note, however, a rethinking of the nude in Victorian art in the exhibition The Victorian Nude, held at the Brooklyn Museum of Art in 2002.

4 See, e.g., Köymen's analysis in "The Advent and Consequences of Free Trade in the Ottoman Empire." See also the more recent study by Owen, "The 1838 Anglo-Turkish Convention."

5 The figures are taken from *Encyclopaedia Britannica*, 11th ed., s.v. "Turkey."

6 When, in 1872, Ruskin said that "the delight in 'divers colours of needlework,' and in fantasy of embroidery, gradually refine and illume the design of Eastern dress" (*Works of John Ruskin*, 22:275), he may have been referring to tourist art, as the manufacture of indigenous Ottoman handicraft arts had fallen off as a result of competition.

7 'Atiya, *Mudhakkirat fi biqa' al-'ahirat*, 62.

8 In its day, it served as a rallying point to either defend or excoriate the neoclassical school of art lead by Ingres, which fought valiantly to retain older academic values against the newer romantic colorists led by Eugène Delacroix. Indeed, responses to the work from outraged critics who counted too many vertebrae in the woman's back has become an apocryphal story about the French master's breaking the rules for the sake of design principles, anticipating the development of the avant-garde.

   Feminist art historians since the 1970s, notably John Connolly and Carol Duncan, have constructed the *Grande Odalisque* as a representation of an utterly passive female body visually consumed by the active male gaze. In *Ingres's Eroticized Bodies*, Carol Ockman's recent analysis of the erotics of Ingres's pictures struggles with the older feminist inheritance, which had developed an important psychoanalytic dimension borrowed from the 1970s film theory of Laura Mulvey. Ockman brings out the fact that the painting was commissioned by a woman, Queen Caroline Bonaparte Murat, the youngest of Napoleon's three sisters—as a pendant to the now-lost *Sleeper of Naples*, bought by King Murat but destroyed in the riots of 1815. Ockman suggests that the work offers erotic pleasure not only to men but also to women, including both the queen and the author herself, indicating that politicized questions in the present affect our writing of art's history. She argues that the *Grande Odalisque*'s "abjection," a concept she borrows from Julia Kristeva, can be used as a means of feminist resistance, an argument criticized by the feminist art historian Abigail Solomon-Godeau ("Problems and Pleasures for Feminists") primarily for its application of Kristeva. See also Norman Bryson's problematic contention more than twenty years ago that Ingres's *Grande Odalisque* represents a "'failure' to portray convincingly the interior of the harem" (*Tradition and Desire*, 142).

9 Ribeiro, *Ingres in Fashion*, 204.

10 Philippe Perrot contends: "Because clothing one's self is an act of differentiation, it is essentially an act of signification." This has resonance for the study of art, in which artists and cultures contribute to the process of clothing the individual (*Fashioning the Bourgeoisie*, 8).

11 It was an event memorialized in the sixty-six-foot-long panoramic canvas by

Horace Vernet now housed in the Versailles Museum, and sketched in the pages of *L'Illustration*. On this official painting, which more than any other I have discovered celebrates the desecration of a harem in one of its segments, see DelPlato, *Multiple Wives, Multiple Pleasures*, 54–56.

12 *Tigersprung*, 4.

13 Ribeiro reminds us that French nudes are by definition uncorseted (*Ingres in Fashion*, 200). Théophile Gautier (discussed below) finds remarkable the absence of harem women's corseting, calling the corset "that instrument of torture" and claiming that it is "unknown in the East, or replaced only by the bowstring or *bastinadeo*" (*Constantinople*, 197).

14 Hollander, *Seeing through Clothes*, 159. See also Hollander, *Fabric of Vision*, 22.

15 Perrot, *Fashioning the Bourgeoisie*, 164–65.

16 Perrot continues that the bedroom was by the mid-nineteenth-century a private section of the bourgeois home (ibid., 165).

17 Correspondingly, in British and French cultural discourse, sharper distinctions were being made in visual art and other forms of representations between male and female spheres, public and private behaviors, and the wealthy and indigent social strata.

18 Hollander, *Seeing through Clothes*, 163. For example, compare the appearance of the garments in Giorgione's 1510 Venetian painting, *Sleeping Venus*.

19 See DelPlato, "A British 'Feminist' in the Turkish Harem."

20 Brown, "The Harem De-Historicized," 60.

21 Lady Mary Wortley Montagu, *Letters*, Isobel Grundy, ed. (London: Penguin, 1997), 164. Note the similarity to what Ribeiro calls the ankle-length shift, a *gömlek* (*Ingres in Fashion*, 213–14).

22 Montagu, *Letters*, 164. Lady Mary also writes of her hair "braided . . . with pearl" (148).

23 Ibid., 165.

24 WorldCat.org lists at least thirteen printings in French (Paris and Bordeaux) and eighteen in English (London) from 1800 to 1899.

25 Lady Mary's avowed pleasure in looking at "the beauteous Fatima" records a female pleasure in looking at females and suggests an aristocratic and pre-Victorian unabashedness in homoscopophilia (if I may be permitted a neologism) that functions as a rhetorical device to empower the female writer by likening her pleasure to a male writer's. The full sentence reads: "For me, I am not asham'd to own I took more pleasure in looking on the beauteous Fatima than the finest piece of Sculpture could have given me" (*Montagu, Letters*, 164). Of course, in her comparison to gazing at art, Lady Mary still maintains Georgian standards of propriety.

26 Ibid., 161.

27 And the obverse also seems to apply. Just as drapery implies nudity, "the nude implies drapery" (Hollander, *Seeing through Clothes*, 157).

28 Perrot, *Fashioning the Bourgeoisie*, 12.

29 Nead, *Female Nude*, 6.

30 Edward Said, *Orientalism*.

31 Ockman has unearthed a valuable body of critical reaction to the *Grande Odalisque* in her *Ingres's Eroticized Bodies*.

32 Gautier, *Constantinople*, 188.

33 In the original French edition: "sein de Vénus grecque, sculptée par Cléomène pour le temple de Chypre et transportée dans le sérail du padischa" (272). Although "padischa" and "pasha" carry different meanings in the Middle East, in France they were often used interchangeably.

34 Relatedly, Ribeiro writes that the predominance of blue in Ingres's *Odalisque with Slave* suggests a Christian woman, as blue was the color of the Virgin Mary's cloak (*Ingres in Fashion*, 234).

35 Gautier, *Critique d'Art*: "Soulevée à demi sur son coude noyé dans les cousins, l'odalisque, tournant la tête vers le spectateur par une flexion pleine de grâce, montre des épaules d'une blancheur dorée, un dos où court dans la chair souple une délicieuse ligne serpentine" (272).

36 Perniola, "Between Clothing and Nudity," 245. Perniola quotes from Bataille's *Eroticism: Death and Sensuality*.

37 Gautier, *Critique d'Art*: "s'étala dans sa chaste nudité"; "un sein vierge" (272).

38 See Booth's comment, in her chapter in this volume, that the reader "is implicitly male."

39 Within this volume, two other scholars offer studies of texts that struggle with the lines of demarcation between a woman of the harem and a prostitute. A. Holly Shissler locates a text in which Canan, the "good" odalik, is defined by her exclusive devotion to one man, and is distinguishable from the "bad" prostitute who works for pay to please many. The ideal is that Canan behaves more like a devoted monogamous wife, while her master's polygynous practice is not the point. In Booth's chapter, *Mudhakkirat wasifa misriyya* (memoirs of an Egyptian lady's companion) offers a very different viewpoint, presenting the positioning of Zaynab within the spaces of the street as liberating her from the stifling space of her father's haremlik.

40 Lacan, "The Signification of the Phallus," 277.

41 Perniola, "Between Clothing and Nudity," 237.

42 Gautier, *Critique d'Art*: "jetés ça et là!" (273).

43 Hollander, *Seeing through Clothes*, 175.

44 Gautier, *Critique d'Art*: "retenant de la main un éventail de plumes qui s'échappe, en s'écartant assez du corps pour laisser voir un sein vierge d'une coupe exquise" (272).

45 Lacan, "The Instance of the Letter in the Unconscious," 166.

46 Ibid., 158.

47 Brown, "The Harem De-Historicized," 64 and endnote 80.

48 See note 8 above.

49 This is a commonplace in nineteenth-century writing about the harem. On this point, see A. Holly Shissler's chapter in this volume.

50 *Arabian Nights*, 1:4. I use the spellings of characters' names found in this translation. As for location, the narrative of the scene in question from the *Arabian*

Nights in Forster's translation is Samarcand, Tartary, announced in the opening of the story (1:2), while Maurin's title, *Constantinople*, gives his picture a less obscure locale.

51 Gautier, *Constantinople*, 188–89.

52 Alloula, *The Colonial Harem*, 95.

53 *Athenaeum*, May 6, 1865, 626.

54 Ibid., 626–27.

55 Hibbert, *Catalogue of the Pictures and Drawings*, 5. Richard Newsham would bequeath *Bey's Garden* as part of his entire art collection to the town of Preston, where he was born in 1798; it became the kernel of the municipal art gallery that still stands today. For a more extensive discussion of Lewis's patrons, see DelPlato, "Collecting/ Painting Harem/ Clothing."

56 *The Times*, April 29, 1865, 12.

57 Similarly, see Charles Baudelaire's scathing critique of "daguerreotypomania" in Paris as mechanistic in his well-known essay, "The Modern Public and Photography" (1857).

58 Lane, *Selections from the Kur-an*, 311–12.

59 Schimmel, "Celestial Garden in Islam," 13.

60 Lane, *An Account of the Manners and Customs of the Modern Egyptians*, 1:60.

61 Lewis and Lane are parallel figures in many ways. While Lewis was born in 1805, Lane was born in 1801. Both were well educated and from well-to-do families. Each traveled to Egypt and lived there for an extended period, Lane from 1825 on and off until 1835 and again in 1842–49, Lewis in 1840–50. Each became immersed in Egyptian society and wore native dress there, entertaining British artists and intellectuals who passed through. Though neither Lewis nor Lane became Muslim, each retained Egyptian habits upon his return to England.

62 Lane, *An Account of the Manners and Customs of the Modern Egyptians*, 1:58.

63 In contrast to Lewis, Lane returned with a woman of Greek ancestry, Nefeeseh, who had been his slave, a gift from the artist Robert Hay. Lane finally married her in England in 1840. On Nefeeseh, see Leila Ahmed, *Edward W. Lane*, 39. Lewis had traveled to Egypt in the 1840s and returned to England in 1850, where he remained until his death in 1876. He made his reputation largely with his Orientalist paintings, works which allowed him promotion from membership in the Old Watercolour Society through the ranks to full membership in the Royal Academy by 1865.

64 Lane, *An Account of the Manners and Customs of the Modern Egyptians*, 1:58.

65 Ibid., 1:61.

66 Ibid., 1:63.

67 Ibid., 1:61.

68 Foucault, *History of Sexuality*, vol. 1, part 2, "The Repressive Hypothesis."

69 Said, *Orientalism*, 223.

70 Ibid., 176.

71 Forster writes in the preface: "I shall now cite a few authors, who have spoken of the Arabian Nights as containing faithful delineations of the manners and customs

of Oriental nations; and begin with our fair countrywoman, Lady Mary Wortley Montague [*sic*], from whose entertaining, and I believe accurate, letters I shall make two extracts" (*Arabian Nights*, xxxi).

72 Said, *Orientalism*, 176.

73 Perniola makes a broad, anthropological statement on the unclothed for "Near Eastern" populations: "Clothing gives human beings their anthropological social and religion identity, in a word—their being. From this perspective nudity is a negative state, a privation, loss, dispossession. The adjectives denuded, stripped, and divested described a person who is deprived of something he or she ought to have. Within the sphere of this concept—which extended broadly through the Near Eastern populations (Egyptians, Babylonians and Hebrew)—being unclothed meant finding oneself in a degraded and shamed position, typical of prison, slaves or prostitutes, of these who are demented, cursed or profaned" ("Between Clothing and Nudity," 237).

74 Lady Mary's final comment in Letter 110 is that while she was in the harem she "could not help fancying I had been some time in Mahomet's Paradice, so much I was charm'd with what I had seen" (Montagu, *Letters*, 165).

75 Alloula, *The Colonial Harem*, 120.

11 ✦ HAREMS, WOMEN, AND POLITICAL TYRANNY IN THE WORKS OF JURJI ZAYDAN

Orit Bashkin

 In this chapter, I examine the depiction of the harem (harīm) in several historical novels written in Arabic around the beginning of the twentieth century. Female protagonists and the harem become focuses for discussing problems relating to female seclusion and opportunities to denounce political tyranny and despotism.

These novels I discuss were written by Jurji Zaydan (1861–1914), a prolific historian, novelist, and journalist. Born to a lower-middle-class family in Beirut, Zaydan studied medicine at the Syrian Protestant College in Beirut, yet never completed his studies. He moved to Egypt, where he contributed articles to the growing Egyptian press. Beginning in the second half of the nineteenth century, many Christian Syrians—especially journalists, publishers, and other intellectuals—had immigrated to Egypt. Although some were criticized by the native Egyptian elite for opportunism and cooperation with the British, many Syrian Christians assumed dominant positions in the Egyptian print market as publishers, translators, novelists, and journalists.[1] Zaydan is one prominent representative of this cultural phenomenon. In 1891, he established his own journal, the famous and still published *al-Hilal*, and in the next year he founded a publishing house (Dar al-Hilal). He also produced voluminous studies of history which dealt with such topics as global history, the history of the Arabs in the pre-Islamic era, and the history of Arabic language and literature. Zaydan was denied a position as a history professor at Egyptian (later Cairo) University because of opposition from conservative circles. He attributed this rejection to the fact that he was a Christian.[2] He wrote twenty-two novels, all but one of which were historical novels. The texts enjoyed immediate success: between 1893 and 1919, many of the novels were printed in several editions; some were later translated into Turkish and Persian. As Zaydan himself recognized, his success inspired a host of local imitators. Fellow intellectuals like Farah Antun followed suit, using historical novels to attack political oppression, seclusion of women, and despotism.[3]

Zaydan's novels introduce a relatively large number of female characters (including queens, slave girls, modern educated women, concubines, and tribal women) and spaces that are associated exclusively with women, especially the harem. This might be the outcome of the novels' schematic structure, which invariably opposes a just and kindhearted hero and heroine with a male and a female villain. Nonetheless, the appearance of female names in the titles of some of the novels and the attention dedicated to the histories of female heroines in Zaydan's fiction suggest that gendered considerations played a vital role in his choices of historical narratives.

The choice of women as subjects of historical novels is connected to the rise of a leisure-reading culture among the Egyptian educated middle classes. Egyptians began to read more in the late nineteenth century and the early twentieth. They were exposed to newspapers and literary and scientific magazines, which they read at home and in societies and clubs.[4] Marilyn Booth and Beth Baron have highlighted the significance of female readership: literary and journalistic products were aimed at and often written by women, and disseminated new ideas about education, domesticity, and social conduct.[5] Interestingly, the women's press included popular Arabic novels and translations of European novels. Booth, in particular, calls attention to the important function of historical narratives and historical role models in the formation of female identity in this period.[6] Journals such as *al-Hilal* and *al-Muqtataf* also dealt with themes related to domesticity and gender in advice columns and in essays about changes in the lives of women around the globe.

Readers in Egypt also learned much about female identity, sensuality, and domesticity from a popular literary genre that the Egyptian literary critic 'Abd al-Muhsin Taha Badr called "novels of entertainment and amusement" (*riwayat al-tasliya wa al-tarfih*), which often described romantic pursuits of young women (and, naturally, of young men). Often, these narratives were both chronologically and spatially detached from the Egyptian milieu and focused on events in faraway locations (like Japan or Russia) and on foreign women such as "the Japanese Girl" (in the novel *al-Fatat al-yabaniyya*, 1903) or "the Amazing Jewish Woman" (in the novel *al-Yahudiyya al-'ajiba aw fatat Isra'il*, 1903). The very genre of entertainment novel seems to have been largely created by the Syrian-Egyptian press, and many of the writers or translators were Christians.[7] Zaydan's novels competed with such products. A typical Zaydan novel took readers to at least three or four settings, covered three or four major historical events, and introduced a mélange of romance, sexuality, and adventure. The novels were serialized in *al-Hilal* and later published by Dar al-Hilal as books. As we shall see, the use of this genre allowed Zaydan, as a Christian, to convey radical political suggestions about the rights of women by situating his plots in distant locations and in the medieval past.

What is the significance of the appearance of female characters in Zaydan's novels? First, as I have noted, these works gained extraordinary popularity in the Middle East, which lasted well after their author's death. The novels, moreover, were read not only by adults, but also by children,[8] and consequently their ideas reached a very large audience. Second, the novels illustrate Zaydan's attentiveness to the debates concerning both political theory and women's rights that were articulated by a variety of both Christian and Muslim intellectuals at the time. His conceptualizations, in other words, respond to discourses that were occurring in the public spheres of urban Middle East centers and, concurrently, appropriate and discuss themes debated among Orientalists and Western scholars. Third, despite the recognition of Zaydan's importance to Arab thought, only recently have his novels begun to be read as an important medium for channeling political and social ideas.[9] This chapter adds gendered dimensions to these new readings.[10]

Zaydan's construction of harems in his novels thus mirrors important conversations about the role of women's domesticity and consumption habits as well as polemics on how well-trained women should order and arrange their homes, topics much in evidence in the Ottoman and Egyptian public spheres. This prevalence is shown, for example, in chapters in this book by A. Holly Shissler and Nancy Micklewright. Both illustrate how themes of self-reliance, marriage, and household management were highly important to elites and the rising middle classes, as well as to intellectuals debating the meanings of these processes. Shissler and Micklewright show the image of the harem assuming a vital function in these discourses. Booth further demonstrates that debates about prostitution in Egypt found their way into the representations of female voices in popular narratives. It is within this new conversation about the modern household, notions of public and private, and ideas about domesticity and propriety that we should come to the novels of Zaydan.[11]

Three important discourses about women and their roles in society which were concurrent with Zaydan's production of historical novels are echoed in these novels. The first was a debate about women's seclusion, isolation, and lack of education. The feminist intellectual Malak Hifni Nasif (1886–1918), for example, compared women's seclusion to the practice of burying girls alive in pre-Islamic Arabia.[12] The works of the influential Egyptian intellectual Qasim Amin (1863–1908) that denounced women's seclusion and called for women's education generated important discussions about womanhood in Egypt. Many important intellectuals participated in this conversation and took sides for and against Amin's arguments against seclusion.[13] It was a debate that had begun at least as early as the 1870s. Zaydan's historical novels thus belong to this contemporary conversation about seclusion.

A second discourse that inspired the novels explored political theory and emphasized the important roles of representative governments and legislative bodies to curb the power of autocratic leaders. Polemics about tyranny and constitutionalism had been prominent in the Middle Eastern intellectual arena since the mid-nineteenth century. The 1908 constitutional revolution in the Ottoman Empire—which forced Sultan 'Abd al-Hamid II (1876–1909) to reinstitute the 1876 constitution and recall the legislature—was an important event for intellectuals like Zaydan. Previous limitations on freedom of expression were lifted briefly after the revolution, and many enthusiastic journalists and intellectuals marked the event as the beginning of a new constitutional era. The revolution, then, was perceived by many Arab intellectuals as a much-needed safeguard against an authoritarian regime.[14] Zaydan integrated this discourse into his historical novels and underlined the relationship between political oppression and women's oppression.

Third, Zaydan was part of an Orientalist discourse. As noted by Donald

Reid, Cairo University was a magnet for important Orientalists; Zaydan had become familiar with such scholars, and admired their theories. He "had discovered European Orientalism in the reading room of the British Museum in 1866" and thus "came to see Arabic and Islamic history—so central to the cultural revival—largely through Orientalist eyes."[15] As Inge Boer notes, images of harems were dominant in the Orientalist imagination "because of themes commonly related to despotism, such as polygamy, . . . and the presumed oppressed positions of women under despotism."[16] *The Persian Letters* by Montesquieu is a case in point. The Orient in the works of Montesquieu, Diderot, and Voltaire was a fancifully elaborated one— more fabricated, we might suggest, than the Orient portrayed by travelers or missionaries who actually dwelled in the Middle East. And the French writers utilized the Orient mainly to discuss European politics.[17] *The Persian Letters* narrates the story of a rebellion in a Persian harem to contrast its tyranny with a representative government, the irrationality of the Persian patriarch and his eunuch with French rationalism and law, and the isolation of Persian wives with the freedom of French women.[18] Zaydan did indeed utilize the harem as a symbol of idleness, sexuality, and eroticism.[19] Most important, however, is the fact that he exploited the metaphor of the harem as a site of political oppression by transforming the allegorical French political references to reflect on contemporary Egyptian and Ottoman politics.

The historical novels intertwine themes from past and present. Important premodern historical and religious texts—by the likes of al-Tabari, al-Khatib al-Baghdadi, Ibn al-Athir, and Ibn Khaldun—are listed as sources for the novels, and in certain cases, Zaydan even footnotes texts as sources from which he took his information. Characters in the novels, in fact, recite entire texts taken from medieval chronicles. The novels also integrate popular genres and stories such as biographies of heroes of Arab and Muslim cultures (*siyar*) and the *Arabian Nights*, which were recounted by musicians and storytellers to the urban poor and narrated in cheap books.[20]

Classical medieval literature must have revealed much to Zaydan. He also recognized the phenomena pointed out by Nadia Maria El Cheikh in her chapter in this volume—relating to the key roles women played in power struggles in Abbasid palaces, and the significance of proximity to the caliph or to his mother—as well as the fact that one could salvage precious information regarding the political and social roles of women from medieval belletristic collections.[21] The fact, however, that Zaydan employed such medieval narratives to discuss contemporary tyranny and political oppression gave them an entirely new meaning. More radically, the novels' repetition of similar themes (minority rights, and resistance to seclusion and oppression) in different historical times generated the impression that the concept of progress did not exist at all in the books. The novels, then, were not an attempt to create a romantic image of the past as Sir Walter Scott had done,[22] but rather, as Thomas Philipp has argued convincingly, an understanding of history as an eternal cycle of struggle between good and evil.[23] Such texts hybridized and synthesized colonial and local knowledge.[24]

Below I closely examine Zaydan's understanding of harems in order to explore his positions toward women and their role in society. I highlight the important spatial meanings the harem acquires in such works, as a site connoting female camaraderie, on the one hand, and as a representation of political oppression and the power of despots to seclude their women and oppress their people, on the other hand. Although such depictions appear in various contexts (Abbasid, Mamluk, and Ottoman), all of Zaydan's novels, in my opinion, should be looked at as political allegories which link tyranny in general to the oppression of women in particular, in a way that reflects his present, rather than the Islamic past. Finally, I wish to emphasize that Zaydan both appropriated and subverted imagery related to the Orientalist construction of the harem, as a site of sexuality, idleness, and immorality. I focus first on his novels that deal with harems in the modern and early modern periods. Second, I examine his use of Egyptian and Ottoman harems in a novel set in Baghdad during the reign of Harun al-Rashid (786–809).

TEXTS AND REPRESENTATIONS: THE HAMIDIAN LETTERS

Zaydan's first novels deal with the more recent history of Egypt and the Middle East. *Al-Mamluk al-sharid* (the fugitive Mamluk) is set in the era of Muhammad 'Ali (1805–49).[25] Other early novels recreate the events of the 'Urabi revolt (1879–82), the Mahdi state in the Sudan,[26] and the reign of 'Ali Bey al-Kabir (1760–72).[27] The novels present multifaceted representations of women in the harem. These women, submissive to and subjugated by a tyrannical and capricious patriarch, are viewed as the antithesis of modern, literate women whose marriages are based on love and friendship. In this context, Zaydan employs the harem as an allegory for authoritarian rule.

However, he also depicts the positive attributes of the harem as a unique, women-only space in which women assist one another and find refuge from masculine rage and tyranny.

Nowhere is the relationship between political oppression and seclusion of women more apparent than in the relatively late novel *al-Inqilab al-'uthmani* (the Ottoman revolution).[28] The novel's malicious tyrant, the quintessential Zaydan villain, is the Ottoman Sultan 'Abd al-Hamid II. This character is a sadistic, paranoid, chain-smoking tyrant who combines the image of a Hollywood-style Mafioso with an Oriental despot. It is to a significant extent an Arabized version of the French text *Abdul Hamid: Sa vie politique et intime*, an anti-Hamidian sensational account.[29]

Being either married to or ruled by 'Abd al-Hamid was indeed a horrifying experience. The sultan's political philosophy is presented in an imaginary conversation that he has with Machiavelli, "one of the greatest rational philosophers."[30] Taking an oath not to cease slaughtering until the world is rid of his enemies, both real and imagined, the sultan confesses that he concurs with Machiavelli's worldview. "You were right, Machiavelli," the sultan says, to argue that great men should sacrifice ethical values in order to preserve their control over the state.[31] The sultan feels that this philosophy was shared by other great men, such as Abu Muslim al-Khurasani,[32] who killed on behalf of the Abbasid revolution, and of the Abbasids themselves, who killed Abu Muslim after consolidating their power.

Machiavelli is invoked to show that the sultan sees himself as a modern ruler. He reads newspapers and listens to the phonograph, and his empire is depicted (in historically correct fashion) as sustained by modern technologies like the telegraph. At the same time, however, he is inspired by the Abbasid regime and imagines himself as belonging to a long line of Oriental despots. This mélange of old and new, modern and medieval, universalizes the Hamidian autocracy and places it outside the realm of the East-West binary. The image of the harem, however, revives the East-West opposition, though in a more complex format.

The novel introduces two female characters: Shirin, a modern, educated Turkish girl from Albania, and the sultan's favorite concubine (*kadın*), known only by her initial, J.[33] The story of Concubine J and Shirin is one of the two main narratives in the plot, the second being the story of the 1908 revolution. The juxtaposition of the two narratives equates a revolt in the harem to the quest for political freedom.

Shirin is a modern girl. We first meet her sitting next to her mother, dressed in European fashion and reading a French-language journal in which her beloved, Ramiz, anonymously publishes articles against the sultan's tyranny. Shirin's categorization as a modern woman is sealed by her decision not to marry the man her mother selects for her, because she loves the freedom-loving Ramiz. Her French journal also aligns her with modernity. In *Asir al-Mutamahdi* (the prisoner of al-Mutamahdi), the educated heroine, Suda, reads "the scientific magazine *al-Muqtataf*, which she used to study to entertain herself."[34] Baron has noted that "a book became a symbol . . . , signifying a new attitude towards literacy and literature." She points out that the intellectual Labiba Hashim took note of the tendencies of modern women to carry books and journals, and her colleague, Malaka Sa'd, also advised women to place books, journals, and newspapers on a table in a reception hall.[35] Women in Zaydan's novels do the same. The presence of Shirin's journal, however, also suggests that the relationship between the reader and the journalist is a loving, positive one because the modern woman's fiancé publishes articles as a way of communicating with his beloved.[36]

Ramiz is imprisoned for his proconstitutional activities. Attempting to learn his whereabouts, Shirin finds herself at Yildiz, the imperial palace in Istanbul which 'Abd al-Hamid made his home. Shirin is brought to the Yildiz harem, where she is to stay under the auspices of Concubine J, an Armenian slave used by 'Abd al-Hamid as a spy against his much-detested Armenian enemies.[37] Concubine J is pregnant with the sultan's child and being pressured to abort the fetus. Various officials are ordered by the sultan to dispose of the child and, if necessary, the mother as well.

Zaydan uses this opportunity to describe the harem in Yildiz. He introduces the various kinds of slaves, mistresses, and concubines in the palace, and categorizes them racially and religiously. The women in the harem are subservient to the desires of the sultan. The modern Shirin is astonished when she is confronted by the many unveiled women in the harem whose only wish is "to please the Sultan of the family of Osman"[38] and who "are all slaves of the commander of the faithful."[39] The text portrays the practices and norms in the harem through the modern gaze of Shirin. She watches the women chat idly, dance, or play with animals. Concubine J senses Shirin's loneliness, which she attributes to the unfamiliar environment (*wasat*). One of the ways in which the women in the palace attempt to entertain Shirin is to bring a black slave girl to amuse her by mimicking all types of animal sounds. Readers learn, through Shirin's eyes, that "the harem in Yildiz is nothing but a domain of pleasure [*malha*] for 'Abd al-Hamid and he does not come there unless he wants to pleasure himself." The pursuit of pleasure dictates the nature of the women in the harem. The authoritative voice of the omniscient narrator underlines the point: "What could be expected from women who have no responsibilities other than eating and drinking and who are ignorant for much of their lives? How can they make use of their time with anything but games, singing, dancing, cultivating cats and birds, and occupying themselves with eating and chewing, or idle talk about jinnis and demons?"[40]

Loyal to her modern ideals, Shirin refuses to be absorbed into this type of life. She does notice that Concubine J is intelligent but that because the "surroundings [*wasat*] influence ethics," she does not live the sort of life she clearly deserves. Shirin is distressed by the ill-gotten wealth of the palace and "by how a bloodthirsty man [*saffah*] like 'Abd al-Hamid governs and arrests a free honorable man like Ramiz and others like him."[41] Thus oppression of women is contextualized in a more general discussion of political and economic oppression within the Ottoman Empire. The two women become good friends, despite the sultan's constant attempts to play them off against each other. When Shirin argues that millions of women in the empire desire to be the sultan's wives,[42] the concubine replies: "No one among the Ottoman people is more miserable than the wives of the sultan. Even our slaves are happier than we are." And again: "The freedom that our dogs enjoy, our birds, . . . even the mosquitoes and flies . . . this is the freedom we are deprived of, unlike other people. When a woman becomes a slave, she is buried in her palace."[43]

Confined to her palace, Concubine J is deprived of the freedom to go out and enjoy nature. Shirin, in reply, says: "Freedom, my lady, is the demand of the free men who struggle against the Sultan."[44] The concubine thus asks Shirin to "rescue her from this jail."[45] The atmosphere of imprisonment is also evident in the description of the concubine's dark, gloomy room, with only a few rays of light entering it through cracks in the window.[46]

Through Shirin, the concubine is introduced to the ideas of the Young Turks, the officers, soldiers, and college students who led the 1908 revolution and curbed the sultan's power. Zaydan, believing the Young Turk leadership was comprised of intellectuals, was impressed by their resentment of Hamidian despotism as well as their modernizing plans.[47] Initially, Concubine J is not convinced of the new ideas that Shirin brings with her. Slowly but surely, however, she changes her mind. Finally, she discovers that her Armenian background threatens her life, since the sultan has heard that his regime would be terminated by the son of an Armenian woman.[48] 'Abd al-Hamid's mistreatment of his concubine is thus linked not only to his abhorrence of freedom but also to his xenophobic hatred of minorities, especially the Armenians. The concubine consequently escapes the palace with Shirin and gives birth to her child and Shirin marries Ramiz following the 1908 revolution.

The concubine's story includes many important elements. Zaydan's harem, in effect, contains the European checklist of negative qualities associated with the institution: sexuality, polygamy, lavish opulence, lethargy, imprisonment, and idleness of women that reduces them to mere animals,[49] as reflected in the references to birds, cats, dogs, and roosters in the novel. The text, then, deftly manipulates the Orientalist image of the harem to intertwine narratives of sexuality and sensuality, race (comparing the black slave to an animal), and theories about the effects of the environment on a person's character. However, the text also equates woman's seclusion with political tyranny, thus mirroring similar claims of Middle Eastern intellectuals. The symmetry between the rebellion against Hamidian authoritarianism and the escape of the concubine associates authoritarianism with the seclusion of women. Seen from this perspective, the harem becomes synonymous with a system of surveillance that characterizes the entire empire.

A useful way to explore Zaydan's claims is to juxtapose them with prevailing Ottoman views of slavery. Ehud Toledano has demonstrated that polemics concerning Ottoman slavery, a "fascinating cultural translation," produced, among other things, plays, novels, and poems. Within this debate, a "rags to riches" narrative was employed in defense of the harem system, as the harem elevated female slaves from their lowly rank to the top of the imperial system. Concurrently, however, politically activist reforming groups such as the Young Turks utilized the image of slavery as a powerful metaphor for political and social oppression.[50] Zaydan, too, could be positioned within these polemics. He uses the metaphor of the slave girl in the harem to signify political oppression, on the one hand, yet also to fiercely denounce the narrative that women lived a comfortable, happy life in the harem, on the other hand. In al-Inqilab al-'uthmani, the women in the harem are oppressed prisoners of the sultan's irrational whims, not symbols of imperial success.

Another theme that emerges in the construction of the Hamidian harem is that authoritarian control of the husband/master is destructive to the structure of the family. Zaydan's story reflects the belief that marriages between uneducated women and educated husbands, as well as marriages based only on sexual relations between a husband and a wife who have nothing else in common, are doomed to fail.[51]

The Hamidian regime is clearly portrayed as a dysfunctional household. The sultan himself is a rather melancholic man who suffers from nightmares and insomnia and wanders aimlessly through his palace at night, tormented by guilt and fear. One scene places him in his garden, surrounded by magnificent animals and blooming flowers: "Every being in this garden was blissful, smiling, except for 'Abd al-Hamid."[52] The existence of unhealthy relationships in the household is evident in the father-son relationship. When 'Abd al-Hamid's son becomes fond of a parrot, the sultan demands to know whom the child likes more and finally orders the parrot killed out of jealousy. 'Abd al-Hamid's desire to kill the child of his Armenian concubine is also indicative of the ways in which a tyrant can destroy his family.[53] The ignorance of the women in the court, moreover, proves physically dangerous since it makes them believe that a drug given by an assassin to a child is just a potion prepared by a magician.

The politics of surveillance and oppression which typify the Hamidian rule are metamorphosed here into the relationships in a very troubled, dysfunctional family unit, with a father ('Abd al-Hamid), his wives, and his son. In this context, it is worthwhile to note that many of Zaydan's novels narrate an account of the destruction of a family unit: a son disappears, a father is abducted, or a woman is forced to marry a man whom she detests. In our case, both the harem and the household represent the state of the Ottoman Empire. An alternative to these dysfunctional relations is provided at the end of the novel, in a chapter titled "The Greatest Victory" (*al-fawz al-akbar*). The chapter celebrates the monogamous marriage of the modern Shirin and Ramiz, a marriage based on love and respect that corresponds to the beginning of the constitutional regime. The marriage and the new management of the nation signify a brighter, better future.[54]

The negative portrayal of 'Abd al-Hamid should not be surprising, given prevailing attitudes among Christian Syrian immigrants toward his regime and the anti-Hamidian propaganda which preceded the 1908 revolution.[55] Depictions of tyranny and oppression, however, also typify Zaydan's 1890s novels, which portray Egypt under the Mamluks. These texts, nonetheless, also highlight the solidarity and feelings of shared identity between women that were hinted at in *al-Inqilab al-'uthmani* (in the friendships between

Shirin and the concubine, vis-à-vis the sultan's power). The harem is presented as a site of female unity and harmony, contrasted to male authoritarianism.

In the novel bearing the self-explanatory title *Istibdad al-Mamalik* (the
tyranny of the Mamluks), readers are introduced to the grievances of the
people of Egypt concerning the Mamluks' wrongdoings. One innocent victim of the regime is 'Abd al-Rahman, a merchant who sells soap in Cairo
during the reign of 'Ali Bey al-Kabir (1760–72). 'Abd al-Rahman's household is composed of himself, his wife, and his son, as well as a few female
slaves, both black and white. Zaydan writes: "He could have been the happiest of men — thanks to his enormous wealth, prosperous business, and
tranquil domestic life — if not for the tyranny and oppression of the Mamluks and their heavy tax load."[56]

Intrigues, however, cause 'Abd al-Rahman to lose his wealth. When his
wife, Salima, hears that their son has been drafted, she cries bitter tears
"and all their female slaves and servants who were in the house shared their
tears." Salima eventually finds herself in the harem of 'Ali Bey al-Kabir,
"among the tens of slaves serving in the palace."[57] 'Ali Bey's chief wife is
presented as beautiful and blessed with intelligence, good judgment, and
compassion for the unfortunate. She is kind to Salima: "Her mercy grew
and she approached her, placed her hand on Salima's head, displaying her
gentleness."[58] Despite her good will, 'Ali Bey's wife is powerless to act because she is fearful of her husband's rage: "His rage might lead him to take
revenge by killing her, throwing her in the Nile, or banishing her from the
palace in the most humiliating fashion imaginable. She had no doubt that
he loved her, and preferred her over all his other wives and concubines.
She was, nevertheless, unsafe from his wrath, and she knew he was quick
to take revenge, and incapable of having anyone contradict his orders. She
knew that no Mamluk respects women, and nothing is easier to them than
divorcing their wives."[59]

When the bey orders the execution of Salima, she thanks the slaves in
the harem for their kindness: "I thank you my dear sisters, for your delicate,
noble feelings, and all I ask from you is . . . to tell your honorable mistress
that I shall never forget her grace and nobility."[60] These words left a great
impression in the hearts of the slaves, and they could not hold back their
tears.[61]

In Zaydan's first novel, *al-Mamluk al-sharid*, we find ourselves in Muhammad 'Ali's Egypt (1805–49). A son, Ghurayb, is separated from his mother,

Jamila. The independent Jamila had refused to marry the man her family chose for her and had settled in Egypt with her beloved.[62] Again, intrigues and family tragedy place Jamila in the royal harem, where the women of the harem display great kindness to her. She befriends them, and they try to comfort her.[63] Her son, Ghurayb, rescues a woman named Karima from her husband, a drunken emir who constantly abuses her. When he takes her away from her husband, he protests, shouting: "Why do you take my wife [away] from me? Is she not my property with whom I can behave as I wish?"[64]

The texts introduce both new and old elements from Zaydan's political philosophy. A liberal and an admirer of the worldwide bestseller *Self-Help* by Samuel Smiles (translated into Arabic in 1880), Zaydan bemoans the state in which political oppression causes an industrious merchant to lose his business and all his wealth.[65] The texts, interestingly, distinguish between the slaves of the ruler and domestic slaves — that is, slaves owned by private individuals. The latter are presented as being part of the family, sharing its joys and miseries, and being as upset as their masters are when a son is taken away.[66] 'Abd al-Rahman's family is by no means a dysfunctional household, as was the case with the Hamidian family. Moreover, these texts accentuate the closeness between women in the harem, the supportive relationship between the kind female slaves (who are not presented as idle or animalistic), and the general feeling of companionship. The company of women seems to save both Salima and Karima from angry despots. Writing on women's camaraderie and social gatherings in harems of the past, Zaydan could have been thinking about the women's associations which existed in the Egypt of his day. Women's solidarity, in other words, might relate to the modern phenomenon of women's salons, reading groups, and societies. In such venues, women gathered to discuss social and cultural themes and devoted much effort to increasing other women's education, exposure to literature, and knowledge of hygiene and household management. In 1909, for example, one of Egypt's most famous feminists, Huda Sha'rawi (1879–1947), argued that upper-class women should instruct working-class women in hygiene and health for their families.[67] The novels' slaves and mistresses, both old and young, thus consult and comfort each other in the harem, and act as a unified group of women.

Alternatively, the wife's fear of the bey's temper — which, unsurprisingly, bears distinct similarities to the temperament of Sultan 'Abd al-Hamid — links the text to Zaydan's later work. In *Al-Mamluk al-sharid*, abuse of women is associated, at least in the mind of the emir, with Islamic law: he justifies his abuse by claiming that Islamic law permits him to act in such a way. The novel *Shajarat al-Durr* also features the manipulation of Islamic law by politically corrupt elements. The female villain of the text is furious that her rival, Shajarat al-Durr, is to become "the first queen in Islam" and claims that political power given to women is an unwanted innovation (*bid'a*).[68] The villain explains: "I know womankind [*jins al-nisa'*]. *They do not keep promises*. I am not saying that Shajarat al-Durr is like this, but women in general are like that. And this is supported by what the books of religion say about women as well."[69] Like the violent emir, she uses Islam (here represented by "books of religion") to oppress fellow women and to obstruct the rise of a new and just form of political governance.

One can hear a multiplicity of voices in Zaydan's novels: the residents of harems, slaves, and women all echo a plethora of colonial, Arab, Egyptian, Syrian Christian, and Ottoman discourses. The texts of Zaydan examine the seclusion and marginality of women and slaves. Trying to look beyond the paralyzing gaze of the male despot, the novels redefine feminine marginality by portraying a series of binaries (men/women, despot/liberal, harem/modern household) that records the influence of the male gaze and breaks down its power. At the same time, however, the texts speak with a European voice, with images of female idleness associated with the harem—a view that also became prominent in Arabic publications. The representations of women in these texts, in other words, constantly shift between the readings of colonizers and those of local males, and simultaneously introduce new Arab and Ottoman discourses that attempted to reverse the terms of these colonial and male perceptions.[70]

A CAGED DESPOT: SECLUSION AND TYRANNY IN *AL-'ABBASA UKHT AL-RASHID*

The contemporaneous nature of Zaydan's medieval novels confirms previous assumptions conveyed in the Mamluk/Ottoman novels. The Abbasid novels (*Abu Muslim al-Khurasani* and *al-Amin wa al-Ma'mun*) analyze political despotism and women's rights, containing abundant descriptions of Abbasid slave girls, mistresses, and wives. To investigate how these relationships of power operate within the medieval novels, let us now turn to *al-'Abbasa ukht al-Rashid aw nakbat al-Baramika* ('Abbasa, sister of [Harun] al-Rashid, or the catastrophe of the Barmakids), a novel first serialized in *al-Hilal* in 1906 and published as a book in 1911. It narrates the marriage of Ja'far al-Barmaki, the Persian vizier of the Caliph Harun al-Rashid (786–809), and the caliph's sister, 'Abbasa. According to the story, Harun al-Rashid did not know of the relationship, and its discovery resulted in tragic events that altered the fate of the Abbasid regime.

Although the word *harīm* is never mentioned, the novel examines many themes prevalent in harem-related literature: liberation of slaves, criticism of arranged marriages, and the hypocrisy of men who selectively apply and manipulate religious law. These themes position the text in a realm far beyond the confines of the Abbasid period. Like its Ottoman counterpart, the Abbasid harem is constructed according to Orientalist imagery, as a space of dubious morality, espionage, surveillance, rivalry between women competing for power, and illicit sexuality.

In Zaydan's imaginary, the Abbasid golden age is quite similar to the period of the Mamluks' rule in Cairo and to the Hamidian era. Harun al-Rashid and 'Abd al-Hamid have similar characteristics: like 'Abd al-Hamid, Harun al-Rashid is paranoid, and his paranoia is manifested spatially by means of the construction of secluded spaces in Baghdad. The city is thus divided into separate spaces for men and women, for Arabs and Persians, for rulers and ruled. Baghdad is depicted as having walls and fortified palaces, revealing a city whose rulers fear their subjects. The opening paragraph of the novel cleverly sets the atmosphere by informing the reader that Baghdad was fortified by the second Abbasid caliph, al-Mansur (r. 754–75), to guard the elite from Shiʿi and Khurasani rebels. Al-Mansur, therefore, encircled the city with three walls and created separate quarters for himself. The image of Baghdad as the prototype of a tyrant kingdom is reflected in the fact that Baghdad's famous name, *madinat al-salam* (city of peace), is nowhere mentioned in the novel.[71]

Harun al-Rashid's temper and constant caprices make him a duplicate of 'Abd al-Hamid. Like 'Abd al-Hamid, he suffers from insomnia, walks around his palace garden in order to relax, and is cruel to animals out of an innate sadism. One key scene sets Harun al-Rashid in the palace garden, near the cages of the wild animals, where he sees a caged lion: "Possibly, the admiration for the lion's power and the astonishment produced by watching it tempt one's soul to resemble a creature of that sort." He asks the keeper to throw food to the lion, and, after a while, to hold the food at a distance, evidently to tease the hungry lion. In response, the animal walks irritably back and forth in its cage, as the keeper laughs at its hunger.

Harun al-Rashid, the narrator tells us, shared the lion's anger: "A beast has nothing to prevent it from showing its emotions; it roars in its fright in its cage, whereas a reasonable man ['aqil] controls his fury and prevents himself from killing his prey . . . [Al-Rashid] thought of himself as a wise lion . . . The lion's roar suddenly scared al-Rashid and so he hinted to the keeper to feed the beast . . . Al-Rashid spent a while pondering this [scene], and he became convinced that if he could control his anger against his subjects, and if he could overpower his own rage, he would be a prudent lion."[72]

The Abbasid monarch, like the Ottoman autocrat, is a prisoner of his temper and beastly desires. Caged and secluded himself, he is torn between rationality and animal-like behavior. At the end of the novel, his inhumane, animalistic qualities will take over. When Harun hears that his sister, 'Abbasa, had clandestinely married Ja'far, the narrator depicts the caliph using the same vocabulary in which he had described the caged lion. Enraged, Harun al-Rashid decides to kill both his sister and her husband. After his sister's execution, he is depicted as striding back and forth in his chambers, exactly as the lion paced in its cage.[73]

Philipp believes that Herbert Spencer's political theory inspired Zaydan's philosophy. According to Spencer's theory, man and beast are born with innate love for themselves and everything that is of use to them. The type of animal-like government epitomized in Harun al-Rashid's character eliminates possible differences between animal and man.[74] More importantly, the text reveals how, in the absence of legal mechanisms to restrain imperial power, both monarch and subjects turn into caged, fearful, animal-like creatures. The paranoia and fears of the ruler thus force seclusion on himself and his subjects.

As in al-Inqilab al-'uthmani, women in this novel pay a tragic price for the autocrat's unrestrained power. The racist Harun al-Rashid does not allow his sister to marry a descendant of the mawali (Persian converts to Islam) and kills her when she defies him. Shortly before her execution, 'Abbasa turns to her brother and says: "I wish to remind you of the slave girls and mistresses you have in your palace. They are many. You do not see anything wrong in enjoying them, although Islamic law forbade them to you. How, then, can you thus forbid my legal marriage to a man? Is this not oppression?"[75]

'Abbasa also notes that the caliph's wife provides him with concubines and slaves that roam his palace in the hundreds. 'Abbasa's miserable state is yet again an outcome of autocratic rule. Both as political ruler (the caliph) and as the oldest man in the family, Harun al-Rashid enjoys an authority that places him above the law. He can therefore denounce his sister's marriage as illicit and sinful, even though it is legal according to Islamic norms. The true reason for his objections to the marriage is his xenophobic stance—namely, his rejection of Persian converts to Islam in favor of "pure" Arabs. Given the very contemporary nature of this political allegory, it is no wonder that 'Abbasa's passionate speech against polygamy, which highlights the virtues of marrying for love, sounds more like a speech by Huda Sha'rawi than the utterance of an Abbasid princess.

Thus, al-Rashid's patriarchal role is closely associated with tyranny, echoing the characters of 'Abd al-Hamid and the oppressive Mamluks from Zaydan's modern novels. In all of these cases, the rulers are tyrannical, erratic, and short-tempered. Nonetheless, when discussing slavery, *al-'Abbasa ukht al-Rashid aw nakbat al-Baramika* introduces new points regarding women's seclusion. The novel's opening chapters are devoted exclusively to the slave trade and introduce us to a Jewish slave trader by the name of Pinhas.[76] One of his clients is the evil politician al-Fadl ibn al-Rabi', the rival of Ja'far al-Barmaki. Pinhas offers Fadl a wide selection of slaves, of both sexes and all races: white, yellow, and black, including Slavs, Turks, Persians, Armenians, and Berbers. Young white girls go for the highest prices. The differences between the slaves are marked spatially: Fadl moves from room to room, and in each room he sees another ethnic or racial group of slave girls. In the first room, he observes "a group of white, extremely young, girls, the oldest of which was barely ten. They were all naked, covered with nothing but rags that barely concealed their genitals. The harshness of the desert was evident on them; their hair, not touched by a comb since the day they were born, was let loose. But the sight of natural beauty was evident in the glowing whiteness of their faces, mixed with a touch of redness, attesting to the health of their bodies . . . Among them were blondes, green-eyed women, and brunettes . . . Every time the door was opened and they saw Fadl and his men, they bolted like gazelles escaping the hunters. Fear appeared on their faces, but the room was too narrow to allow their escape."[77]

When Fadl appears uncomfortable that these girls are so young, Pinhas repeats the "rags to riches" narrative (also used in the Ottoman context to justify slavery): being sold into slavery, he says, saved them and brought them to civilization (*madaniyya*) and a comfortable life. In the next room, Fadl sees "girls of black flesh, with curly hair, and flat noses. Fadl knew they were the daughters of the black races [*zunuj*]. They were the closest to filthiness and barbarism in comparison to the slaves of the first room. Black is the ugliest of colors and is only rarely compatible with beauty."[78] These black slaves, the reader is informed, are sold cheaply and are used either for hard labor or as servants of white female slaves. The last rooms contain white slaves in their teens, who arouse the sexual appetite of all the men present.

The racial hierarchy of the slaves is interesting. On the one hand, the text parodies the language of both modern colonizers and champions of slavery, since the vicious slave trader justifies himself by saying that enslavement is a way of bringing female slaves into civilization. On the other hand, as it seems to echo the descriptions of slave girls for sale by the French writer and traveler Gérard de Nerval, the text exposes the racism of Zaydan himself because it is the authoritative narrator—and not Fadl or Pinhas—who describes the blacks as ugly and filthy. The depiction of blacks as animalistic creatures is analogous to the animal-like description of the black slave in the Ottoman harem. We view the slave girls from the perspective of the men who gaze at them (Pinhas and Fadl) from open doors and windows.

Commenting on the racial categories evident in *al-Mamluk al-sharid*, Stephen Sheehi translates the following passage: "One of the monks opened the door. The person who was knocking was a tall, black slave [*'abd aswad*]. . . . At his side there was a breathtaking woman wearing black clothes of mourning, and in the hands of the slave, a child. . . . The monks were amazed by the great contrast between the beauty and pure whiteness of Jamila and the ugly face of her black servant."[79]

Sheehi notes that the racial comments are used to establish a contrast between races and colors, and concurrently to signify an aberrant, irregular family structure in which a black slave—rather than a wife—is holding the baby. The abnormality of the family is therefore established by the dichotomies between beautiful and ugly, white and black, and princess and slave.[80]

Although the description of slaves in the text is accompanied by quotations from Abu al-Faraj al-Isfahani's *Kitab al-aghani*, this portrayal also refers to a modern Egyptian context.[81] While slavery in Egypt was abolished in 1877, the slavery discourse continued to take place in the public sphere. Some of Zaydan's descriptions of the Abbasid slave trade must have sounded familiar to Egyptian readers. As Gabriel Baer has shown, in the nineteenth century, slaves in Egypt were classified and assessed according to skin color, race, and sex. While white slaves were far more expensive, black female slaves were used for domestic service and as concubines.[82] Further-more, the question of marriage, so central in the novel, was critical to the Egyptian culture as *qadis* (judges) refused to perform marriages of manu-mitted female slaves.[83] There were evidently similarities between Abbasid slavery, as depicted in the novel, and nineteenth-century Egyptian slavery. Therefore, Zaydan's stance on slavery was not just a metaphor for despotic power but also a contemporary commentary on the practices of selling and buying humans during the first seventy years of the nineteenth century, practices whose abolition was discussed in print.[84]

The issue of slavery was also intertwined with the fact of Western inter-vention in the practice. Western consuls (especially British ones) pressured the Egyptian government to free the slaves. In the 1870s, European offi-cials were involved in expeditions against slave dealers.[85] Zaydan, we should note, joined the 1884 British expedition to the Sudan to rescue General Charles Gordon, serving as a war correspondent and interpreter.[86] Zaydan might have thus been influenced by the dominant Western view of his time that portrayed Africans as laggards in the march for progress.

Zaydan's description of al-Amin's slaves is yet another interesting blend of Orientalist and medieval Islamic sources. Al-Amin, a strong and beauti-ful boy of seventeen, has discovered the joys of youth; he has become par-ticularly fond of slaves. The medieval sources emphasize his indulgences even more. He spent most of his time in his palace and was so enamored of his male slaves that his mother had to dress his female slaves as young men in order to lure him to sleep with them.[87] Zaydan describes al-Amin's re-lationship to his slaves more modestly: "Al-Amin clapped his hands and a Turkish boy entered. He was beautiful and was not yet in full youth . . . This boy resembled a girl . . . if you heard him speak you would be certain he was a girl . . . and the palace of al-Amin had many slaves like him. Al-Amin made it a point to bring them from the furthest parts of the Turkish lands to serve him."[88]

The narrator also emphasizes that the slaves were not Arab: "As soon as they uttered a word, the listener realized that Arabic was not their lan-guage. Some of them were Slavs and others Turks or Byzantines, and most were new to Baghdad."[89] Al-Amin's palace has strong feminine over-tones; it is a colorful site decorated with flowers and populated by exotic birds, and a place of singing and dancing. Unlike other male characters, who are portrayed as performing manly actions (riding horses, carrying weapons, coming back from wars), al-Amin spends most of his time inside his palace, behind sealed walls, a behavior more associated with women in the harem. The only time al-Amin leaves his palace is to visit his mother. Inside the palace, we find items—such as silk cloths, flowers, and musical instruments—that are usually associated with females rather than males. Al-Amin's clothes (colorful garb, a bonnet of flowers) and his choice of companions stress his feminized traits.

Although al-Amin is not a significant character in the plot, the descriptions of his palace, feasts, and behavior take up almost thirty pages in the novel.[90] These descriptions are important to the plot because they show how al-Amin, the future caliph, lacks political capabilities, and this is viewed as the unfortunate outcome of his father's disciplinary methods. In the same manner that 'Abd al-Hamid corrupted his son, al-Rashid's self-seclusion created a feminized male who does not even desire to leave the palace, and whose future capabilities to rule as caliph are questionable at best.

There remains, however, another problematic issue, which is al-Amin's homosexuality. Zaydan had to take into account notions of middle-class propriety among his readers. As Michel Foucault has shown, the Victorian discourse on sex, particularly homosexuality, became confined to the medical, professional field (under the purview of psychiatrists, physicians, and so on), and moved outside of the realm of daily conversation.[91] In the Middle Eastern context, Qasim Amin concurred with the Victorian approach when he complained that Egyptians discussed inappropriate sexual themes in public and in front of their children.[92] Zaydan, then, could not talk freely about such themes, and thus he adopts a complex writing technique in which his text addresses its audience on two different levels. The first level is for readers who were familiar with the medieval sources and, hence, with much more graphic descriptions of al-Amin's interaction with his slaves. For such readers, each of the details provided by the author about al-Amin is linked to a network of intertextual references. The second level is for readers who were not familiar with the medieval sources and relied on the text itself for information. For them, such descriptions would imply only that the caliph failed in disciplining his son.

Most significant, however, is the depiction of feminized space and the existence of slavery. If al-Rashid's (and 'Abd al-Hamid's) tyranny was apparent in his irrational and violent behavior both within his household (concerning his sister) and outside it (concerning his subjects), al-Amin is an Oriental monarch of a different sort: sexualized, idle, and indifferent.

The presence of male slaves, al-Amin's homosexuality, and indulgences in the pleasures of the flesh all evoke the ambience of the palace as a harem. Al-Amin himself has taken on the role of the feminized male who seeks seclusion.

Badr classifies *al-'Abbasa ukht al-Rashid aw nakbat al-Baramika* as an educational novel based on Zaydan's introduction, in which he states: "We have tried in this novel to simplify Islamic history and to describe the events of the Arabs and the rest of the Muslims."[93] The novel, as we have seen, also alluded to very contemporary issues, such as women's seclusion and the relationship between slavery and tyranny. Zaydan wrote in *al-Hilal* that the Abbasids were often unjust to their subjects, as exemplified in the behavior of both Amin and al-Rashid and the brutal massacres that occurred when the dynasty came to power.[94] Zaydan could have stressed other, more positive aspects of al-Rashid's period, such as his alleged contacts with Europe and the development of trade. Al-Rashid enjoys a positive image in some Islamic sources as a benevolent and religious caliph. The popular image of Harun al-Rashid in the *Arabian Nights* portrays him dressed in simple clothes to conceal his identity, so that he could learn about his subjects' problems.[95] Zaydan, however, chose to ignore all these positive traits as they interfered with his desire to depict Baghdad as analogous to the corrupt Hamidian space. In his historical studies, but not in this novel, Zaydan divided the Abbasid period in two: first, a prosperous period of golden days (*izdihar*), which included al-Rashid's period, and then an era of decline.[96] Thus the Baghdad of Harun al-Rashid in Zaydan's novel—as opposed to its representation in his historical texts—is a nest of political intrigues and characterized by racism and violence.

Zaydan insisted on the historical veracity of his novels and told his readers that he offered an accurate account of the past. Although he noted that historians and storytellers disagreed as to the causes of the fall of the Barmakids, his novel was to "put forward the political, cultural and historical reasons" for their fall, using the "form of a love story [*qissa*]." He underscored the variety of historical sources he used to further indicate the truthfulness of his representations.[97] Yet the educational and pedagogical aims of the novel distanced it from its presumed historical authenticity, and brought the past much closer to the present.

In discussing timid and mistrustful monarchs like al-Rashid and 'Abd al-Hamid, Zaydan created the impression that tyrants were afraid of their subjects. Tyrants, we are repeatedly told, wish to seclude themselves from people, be it women or their own male subjects, because they fear to share power. The construction of al-Rashid and 'Abd al-Hamid as emblems of autocracy prevailed in intellectual debates of the future generations. Salama Musa noted that "it is not in the interest of our constitutional nation to praise Harun al-Rashid or al-Ma'mun since both were dictatorial rulers just like 'Abd al-Hamid."[98] Sati' al-Husri, however, asserted that the regimes of 'Abd al-Hamid and Muhammad 'Ali were inspired by absolutist European models as much as they were by Islamic forms of governance.[99] The basis for this comparison, and for characterizing both 'Abd al-Hamid and al-Rashid as oppressive rulers, had been established in Zaydan's historical novels.

CONCLUSIONS: QUEEN VICTORIA IN THE AZBAKIYYA GARDENS

Although this chapter has presented a few fictional texts by Jurji Zaydan that comment on harems and political tyranny, my (modest) claims about Zaydan's novels are historical. Zaydan was a participant in the discourse on women and strongly protested against their seclusion. He likewise cautioned that the unsupervised powers of autocrats had devastating political, social, and cultural effects. Spatially, he used the harem as both a domain under the sultan's coercive grip and, concurrently, a site of female compassion that protects women from imperial and irrational power. Zaydan's historical novels should be read as political allegories that examine the problem of tyranny, while linking tyranny in general to the oppression of women in particular—and as written in a multilevel style appropriate for vastly different audiences.

The similarities between Harun al-Rashid and 'Abd al-Hamid indicate that Zaydan wrote at a time when the national Arab narrative that contrasted a golden Arab past and Ottoman decadence had not fully crystallized. A letter that Zaydan wrote to his son may elucidate his approach:

> Your decision to learn Turkish made me very happy. It is the language of our government, after the gloom of tyranny has been disappeared, after knowledge has prevailed over ignorance and after the constitution has been proclaimed, our time has come to demonstrate to the other nations that we are a living nation who know to gather and unite and that we help our government with our tongues . . . The rise of the Committee of Union and Progress and its victory over the old and despotic party, is a

sign of the prevalence of knowledge over ignorance, because the men of that party were ignorant, greedy and despotic people, while the members of the Committee of Union and Progress are all philosophers, poets, and educated people. The former shed blood, the latter avoid it.[100]

Zaydan, whose images of slavery and freedom appeared in Ottoman plays and novels, was still thinking in Ottoman-imperial terms. However, his portrayal of 'Abd al-Hamid as an emblem of tyrannical, anti-Christian terror was an image that became dominant in later years among Arab nationalists, most noticeably George Antonius. Nonetheless, the negative image of the sultan as an autocrat was already taking shape in Arab, Ottoman, and European circles of the time. Incidentally, the mélange of almost every possible negative quality in the persona of 'Abd al-Hamid (sadism, paranoia, misogyny, despotism, irrationality, and a hot temper), synthesized from both local and European sources, is what makes his character so entertaining (at least for this reader).

Zaydan's novels responded to, appropriated, and commented on themes discussed by prominent intellectuals in print and in the writings of Muhammad 'Abduh, Qasim Amin, and Tal'at Harb. His historical novels convey the modern ideas that women should be educated in order to improve the quality of their households; that an egalitarian relationship between an educated man and an educated woman is the key to a good marriage; and, finally, that seclusion of women is simply unjust and unfair. These ideas are exemplified by Zaydan's portrayal of the idle concubines in the harem of Yildiz; the suffering of 'Abbasa and Shirin, who cannot (at least initially) marry the men they love; the resemblance of the imperial harem to a jail; and the incessant secrets and intrigues in the households of imperial tyrants. A man who is a polygamous tyrant in his own household, in other words, can never be a civilized person either inside or outside his house. As Montesquieu's *Persian Letters* suggests, the rebellion against the harem system, as shown in *al-Inqilab al-'uthmani*, is indeed *the* revolution against authoritarianism and is equated with the moment of political liberation in 1908.

Reading against the grain, however, exposes Zaydan's own racism and the implication of the hybridization of colonial knowledge by a colonized subject. His novels are also acts of appropriation, in which the colonized wishes to claim the right to reform himself, and to reform by himself his own subaltern population (in this case, women) by employing the colonizers' language. The appropriation of Western voices introduced new ideas

to Zaydan's texts: the Oriental images of black slave girls who resemble
animals, and the coded talk about homosexuality (acknowledging its existence, yet avoiding describing it directly because of notions of middle-class
propriety).

The novels of Zaydan point to the impossibility of regarding East and
West as separate entities since they merge together in each novel and, in a
sense, in each harem. Seen from this perspective, it is interesting to examine the opening lines of Zaydan's 1893 nonhistorical novel *Jihad al-muhibbin*
(the battle of lovers): "On June 21, in the year 1887, the people of Cairo celebrated fifty years of the rule of Queen Victoria, the Queen of England. They
decorated the Azbakiyya gardens with lights. Alone and in groups, people
gathered in the garden: women, men, and children, from all communities
and all walks of life."[101]

Although the rule of Queen Victoria began before the occupation of
Egypt, it becomes part of Egyptian time. This conception of time, moreover, becomes part of the Egyptian novel that uses the date as a point of reference. This date likewise affects Egyptian space itself (the decoration of the
Azbakiyya gardens). The images of women, harems, and despots similarly
collapse the categories of East and West as these images are amalgamated
into new metaphors borrowing from both Middle Eastern and Western
sources.

NOTES

I thank Samah Selim, Farouk Mustafa, Marilyn Booth, and the press's readers for
their comments. All translations are mine, unless otherwise indicated.

1 For Arab Syrian intellectual production in Egypt, see Reid, "The Syrian Christians
and Early Socialism in the Arab World," *The Odyssey of Farah Antun*, and "Syrian
Christians, the Rags-To-Riches Story, and Free Enterprise"; Kenny, "East versus
West in *al-Muqtataf*, 1875–1900."

2 Philipp, *Gurgi Zaydan* and "National Consciousness in the Thought of Jurji Zaydan"; Crabbs, *The Writing of History in Nineteenth-Century Egypt*; Di-Capua, "The
Thought and Practice of Modern Egyptian Historiography, 1890–1970"; Reid,
"Cairo University and the Orientalists," 62–64. On Zaydan's perception of his
dismissal from the university, see his letter dated October 12, 1910, translated and
quoted in Philipp, *Gurgi Zaydan*, 210–14.

3 In a letter to his son, dated March 28, 1912, Zaydan claimed that other authors
"tried to imitate me in writing historical novels about Islam and were unsuccessful."
Zaydan influenced, and was influenced by, other authors of historical novels. This
similarity is manifested in choice of titles. Zaydan often used "Maiden[s] of . . ." in
his titles (*'Adhra' Quraysh*, 1889; *Ghadat Karbala'*, 1901; *Fatat Ghassan*, 1898, *Fatat*

al-Qayrawan, 1912); this phrase also appeared in the titles of many historical novels of the time (for example, Ahmad Sa'id Baghdadi, *Ghadat Jabal Anasiya*, 1897; Ahmad Shawqi, *'Adhra' al-Hind*, 1897; 'Abd al-Rahman Isma'il, *Ghadat al-Andalus*, 1899; 'Abd al-Masih al-Antaki, *'Adhra' al-Yaban*, 1906; and Sa'ada Murli, *Fatat al-Busfur*, 1911). 'Abd al-Muhsin Taha Badr and Matti Moosa note that other historical novels, such as Khalil Bey Sa'ada's *Asrar al-thawra al-rusiyya* (1905), Farah Antun's *Urshalim al-Jadida* (1904), and Ya'qub Sarruf's *Fatat Misr* (1905) dealt with themes similar to the ones discussed by Zaydan. Labiba Hashim's *Qalb al-rajul* (1904), for example, examined religious minorities, a theme explored in Zaydan's novels. In *Shirin* (1907), she situated an Armenian woman in a Sassanid palace; it might be the case that Zaydan's *al-Inqilab al-'uthmani* was inspired by Hashim's *Shirin*. See Philipp, *Gurgi Zaydan*, 217; Badr, *Tatawwur al-riwaya al-'arabiyya al-haditha fi Misr*, 409–21, 116–84; Moosa, *The Origins of Modern Arabic Fiction*, 219–52.

4   For the rise of the press in Egypt, see Ayalon, *The Press in the Arab Middle East*; Cole, "Printing and Urban Islam in the Mediteranean World, 1890–1920."

5   Baron, *The Women's Awakening in Egypt* and "Readers and the Women's Press in Egypt"; Booth, *May Her Likes Be Multiplied*; Ziegler, "Al-Haraka Baraka!"; Cannon, "Nineteenth-Century Arabic Writings on Women and Society."

6   Booth, *May Her Likes Be Multiplied*, especially chaps. 1–3 and 5–7; see also the comparison between Zaydan and Zaynab Fawwaz in her "On Gender History . . . and Fiction." See also Badr, *Tatawwur*, 123 (on translations in *Fatat al-Sharq*) and Moosa, *The Origins of Modern Arabic Fiction*, 91–121 (on Egyptian and Syrian translators in the nineteenth century).

7   On the genre, see Badr, *Tatawwur*, 116–84.

8   Sheehi, "Doubleness and Duality," 90–105; Musa, *Al-Yawm wa al-ghad*, 236; Ayyub, "Mu'amarat al-aghbiya'," in *al-Athar al-kamila li-adab Dhi al-Nun Ayyub*, vol. 1, pp. 3–50.

9   Two notable exceptions are Di-Capua and Sheehi.

10 See also Booth's brief comparative reading of Zaydan's novel *Armanusa al-Misriyya* in Booth, "On Gender, History . . . and Fiction," 234–37.

11 See the chapters by Shissler, Micklewright, and Booth in this volume.

12 Cole, "Printing and Urban Islam in the Mediterranean World, 1890–1920," 344–64.

13 Amin, *Tahrir al-mar'a* and *al-Mar'a al-jadida*. On the debate, see Ahmed, *Women and Gender in Islam*, 144–68; Cole, "Feminism, Class, and Islam in Turn-of-the-Century Egypt."

14 See Hourani, *Arabic Thought in the Liberal Age, 1798–1939*, in particular 73–83 (on the opinions of Tahtawi), 88–94 (on the opinions of Khayr al-Din al-Tunisi), 173–92 (on debates among Lutfi al-Sayyid, 'Ali 'Abd al-Raziq, and others, and the question of the caliphate). On debates about the meanings of 1876, see Cole, *Colonialism and Revolution in the Middle East*, 118–22. On the 1876–1909 period, see Kayali, "Elections and the Electoral Process in the Ottoman Empire, 1876–1919" and *Arabs and Young Turks*, chaps. 1 and 2.

15 Reid, "Cairo University and the Orientalists," 62.

16 Boer, "Despotism from under the Veil," 43. See also Zonana, "The Sultan and the Slave." See also the critique of the Orientalist construction of the harem in the chapters in this volume by El Cheikh, Schick, and Micklewright, as well as Micklewright's discussion in her chapter of the ways in which Ottoman elites appropriated Orientalist imagery.

17 Lowe, "Rereadings in Orientalism," 119.

18 Ibid., 124.

19 See Inge E. Boer, "Despotism from under the Veil: Masculine and Feminine Readings of the Despot and the Harem, *Cultural Critique*, no. 32 (Winter, 1995–1996), 43–73.

20 Connelly, *Arab Folk Epic and Identity*, 3–25.

21 See Nadia Maria El Cheikh's chapter in this volume.

22 Hourani, *Arabic Thought in the Liberal Age, 1797–1939*, 277.

23 Philipp, *Gurgi Zaydan*, 78.

24 See Homi Bhabha's formulation of colonial hybridity in "Signs Taken for Wonders." See also Partha Chatterjee's comments on the Bengali novel in *The Nation and Its Fragments*, 8.

25 The first edition of Zaydan's *al-Mamluk al-sharid* appeared in 1891.

26 The first edition of Zaydan's *Asir al-Mutamahdi* appeared in 1891.

27 The second edition of Zaydan's *Istibdad al-Mamalik* appeared in 1893.

28 The first edition of Zaydan's *al-Inqilab al-'uthmani* appeared in 1911.

29 Rizas, *Abdul Hamid*. See also Dorys, *The Private Life of the Sultan of Turkey*. The English translation by Hornblow informed its readers that Dorys was the pen name of the son of "the late Prince of Samos." The author's father had worked as the sultan's minister and gave the author information about the sultan's private life. Dorys was a member of the Young Turks. Many of the novel's descriptions of the physical structure of the Yildiz Palace, its inner politics and intrigues, and its harem are taken from Dorys's book.

30 Zaydan, *al-Inqilab al-'uthmani*, 228. Dorys also says the sultan was fond of Machiavelli's *Prince* (Dorys, *The Private Life of the Sultan of Turkey*, 176–77).

31 Zaydan, *al-Inqilab al-'uthmani*, 227.

32 Abu Muslim al-Khurasani (700–55), a general of Persian origins, was killed by the Abbasid Caliph al-Mansur, despite the seminal role he had played in the Abbasid revolution and in their rise to power.

33 On the development of the term *kadın*, see Peirce, *The Imperial Harem*, 108.

34 Zaydan, *Asir al-Mutamahdi*, 12.

35 Baron, "Readers and the Women's Press in Egypt," 222. See also the analysis of the educated girl as a model of virtue in the writings of Salim Bustani, in Moosa, *The Origins of Modern Arabic Fiction*, 162.

36 Young female characters in early novels by Arab women and men were often portrayed in the acts of reading and writing, Booth has argued, acts that sometimes saved them. See Booth's chapter in this volume and her "Fiction's Imaginative Archive," 282.

37 On the Armenian spies, see Dorys, *The Private Life of the Sultan of Turkey*, 234–35.

38 Zaydan, *al-Inqilab al-'uthmani*, 265.

39 Ibid. Dorys also provides descriptions of the imperial harem, in which women are smoking, playing with animals, and busy with intrigues, on the one hand, and fearful of the sultan's rage, on the other hand (*The Private Life of the Sultan of Turkey*, 241–43).

40 Zaydan, *al-Inqilab al-'uthmani*, 270.

41 Ibid.

42 Ibid., 278.

43 Ibid.

44 Ibid., 279.

45 Ibid.

46 Ibid., 280.

47 Philipp, *Gurgi Zaydan*, 78.

48 Zaydan, *al-Inqilab al-'Uthmani*, 292. Dorys devotes much space to the sultan's hate of the Armenians and argues that the sultan's mother was Armenian, although the sultan refused to acknowledge this. Zaydan repeats this claim. See Dorys, *The Private Life of the Sultan of Turkey*, 1–3, 81.

49 Zonana, "The Sultan and the Slave," 602.

50 Toledano, "Late Ottoman Concepts of Slavery (1830s–1880s)," 490–94, 503–1. See also Toledano, *Slavery and Abolition in the Ottoman Middle East*, 112–35.

51 See the similar assertions of Amin, *Tahrir al-Mar'a*, 60–63; see also his views on the connection between veiling and idleness (*batala*) in *al-Mar'a al-jadida*, 61–62.

52 Zaydan, *al-Inqilab al-'uthmani*, 96. Dorys also speaks about the sultan's inability to sleep and recurrent nightmares (*The Private Life of the Sultan of Turkey*, 177–79).

53 Zaydan, *al-Inqilab al-'uthmani*, 96–102.

54 The text refers to two victories. One is that of chapter 70, titled "A Glorious Victory" (*fawz bahir*), in which the concubine decides to escape the harem; the second is "The Greatest Victory," that of the Young Turks.

55 On the period, see Hanioğlu, *Preparation for a Revolution*.

56 Zaydan, *Istibdad al-mamalik*, 7–8.

57 Ibid., 70.

58 Ibid., 71.

59 Ibid., 74.

60 Ibid., 76.

61 Ibid.

62 Zaydan, *al-Mamluk al-sharid*, 110.

63 Ibid., 27.

64 Ibid., 27. Karima, it should be noted, used to be married to another Mamluk, before their massacre by Muhammad 'Ali. The drunken emir, described by her as a beast (*insan mutawahhish*), is her second husband.

65 Philipp, *Gurgi Zaydan*, 12, 68–69. On Smiles, see also T. Mitchell, *Colonising Egypt*, 108–11. Zaydan often celebrated those who strove for personal achievements. Writing about his mother, he noted that although she was illiterate, she hated laziness, admired hard work, and "found time to conduct some business at home" (Zaydan, *The Autobiography of Jurji Zaydan*, 27).

66 For a more realistic depiction of the harshness of domestic slavery, see Toledano, *Slavery and Abolition in the Ottoman Middle East*, 54–80.

67 Badran, "Dual Liberation," 16.

68 Zaydan, *Shajarat al-Durr*, 42.

69 Ibid., 74. Emphasis added.

70 I am paraphrasing in this paragraph the words of Eric Meyer about the ways in which one could look at the European harem literature. See Meyer, "'I Know thee Not, I Loathe Thy Race,'" 683.

71 Zaydan, *Al-'Abbasa ukht al-Rashid aw nakbat al-baramika*, 5–7.

72 Ibid., 214–16.

73 Ibid., 297.

74 Philipp, *Gurgi Zaydan*, 80.

75 Zaydan, *Al-'Abbasa ukht al-Rashid aw nakbat al-baramika*, 269.

76 Ibid., 12. On Jewish slave traders in the ninth century and their role in the traffic of slaves from central and western Europe to the Islamic empire, see "'Abd" in *EI*², 1:24–40.

77 Zaydan, *Al-'Abbasa ukht al-Rashid aw nakbat al-baramika*, 50.

78 Ibid.

79 Sheehi's translation ("Doubleness and Duality," 96) is of *al-Mamluk al-sharid*, in volume 7 of *Mu'allafat Jurji Zaydan al-kamilah* (Beirut: Dar al-Jil, 1981), 232–33.

80 Sheehi, "Doubleness and Duality," 96.

81 On the integration of colonial and Egyptian discourses about race, see Troutt Powell, *A Different Shade of Colonialism*.

82 Baer, "Slavery in Nineteenth Century Egypt." See also Toledano, *The Ottoman Slave Trade and Its Suppression, 1840–1890*, 205–19.

83 The documents Baer uses referred to manumissions of 1878–80. See Baer, "Slavery in Nineteenth Century Egypt," 436 (n. 130), 438 (n. 140).

84 See Troutt Powell, *A Different Shade of Colonialism*. See also Shafiq's 1892 treatise *Al-Riqq fi al-islam* (113–20), which includes articles that both Shafiq and Ahmad Zaki had published on slavery in *al-Mu'ayyad* and speeches delivered by Shafiq on the subject. On the effects of Shafiq's book, see Toledano, *The Ottoman Slave Trade and Its Suppression, 1840–1890*, 276–78; Baer, "Slavery in Nineteenth Century Egypt," 440 (Baer also refers to ideas published in *al-Manar*).

85 Baer, "Slavery in Nineteenth Century Egypt," 430–36.

86 Moosa, *The Origins of Modern Arabic Fiction*, 197.

87 El-Hibri, *Reinterpreting Islamic Historiography*, chap. 3.

88 Zaydan, *al-'Abbasa ukht al-Rashid aw nakbat al-baramika*, 123.

89 Ibid., 122.

90 The following chapters in *al-'Abbasa ukht al-Rashid aw nakbat al-baramika* deal with al-Amin and his palace: 20, "The Palace of al-Amin"; 22, "Muhammad al-Amin"; 23, "The Brining of the Rams"; 24, "The Harem"; 25, "A Singing Party"; 26, "The Singers and Abu Nuwas"; and 27, "Satirical Poems."

91 Foucault, *History of Sexuality*, vol. 1.

92 See Amin, *Tahrir al-mar'a*, 61 (a complaint about the fact that when women gather, they talk about explicitly sexual topics), *al-Mar'a al-jadida*, 65–66 (a complaint

about the fact that Egyptian children were exposed to talk about sex when their relatives were present in their homes, hearing stories about what happens between a man and his wife, listening to songs about sensual love, and seeing sensual dances).

93 Quoted in Badr, *Tatawwur*, 94; see also 93–107.

94 Zaydan, *Al-Hilal* 18, no. 2 (November 1909): 119–22.

95 El-Hibri, *Reinterpreting Islamic Historiography*, chap. 2. See "al-Baramika," *EI²*, 1:1033–36.

96 Zaydan, *Ta'rikh al-tamaddun al-Islami*, 2:37–119.

97 Zaydan, *Al-Hilal* 18, no. 2 (November 1909): 119–22.

98 Musa, *al-Yawm wa al-ghad*, 236.

99 al-Husri, "On Islamic Unity and Arab Unity," in *Abhath mukhtara*.

100 Philipp, *Gurgi Zaydan*, 78.

101 Zaydan, *Jihad al-muhibbin*, 1.

12 • THE HAREM AS THE SEAT OF MIDDLE-CLASS INDUSTRY AND MORALITY

The Fiction of Ahmet Midhat Efendi

A. Holly Shissler

 Ahmet Midhat Efendi (1844–1912) was an essayist, novelist, translator, and newspaper editor. During his career he produced more than two hundred works, and the newspaper he founded, *Tercüman-i Hakikat*, which appeared from 1878 to 1922, was one of the most important serial publications of the nineteenth century.[1] He was known for producing popular treatises on philosophy, religion, history, and economics, and his fiction was so successful in his own day that one of the leading contemporaneous works of Western scholarship on the Middle East called him "the most important author of modern Turkey [*sic*]."[2] Though modern scholars have sometimes dismissed his treatises as mere vulgarizations and his fiction as ham-handed teaching tools rather than works of art, it is undeniably the case that Ahmet Midhat's interest in reaching a broad audience led him to adopt a writing style that was both engaging and remarkable for its clarity.[3] His success as a popular writer made him influential, and his fiction, in particular, allowed him to expound his ideas to the widest possible public without attracting too much attention from the censor.

Ahmet Midhat's works concern themselves with issues that were deemed of immediate importance in his own day, and because this is as true of his fiction as it is of his essays, one finds many of the same underlying themes in both. One of his principal areas of concern was economics, since he saw capitalism as a fundamental aspect and cause of progress. In fact, Hilmi Ziya Ülken has pointed out that economics occupied Ahmet Midhat's attention more consistently than any other topic, and his writings on the subject were among his most deeply thought through. From the 1850s onward, as François Georgeon has shown, economics had assumed importance among Ottoman intellectuals as an object of study and discussion. Many who engaged the topic accepted the principles of liberal economics, and indeed of liberalism more generally. Those thinkers gave credence to the idea of individual freedom and individual enterprise as the engines of innovation and prosperity.[4] At the same time, many Ottoman intellectuals of the nineteenth century, familiar as they were with the explanation for European progress and capitalist development prevalent among European writers, believed that the nuclear family and companionate marriage correlated with the development of modernity and modern capitalism. The idea that the move from the patriarchal family and arranged marriages to the nuclear family, companionate marriage, and the development of "modern" sentiments within the couple was connected to the rise of capitalism had been present in European thinking since the late eighteenth century.[5] Ottoman thinkers therefore came to see companionate marriage as the incubator of men who possessed the qualities of individualism and were capable of exercising personal, economic, and political freedoms.

Ahmet Midhat's approach to economics, embodied in four works that appeared between 1879 and 1889, differed from the dominant laissez-faire economic attitudes in several important ways. While he extolled the modern, disciplined workforce and advocated a strong work ethic, he also defended social provisions for the poor and rejected the classical notion that charity encouraged laziness or subsidized low wages. While praising the enterprising spirit of the private individual, he dwelt on the need for social solidarity, including measures like protective tariffs, if conditions such as relatively late industrial development or the existence of unequal trade agreements and concessions between the Ottoman Empire and European powers made them necessary. In similar fashion, Ahmet Midhat embraced the supposed link between family structure and capitalist development, with its emphasis on companionate marriage. He believed that family life should not be autocratic and ill-matched strangers should not marry, if one wished to construct a productive and healthy society. But at the same time, in his novels as in his economic essays, Ahmet Midhat privileged social solidarity over the notion that private vice produces public good. Contrary to that notion, he thought that private virtue produced public good, and that public good had a role in securing private virtue. He viewed the couple and the private life of the family, properly constituted, as the first and most perfect embodiment of a principle of social solidarity. Thus, many of his stories deal with domestic arrangements and address questions like companionate marriage, the seclusion of women, slavery, and prostitution, and they often pay a remarkable amount of attention to financial arrangements and the financial or economic underpinnings of various situations.

The institution of the harem—that is, the removal of women from the world and their placement under male protection, even while leaving them the freedom to move about, properly accompanied, wherever they wish— is seen by Ahmet Midhat as protecting the deepest structure of the family from market forces. The harem is for him the manifestation of a man's obligation to maintain his family, an obligation that is the cornerstone of the family understood as a unit of complementarity and love. A man who assumes the responsibility of maintaining a household with dependent women in it is both happier and a more productive member of society than a man without such a household. Above all, Ahmet Midhat's depictions of the life of the well-ordered harem are a rejection of the principles of self-interest, competition, and unfettered individualism as the drivers of progress. His fiction urges a different understanding of self-interest, one that values individual choice and freedom, but sees real self-interest as distinct from selfishness. The well-grounded individual in the bosom of a happy family feels a sense of responsibility to himself and others. He is industrious and also inclined to altruism. To illustrate this, I will contrast two of Ahmet Midhat's novels: *Felâtun Bey ile Râkım Efendi* (Felâtun Bey and Râkım Efendi), published in 1875, and *Henüz 17 Yaşında* (just seventeen), published in 1881, and I will attempt to show what aspects of the institution of the harem, properly realized, were regarded by Ahmet Midhat as central to the construction of a good society. Before undertaking such a comparison, a brief clarification of what I mean by harem—or rather, what I think Ahmet Midhat meant by it—is necessary, as well as a brief plot summary of each of the two novels.

The term *harem* often calls to mind the elaborate and sensually imagined women's quarters in the house of a great and wealthy man or dynasty, as in the case of the Ottoman imperial harem. But in the Ottoman Empire and other parts of the Middle East, the term had a much broader meaning. As Leslie Peirce has defined it: "A harem is by definition a sanctuary or a sacred precinct. By implication it is space to which general access is forbidden or controlled and in which the presence of certain individuals or certain modes of behavior are forbidden. That the private quarters in a residence, and by extension its female residents are also referred to as a 'harem' comes from the Islamic practice of restricting access to these quarters, specifically access by males beyond a particular degree of consanguinity with the resident females."[6]

In this chapter, I will broadly follow Peirce's definition. However, Ahmet Midhat's novels depict the domestic arrangements of modest households in the nineteenth century, not the Ottoman imperial harem in the early modern period. Since his protagonists did not dispose of large living spaces with numerous rooms, I will use *harem* to mean the women in a household that was organized in such a way that the women restricted their social contacts to other women and to men of their immediate family circles, never going out without the protection of a male guardian or a much older slave woman, while male visitors were confined to a specific room or two when they called on the family. In *Henüz 17 Yaşında* and *Felâtun Bey ile Râkım Efendi*, Ahmet Midhat does not use the word *harem* much, though the books have this arrangement of a family's affairs and the consequences of those arrangements for society at their core. However, his satirical short story of 1875, "Bekârlık Sultanlık mı Dedin?" (so the bachelor life is a king's life, you say?), does mention the word in its lively description of the implications of such arrangements for personal happiness and household thrift:

> In Cihangir [a neighborhood of Istanbul] in a tight little four-room box of a house one can see an ordinary family made up of a mother, a daughter, and a son-in-law. There is a male servant in the public rooms and a black slave woman [Fedayî Kalfa] in the harem to serve the family. Nevertheless, the mother-in-law, because she is solicitous to make sure that her son-in-law's property isn't going to waste and that everything is running smoothly and because she is a real women's woman, reviews one by one the price of each item the servant orders from the market and afterward pays the money accordingly, and every day she goes down to the kitchen five or ten times to carefully oversee the slave woman's work. The young wife for her part spruces herself up each day

as though she were a new bride. And only she looks after her husband's evening tray and takes care [of him] . . . And so this happy son-in-law cannot understand the validity of the judgment expressed in the saying "the bachelor life is a king's life" nor the cleverness of refusing to emerge from bachelorhood and enter the house of life. And even [his] budget is so well on track that the expenses of the [whole] large household are covered by fifteen gold *lira* each month and the addition of ten gold *lira* to his estate [through savings] enhances his well-being.[7]

If we consider the description of Râkım Efendi's home in *Felâtun Bey ile Râkım Efendi*, with its three little rooms and kitchen below the stairs, inhabited by the master of the house, Râkım; his concubine and future wife, Canan; and his old black slave woman, Dadı Kalfa, who carries out all the heavy labor of the household, we can see that the environment being described is almost identical.[8]

SYNOPSIS OF THE NOVELS

Felâtun Bey ile Râkım Efendi compares the progress of its two eponymous heroes, Felâtun Bey, the spoiled scion of a wealthy family who squanders his patrimony on chasing women and senseless entertainments, and Râkım Efendi, the product of a modest background who, through hard work and thrift, establishes himself comfortably in the world. The real hero of the story, who occupies most of the reader's attention, is Râkım Efendi. Râkım was left fatherless at a young age. His mother and her black slave, Fedayî Dadı (also referred to as Dadı Kalfa), get him through his childhood by dint of hard work and sacrifice, with his mother taking in sewing and Dadı Kalfa hiring herself out as a washerwoman. Râkım studies French and begins to earn a modest living as a translator and scribe at a young age. After his mother dies, he lives alone with Dadı Kalfa, who keeps his house and manages the money. Râkım's unstinting efforts lead to additional work translating documents for private clients and teaching Ottoman Turkish to foreigners. His work ethic and sober habits place his life on a stable footing. Thus we see Râkım as an attractive, intelligent, energetic young man, now well fixed professionally and financially, with an impeccable reputation. Felâtun Bey, by contrast, is the only son of a wealthy man. His father, Mustafa Merakî Efendi, entranced with all things modern and fashionable, insisted that Felâtun be taught at a Western-inspired school and dressed in the latest European fashions. Upon leaving school, Felâtun received a sinecure in a government office where he rarely deigned to appear, though he was a regular in all the European-style nightclubs and theaters.

One day Râkım sees a Circassian girl of fourteen for sale, and on impulse he buys her. He names her Canan, and over the next year he attends to her education, teaching her to speak Turkish and French; to read and write in Ottoman Turkish, Persian, and Arabic; and to recite Persian poetry. Her education is topped off by piano lessons from a Christian woman, Madame Josefino, who is a friend of Râkım's and who gives lessons to the *cariyeler* (female house slaves) of neighboring wealthy households. Canan, who is very innocent, quickly becomes enamored of her master, but is unable to articulate her feelings.

During the course of this year, Râkım's friendship with Madame Josefino deepens, and he begins an affair with her. At the same time, he is giving Turkish lessons to the daughters of an Englishman, Mr. Ziklas, and the elder of these, Jan, is gradually becoming infatuated with Râkım. Felâtun, meanwhile, is catting about town, playing the dandy and making a fool of himself. When his father dies, he inherits a large fortune and in short order takes up with a French actress, Mademoiselle Polini. He spends enormous sums entertaining her and begins to gamble.

Madame Josefino, who is considerably older than Râkım, is fond of him and also of Canan. Over time, therefore, she deflects Râkım's affection for herself onto Canan, encouraging his feelings for her. Eventually, Râkım begins having sexual relations with the slave girl. One day, the Ziklas family visits Râkım's house, and Jan Ziklas perceives the nature of the relationship between Râkım and Canan. She falls seriously ill as a result of melancholy and frustrated love. In desperation, her father offers her in marriage to Râkım, even promising him great sums of money if he will agree, but Râkım refuses, saying that his heart is already engaged. Felâtun, meantime, has lost all his money through his entanglement with Mademoiselle Polini. Once his money is gone, their relationship founders. Then the scales fall from Felâtun's eyes. He seeks a real and respectable position as a provincial administrator and bids Râkım farewell, swearing that he will live a modest life and repay all of his debts honorably. Jan Ziklas recovers in the end from her heartsick condition, and Râkım marries Canan and becomes the father of a son.

In this novel, Râkım Efendi is the very spirit of capitalism—sober, hardworking, educated, and aware of his familial and professional responsibilities. Felâtun Bey is his lackadaisical opposite. The son of a wealthy family, he is a product of privilege and dependence, relying first on money from his father and a government sinecure, and later on his inheritance. Only superficially educated, he is a slave to the latest fashions, a spendthrift, a skirt chaser, a gambler, and a blowhard.

Henüz 17 Yaşında begins with two friends of the *esnaf* (organized guilds) class, Hulusi and Ahmet Efendi, going to the theater one night in Beyoğlu, where they get caught in a rainstorm after the show. This, combined with their having had rather too much to drink, leads to their being unable to get a cab home and also unable to find a room for the night in Beyoğlu. They wind up spending the night in a nearby brothel. There the philosophical Ahmet Efendi meets Kalyopi. Though uninterested in her physically, he becomes fascinated with Kalyopi's situation and keeps returning to the brothel, where he questions her minutely to learn both her story and the details of her arrangements with the establishment. Kalyopi comes from an upper-middle-class Christian family in Aya Stefanos (Yeşilköy). Her father made his money in the tobacco business. When that sector began to contract because of the Régie,[9] he opened a nightclub (*meyhane*) on the first floor of his house. There, Kalyopi came into contact with a young Muslim man who secretly courted her with sweet talk and gifts. Kalyopi was encouraged to pursue this connection by her older sister, who saw it as a way for the sisters to get the jewelry — so necessary for their dowries — that their father could no longer afford. When it became clear to the suitor, Yümni Bey, that the girls would never present his case for marriage to their father, he kidnapped Kalyopi and married her legally before witnesses. Kalyopi was happy and her family resigned, but the Christians in the village were infuriated by what they viewed as a Muslim outrage. They brought the case before a judge and intimidated Kalyopi, promising that if she told the judge she didn't want to be with Yümni Bey, they would give her money for a dowry to marry a Christian, but saying that if she stuck with Yümni Bey, sooner or later they would kill her. Out of fear and naiveté, Kalyopi renounced Yümni Bey. Thereafter, however, her family was forced to leave the village, their reputations and fortunes ruined.

They moved to a poor section of Istanbul, where her father could not find work and the women tried to earn money by taking in laundry. The family was starving. An old female friend of the family appeared, offering to take Kalyopi with her to her house in Beyoğlu, where she could work as a seamstress. In reality, however, this woman earned her living more as a call girl than as a seamstress, and soon Kalyopi was in the same situation.

This, however, required her to have new clothes, perfume, jewelry, and so on, and she was also trying to send money home to her family. She soon fell into debt with local merchants. Shortly thereafter, a spurned suitor mortally stabbed her older sister. The medical and funeral bills made Kalyopi's debt unmanageable, and she sold herself to a brothel, managed by Dudu, for money to pay off her debt. This, of course, meant that Kalyopi could not leave the brothel until she paid back the money. The financial arrangements at the brothel were managed in the following way. The girls—and they were girls, often as young as thirteen—gave a portion of every client's fee to the house. In addition, they paid the house for meals, laundry, toiletries, and necessary clothing items like socks and underwear, all at exorbitant prices. Thus, no matter how many clients they saw, night after night, their debt to the house only grew. This section of the story, where Ahmet Efendi questions Kalyopi in detail about the functioning of the brothel, is remarkable for its frankness in discussing the young age of the girls, the fact that many were sold to the brothel by their parents, the danger of disease, and the frequent physical violence endured by the girls and women of the house.

After understanding all of this, Ahmet Efendi determines to rescue Kalyopi. He pays off her debt, though it is big enough to be a burden to him. He sets her up with her parents in a rented house of her own. He assures her that his only desire is her freedom, and he promises her that if she ever finds a suitable man whom she wants, he will help her to marry. After a year, Ahmet Efendi takes aside a Christian lad, who is an employee in a friend's establishment. He tells the young man Kalyopi's whole story and arranges the marriage she has always desired. Thus, in the end, Kalyopi is married in white in a joyous church ceremony.

MARRIAGE, FREEDOM, AND THE HOUSEHOLD

A number of Ahmet Midhat's views on the role of the family, love, and social solidarity can be seen in these story lines, with the complementary relationship of helpmates embodied in an upright man and his properly arranged harem standing for social solidarity and the productivity and good order it engenders. First among these is the idea that productive marriages are companionate marriages, based on a choice made by two individuals who feel affection for one another (or at least who are so well suited to one another that such an affection might be expected to grow between them), who are free to make the choice to marry, and who have the capacity to do so. Flowing from this is the further idea that the two spouses should be appropriate to one another in terms of age, education, intelligence, and beauty. Unions made without choice or between individuals who are not suitable for each other will be lacking in genuine affection and will result in misfortune. It is worth emphasizing here that while genuine affection is key, this conception is not a plea for romantic love, which Ahmet Midhat regards as an ill-conceived flight of passion. Rather, affection is the outgrowth of appropriateness. Both novels address head-on the issues of the freedom and ability to choose one's mate, and of the suitability of one's choice. They are an assault on the cold, authoritarian marriages of patriarchal tradition, but they equally condemn romantic liaisons based solely on lust or emotion and lacking pragmatic foundations.

In the case of *Felâtun Bey ile Râkım Efendi*, the contrasting fates of the two title characters could hardly be any sharper. Râkım marries a woman he knows well and has come to love, after he has seen the world and had the chance to meet a number of women. For her part, Canan is sufficiently educated, thanks to Râkım's generosity and her native intelligence and industry, to be a real companion to him. Râkım has facilitated, under the proper protection, Canan's getting out a bit, seeing things, meeting other women, and being offered different possibilities. Early in their relationship, Râkım stresses that Canan is free to go anywhere she wishes (though never alone—only if Dadı Fedayî is with her). So, when she chooses him, he can be assured that her choice is based on genuine sentiments and not because she lacks other opportunities. Râkım's own affection for Canan is put to the test by Madame Josefino, who informs him that one of her wealthy clients has offered to purchase the girl for 1,500 pieces of gold, a great sum of money and ten times more than Râkım paid for her. Râkım rejects the idea with evident discomfort, but feels compelled to mention the offer to Canan. Here it must be remembered that being sold to a wealthy Ottoman gentleman was considered a great chance at upward mobility for a Circassian slave girl, especially since, if she became an odalık (i.e., sexually involved with her owner) and bore him sons, she gained considerable status and power.[10] Thus Râkım is understood to be offering Canan a kind of golden opportunity. Canan shows herself resigned to accepting Râkım's will in the matter, but is deeply distressed at the idea of leaving him. Râkım urges her to accept the offer, saying that surely she would be made an odalık in her new home, and in addition he would send with her all the clothes and gifts he had already given her, and would give her whatever sum the buyer paid for her. She would become a rich woman in a great house, with a strong possibility of becoming the mother of an heir. Canan refuses the offer tearfully. Thus, when Canan and Râkım do become sexually involved, Ahmet Midhat has made it very clear that theirs is a real choice based on real affection, other options having been considered and rejected. Moreover, the appropriateness of the two lovers is repeatedly emphasized. At several junctures in the novel, Madame Josefino points out that Râkım and Canan are both young, attractive, diligent, and respectable. Madame Josefino, though a good woman of whom Râkım is genuinely enamored, is ultimately to be avoided as a partner in life because she is inappropriate, particularly as regards her age (she is forty, he is twenty-five). When Râkım expresses surprise that she is pushing him into Canan's arms, Josefino exclaims: "Did you really take me for one of those theater whores? I have a heart! A heart!"[11] She herself later tells Râkım that had he become more deeply bound to her, a great deal of harm could have ensued. Yet the genuine and constructive love that arose between Râkım and Canan was not the fruit of a sudden passion, of love at first sight, but of a gradual sympathy that grew up between two individuals who were properly suited to one another.

Felâtun's emotional life and family background provide a contrast to Râkım's happy choices. In Felâtun, we see the effects of marriages that are not based on the principles of choice and appropriateness — the wellsprings of genuine affection — but rather are grounded in transitory and superficial emotions like lust and the desire to be fashionable. Felâtun's grandfather believed in early marriages and, as a result, Felâtun's father, Mustafa Merakî Efendi, was married at the age of sixteen to a girl of twelve. Though these family arrangements might be viewed as in some sense traditional, they are not the type that Ahmet Midhat viewed as the cornerstone of a modern, progressive society, and he is quick to show their negative effects. Felâtun's mother, a bride in an arranged marriage to a boy who never knew what it was to make his own way in the world, and then a mother at a very tender age, was dead at twenty-six. Felâtun, the product of that union, was raised in a manner that was both indulgent and subject to his father's whims.

As a man, Felâtun is never required to work for a living or to show any self-discipline. He seeks only inappropriate objects of desire that flatter his vanity or slake an immediate thirst for pleasure. First he trifles with one of the Ziklas family's serving girls, a young woman he does not really know and toward whom he has no real feelings. After his father's death, Felâtun, now a wealthy man in his own right, gets involved with the French actress, Mademoiselle Polini, but their relations are superficial and based purely on each one's desire for self-gratification, not on any real meeting of the minds. Thus, for example, Ahmet Midhat describes an argument between Mademoiselle Polini and Felâtun where she derides him for not taking his gambling losses like a man, then orders him to leave when he complains that he doesn't like her telling him what to do at the gaming tables. The author explains that a woman of Mademoiselle Polini's type is always looking for a pretext to quarrel with a man, seeking ultimately to enthrall him more fully and make him pay more dearly for the privilege of her company. During their rupture, Felâtun can think only that a man of his superior qualities ought to be able to buy a dozen Mademoiselle Polinis.[12]

THE MUTUALITY OF HAPPINESS

One of the most important factors to note in these stories is that in the case of Felâtun and Polini, their passion is based entirely on the vanity, selfishness, and desire for self-gratification of each, whereas Râkım and Canan's love takes the shape of each one striving to see to the well-being and happiness of the other. No sacrifice is too great in this regard, and no limitation deriving from this desire is really experienced as a limitation. In particular, both Râkım and Canan reject offers of pecuniary gain and social advancement for the sake of love, and both, though they have certain rights or liberties, decline out of love to make use of them. Though Râkım had the legal right of sexual access to Canan, he could not conceive of employing it unless she wished it. Though he had the right to refuse to sell Canan as well as the right to profit from her sale, he recoils from both notions—the decision is hers, and the profit of any sale must be hers as well. Though legally Râkım was free to contract a marriage with Jan Ziklas, with its attendant possibilities of social advancement and an offer of considerable wealth, his love for Canan causes him to refuse. For her part, Canan is passionately eloquent in embracing the bonds of love. Offered the chance to attach herself to another household as a rich woman, she replies tearfully: "I don't want 1,500 pieces of gold, I don't want clothes, I don't want diamonds. I want you, sir! I want you. Let me be your slave, let me be your chattel. That's enough happiness for me." Râkım then says that she should stay with him, but as his sister rather than his slave. This Canan also tearfully rejects, saying only that she wants everything to be as it was before: "I won't be your sister. To be your sister won't give me the same pleasure as being your slave. I say that I have been happy with my situation up till now. If you are not going to sell me to make a profit and tend your own interests, then let me kiss your feet and serve you, sir. Leave me as I was. When you say 'Canan' again (as you used to do), all the world is mine, while if you say 'my sister,' I won't be able to feel the pleasure that I used to feel in my heart."[13]

The important point here is the presence of possibilities that the parties choose not to pursue out of love. This is self-interest rightly understood; truly free individuals grasp that human relations cannot be commodified, because the real benefit to the self is in benefiting the other. To fail to grasp this has distinct consequences for the economic and moral well-being of both individuals and society.

THE HAREM AND TRUE FREEDOM

Both *Felâtun Bey ile Râkım Efendi* and *Henüz 17 Yaşında* make vivid comparisons between the apparent freedoms of a totally selfish and mercenary system and the supposed oppression of being shut up in a harem. Canan the cariye is a harem girl—her master is uncomfortable with her going outside the confines of the house without supervision ("If you are not with her," he says to Dadı Kalfa, "I cannot accept Canan's setting foot outside the front door") and when he finds her going to the neighbors' house for piano lessons, he prefers to buy a piano and arrange for lessons at home.[14] Likewise, when the Ziklas family visits his house in order to experience authentic *alaturka* life, Râkım explains to them that strict segregation of the sexes will be maintained at his house: "You won't be able to see any women; you will only see a black [woman's] arm thrusting a platter through the room's door."[15] Yet Canan is free in Ahmet Midhat's conception: she can visit any part of the city in Dadı Kalfa's company, and her every want is supplied in the three rooms with kitchen and garden that are the family home. Râkım ensures that the world comes to her there. After all, Canan does get her piano lessons.

Kalyopi's forced entrance into the world, in contrast, is the cruelest oppression. Ahmet Midhat consistently uses the symbol of the cariye and the imagery of slavery to emphasize the difference between the false freedoms of a market-driven intimacy and the real liberation of the bonds of affection. Even the story of Kalyopi's first marriage is designed to emphasize the contrast: Yümni Bey kidnaps and marries the young Kalyopi after his long, secret courtship of her fails to result in her father's permission for them to marry. Yet this marriage born of abduction is portrayed as a happy one. Yümni Bey experiences marriage as an incentive to a sober and responsible life, and he is a good provider to Kalyopi, who has grown fond of him.[16] Her subsequent forced separation from him and entry into the outside world is an act of tyranny and the root of all her subsequent misfortunes. As we shall see, Ahmet Midhat always casts Kalyopi's indebtedness and her being forced to give herself to any client who comes along in terms of slavery and of buying and selling for money. He regards prostitution as a European innovation, and he compares the condition of a prostitute very unfavorably with that of a cariye: "Hey, Europeans! Here you are tossing around a few words about the promotion of civilization and the love of freedom and trying to block slavery in Turkey. Among us, however, no slave would ever be sold in whorehouses like these to service the lowliest scoundrels."[17] And he further observes that whereas Ottoman Christian girls are more likely to fall into prostitution than Muslim girls because of the burdens the dowry system places on poor families, this system is also a European innovation: "Nowadays, the thing which is called the 'apparatus' by Christian peoples who wear local coverings on their heads is of the same style as it is among us Muslims. But a lot of local Christians took on European customs as soon as they put [European-style] hats on their heads, and they have come to deem the dowry as a fundamental part of marriage. Have we forgotten that until yesterday Armenian women were veiled? And don't we see that in Anatolia and Arabia Christian women are still as virtuous and veiled (*mestur*) as Muslim women?"[18]

Once Kalyopi is free of the brothel, she wishes to seclude herself entirely and not be seen by any strange man, not even a doctor. The return to placing herself under the protection of an individual man, first Ahmet Efendi and later a second husband, and her withdrawal from the world and gradual seclusion from the company of strange men, are her choice and the utmost expression of her freedom. Kalyopi is both a Christian and a fallen woman, so her circumstances and options are naturally different from, say, Canan's; Kalyopi can never recapture what her life would have been with Yümni Bey. The possibility of romantic love between Kalyopi and her benefactor, Ahmet Efendi, a respectable Muslim man, is discounted in the novel. Such a joining could not lead to happiness, given the inappropriate disparities between the two parties. But Ahmet Efendi's protection can slowly recreate the conditions of spacial and social boundaries and inner freedom that do allow for Kalyopi's ultimate happy marriage to a poor, but honorable and hard-working, man. Ahmet Efendi tells her after he has rescued her from Dudu's establishment and begun to set her up in a home of her own: "You are going to be completely free and act in whatever way your spirit moves you . . . Not even I am going to accost you . . . What I want from you is not for you to be a slave . . . [rather] what I want from you is a very great thing: first, to know that I am really and truly your friend and second to tell me if there is any man your heart desires without hiding from me anything that is in it. [That way] I may unite you with that man decently."[19]

The considerable space that Ahmet Midhat devotes to explaining the economic and financial circumstances of Kalyopi's fall into prostitution, and especially of the operations of the brothel, allows him to display the slavery and impoverishment that arise from seeking selfish individual plea-sures in the absence of any feeling of responsibility or human regard. A crass and monetary conception of self-interest and human worth is put on display and judged harshly. First of all, the utilitarian attitudes of the brothel's clients are juxtaposed with the duplicity of the girls, and the two are clearly revealed to be the result of one another. Kalyopi says of herself and the others working in the house: "What are we? We are creatures, like animals, who can never love anyone in the world. When a client buys us, he expects affection from us, and pleasure, but no matter how much affection, desire, and pleasure we show for him, it is all a lie. Isn't this the way it is? We don't go to him because we want to; we go to earn our fees."[20]

The flip side of this dynamic is revealed when, in explaining the workings of the brothel to Ahmet Efendi, Kalyopi recounts the story of Cüneyd, a regular client of one of the young women in the brothel, Lasimaki. Lasi-maki is fond of Cüneyd and laments all the money he is wasting on fre-quenting the establishment. She often urges him to buy up her debt, saying that they could live together for a fraction of what the brothel is costing him, and he wouldn't have to share her with anyone. Cüneyd's answer is always the same: "If I were going to shut myself up and stay at home with a woman who would be only mine, I would get married. I don't need a wife, I need a turn-on. She swishes her hair around the way I like and I enjoy myself freely. I do whatever I want. When I get bored [with her], I'll take a fancy to someone else. So, that's the way that is."[21]

The mercenary relations between the men and the girls are further con-textualized in terms of the relationship of the young women and the clients to the brothel and its proprietress, Dudu. When Ahmet Efendi and Hulusi leave the place after their first visit, Kalyopi says to her friend and fellow prostitute, Agavni, that it's a shame that Dudu has overcharged the men so much. Agavni replies: "Shame shmame! What are they to me? The stupid asses shouldn't have paid [so much]." When Kalyopi protests that they were nice guys, not asses, Agavni replies sharply: "Men who are not stupid asses don't come here." She adds: "I've met a lot of smart guys like them. They talk a good game, but in the end when it comes time to pay, even they know that if there is one true thing in the world, it's money." Then Agavni gives Kalyopi this advice:

> Anyway, since you like Ahmet Efendi, try to make him like you . . . [Then] when the guy shows up, order the best *rakı* and *mezeler*, and lots of it. None of this bean salad and salted mackerel stuff! Do you understand? Good food! Fine food! Get Dudu invited as well. Even ask for a present for Dudu, if you can talk the guy into it. Get it? Don't be in a hurry for yourself; once he's given something to Dudu, he'll definitely give you something for yourself too. That way, Dudu won't treat you like the other girls. Listen to what I am telling you: if you want to be somebody, do as I say. Otherwise, you'll stay in the brothels with [nothing but] your nightly fees, and you won't earn a thing; it'll all be for nothing.[22]

Kalyopi explains the situation with brutal clarity to Ahmet Efendi. She and the other women were either sold to the house by their parents or else sold themselves to pay off debts or because they were starving: "Anyway, I came here and settled and stayed because of that debt [of mine]. I became Dudu's chief capital."[23]

That these arrangements are soul killing seems obvious, but Ahmet Midhat also lays out the larger social and economic implications. Sparked by a comment of Kalyopi's, Ahmet Efendi calculates in his mind the value of the money wasted in such establishments:

> The nightly fee for a man to stay in a place like this is a *lira* and a half. If nothing else, there will be a half *mecidiye* in tips for the guide. Add on the money for three or four bottles of raki and that makes two [more] *mecidiye*. In the morning, a *mecidiye* in tips to the waiters. Another *mecidiye* in the bathhouse for a bar of soap. It comes out to 260 to 270 *kuruş*. But what's the capital of a man who sells fruit and vegetables with a basket on his back from morning till night? If he had fifty *okka* of grapes

on his back and he sold them with his profit included at forty *para* each, it comes to fifty *kuruş*. That is, fifty *kuruş* could be the capital of a poor man. That means 270 *kuruş* is the capital not of one poor man but of five . . . A man who came here from Anatolia with that much money would be able to start a business and both take care of himself and pay his taxes back home. What's more, in three to five years he'd save up five or ten thousand *kuruş* and go back. Uff!! The money we squandered in one night was really a great sum [when you think about it that way]. We up and threw away enough money to set up not one but several poor men. But anyway most of us don't come here with money we earned ourselves. We come here with money that our parents either earned or got from a government post which they were appointed to on account of having connections.[24]

The men who frequent houses like Dudu's are men with inherited wealth and government sinecures—that is, men like Felâtun Bey. Having failed, for whatever reason, to establish happy nests with women and children whom they take responsibility for protecting and maintaining, they waste their substance and the country's. The commodification of human relations, especially those between men and women, is demonstrated to have ruinous economic and moral effects on the individual and the larger society. A perfect illustration is the separate expeditions made by Felâtun Bey and Râkım Efendi to the popular Istanbul picnic site at Kağıthane. Râkım organizes a trip with Canan, Fedayî Dadı, and his friend and erstwhile mistress, Madame Josefino. The trip takes place on a weekday when the location will be deserted. The group leaves in the dark, traveling by rowboat up the Golden Horn by the light of the moon and stars. They bring their own food with them; near dawn, they stop to drink some fresh milk that they buy from a shepherd. Finally they come to an idyllic spot on the riverbank, where they spend the rest of the day hardly seeing anyone else. They eat, drink tea, swim, play tag, and stroll along the river. In the evening after a final meal, they row home again.

A few days later—on a Friday, when the riverbanks are swarming with people—Mademoiselle Polini appears in an open carriage drawn by two horses. She is loaded down with jewelry, and Felâtun follows her, mounted on a fine horse. The two of them spend a couple of hours there listening, together with five or six seated gentlemen, to two troupes of musicians. They are attended by vendors with an endless stream of trays offering ice cream, sweets, and other delicacies. The patrons throw money to the musi-

cians as the latter play requests, both Turkish and European. Finally Felâtun and Polini move on, while the crowds follow them with their eyes and
comment that the gentleman is throwing money away with both hands, but
is surely enjoying himself in princely fashion. The money, we later learn,
comes from gambling.[25]

The contrast between Râkım's day and Felâtun's — the one private, intimate, long-lasting, based on simple pleasures and well within the man's
means; the other a public spectacle devoid of real human contact, short-
lived, ridiculously expensive, and beyond the man's means — could hardly
be more extreme.

The two novels are eloquent throughout on the connection between
good finances and economy on the one hand, and happy, moral families
on the other hand. Râkım is an industrious, self-made man, the product of
a loving harem inhabited by his mother — for a time — and a devoted slave
who has raised him from childhood and loves him like a son. Once he is
securely established in life, he purchases the cariye who over time develops
into a young woman suitable to be his wife. Though free to move about as
she wishes, she is at all times under his protection and is never in the world
without that protection. He continues to work hard in order to be able to
provide that security, and the women in his harem — Canan and Fedayî
Dadı, both nominally slaves — manage his money and house with supreme
efficiency and economy. Canan is free to come and go as she pleases, but
she wants for nothing and seldom goes out. Ahmet Midhat describes her
circumstances:

> As we said before, whatever fashion took hold in Istanbul, Canan was
> one of the first to sport it. Besides this she had in her closet patterned
> fabrics of the highest quality. A few diamond brooches, some earrings,
> and rings were not lacking in her dresser. A week didn't go by that Râkım
> didn't give Canan for her own use eighty or a hundred kuruş in bright
> gold or silver coin. But what was Canan going to do with the money? She
> never went out and lacked for nothing, so what was there to spend it on?
> She gave it all to Dadı Kalfa, and Kalfa put it aside and after it had accu-
> mulated at bit she would have Râkım Efendi use it to purchase a new
> ring, watch, necklace or some other little piece of fine workmanship for
> Canan. Is it necessary to say more?[26]

Felâtun, on the other hand, spends money freely on gambling, theaters,
nightclubs, and living in expensive hotels with a mistress. He even re-

proaches Râkım for working too hard and never enjoying life: "Work, work, work! What is all this work? When are you going to be done, man? The money you've earned already is enough. Look to spending those earnings a little." Without knowing the truth of Râkım's domestic situation, he tells Râkım that he needs to get himself a foreign mistress because Ottoman ladies are stuffy, stiff, and uninteresting, while in the case of a cariye: "What pleasure can free men like ourselves take from a slave? Who knows where her heart [really] is? Because she is your slave she is compelled to submit to you." The irony here, of course, is that Mademoiselle Polini doesn't love Felâtun at all and leaves him as soon as his money runs out, whereas Canan becomes the perfect loving wife. Listening to Felâtun, Râkım almost lets out a belly laugh and thinks to himself: "Hey stupid, doesn't a slave have a heart? It's not a matter of buying a girl's freedom for five or ten kuruş. Gain her heart and see what a helpmate she turns out to be!"[27]

Just as the stories of Râkım and Felâtun show us the best and worst that different models of family life can to do to society and the economy, so *Henüz 17 Yaşında* shows us the moral and familial evils of a breakdown in the economic order. The first factor in the chain of events that results in Kalyopi's downfall is the interjection of foreign powers in the Ottoman economy in the form of the Régie, and the collapse of the tobacco business of her father, Yorgaki. As the story continues, Yorgaki's economic circumstances deteriorate ever more, and with them his ability to protect the women in his family and his moral compass. From tobacco merchant he moves to meyhane operator and finally to beggar. For a time, his wife and daughters support him and the family through washing and sewing, and finally Kalyopi enters into prostitution. The utter failure of the father's ability to protect his family materially and spiritually is embodied by the fact that he knows how Kalyopi is supporting him and the rest of the family, but he does not act to stop her, simply turning away from the truth. In fact, the women of his family have become a kind of unacknowledged capital for him, as Kalyopi is for Dudu. Harsh economic circumstances have broken down the fabric of the family and exposed it to the brutal and corrosive forces of the market. Ahmet Midhat sees this as a failure of the state and the society at large, and also as the root of the moral destruction of all members of the family.[28]

This is why, in order to free Kalyopi from the slavery of prostitution, not only must she be removed from the scene of her enslavement and restored to a virtuous life of freedom and seclusion, but her father also must be restored to his role as protector. Though initially Kalyopi is returned to her family home, her rescuers, Ahmet Efendi and Hulusi, do not regard Yorgaki as trustworthy. Hulusi warns Yorgaki that Kalyopi is now under Ahmet Efendi's protection [himaye] though she may be living in her father's house, and so Yorgaki had better not try to compromise the girl again. Hulusi berates Yorgaki: "If nothing else, couldn't you have worked selling water on a bridge? How could you not be ashamed to subject such a girl, seventeen years old and [innocent] like an angel, to the worst [possible] house of horrors? . . . After this, if you ruin the girl again, you are the one who will end up ruined. But Kalyopi won't be ruined again [for] she will not lack Ahmet Efendi's protection."[29]

Very soon after, Ahmet Efendi decides that it is necessary to move the whole family to a new house, in a new neighborhood. There, over a period of months, he works to restore both the fortunes of the family and also their morals—which, of course, he sees as inextricably intertwined. He rents a house for the family and furnishes it bit by bit; he and Hulusi often visit Kalyopi to share meals with her, and often when they do so, they also make her gifts of jewelry in a brotherly way so that she will be outfitted like any other nice, marriageable young woman. Yet at the same time, Ahmet Efendi hires strange men to go to Kalyopi's house and offer her large sums of money if she will agree to "entertain" them. He wishes to be assured not only that she has been removed from the material causes of her fall, but that its mark on her consciousness has been removed—that is, he wishes to be sure that, once properly protected, she will trust in that protection and not fall back into forming purely monetary relationships with men. Her choice of seclusion and chastity are understood by Ahmet Efendi as indicators that this has been achieved. An inability to trust herself fully to a man's protection would indicate the failure of his efforts to save her. Such an inability is the reason Agavni, the other girl from the brothel, cannot be saved. When, at the time of Kalyopi's rescue, Agavni and Dudu hear that Ahmet Efendi has not offered Kalyopi a large sum of money or bought her a house of her own, they feel sure that she will end up back in the brothels after a few months, and Agavni makes it clear that she would not accept such an offer. She says to Hulusi: "Look! If he were to buy the girl a house or give her piles of money or buy her rings, necklaces, or similar presents and gifts that could be turned into cash later, in short, if he were to make Kalyopi rich, things wouldn't turn out as I have said. I would leave here to become somebody's mistress, but I'd leave that way [i.e., with money].

Then, if my friend grew cold [toward me] and left me, I would be able to make my own way with resources I held in my own hands."[30] By contrast, Kalyopi chases off the men who solicit her in her new home, saying: "I lack for nothing. If I felt the need to have ten lira in hand, the man who sees to the accomplishment of my every desire would provide them."[31]

In tandem with the rehabilitation of Kalyopi, Yorgaki is also being rehabilitated through Ahmet Efendi's efforts. He tells Yorgaki that all the living expenses of the family are covered—the food on the table, the rent of the house—and then he gives Yorgaki some money to start a business. Whatever profits Yorgaki makes in the business, Ahmet Efendi promises that he will contribute a matching amount until the business is firmly established and profitable enough to support the family. It is worth noting here that Ahmet Efendi doesn't simply take the money he is spending on the maintenance of the family and give it to Yorgaki. In order to be restored to his proper social and economic role as provider and protector, Yorgaki needs to earn that position himself, albeit with help and support.

As these episodes illustrate, morality, of which chastity is one aspect, is a quality of the heart, as well as having economic preconditions and consequences. The failure of the necessary economic context can destroy the fabric of a loving, moral family, as in the case of Yorgaki; but even when the material conditions are in place, they will avail nothing if the requisite emotional conditions are not also in place. For Ahmet Midhat, the real engine of virtue and of enterprise is the bond of love freely assumed, and the most fundamental embodiment of that love is the companionate couple with its complementary roles—the woman trusting in the support and protection of the man, the man happily and soberly putting his shoulder to that responsibility. Kalyopi's virtue and honor are in her heart; even her fall was based on her love for her family and her desire to help them. She is able to love, trust, and accept protection, and so, the moment she is put in the right conditions, she thrives. When her protector, Ahmet Efendi, approaches a friend's hired hand about marrying her, he tells the man her whole story. The man responds that he is more interested in the future than in the past, and has no reason to stir up the history of a calamity that the girl has survived.[32] It seems clear that their future will be a happy one, for within months of being removed from the brothel and allowed to settle in a home of her own, Kalyopi has shown herself to be not only a model of virtue, but also a model of thrifty housekeeping. The author notes with approval that although Kalyopi lives with her parents and siblings, which means that the household consists of eight people, and although Hulusi, Ahmet Efendi, and often several of their friends join the family for meals at the house four or five times a week, Kalyopi's household expenses "did not exceed eight or nine lira by much in a month and never went as high as ten."[33] Moreover, just to be sure that the right conditions are maintained, Ahmet Efendi gives Kalyopi's future husband a gift of money that will allow him to join Yorgaki's now-thriving business as a partner. Thus, when the wedding is celebrated, "the judgment of fate fell into its [proper] place" and the good order of things was restored.[34]

Ahmet Midhat's middle-class harem is the place where people learn that the sacrifice of selfish interests and desires for the sake of love brings with it not suffering but happiness. In other words, it is a place where members of society learn what true self-interest is, and from this comes industry, contentment, and a sense of responsibility not only to one's friends and family, but also to others. The hero of *Henüz 17 Yaşında*, Ahmet Efendi, is not a rich man. It takes him considerable effort to come up with the money to pay off Kalyopi's debts, rent a house for her and her family, furnish it properly, get her father back on his feet in a business, and provide the nest egg that will allow the young man he has selected for her to marry her in proper economic conditions. It is explicit throughout the story that Ahmet Efendi has no sexual interest in Kalyopi. His motives are altruistic, and his articulation of them makes clear what a man owes to society and what the right definition of self-interest is. As he says to Kalyopi: "Aren't sums like this spent quite commonly in the pursuit of pleasure? But who says that the thing called enjoyment [or] pleasure consists solely of drunkenness and lasciviousness? We determined earlier that it would be a happy and joyous achievement to rescue a bird from the clutches of a cat. To save a girl like you from the clutches of prostitution, that is, from the most terrible clutches of all, and to send her home — is that a small joy, a small pleasure?"[35]

In the simplest terms, Ahmet Midhat believed that a properly constructed, freely contracted companionate marriage, with the roles of the sexes defined in complementary fashion, produced enterprising and altruistic citizens and resulted in a prosperous economy and a moral society. As an economic unit, the companionate couple was efficient: the man earned the collective living, and the woman managed the household and their finances. In social terms, the man functioned as a protector, while the woman acted as a steadying influence, channeling his energies in a productive direction.

Because their association is based, according to Ahmet Midhat Efendi, on true love properly understood—that is, on attraction, free choice, and appropriateness—the man does not feel confined by his obligations, and the woman does not feel limited by her circumscribed sphere of activity; he is spurred to industry, she to frugality, and both find contentment. This is Ahmet Midhat's middle-class harem: it is not the traditional affluent, capricious, and loveless harem of Mustafa Merakî Efendi; still less is it the opening of the harem and the entrance of women into the world, or an embrace of spontaneous and ill-conceived passions. Ahmet Midhat believed that deviation from this ideal family structure produced citizens who were vain, shortsighted, lazy, and selfish. Unacquainted with the true nature of love, they commodified all relations, and their unwillingness to accept any responsibilities made them unable to perceive where their own self-interest really lay or to understand the nature of happiness. They wasted their lives and their substance on meaningless, immediate pleasures to the detriment of themselves, the economy, and the fiber of society at large. The well-ordered harem is society's bulwark against such misfortunes.

NOTES

All translations are mine, unless otherwise indicated.

1 For details of his life, see Gövsa, "Ahmet Midhat Efendi" and Siyavuşgil, "Ahmet Midhat Efendi."

2 Oestrup, "Ahmed Midhat," 199.

3 Relatively dismissive assessments of his fiction can be found in Tanpınar, *XIX. Asır Türk Edebiyatı Tarihi*, 464; Finn, *The Early Turkish Novel*, 13–21. For a contrasting view, see Berkes, *The Development of Secularism in Turkey*, 282.

4 For a discussion of Ahmet Midhat's writings on economics, see Ülken, *Türkiye'de Çağdaş Düşünce Tarihi*, 166–74; Georgeon, "L'Économie politique selon Ahmed Midhat." The latter also contains a good discussion of Ottoman economic thought in the nineteenth century more generally.

5 A discussion of the development and impact of this idea, which is now widely questioned by historical demographers, can be found in Thornton, "The Developmental Paradigm, Reading History Sideways, and Family Change." I am grateful to Ken Cuno for drawing my attention to this article. Chapter 14 of Macfarlane's *The Savage Wars of Peace* also contains a most interesting discussion of the connection between companionate marriage and economic life.

6 Peirce, *The Imperial Harem*, 4–5.

7 Ahmet Midhat Efendi, "Bekârlık Sultanlık mı Dedin?" 280–81.

8 Ahmet Midhat Efendi, *Felâtun Bey ile Râkım Efendi*, 153.

9 The Régie was the foreign-operated monopoly on the distribution and sale of to-

bacco and tobacco products in the Ottoman Empire, established by the Public
Debt Commission after the Ottoman government declared bankruptcy and consolidated its debt in 1881.

10 On this topic see, for example, Davis, *The Ottoman Lady*, 99–114.

11 Ahmet Midhat Efendi, *Felâtun Bey ile Râkım Efendi*, 181.

12 Ibid., 222–23.

13 Ibid., 190.

14 Ibid., 150.

15 Ibid., 105–7.

16 Ahmet Midhat Efendi, *Henüz 17 Yaşında*, 139–41.

17 Ibid., 104–5.

18 Ibid., 123.

19 Ibid., 199.

20 Ibid., 44.

21 Ibid., 69.

22 Ibid., 79.

23 Ibid., 172. The word *sermaye* here is something of a double-entendre: it is a common slang term for a prostitute in a brothel, and it is also the word for capital in
the economic sense.

24 Ibid., 64–65. *Lira, mecidiye, kuruş,* and *para* are all Ottoman units of money. Forty
paras equal one *kuruş,* twenty *kuruş* equal one *mecidiye,* and five *mecidiye* equal one
gold *lira.* The actual figure for a night in the brothel by Ahmet Efendi's calculation
comes to 240 *kuruş* but he rounds up to 260–70. An *okka* is an Ottoman measure
of weight equivalent to 2.8 pounds.

25 Ahmet Midhat Efendi, *Felâtun Bey ile Râkım Efendi*, 212–21.

26 Ibid., 174–75.

27 Ibid., 194–98.

28 Ahmet Midhat describes the state as the father of the nation and says it ought to
protect its people, but it can only do so effectively when a preponderance of opinion—the general will—supports state action (*Henüz 17 Yaşında*, 124–25).

29 Ibid., 192.

30 Ibid., 182.

31 Ibid., 210.

32 Ibid., 212–13.

33 Ibid., 210.

34 Ibid., 213.

35 Ibid., 174–75.

13 · BETWEEN HAREM AND HOUSEBOAT

"Fallenness," Gendered Spaces, and the Female
National Subject in 1920s Egypt

Marilyn Booth

 When Egypt achieved partial independence from
British rule in the early 1920s, contests among
elites over the state's constitutional form and
future intensified. One form this took was debate over who
had rights to occupy what spaces. Questions of gendered subjectivity and gendered spaces (Were they changing? Should
they change?) had been debated in the local press since the
late 1880s. By the 1920s, elite women's visible activism in national politics gave immediacy to the question of what physical spaces and social manifestations a modern femininity
might occupy in Egypt. Meanwhile, some male politicians
hoped that gendered formations of place would resume their
accustomed, precrisis forms and worried out loud about the
moral consequences of women appearing in public.

It seems no accident that the same decade witnessed the
appearance of a new literary genre, the first-person, memoiristic narrative of sociosexual, gendered "fallenness." Such
narratives address an immediate political issue—whether
prostitution should remain regulated and therefore politically legitimated. But these texts link debates over prostitution to a more general question: How should arrangements

of gendered social space change, in a society poised for nationalist modernity? I argue that these texts carry out such a debate via representations of space, specifically, the space of the home versus that of the street. Narrating girls' and women's movements out of—and presence within—the harem as supposedly protected and secluded domestic space, they show that space as anything but protected.

Mapping urban space, these texts highlight young female figures who step across spatial boundaries that, the narratives imply, had heretofore marked the experiential limits of their lives. Such boundaries inscribed, and stood in for, conventional notions of where honor's limits lay, notions given disciplinary force by their embedding in Islamicized codes of conduct. In these memoirs, transgressions of spatial boundaries mark out a discourse on the fallen woman (al-saqita), whose excursions through space are said to breach moral boundaries. But the figure they construct at the text's center is above all the *falling* woman, as potential prostitute: the young woman who, having left the house of her father, necessarily falls into a space—or void—of impending sexual danger. Lacking the boundaries drawn by others, and thrown into public, urban space, the daughter has left the status of the *masuna*, the female protected by male guardians, although the protection of those male guardians is shown in these texts as a sham. To be protected is to be "respectable"; *masuna*, a descriptive term, thus becomes a title of respectability. The houses—always pluralized—that shelter the daughter who has fled the protection of the harem are the houses of prostitutes, conventionally the ultimate contrast to the house of the father. The rupturing of idealized notions of home and the exposure of domestic space as dangerous rather than protective are consistent motifs in these and other memoir texts from this decade.

Many backdrops offer themselves against which to analytically pose these narrated figures of fallenness. I contextualize these texts briefly in contrast to elite memoirs and biographies of female experience, and I read them against a specific and contemporaneous campaign against legalized prostitution.[1]

A GENRE OF THE 1920S

Mudhakkirat wasifa misriyya (memoirs of an Egyptian lady's companion; hereinafter *Memoirs*) appeared serially in 1927 in several cheaply printed booklets of thirty to forty pages each and was followed shortly thereafter by *Asrar wasifa misriyya* (secrets of an Egyptian lady's companion; here-inafter *Secrets*).[2] Both works bear a female signature: as described on the cover of *Memoirs*, they were written by "the bold young woman Zaynab Muhammad." They therefore claim to fulfill the "autobiographical pact" between author and reader: the latter trusts that the first-person narrator in the text and the author of the text are the same, and the author is to fulfill that trust.[3] This pact sustains a reality effect: the reader assumes that the author-narrator is telling the truth about her or his life. Although much recent scholarship—and, in North America, scandals over the contents and truth claims of some popular memoirs—demonstrates the constructed nature of autobiography, this reality effect remains a dominant attraction of autobiographical writing.

To all appearances, the author and the narrator of *Memoirs* and *Secrets* are identical. "Zaynab," the narrator, is "Zaynab Muhammad," the author. Yet this attribution is complicated by a further explanation: each install-ment's cover announces that the work was "put into novelistic form, cor-rected and polished [or revised] by the two famous writers Muhammad Bek Ahmad al-Buhaydi and Mahmud Effendi Kamil Farid." This acknowl-edgment seems to imply a more equivocal pact: that both memoir and author may be fictions, but if so, they are fictions that call on memoir's experiential authority and assert a truth claim. That is, only the form is "novelistic." Whether these memoirs would have been considered autobio-graphical documents or whether they would have been read as fictions by their earliest audience remains an intriguing question.[4] Furthermore, the issue of who the real author was—of whether Zaynab Muhammad is a fic-tion—is also muddied by the fact that a collection of what are said to be the nationalist leader Sa'd Zaghlul's "historical speeches," edited by one Zaynab Muhammad, is advertised at the end of one segment of these memoirs.[5] Is this bibliographic information simply a ruse designed to add plausibility to a fiction of female authorship?[6]

My next text, *Mudhakkirat 'amil fi biqa' al-'ahirat* (memoirs of a worker in whores' whereabouts), by 'A. 'Atiya, came out around the same time.[7] This work does not claim to be the voice of a prostitute or a so-called fallen/fall-ing woman, as an autobiographical narrator. Rather, the prostitute is the sympathetic object of discourse, observed, interviewed, and described by a male—and supposedly unfallen—narrator. Several prostitutes and *patro-nas* appear as characters in the work; their first-person narrations are intro-duced through the male narrator's interlocutory and investigative role, as a character in the text and as a speaker to the Egyptian community at large, the constructed audience for the text. The young man establishes his authority to speak on behalf of Egypt's so-called fallen women.

Because they are organized around the comings and goings of female characters across diverse social spaces, these texts interrogate, although they do not name, the institution of the harem. I define *harem* here as that enclosed space in which lived the women and children of households wealthy enough to afford this division of space, and the seclusion of family members within. In other words, the harem was that space which was understood as remaining off-limits to males other than close kin.[8] I use the term *harem* to signify a set-off social space common to the middle and upper strata of urban Egypt (in other words, to those families where female labor outside the home was not essential to collective survival) even into the 1920s. As other contributors to this volume note, the harem is variable over time and across space. In the transitional era of the 1920s in Egypt, if the Arabic word *harīm* signified the females of a household, it also implied the space that nonservitor, middle- and upper-strata women ideally—if not always in reality—inhabited. But this ideal was subject to strong challenge: its breakdown in practice and through discourses that contested it was a subject taken up in print by many anxious writers.

There are other texts similar in form and focus to those that I discuss in this chapter.[9] As an example, another text from this decade, *Yawmiyyat saqita* (diaries of a fallen woman), by Muhammad Ahmad Yusuf, alludes even on the cover to the status of fallenness and its attendant implications for women's habitation of social spaces, for it is subtitled "the most important social issue in novel [or narrative] form." Unlike *Memoirs*, *Yawmiyyat saqita* signals its fictionality in the named separation of (and gendered difference between) author and narrator—Muhammad Yusuf is certainly not a fallen woman.[10] But, rather than being a retrospective narrative, Yusuf's text comprises diary entries that mark the daily rhythm of an unnamed female diarist. She inscribes her own past through flashbacks as her diary progresses, allowing "immediate" interruptions of private female space in the form of violently invasive men. But the author further undermines the pretense of a female voice as he situates his text overtly in a series of male-authored works on prostitution, by prefacing the supposed diary with excerpts from those earlier works.[11] Though not discussed further here, this text illustrates well a publishing context in this decade and the following one, wherein a generalized polemics on prostitution was constituted and sustained partly by alleged narratives of prostitutes' lives printed in cheap, chapbook form. And it parallels a similar interplay of literary structures of memoir and polemical content in eighteenth- and nineteenth-century England.[12]

The sudden appearance of first-person (pseudo)subaltern memoirs in the 1920s is in itself a fascinating question caught up with the history of production of the Arabic novel and with emerging notions of subjecthood and citizenship, as I discuss elsewhere.[13] The conditions of possibility for these texts had to do not only with the shifting place of gender within questions of nation, but also with a shifting culture of the production of print. In urban Egypt during the 1920s, a clamorous, variegated print and visual culture arose at the intersection of new technologies and a public political sphere in which every move of Egypt's young nationalist government was charted critically.

The publishing scene responded to and created a broader readership. Educational opportunities for both girls and boys were expanding, though mostly on the elementary level. Wider literacy promised a bigger audience for locally published texts. And it may well be that cheaply printed, somewhat sensationalist, easy-to-read texts such as these were most popular among those newly armed with an elementary education. Though forces ushering in *al-hadatha* (modernity) had in fact long been at work in and on Egypt, the social effects of this process were under more intense public scrutiny than ever before, with a proliferation of periodicals and cheaply printed books clamoring for the attention of readers. The 1920s was a decade of popular magazines and serial romances, of colloquial poetry and caricatures; this was literally when color burst into the periodical scene. With their readership expanding as never before, publishers were hastening to meet—and to shape—audience demands while also often linking their publications to particular parties' political platforms. Many were the cultural sites in which politics was enacted, sometimes contested from unexpected quarters and often with a raucous openness that looks startling from the more conservative moment of the early twenty-first century.

Since at least the 1880s, and by a few voices before that time, Arabic fictional and essayistic texts had debated the gendering of social space through history and in the present.[14] Novels and conduct books had cautiously plotted a future of more, albeit still limited, choices for young women and young men, particularly with regard to romance and marriage.[15] But the boisterous culture production scene of the 1920s, and perhaps new notions of individual and collective authority, allowed the issue of girls' and young women's shifting social spaces to be broached in this new form of first-person narratives in ostensibly feminine memoirist voices. Yet a feminine authority to "speak" was curtailed by its framing in masculine editorial authority, echoing the masculine elite project of shaping the educated female citizen as emblematic of the new nation. I see this as a ventriloquizing move: through first-person narratives, male authors (and editors, or editors who were actually the authors) "spoke" the feminine. Yet, in some cases, we simply do not know who penned these memoirs; and I am loath to foreclose the possibility that these texts are, in some sense, autobiographical.

In this era, what *were* clearly autobiographical writings, personal narratives by Arab and Muslim women, began to appear in Arabic (though fragmentary autobiographical narratives had appeared in print earlier). The sparse female-authored autobiographical narratives of the 1910s and 1920s were essayistic "thoughts" (*sawanih*, which also means "good omens") rather than autobiographies or memoirs proper, and their authors were highly respectable intellectual women. Such writings did not entail visits to the harem. Sawanih were an entirely modest, circumspect, intellectualized, "veiled" sort of personal, first-person commentary, therefore sufficiently unassertive and respectable for women to publish under their own names. The Turkish Egyptian princess Qadriya Husayn's *Sawanih al-amira* (ponderings of the princess) appeared in an Arabic translation (from the Turkish) in 1920, and the celebrated Palestinian-Lebanese—but based in Egypt—writer and orator Mayy Ziyada brought out her *Sawanih fatat* (thoughts of a young woman) in 1922 (reprinted from Jurji Zaydan's cultural journal *al-Hilal* [the crescent]). Husayn and Ziyada wrote highly discreet if personal musings. They were intellectual autobiographies and (in Ziyada's case) an exercise in romantic portraiture. They were not a direct intervention in public political debate, nor did they offer the titillating promise of a peep inside the boudoir.

But such peeps—into others' boudoirs—did circulate. While European writers were keeping alive an Orientalist gaze purportedly into the harem through travel accounts, in Arabic, the lives of European women were constructed in print not only through biographies of famous women in the circumspect women's press but also, and more headily, in translated (and sometimes fabricated) memoirs and biographies. The lives of women such as Sarah Bernhardt, Lady Asquith, "al-Comtessa Suzanne de Vincennes," and "Catherine II, most famed of female sinners among wearers of the crown"[16] when "unveiled" in print tracked the private spaces of these socially and geographically distant (European) women, in texts often packaged with a suggestive cover sketch to draw the eyes of the reader or voyeur.

The cheaply printed memoir or diary of a *local* and fallen woman, on the contrary, appeared to offer textual access to the closer, and therefore more intriguingly off-limits, forbidden space of the harem or boudoir — while the referential pretense of memoir seemed to offer (and did advertise) the patent truth of lived experience and inside knowledge. Closer to home in the spaces it depicted, the ventriloquized, confessional memoir with an Arabic-speaking female narrator pledged an inside tour of the house next door, the opposite of the arms-length intellectualism or romantic tenor of Husayn's or Ziyada's personal musings. Memoirs of fallenness uncannily echoed (and perhaps mocked) Orientalist European writings on ("in") the harem by promising to reveal, but endlessly deferring the description of, the inner realms of brothels, particularly the "secret houses" (*al-buyut al-sirriyya*) of illegal prostitution that, according to complaints in the press and petitions to the central government, had been cropping up in the respectable neighborhoods of Cairo, Alexandria, and provincial towns and cities of Egypt at least since the 1890s.[17] Such houses were, literally, becoming the "house next door" for some middle-class readers and writers, yet as presumably immoral territory, their interiors were as (morally) inaccessible as the supposedly respectable harem boudoirs of ladies were physically off-limits.

As represented in these texts, the spaces of brothels — inversions of the harem — were part of a larger underground scene that this genre specific to the 1920s mapped. Overall, the genre of subaltern and probably ventriloquized memoir offered the voyeuristic reader a journey into the underworld — not only into these brothels next door but also into the low-life sites of Cairo's urban fabric, from the gambling dens of Rawd al-Farag to houseboat brothels on the Nile, and from the opulent facades harboring illicit sex on the boulevard Wishsh al-Birka to the hashish dens behind al-Azhar Mosque. Not all of these memoirs of the 1920s were voiced by female narrators. Among the most famous ventriloquized subaltern memoirs are several with male narrators: *Mudhakkirat laqit* (memoirs of a foundling; 1923), *Mudhakkirat 'arbagi* (memoirs of a hackney cab driver; serialized 1923), or *Mudhakkirat futuwwa* (memoirs of a street tough; second printing, 1927).

Yet it is the women's (pseudo) memoirs in particular that suggest anxieties about social change. The figure of the fallen woman roaming the streets may represent—and may well have served to maintain—unease about the perceived blurring effects of modernity on morality, as policed through spatial separation of the sexes. As Deborah Epstein Nord comments about the British and French nineteenth century: "The narratives of prostitutes' lives that began to appear in certain mid-century treatises and investigations encouraged the idea that the woman of the streets was not wholly separable from the respectable bourgeois home."[18]

FLEEING THE FATHER

Memoirs tells the story of its apparent author, Zaynab Muhammad, who begins, conventionally, with her genealogy: she is daughter of a *bek* (bey) of Turkish origin, she explains—thus, a member of Ottoman Egypt's old elite, which was then partially being replaced (and married into) by an indigenous Egyptian elite, although the Egyptian Turkish families produced some of twentieth-century Egypt's leading landowners and politicians as well as some of its reformist voices. The author's home, therefore, is evocative of the upper-class harem so beautifully described by a contemporaneous daughter of the elite, Huda Sha'rawi, in *her* memoirs (dictated and then published long after the 1920s). Giving her birth date as 1896 (and, by giving a birth date at all, acknowledging the referential demands of the memoir genre), Zaynab as a character represents the first generation of elite Egyptian daughters schooled outside the home. Her father, whom she describes as a senior civil servant, is presented initially as a modernized and somewhat anomalous member of his generation and social standing in that he sends his daughter to school. The father thus signifies the first generation of elite men in Egypt to support girls' education publicly and to send their daughters to school. Such men were praised in the late-nineteenth-century Egyptian press for doing so—but most were probably native Egyptian or immigrant Syrian men, Christian as well as Muslim, rather than scions of the old Turkish Muslim aristocracy like the father here, "Muhammad Bek Question-Mark."

Zaynab's description of her childhood offers a tranquil scene of emerging modernity in the form of a model father-daughter relationship that emphasizes his attention to her education first at home and then in the precedent-setting and prestigious Saniyya School for girls, where Zaynab "entered a new life of knowledge . . . overjoyed to be in this great school. I went there each morning in my father's carriage. The driver would return home to drive my father to the Diwan. At four p.m. the carriage would be in front of the school entrance, and I would ride home."[19]

These details are not extraneous. They map out acceptable space for girls of the elite. Riding in her father's enclosed carriage from the school entrance directly home—a route that is articulated as exactly parallel to the father's movement between home and his state office—Zaynab traverses an extension of the harem that made going to school thinkable and that constructs her from the beginning as respectably *masuna* (protected; by extension, respectable) by her separation from the life of the street. Paralleling her father's path as he does the work of the state, Zaynab does her work as a feminine subject, educatable yet—in her father's carriage—tractable and ever-secluded. Yet Zaynab's path is perhaps more ambiguous than it appears, for her protected and temporary departure from the home is the result of a projection forward: "When my mental quickness gave my father reason to attend to the question of my future, he entered me in the Saniyya School."[20] Perhaps even to refer to the girl's "future" marks the text as modern. Perhaps only in the context of recognizing education as separate from (if implicated with) the home were girls to have something called a "future," even if it was almost inevitably one of marriage and motherhood. To articulate the notion of "having a future" was to recognize the possibility of new social spaces for feminine agency.

What interrupts and destroys Zaynab's tranquil life of social privilege and cautious modernist exploration is the unmitigated exercise of patriarchal right: specifically, the father's right to obtain a divorce unilaterally, without recourse to higher authorities. Zaynab's sheltering class privilege and her education cannot protect her from vulnerability enshrined in canon law and upheld by the state: "My life was one that very few daughters of Eve enjoyed. I spent nearly two years at school until fate stunned me in the form of my father's divorce of my mother."[21] This life event—brought on not so much by "fate" as by the father and (the nonintervention of) the state—cracks the walls of the harem, exposing it as anything but a protective enclosure around women's and children's lives. As the father remarries his first (apparently also once repudiated) wife, Zaynab is placed outside the family circle. It is not just that she is no longer her father's adored object of attention as an extension of her mother. With her father's shift of his interests to his son (Zaynab's half-brother), she is no longer protected. This is stunningly represented in her half-brother's repeated attempts to seduce her. The walls of home no longer protect her, for the threat is within. Indeed, the walls of the harem, which keep her inside and allow her brother entrance into a space she cannot escape, now jeopardize her bodily integrity.

The unspeakable menace of incest literally haunts Zaynab's dreams. On an allegorical level, the brother, Nu'man, embodies the threat of Europeanizing practices to the nation's social and moral health. His attempted seduction is spoken through erotic European postcards that he waves in his sister's face and insists that she keep for him in her room. The supposedly chaste and unchallengeable space of female virtue is thus invaded, against its inhabitant's will, by the cultural economy of Westernization in its most salacious forms.[22] Yet this takes place through the most local and intimate of agents, the (admittedly only half-) brother. And the brother's seduction is also spoken through a reading of ancient Egyptian history: "How beautiful were ancient times," exclaims Nu'man, "those eras in which a brother would marry his sister. If only I had been with you in that time, I would have married you . . ." In response, Zaynab lashes back, labeling "those eras" as *ayyam al-jahiliyya* (the days of ignorance).[23] The jahiliyya separates pre-Islamic from Islamic time temporally. More importantly, it separates the two eras morally and thus timelessly: in the context of modernity, jahiliyya came to signify conduct that was not regarded (by some, at least) as properly Islamic, and that more specifically was linked to European social practice. Jahiliyya remains a key concept and rhetorical device in today's Islamist discourses, often deployed particularly in the context of perceived deviations of female behavior. If it is most often associated with the slightly later writings of the Muslim Brotherhood theorist Sayyid Qutb, its use here suggests that this concept was already in formation in the 1920s; indeed, its use in a work of popular literature suggests it resonated amongst more than a few readers. For Zaynab, the harem has become a space of jahiliyya — not because of wayward female behavior but due to a male family member's morally reprehensible conduct.

With the harem compromised, Zaynab, asserting bodily honor and a moral outlook based on her practice of her faith, must leave. The distance between her assertion of an Islamic moral probity and her brother's pornographic postcards is formally represented in his physical and verbal crudeness, and in the weighted linguistic practice of their exchanges, wherein she speaks the modern literary Arabic of educated, written exchange while he prefers — or can only muster — a crudely represented colloquial speech.[24]

But Zaynab's naiveté—supposedly the appropriate, sanctioned sign of a protected, therefore honorable, female (masuna)—is also at issue. The text implies that old forms of protection no longer work, that they expose young women to threats of sexual assault rather than protect them.

In this sense, Zaynab's narrative challenges both older, customary notions of seclusion as protective and the reworked patriarchy of modernity. To place girls in school (as opposed to educating them at home) was to acknowledge the possibility of expanding the social space of (some) females' movement and habitation. This entailed training elite girls in self-surveillance that would make possible their entry, though invisibly, into public space. Covered faces and covered spaces (the father's carriage) could extend the harem.[25] If the nationalist ideal is a reworked set of gendered norms based on carefully revised but ultimately stable spatial adherences, where modern elite feminine selfhood will be enacted on trained self-policing in public and the maintenance of domestic-centered identity, then what is questioned here is the transferability of older patterns of female sequestration to the demands (and international reputation?) of an emerging postcolonial state. What the text also questions is the educability of a younger (male) generation seduced by the West (*al-gharb*). Perhaps young men are the ones who need to be kept at home.

Zaynab fends off her brother's attack in the family's walled garden—supposedly a safe, because secluded, extension of domestic space—and later in her bedroom, the heart of the harem. Failing to trap her there (perhaps the harem—the lock on the door of her bedroom—retains some protective force!), Nu'man is more successful outside the house, where his sister's honor is assumed to be always imminently at risk. Occurring in the street *just outside* the home, between the home and the family carriage, Nu'man's ruse is sited literally on the threshold of family honor and its success exposes the fragility of a new doctrine of girls' self-surveillance. Nu'man makes sure that his father is in the street precisely at the moment when his sister steps down from their carriage onto the street, whereupon he traps her into an exchange of words with one of his male companions. This puts Zaynab's honor (and therefore her father's) publicly into question, while possibly also satirizing or critiquing the notion, held by some, that women's voices were *'awra*, part of that which must remain hidden, or covered. As a modern daughter (the first generation of "modern daughters"), she has been able to traverse the streets, though only fully veiled, silent, and in her father's carriage, thus in a mobile, transportable harem.

Outside of this family space, she has violated the rules by allowing her voice to enter the street. Now, the father denounces her as a "whore" and locks her inside the house.[26]

PROSTITUTION AND PUBLIC DISCOURSE

The elite household, the space where the ideology of the harem is enacted, does not protect: it imprisons and it threatens female bodily integrity. Yet this "fall" (potential as well as actual, and social as much as moral) is not portrayed as attributable to poverty or to sexual desire. Rather, it is the inevitable end of the road after a girl has fled threats of sexual aggression in the family, and/or after she has run away from coerced marriage, rape by another name, arranged by her father against her will. The marital home is a space—a harem—directly antithetical to her hoped-for future, as a girl educated at school.[27] Nu'man's attempted rape of his half-sister in the home—in the harem—may simply be a more dramatically shocking version of many women's lives.

Yet there is a specific and sexualized discursive context here. If anxieties over female visibility and feminist activism were among the forces leading to these memoiristic texts, surely it also mattered that the immediate historical moment was one of verbalized public concern about prostitution as a problem for the nation—a discourse that touched upon the visibility of all women. Although prostitutes had experienced Egyptian state intervention in the nineteenth century (indeed, for a long period they were banished from Cairo), government oversight of prostitutes was formally established only at that century's end, by an administrative order issued in 1896, after a period of closer policing following the start of the British occupation in 1882.[28] Late-nineteenth-century newspapers consistently drew attention to community disaffection with the presence of houses of prostitution in various urban centers.[29] After the First World War, prostitution was more widely represented in texts, corresponding to what may have been an increasing visibility of the practice in urban centers and its increasing proximity to the lives of the literate and well-off. Political controversy and local sensitivities over the state's role in its regulation, evident in the nineteenth century, did not decrease in an era when British imperial troops were ubiquitous in Cairo, Alexandria, and beyond (many of them from British colonies, notably Australia), and when local observers bemoaned that Egypt was a locus of what was called white slavery.[30]

Thus, prostitution was an issue of imperial reach, but not only that. The nationalist ferment of the immediate postwar period generated intensive public discourse on a range of social ills, as diverse factions sought political legitimacy in the national independence struggle. Many essays in the press voiced unease about what elite writers saw as greater spatial freedom for young women and young men; this discourse of anxiety mirrored but also fueled public unease concerning the status of all sorts of social boundaries and implicated pro-Westernization tendencies in local rearrangements of gendered space. Indeed, that the term *saqita* (fallen female) appears in tracts on prostitution as well as in fictional texts in this period reveals the ubiquitous presence of the European metropole in local discourses. I have not been able to trace the first appearance of the term *saqita* (and the associated verbal noun *suqut*, meaning fall) as referring to prostitutes, but I suspect it is a direct borrowing from Victorian discourse, wherein the specifically Christian notion of fallenness had become secularized. Amanda Anderson notes in her important study of the trope of fallenness in nineteenth-century Britain: "Fallenness was rearticulated to secular and scientific paradigms during the Victorian era and ultimately served to loosen religious and ethical moorings."[31] It was in this secular (but still highly moralized) sense that the term resonated in Egypt, retaining a specifically gendered force through its grammatical form, a feminine adjective — a gendered specificity that is not of course present in its English usage.

Early feminists in Egypt practiced their activism on prostitutes, regarding this as an important focus of paternalizing elite social reform. Beginning in the early 1920s, they instituted projects designed to draw poor young women away from prostitution. The Egyptian Feminist Union (founded in 1923 out of the frustration of a group of elite women who were angry that male nationalist leaders had declined to support women's suffrage as a constitutional right) campaigned against legal prostitution and protested the irony that prostitution was sanctioned by legislation while prostitutes — but not their customers — were vilified and victimized.[32] Published debates and activism may have moved the state to curtail activism (if not prostitution) by introducing new regulatory legislation and by reducing prostitutes' visibility, moving their places of work to socially liminal sites at the city limits while maintaining control over prostitutes' bodies through medical checks (which had been proposed for prostitutes in Egypt as early as the period of Muhammad 'Ali, by his chief medical officer, the Frenchman Clot Bey).[33]

To retain legalized prostitution was, opponents argued, to follow imperial patterns. Since prostitution had been legalized under the British Protectorate, opponents of legalization saw the first ministry of the allegedly independent Egypt as complicit with the imperial masters. Thomas Russell, Cairo's chief of police for many years and a mainstay of the British Egyptian Service, recalled that in 1924 the government "closed down the brothels" on Wishsh al-Birka and "restored the district's respectability."[34] But two years later—and one year before the publication of *Memoirs* and *Mudhakkirat ʿamil fi biqaʿ al-ʿahirat*—the issue was saturating the local press. In 1923, Shaykh Mahmud Abu al-ʿUyun (1882–1951; his last name means "he of the eyes") had launched a campaign to abolish legalized prostitution.[35] Abu al-ʿUyun was a man of unassailable credentials, as a graduate and then a professor and curricula and teaching inspector at al-Azhar University and its affiliated Islamic Institutes, and a vigorous anti-imperialist activist before 1923. He knew how to embarrass politicians into action. Described in the press and in volumes of republished essays, Abu al-ʿUyun's activism reached its rhetorical height with his second campaign in 1926. Supported by Dawud Barakat, the editor-in-chief of the major Cairene daily *al-Ahram* (the pyramids), Abu al-ʿUyun not only published article after article but also made the rounds of government ministers and other leading political lights. Interviewing them to elicit their thoughts on prostitution, he published their comments in *al-Ahram* and then in book form. Thus, he produced a battery of proclamations against prostitution that cannily implied that to support government regulation—labeled by Abu al-ʿUyun's partisanship as the "legalization of adultery" and a "system of licentiousness"—was to favor the morally out-of-bounds practice itself.[36] Abu al-ʿUyun linked Egypt's loss of political independence to a loss of not only economic but also moral independence. He noted the "long and difficult struggle [jihad]" that Egyptians must wage to "liberate ourselves from the shackles of tyrannical appetites."[37]

Prostitutes blurred spatial boundaries that were meant to articulate and guarantee acceptable behavior: "Members of infamous occupations were often physically segregated as dishonorable persons and could be distinguished by their outward appearance."[38] State policy had repeatedly tried to place prostitutes "outside," on the edges of Cairo and other cities, far away from the "protected" spaces of respectable families—the inside/outside dichotomy of the harem system writ larger. Since at least the late nineteenth century, prostitutes had countered this policy of separation by inserting themselves into "good" neighborhoods, leaving their new neighbors aghast. Local news items in national newspapers had called on the authorities to disrupt prostitutes' permeation of these neighborhoods since the 1890s. The lawyer Muhammad Sa'id al-Bayyumi was motivated to write his 1919 treatise on "secret houses"—houses of prostitution not licensed by the state—when he discovered that one of these houses had opened near his own residence.[39]

Even bodily markers were no longer clear: in press polemics from the 1890s on, commentators bemoaned the impossibility of distinguishing "respectable women" from "fallen women" in an era when some urban middle-strata and elite women were just beginning to emerge from customary strictures on their movement through public space. If young women were removing their face veils and dressing "like prostitutes," who was to know the difference between the *'adhra'* (virgin) and the *'ahira* (prostitute)? The divisions and distances both metaphorized and policed by the harem system as a division of family versus public space seemed threatened. And protests against allegedly widespread prostitution might work in more than one way: were they aimed at prostitution, or were they protests against feminine assertions of prerogatives in public space? Was the aim to efface prostitution, or to send women home? Texts excoriating male predators could be deployed to insist that women belonged at home. "The precious daughters of homes and the respectable women of families are being chased through suburbs and public squares!" exclaimed Abu al-'Uyun.[40]

We cannot know how widely *Memoirs* and similar texts were disseminated and read. But I suggest that their production in the 1920s signals a wider public concern, or an attempt to create a wider concern, about such social issues. As the texts center issues of agency by constructing "autobiographical voices" claiming the right to narrate feminine experience, the works—even as ventriloquized, simulated voices—offer a different mapping of urban space than that found in the antiprostitution discourse. In these texts, the house of refuge is not that of the husband or father—where the female figure is either locked up or from which she is expelled—but rather that of the female community in and around the house of prostitution. The space of the harem is the space that imprisons the young female subject; it is the space that produces coerced marriages and sexual dangers. One could certainly argue that the issue here is the failure of the father and brother to properly implement the harem system; they are at fault for its fissuring. On the other hand, for the female characters of this work and others, it is the spaces of the street and the brothel that provide refuge, albeit temporarily, from the violence of home as they provide sustaining female companionship rather than the father's whip and the half-brother's attempted rape.

WHOSE HONOR IS IT, AND WHERE DOES ONE FIND IT?

One can read Zaynab's story allegorically as a commentary on national honor, compromised by the "caring" threats of the paternalist imperial ruler under the guise of a "protectorate" continued under other names, and then insultingly seduced by the pornography of imported cultural artifacts. Yet the honor at stake here, highlighted through compellingly told first-person stories, is that of the young woman who—as so many commentators reminded readers—held the future of the nation in her hands. The narrative makes this point all the more forcefully in that Zaynab isolates herself, her brother's whispered hints of his sexual attraction to her forcing her to lock herself in her room before she is incarcerated by her father in a travesty of "honorable" seclusion.[41] That the obedient and well-trained Zaynab "sits at her small desk and reads some novels and stories"[42] contrasts with her brother's reading and viewing material, which comprise (along with the postcards) a republished premodern sex manual and the nationalist newspaper al-Mu'ayyad. The image of Zaynab seated obediently at her desk seems to challenge a long-standing critique in the local press: that girls deliberately read fiction as a map for misbehavior, or as a means of breaching the walls of the paternal home, transgressing the harem.[43]

Perhaps the reading girl does learn something from her novels—something about survival. Fourteen-year-old Zaynab escapes from her father's imprisonment, arming herself against starvation by hiding her jewelry on her body and wrapping herself in a milaya baladi, the black wrap of a non-elite woman (who would not have the luxury of sequestration) to mask her departure from the harem. But, leaving her enclosure, she has no truly safe destination, for sequestration has left her without experience of the world, literally without a place to go. The elite girls' school, with its carefully circumscribed space—its alternative harem—has not prepared her for this jolting entry into the world (although the point may also be that only having spent two years there, and then being plucked out due to her father's divorce, did not allow her sufficient time and training). Zaynab is promptly picked up by a woman who takes her in under the terms of filial protection, as a daughter. Yet this woman's wealth of domestic space satirically spells a different trajectory—her "three houses" do not signify a domestic hearth but rather are an unmistakable allusion to houses of prostitution, especially since the neighborhood to which they go, and where these houses are located, al-Baghghala, was an infamous Cairo red-light precinct.

Throughout the installments of the text, Zaynab disappears inside the doorways of various police stations and into the walled gardens of elite homes that—like hers—incarcerate daughters in webs of hypocrisy rather than protecting them. She spends time on a Nile houseboat; these floating "homes" were infamous at the time as illegal elite brothels often "protected" through the fiction of European ownership and hence immune from Egyptian prosecution.[44] (Today, boats anchored on the Nile at Cairo house expensive fish restaurants, nightclubs, and a T.G.I. Friday's.) These floating pleasure palaces were the antithesis of the harem ideal, not only in their transgressions of honor but also as spaces that the patriarchal state could not control—and, indeed, that its male employees patronized. Visiting Prime Minister 'Adli Yakan Pasha to present him with a copy of a tract on prostitution, the indefatigable Abu al-'Uyun mentioned not only Cairo's official prostitution zones but also "areas beyond enumeration [or containment], such as the dahabeahs and [other] houseboats ['awamat], shacks on the Nile banks, *pensiones*."[45]

Now always wrapped in coverings that middle- and upper-class Egyptian women wore outside the home (as she is consistently careful to note), Zaynab moves through urban space protected by her own sense of virtue, marking out an alternative to the patriarchally defined harem—an alternative constructed in this text as a safer space. Here, there is a clear relationship between the appearance of the body and a gendered spatial trade-off: now that Zaynab is in the masculine space of the street—a space certainly traversed by many females, if not usually those of her class—she must make her body conform to a kind of traveling seclusion, an all-covering wrap that labels her as respectable. Whereas, in domestic space, she need not describe her clothing—for it is irrelevant—when she strides into the street, the covering in a sense is her, and it must be presented as the outward sign of her presence.

Zaynab takes on the role of roving reporter, conveying to the audience the "memoirs" of other women, who tell her their stories. These embedded narratives may evoke traditions of women's oral storytelling. But the content of their tales (forced marriage, forced concubinage, refuge from oppressive husbands and fathers in whorehouses, and so forth) seems to satirically and sadly reverse the moral compass of stories that women may have been telling their daughters at home.[46]

The major embedded narrative in *Memoirs* is that of a woman Zaynab meets on the houseboat, whence this woman has fled after being forced by her father into marriage to a much older man.[47] Likewise, telling a later installment of her own story in the second volume of her memoir, *Secrets*, Zaynab herself makes a second escape from the paternal home in order to avoid an arranged marriage. She attempts to find employment through a "domestic service office," but this simply results in her being led off by another procuress: "The fates dropped me into one of the houses of prostitution. The honorable readers will read all of that in due course."[48] In this volume, the text is structured around a series of contrasts between Zaynab and women she encounters who have fallen irretrievably and are distinguished by their European dress, metonymic of the societal fall into European ways that Abu al-'Uyun and his associates bemoan.[49] Thus, the encounter of the young Egyptian woman with the lures of the West occurs because of, not in spite of, an early and coerced marriage. Moreover, the fall into European ways is narrated as seductive in a way that the fall into sexual disrepute is not. Where does the honor that the harem is supposed to guarantee lie?

Introducing the issue of arranged marriage as a transaction between fathers and wealthy older suitors, *Memoirs* and *Secrets* serve as commentary not only on prostitution but also on Egyptian and Arab feminist activism against coerced and early marriages. Implicitly, the works also confront those conservative men in the movement against legalized prostitution who were calling for the reinstitution of early marriage as a way to take young Egyptian men off the sexual streets—who were, in other words, calling for a reinvention of the harem, with its attendant patriarchal privileges.[50] This is one way in which *Memoirs* might almost be a direct response to the debate among men on legalized prostitution then pervading the mainstream press. It is no wonder that Zaynab voices an implicit critique of coerced and early marriage as parallel to legalized prostitution, when these men of the government and the official religious establishment were making statements like the following: "Early marriage was made lawful for no other reason than to protect society and immunize it against the need for prostitution. So propagate the idea of early marriage, call for good moral behavior, and desist from the shameful infamies of civilizations that lead one astray [i.e., Europe]."[51] In the same context, Abu al-'Uyun's interlocutors—in this case, writers of anonymous letters to the newspaper—noted the real danger of women's economic independence: "Independent with her earnings and her property, she will find that she need not follow a particular man but rather can choose among the finest men who swarm around her."[52]

Thus, at the heart of the heated debate among men over the legalization of prostitution lay worries about what they perceived to be women's emerging freedoms. Zaynab's narrative debunks these worries by showing that her "freedom" to walk the streets is actually a desperate flight from the house of her father, and by presenting prostitution as the last resort of desperate women fleeing patriarchal coercion. The text thus calls attention to the social meanings of place, the ways in which gendered prescriptions of how spaces are to be occupied also prescribe and maintain power relations. Moreover, despite her formal education, it is outside the home that Zaynab learns the world, and where she uses reading to help herself and begin to define her own future. The text thus addresses the link between space and access to knowledge: keeping a person confined may prohibit her or him from knowing, and thus from exercising certain kinds of power, as Daphne Spain in particular has emphasized.[53]

At the tale's end, the narrator chooses to return to her father's home. The latest house in which she has sought shelter has been raided, and return to the father's house is the only available means of escape from the compulsory state medical examination to which prostitutes were subjected. Given a choice between the father and the state, Zaynab opts for the more familiar authority, and for familial space. It seems that the incarceration of home is preferable to that of the state, though the possible dreadfulness of both choices underlines the dubious welcome of home. Zaynab's father finds her at the police station, and she reaps an unexpected reward for choosing to summon him. He tells her that (with the marriage he forced on her still unconsummated, since she fled her father's home on her wedding night) her husband has died the night before—and has left her extensive property in the countryside. What the text foregrounds, though, is her reinstallment in the paternal home as the object of her father's affection and her stepmother's respect. Though she has fallen from grace, the fact that Zaynab somehow remained virginal throughout her adventures means she can reenter the space of the harem. The substance of the tale's happy ending is that all players are tamed by the liberal nationalist ideal of companionate marriage. Zaynab's half-brother Nu'man has been reformed through marriage to a "good woman." Zaynab happily marries her new sister-in-law's brother, after praising him as an outstanding young man—and willingly complying with her father's arrangement of the marriage, including a carefully stage-managed meeting of the pair, a chaperoned viewing of the bride now that she is safely back inside the paternal home.

Yet the politics of space in this text provides a cautionary reminder that domestic space cannot automatically be glossed as female space. As Mieke Bal has noted, this equation is problematic, to say the least, for home is where the patriarch is: "In the house fatherhood establishes itself; the house becomes fatherhood's synechdochic metaphor."[54] For our purposes, this highlights the patriarchal control of domestic space. In this context, Mildred Mortimer points out the significance of the room as refuge, as the Woolfian space of writing—and of dreaming.[55] Incarceration in patriarchal domestic space leads to the seeking of an internal space of freedom— Zaynab's room, her desk with her books, and her dreams. But for her, the dreams are nightmares, and furthermore their predictive role appears realized when her brother breaks into her room and tries to drug her. The room—or, in Zaynab's particular historical context, the miniaturized and modernized harem, as the space of female protection—provides no solution. It is only through escape, but also through return to a now-penitent father, that the girl's future can be a felicitous one. Both father and daughter appear disciplined by the experience.

By exposing the fiction of protection and emphasizing the coercive aspect of the upper-class home, the text questions the doctrine of the harem—and the concept of gendered spatial segregation—as beneficial and benign guarantor of correct social practice. By contrast, the women who come and go in the houseboat and the "houses" are guarantors of their own bodily integrity, as they are also (and importantly) the ones who bind up the wounds of other women. This is not to suggest that this or other texts present sites of prostitution in an unequivocally positive light, for these texts are also inhabited by women and men who are bullies, sadists, thieves, bad mothers who force their daughters into prostitution, and the pathetic detritus of European urban poverty. Such a panorama is on view in my next text, *Mudhakkirat 'amil fi biqa' al-'ahirat* (memoirs of a worker in whores' whereabouts).

SLUMMING WITH THE WHORES

Who is this "worker in whores' whereabouts"? At first glance, the grammatical structure of the title seems to promise a tell-all through the eyes of a male brothel employee. In fact, though, he is an onlooker, and moreover evidently not working class but rather an efendi (an educated, white-collar employee or professional). He is *in* but not *of* these "whereabouts." His "memoir," thus, is not that of a subaltern speaker, but of an at least potentially middle-class observer, emblematic of those who produced and read the popular Egyptian magazines of the 1920s.[56] The active participle *'amil* (worker) is perhaps better understood here as signifying its participial meaning of active, for even as he poses as a sort of *flâneur*, the narrator seems to take on the role of activist as well as observer.[57]

An intertextual circuit links these two texts, through the practice customary at the time of circulating, mutually referential, back-page advertisements that reiterate the mélange of moralizing glosses and titillating allusions found in these and other similar texts. Zaynab's memoir attempts to enlist readers for *Mudhakkirat 'amil fi biqa' al-'ahirat* in the advertising copy on its back pages, making clear the distance that separates this memoirist from his subject:

> We read these memoirs and found them to be the best lesson for everyone immersed in vice, for its writer researched all the harms of prostitution on the ships of decadent living. The writer wrote his memoirs in [the form of] 30 letters on the love of prostitutes, their craftiness and cunning, what binds a man and what harms him. In truth these are a clear and excellent lesson for all. The writer wrote these memoirs as a service to virtue for he has investigated all the caprices and pleasures of prostitutes.[58]

Like Zaynab, this narrator insists on the referentiality of his narrative: "These are not a cluster of fanciful narratives written by a litterateur, or a story collection by a skilled fiction writer, or theories . . . these are true narratives, real stories, important research, candid images, all of which elucidate our social situation."[59] Indeed, "whores' whereabouts" becomes a microcosm of society, as the "memoirist" finds his passion for "the study of life" best satiated here, a collective site "entered by every sort of person . . . every representative of the social structure, from civil servant, administrator, writer, and poet, to student, farmer, craftsman, and merchant. All submit to the rulings of women."[60] That women and prostitutes become blurred and overlapping categories here is a point I want to note, if not to dwell on. And the fact that the title uses the unspecific *biqa'* (singular, *buq'a*), meaning spots, stains, or sites, rather than a more specific term such as *buyut al-da'ara* (houses of prostitution) seems to suggest that "whores' whereabouts" are pervasive rather than contained. They spill over into the street.

The "rulings of women" to which the narrator refers are not, it appears, the clichéd and whimsical rulings of passion, which saturate the popular narratives and translations of this era. In this text, women are constructed to some extent as agents, but not as agents of their own downfall or as tyrants governing men's desires. Their agency consists of a feminized survival strategy, in perfecting wiliness, a streetwise, modern equivalent to the time-attested trope of women's wiles that threads through narratives from North Africa to Iran.[61] In parallel, and yet utterly differently, the male narrator's wiliness is to "act the roles before me, and raise in a single day multiple curtains" — to expose the world of these "wily women": "And this I could do only by frequenting these places, expending my leisure time in them."[62]

But the narrator/author's investment of time is not as innocent as it may seem, for he lets the reader know eventually that he is a civil servant by day, a servant of the state. If this qualifies him to expose what he explicates as the nether regions of his society, it also implicates him directly in the formal power structure responsible for policing boundaries. Here, it is the male narrator who draws his cloak of morality around his body, as he exposes less-protected bodies, shielding himself from the contagion of the tales they tell. He is their interlocutor, observer, and interpreter — but never, to all appearances, their lover. As a narrator, he is Zaynab's equivalent; yet, unlike her, he has the unchecked power to come and go, unmediated by a father's or older brother's will, and certainly undeterred by the walls of the harem. If, at one point, he appears momentarily seduced by another young man, his rejection of that enticement recuperates his authority as social critic within mainstream homosocial discourse, "man to man." Does his hinted vulnerability to the young man's homosexual approach cement a homosocial authority and further exclude a feminine audience?

To his unnamed interlocutor, described as "a [male] friend," and of course to the reader (who is implicitly male), this observer characterizes the age, and the social reality before him, as a "narrative" of ubiquitous corruption and wrongdoing: "I believe you have perused the story of commerce in chastity and honor and the fair sex; [we are in] an age of selling virgins and matrons." This narrator distinguishes himself from the era's supposedly representative characters by declaring that he does not sense himself to be "among the sons of this generation."[63] In this text, suqut — fallenness — is society-wide and only ambiguously gender-specific. It corresponds more closely to Anderson's insights on the trope of fallenness as "dramatiz[ing] predicaments of agency and uncertainties about the nature of selfhood, character, and society."[64] And if prostitutes are allegedly women without men, this narrative (like Zaynab's) shows prostitutes to be women with men—whether husbands, fathers, brothers, or "companions"—who instigate and maintain prostitution. The honorable ones seem to be those who have escaped male-controlled space once and for all.[65]

As the male observer and chronicler watches from the street and occasionally visits the "houses" of his interlocutors, the embedded stories of these individuals construct an inversion of the home/private/safe versus street/public/unsafe dichotomy. As in Zaynab's story, it is "domestic space" that is dangerous, while the street offers (temporary) safety. It is the family that endangers young women: husbands sell wives, mothers sell daughters, and women sell themselves out of abusive marriages, while the state colludes with patriarchal rights. For example, being caught and registered as a prostitute puts an estranged or even divorced woman in a vulnerable situation, for now it is easier for her spouse or former spouse to track her down and claim her. "She feared," explains the narrator, "that he would claim falsely that she had fled from his home, and then she would be arrested. She asked me for advice on getting a lawyer. I was amazed at her tale, and realized that as he had brought her to this place, he was the criminal."[66]

Initially, this narrator appears considerably more sympathetic than does Abu al-'Uyun to the female subjects of reformist concern. Morever, in addition to pointing out the culpability of various men, he narrates forms of women's resistance to the state (as when one female brothel owner has a successful standoff with an entire police detachment). But as the narrative progresses, this observer becomes almost an undercover agent—and not on behalf of the women he observes. His advocacy of increased government intervention—he is not on the side of Abu al-'Uyun, it appears—is evident as he corresponds with the police chief of Azbakiyya. This Cairo district, situated between the old city and the new, was the center of the city's legalized brothel activity and the site of many "secret houses." The narrator writes to the police chief to "inform" him about the presence of cocaine dens. He also mentions "the women who do not go to the pharmacy [for the prescribed medical examination], and those who only go late, and the women who traffic in poisons, and where they hide when the detachment goes by."[67] What is significant here, for a politics of gendered spaces, is that the house of the father or husband—and the spaces of state paternalism and incarceration (police stations, pharmacies)—are grouped together as spaces of danger for women, while the street and the brothel become spaces of (relative) safety as well as of female community. And both texts highlight the ways in which "private" family space, defined by the father, and "public" spaces of government regulation and security, defined by the state, work together and ultimately against the health and happiness of young women.

In this context, let us return briefly to Zaynab. In a scene that is telling for its reference to the increasing newspaper column space that was devoted to crime and policing, the husband of the houseboat (brothel) owner who had taken her in recognizes Zaynab as "the girl the newspapers wrote about."[68] She, to her dismay, recognizes the disciplinary implications: she must flee, or her father will find her. The text invokes simultaneously this new public exposure and the older paternal authority to police the boundaries of appropriate social behavior—even if, in narrating Zaynab's story, it interrogates the validity of those boundaries.

CONCLUSIONS

Not only do these texts historicize the space of the harem as a changing, disappearing social space; they also question the notion of it as a sacrosanct space of respect and protection which the word embodies. They suggest instead that it may be a space of exposure and even danger—that it may engender the opposite of the honor it means to safeguard. By enacting this critique through the (ventriloquized) voices of females who articulate their status as victims of this system and its expectations, these texts appear to make space for the voices of national subjects who were not usually given voice in the era's public discourses. The critique of the harem is powerful because the narrative structure implicitly challenges the right of elite nationalist commentators (whether male or female) to define the space of the abject female subject. Yet, in the end, these texts enact an act of ventriloquism that returns narrative authority to the political center, while perhaps opening up the possibility of broadening that acknowledged center of discursive authority.

As narratives about fallenness, in their careful and extensive spatial mapping, these memoirs respond to a discourse of anxiety about the female body's new—or perhaps simply more visible—mobility. Though this discourse was local, it was shaped and informed by imperial discourses and practices as well. Local and imperial discourses on "the woman question" othered the female body in space and in social discourse, displacing it from a realm of public concern while ostensibly making it the object of sustained public critique. In other words, and proliferating through the local press, a predominant discursive focus on the female body—as a body disconnected from its anchoring in domestic space—seems to have been concerned not so much with and about the fortunes of actual young women as it was with a perceived suspension of spatial gender-determinative boundaries and the consequences of this suspension for familiar patterns of social reproduction. The female body stood in for the family; and for the female to cross boundaries demarcating the territory of honor was to betray the family, and thereby the nation.

These "memoirs" recenter the female body—partly through an endlessly deferred but always promised narrative of sexual violence—as they assert both the failure of the harem system for young women from elite families and the lack of a socially and psychologically acceptable alternative. They show the false respectability of a system of enclosure in a feminized space of "protection" and exclusion (in other words, the harem) by juxtaposing the paternal and patriarchal household with the house of the abandoned woman and the houses of prostitution. They expose a discourse of privileged social respectability—of honor based on female chastity and obedience, and also (crucially) on economic privilege—by narrating the "futures" of young women of the elite and middle strata as shaped by choice, but only a choice between equally painful alternatives. They displace the blame that was put on young women (and, to a lesser extent, young men) in much rhetoric of the time onto the figure of the father and the space of the paternal home, represented as the harem but only in its negative possibilities[69] rather than as a space of feminine sociability and mutual support. Sociability and support are on view amongst women who have been expelled from the harem. Some of these texts—such as Zaynab's narrative—can be read in more than one way. Is it the harem system that has failed? Or is it that the father has failed to implement it properly? By becoming a good father, at the end of the story, he reinstitutes the system as it should work. Yet, the vulnerability of the young woman to the angers and caprices of family men seems to underscore the moral fragility of the system.

Canny memoirs, these texts give only to retrieve. While they advertise the unveiling of real lives, in their layered attributions of authorship and narrative authority, they question the authenticity and authority of experience while claiming to represent it unproblematically. What I have called

simulated or ventriloquized memoirs claim to voice the experiences of subaltern or marginalized social figures and thereby to expose the seams of
elite society in narrating the daily lives of the disprivileged. The analytic, archival, and political dilemma of the researcher is to honor the possibility of
voiced, textually mediated experience while attending to the (further) layers
of representation and responsibility that frame these texts.

Claiming autobiographical authority for subjects who had no voice in
dominant discourses of the time, these texts bisect those discourses and
sometimes echo them. Yet, in the contours of their own narratives, they
highlight the silences of those more official discourses—whether those of
state representatives, feminists, antiprostitution activists, or liberal nationalists in opposition to the government. If the emerging Arabic novel traced
a local elite's concern with society-wide received expectations for female behavior, the simulated memoir took that concern a step further by constructing a first-person narrative voice claiming to speak from (and not only for)
female experience, and purporting to offer readers the narrative authority
of firsthand experience in the Cairo underworld as it traces a route from
the harem to the houseboat. In their organization of space and their particular mapping of urban Egypt, these texts interrogate the institution of
the honorable bayt—house, home, family—by opening it to critical view
and exposing it as fiction. Simultaneously, as these texts demolish the impermeability of the walls of the harem, they construct other houses that
have no impermeability but rather exhibit a free flow of males and females.
And from the spaces of these other houses, the texts voice a critique of elite
politics and spaces of behavior. They speak back to the discourse of anxiety
about growing female visibility in the society at large.

Yet the ultimate trajectory that these texts produce, a trajectory of desire,
is not a one-way street. In fact, the narratives carve out a path of return to
the father's home. The conditions of possibility for that return reside in
the maintenance of honor as female purity, a social value that these texts
do not contest but instead uphold. However, they do so by dissolving the
physical harem, by displacing honor from the walls of the paternal home
to the female body itself. They thus mark out a new space of female respectability, a public space of movement. But the female body, to claim
that space, must remain untouched and unseen: it must remain covered.
That body exchanges *ihtijab* for hijab—roughly, seclusion in the home for
the covering of the mature female body when outside the domain of immediate family. These texts distance themselves not so much from what

Arab feminists were saying as from what feminists were alleged (by their adversaries) to be doing, and more broadly from popular and conservative constructions of classed behavior—for which the accusation of Westernization had come to stand as a shorthand. Hence, the texts endlessly defer the threat of sexual violence as they enact a chaste space in which to produce a female modernity. It is only the uncovered body that cannot return to the father's home. This is the body clothed in Western garb, which constitutes a national threat in its advertisement of imported patterns of consumption. This is the body that marks the ultimate space of fallenness, the space where honor—individual and national, impervious to the rape of the outsider—is marked as irretrievable.

NOTES

I thank three readers for Duke University Press for their very helpful suggestions, and participants at the MIT conference for useful comments on an earlier draft. All translations are mine, unless otherwise indicated.

1 These texts can also be analyzed via the discourse on girls' schooling and reading practices; pronouncements and charity activities of elite early feminists in Egypt; widespread anxiety about Europeanization as expressed in the 1920s Egyptian press; and novels by the male writers of the 1920s through the 1930s who became canonized as the fathers of modern Arabic fiction.

   A further context, of course, is to consider prostitution narratives comparatively. Though I do not have the space to do that here, my work is informed by scholarship on prostitution and concepts and discourses of fallenness produced by Amanda Anderson, Charles Bernheimer, Carol Bernstein, Timothy Gilfoyle, Donna Guy, Gail Hershatter, Dominique Kalifa, Arlette Lafarge, Judith Walkowitz, and others. Moreover, these works can be juxtaposed with confessional fictional memoirs from other cultural contexts: John Cleland's *Fanny Hill, or Memoirs of a Woman of Pleasure* of course comes to mind, as do the works in Peakman, *Whore Biographies 1700–1825*.

2 Muhammad, *Mudhakkirat wasifa misriyya* and *Asrar wasifa misriyya*. The publication history of these texts is complex; they were issued serially and then in book form, and it is not even clear how many parts came out. Eight or ten parts (comprising the two books) are claimed, in the text itself, to have been published or to be in press. I have located seven (they are not numbered). Nusayr lists *Mudhakkirat wasifa misriyya* as published once, in 1927, in seven parts, by Dar al-Ma'arif; I have not found that version. My texts are the serial parts, to which I refer in these endnotes, as each is paginated separately. See Nusayr, *al-Kutub al-'arabiyya alati nushirat fi Misr bayna 'amay 1926–1940*, 166.

3 Philippe Lejeune is generally regarded as the preeminent theorizer of the "autobiographical pact." See Lejeune, *Le pacte autobiographique*.

4 One of the "editors" was certainly a prolific writer of fiction and social commentary, and among his preoccupations was the concept of fallenness. Farid's *Asrar al-shawari' wa al-qusur* (secrets of the streets and palaces: a contemporary moral Egyptian literary narrative) bears no date of publication, but on its cover the "narrative" (or "novel") asserts the status of historical reportage—"Its astonishing events took place in the city of Cairo approximately 1916 to 1919 AD."—and a precise date opens the story. Constructed in the third person, the relatively greater distance of the text from firsthand experience perhaps incites this historical referentiality.

5 I have not been able to locate this book, but it is announced at the end of part 1 of *Asrar wasifa misriyya*, and Zaynab Muhammad's name is mentioned as the editor. See "Majmu'at khutab Sa'd al-tarikhiyya," "Yawmiyyat tilmidh 'ashiq" (diaries of a lover pupil), 48, *Asrar wasifa misriyya*. Muhammad announces at the end of *Asrar wasifa misriyya*'s final part that she will return to her readers with books on "social topics" in the very near future ("Dawlat wa-dawahiha: al-Khatima" [Dawlat and her disasters: the end], 34, *Asrar wasifa misriyya*).

6 For more on this issue, see Booth, "From the Horse's Rump and the Whorehouse Keyhole."

7 The work is advertised in Zaynab Muhammad's text: thus, at least the first volume was probably out by 1927. The cover calls this volume 2, but there is no indication in the text that it is a continuation.

8 Specifically, males who would not be prohibited, by reason of kinds of kinship (colactation as well as consanguinity or relation by marriage), from marrying the female inhabitants of a household.

9 Moreover, the period also saw publication of a few studies and political essays on prostitution, although more of these appeared between the early 1930s and 1949, when legalized prostitution was abolished.

10 Yusuf, *Yawmiyyat saqita*. Another work in this vein is the clearly fictional 1922 *Mudhakkirat baghiy* (memoirs of a prostitute), by Muhammad Ra'fat Jamali, which I do not discuss here. It is of course possible that these works were authored by women using male pseudonyms. My research in periodicals of the time—in which works were often first serialized, advertised, or discussed—has so far yielded no information on these elusive issues of authorship.

11 I discuss this text in Booth, "Un/safe/ly at Home."

12 For a collection of such texts (both memoirs and polemics, which of course are not entirely separate), see Peakman, *Whore Biographies 1700–1825*. There are many parallels between these texts and the ones I analyze, but they are beyond the scope of this essay. I mention such parallels in a review of Peakman's work that appears in *Biography: An Interdisciplinary Quarterly* 31, no. 3 (summer 2008): 468–75.

13 I tackle issues of authorship, politics, and the popular in these texts in Booth, "From the Horse's Rump and the Whorehouse Keyhole."

14 This textualizing of space as gendered was, moreover, intimately linked to the emergence of the Arabic novel in the nineteenth century. See Booth, "Fiction's Imaginative Archive and the Newspaper's Local Scandals."

15 On this theme in nineteenth-century Arabic literature, see ibid; Sheehi, *Foundations of Modern Arab Identity*. And for Ottoman Turkish literature of the same period as representing heterosexual romance, see Shissler's chapter in this volume.

16 The latter is a translation of the title *Katirin al-thaniya, ashhar al-khati'at min sahibat al-tijan*. This pamphlet, produced as a gift supplement for readers of *al-Hilal* magazine in 1922, notes that it was translated specifically for the magazine but gives no author's or translator's name.

17 Booth, "Disruptions of the Local." On the petitions, see Fahmy, "Prostitution in Egypt in the Nineteenth Century."

18 Nord, *Walking the Victorian Streets*, 10. On this anxiety as represented in late-nineteenth-century newspaper reports on local and provincial events, see Booth, "Fiction's Imaginative Archive and the Newspaper's Local Scandals" and "Disruptions of the Local."

19 Muhammad, "'Ashiq ukhtih" [his sister's lover], 4, *Mudhakkirat wasifa misriyya*.

20 Ibid.

21 Ibid.

22 In this case, the postcards are the visual component; the written component is a medieval sex manual republished in Cairo in the 1920s, which Nu'man also waves in Zaynab's face. It may be that this signifies the overtaking (and/or buttressing) of local discourses on sexuality by European representations. The postcards may also be a sly and critical reference to the new presence on the local publishing scene of visual representations, especially of European and then local entertainment stars, in the new radio and film magazines.
    The following discussion is based on my "Un/safe/ly at Home."

23 Muhammad, "'Ashiq ukhtih," 8–9, *Mudhakkirat wasifa misriyya*.

24 In a crescendo of crude advances, his colloquial speech literally silences her articulateness. The crisis comes in his comment to her, after seeing her accompanied home by the brother of a friend: "Bravo, what a guy, so now you've seen the thing that's like the banana" ("'Ashiq ukhtih," 23, *Mudhakkirat wasifa misriyya*).

25 Other "memoirs" of this genre and era, however, expose the fragility of this expectation by narrating sexual assignations that take place "under cover"—specifically, under the cover of hackney cabs and full-face veils. See Booth, "From the Horse's Rump and the Whorehouse Keyhole."

26 Muhammad, "'Ashiq ukhtih," 29, *Mudhakkirat wasifa misriyya*.

27 See Booth, "Un/safe/ly at Home," for an elaboration of this point, concerning an embedded narrative in this same text wherein the speaker expresses her dashed hope to attend medical school.

28 On prostitution in nineteenth-century Egypt, which—in concert with public entertainment—was subjected to increasing regulation, see Hilal, *al-Baghaya fi Misr*; van Nieuwkerk, "A Trade Like Any Other," chap. 2; Tucker, *Women in Nineteenth-Century Egypt*, 150–55; and Fahmy, "Prostitution in Egypt in the Nineteenth Century." As Tucker notes (153), the focus of the 1896 law was on protection of clients from disease rather than on protection of prostitutes in any sense. Fahmy argues convincingly that concern over prostitution, particularly on the part of the

authorities, had less to do with morality than it did with concerns about public safety and (especially earlier in the century) health.

29 Booth, *May Her Likes Be Multiplied*, 141, and "Fiction's Imaginative Archive and the Newspaper's Local Scandals."

30 During the war and through the early 1920s, prostitution expanded enormously, as did venereal disease; see Hilal, *al-Baghaya fi Misr*, 182–92.

31 Anderson, *Tainted Souls and Painted Faces*, 3.

32 Badran, *Feminists, Islam, and Nation*, 192.

33 Fahmy, "Prostitution in Egypt in the Nineteenth Century," 86–87.

34 Russell, quoted in Booth, *Bayram al-Tunisi's Egypt*, 294 note 42. On Azbakiyya and Wishsh al-Birka as prostitution areas and their representation in popular literature (especially colloquial poetry) of the 1920s, see ibid., 150–51, 196–97.

35 For a brief biography of Abu al-'Uyun, see Hilal, *al-Baghaya fi Misr*, 204, note; and on his campaign, 205–14.

36 Indeed, Abu al-'Uyun's political use of the public sphere, especially of publication, is an instance of exemplary politicking: publishing his exchanges with various ministers, he puts them on record and holds them to account. He tells Zaki 'Abd al-Su'ud of the justice administration: "We are publishing these views so that people realize that the Ministry has its men, the government has its heroes . . . and so they will know that these men's views are matched by deeds" (Abu al-'Uyun, *Safha dhahabiyya*, 32).

37 Ibid., 5.

38 Van Nieuwkerk, "*A Trade Like Any Other*," 6.

39 Al-Bayyumi, *Al-Manazil al-sirriyya*, 1. On this topic in the press, see Booth, "Disruptions of the Local."

40 Abu al-'Uyun, *Safha dhahabiyya*, 4. *Karima* (plural, *kara'im*), "daughter," has the basic meaning of "precious thing" or even "body part."

41 I discuss this text's allegorical interface further in Booth, "Un/safe/ly at Home."

42 Muhammad, "'Ashiq ukhtih," 18, *Mudhakkirat wasifa misriyya*.

43 The image of Zaynab reading novels simultaneously supports the respectability of her narrative, giving weight to its potential moral efficacy, albeit one removed from the possible taint of fictionality by its definition as memoir. But the boundary seems porous indeed between these alleged memoirs and the crime novel series advertised in *Secrets* as the publisher's next venture.

44 The text claims, between the publication of one installment and another, to possess reformist efficacy, noting that a "house" (of prostitution) exposed in one installment was closed down before the next came out. See Booth, "From the Horse's Rump and the Whorehouse Keyhole."

45 Abu al-'Uyun, *Safha dhahabiyya*, 11. The prime minister's response was: "You have studied the subject well indeed."

46 This is emphatically *not* to suggest that women's storytelling has been devoid of sexual content or violent and misogynistic scenes. But presumably such stories have not centered on first-person narratives of sojourns in whorehouses.

47 For more on this, see Booth, "Un/safe/ly at Home."

48 Muhammad, "Yawmiyyat tilmidh 'ashiq," 24, *Asrar wasifa misriyya*.

49 These individuals are represented not only by the other women on the house-boat but also and most extensively by Bahiya Hanim, mistress of the husband of Zaynab's houseboat interlocutor, and the husband's consumption patterns are the focus of an extended dialogue. This troped intersection of consumption and dress is a complex one, figuring both classed consumption practices and exhibitionism as infections that endanger the nation, parallel with the infection of "secret diseases" (venereal diseases) and, by extension, the "secret houses" of prostitution. Tropes of disease and infection were ubiquitous in Victorian British and contemporaneous French rhetoric on prostitution. See Bernheimer, *Figures of Ill Repute*, in particular chap. 1, on the work of Parent-Duchâtelet. Indeed, the tropes of containment as well as those of decay and infection — all of it necessitating, in Parent-Duchâtelet's view, constant regulation and vigilance on the part of the government — that Bernheimer finds in this rhetoric are echoed consistently in Egyptian reformist discourse of the 1930s, although that discourse emphasizes the moral reprehensibility of regulating — and thereby on some level accepting — prostitution.

50 See an article by the Azhar shaykh 'Abd al-Baqi Surur Na'im, first published in *al-Ahram* and reprinted by Abu al-'Uyun in *Safha dhahabiyya*, 63–66, especially 66. I discuss *Mudhakkirat wasifa misriyya*'s representation of coerced marriage further in Booth, "Un/safe/ly at Home."

51 'Abd al-Baqi Surur Na'im, reprinted in Abu al-'Uyun, *Safha dhahabiyya*, 66.

52 Reprinted in Abu al-'Uyun, *Safha dhahabiyya*, 57.

53 Spain, *Gendered Spaces*. See also Mernissi, *Dreams of Trespass*, 186, in which the young author's mother tells her that "men keep women in harems to keep them from becoming too smart."

54 Bal, quoted in Mortimer, "Whose House Is This?" 469.

55 Mortimer, "Whose House Is This?"

56 For more on the efendi and this genre, see Booth, "From the Horse's Rump and the Whorehouse Keyhole."

57 'Atiya, *Mudhakkirat fi biqa' al-'ahirat*, 3–4. The carefully editorial cast of the text — "dedicated . . . to probing the personalities of those females, and those who fall in love with them, with a study of the women's situations and information on causes of their fall, and the upbringing and morals of all" — asserts the didactic worth of his enterprise; this writer has been "careful to preserve truthfulness in utterance and transmission . . . he who reads these investigations and observations will find a true lesson, not in grammar but rather one of those important lessons that embrace all of collective life, for those who have completed their ordinary lessons" (4).

58 Muhammad, "Hawanim al-qarn al-'ishrin" (ladies of the twentieth century), 47, *Mudhakkirat wasifa misriyya*. See also the advertisement in *Asrar wasifa misriyya* for *I'tirafat mumis* (confessions of a prostitute): "These are astonishing confessions from which one learns the cause of a young woman's fall, how young men operate to make her fall, offering her to others, who may take what he has taken from her. Two hundred pages, priced at 5 piasters" (Muhammad, "Yawmiyyat tilmidh 'ashiq," 48, *Asrar wasifa misriyya*).

59 'Atiya, *Mudhakkirat fi biqa' al-'ahirat*, 62.

60 Ibid., 3.

61 See Milani, "The Mediatory Guile of the Nanny in Persian Romance" (as well as the other essays in the special issue of the journal in which this appears); Najma-badi, "Reading 'Wiles of Women' Stories as Fictions of Masculinity."

62 'Atiya, *Mudhakkirat fi biqa' al-'ahirat*, 3.

63 Ibid., 5.

64 Anderson, *Tainted Souls and Painted Faces*, 1.

65 See the discussion in Booth, "Un/safe/ly at Home," of the narrator of *Diaries of a Prostitute*, an aging prostitute who has her own home and defines her honorable-ness as stealing money from would-be clients to give to the poor.

66 'Atiya, *Mudhakkirat fi biqa' al-'ahirat*, 6–7.

67 Ibid., 24. Ironically, his complaint to the police chief has the effect of highlight-ing women's resistance to state regulation. His advice to "those working for the 'women's awakening'" — that they "banish" all women who act outside of "accepted moral boundaries" — further suggests a lack of sympathy.

68 Muhammad, "Hawanim al-qarn al-'ishrin," 37, *Mudhakkirat wasifa misriyya*.

69 They are thus silent on aspects of gender segregation in domestic space that shaped mutually supportive homosocial communities, as recalled and constructed, for in-stance, by Fatima Mernissi and Leila Ahmed in their respective works of memoir and reflection, or in Altaf Fatima's novel set among elite Muslim households in India. See Mernissi, *Dreams of Trespass*; Ahmed, *A Border Passage*; Fatima, *The One Who Did Not Ask*.

BIBLIOGRAPHY

Dates of publication are given for the Christian era, the Islamic era, or both, depending on the information available.

'Abd al-'Aziz Badr, Hamza, and Daniel Crecelius. "The *Awqāf* of al-Hajj Bashir Agha in Cairo." *Annales Islamologiques* 27 (1993): 291–308.

'Abd al-Baqi, Muhammad Fu'ad. *Al-Mu'jam al-mufahras li-alfaz al-Qur'an al-Karim.* Istanbul: al-Maktabah al-Islamiyah Mehmed Özdemir, 1982.

'Abd al-Raziq, Ahmad. *La femme au temps des Mamlouks en Egypte.* Cairo: Institut français d'archéologie orientale du Caire, 1973.

Abdesselem, Ahmed. *Les historiens Tunisiens des XVIIe, XVIIIe et XIXe siècles: Essai d'histoire culturelle.* Paris: Klincksieck, 1973.

Abdulac, Samir. "Traditional Housing Design in Arab Countries." In *Designing in Islamic Cultures 2: Urban Housing,* edited by M. B. Sevcenko, 2–9. Cambridge, Mass.: Aga Khan Program for Islamic Architecture, 1982.

Abu al-'Uyun, Mahmud. *Safha dhahabiyya: Ara' wuzara' al-dawla al-misriyya fi al-bagha' wa-ara' rijalin mas'ulina wa-amirin min kibar al-umara'.* Cairo: Matba'at al-ma'arif, 1928.

Afsaruddin, Asma. *Excellence and Precedence: Medieval Islamic Discourse on Legitimate Leadership.* Leiden: Brill, 2002.

———. "The Excellences of the Qur'an: Textual Sacrality and the Organization of Early Islamic Society." *Journal of the American Oriental Society* 122, no. 1
(2002): 1–24.

———. "Introduction: The Hermeneutics of Gendered Space and Discourse."
In *Hermeneutics and Honor: Negotiating Female "Public" Space in Islamic/ate
Societies*, edited by Asma Afsaruddin, 1–28. Harvard Middle East Monographs. Cambridge: Harvard University Press for the Center for Middle Eastern Studies, Harvard University, 1999.

———. "Knowledge, Piety, and Religious Leadership: Re-inserting Women into
the Master Narrative." In *Sisters in Faith: Women, Religion and Leadership in
Christianity and Islam*, edited by Scott Alexander. Lanham, Md.: Rowman and
Littlefield, forthcoming.

Ahmed, Leila. *A Border Passage: From Cairo to America; A Woman's Journey.*
London: Penguin, 1999.

———. *Edward W. Lane: A Study of His Life and Works and of British Ideas of
the Middle East in the Nineteenth Century.* London: Longman, 1978.

———. "Western Ethnocentrism and Perceptions of the Harem." *Feminist
Studies* 8, no. 3 (1982): 521–34.

———. *Women and Gender in Islam.* New Haven: Yale University Press, 1992.

Ahmed Resmi Efendi, Giridı. *Hamîlet ül-kübera': Darüssaade ağaları* (the ostrich
plumes of the great), edited by Ahmet Nezihi Turan. Istanbul: Kitabevi, 2000.

Ahmet Midhat Efendi. "Bekârlık Sultanlık mi Dedin?" 1875. In *Letaif-i Rivayet*,
edited by Fazıl Gökçek and Sabahattin Çağın, 269–81. Istanbul: Çağrı Yayınları, 2001.

———. *Felâtun Bey ile Râkım Efendi.* 1875. In *Ahmet Midhat Efendi Bütün Eserleri: Romanlar I*, edited by Kâzım Yetiş, Necat Birinci, and M. Fatih Andi,
27–273. Ankara: Türk Dil Kurumu Yayınları, 2000.

———. *Henüz 17 Yaşında.* 1881. In *Ahmet Midhat Efendi Bütün Eserleri: Romanlar VII*, edited by Nuri Sağlam, Kâzım Yetis, and M. Fatih Andi, 5–213. Ankara: Türk Dil Kurumu Yayınları, 2000.

Aisen-Elouafi, Amy. "Being Ottoman: Family and the Politics of Modernity in
the Province of Tunisia." Ph.D. diss., University of California, Berkeley, 2007.

Akgündüz, Ahmet. *Osmanlı Kanunnâmeleri ve Hukuki Tahlilleri.* 12 vols. to date.
Istanbul: Fey Vakfı, 1990–.

Alberti, Leon Battista. *On the Art of Building in Ten Books.* Translated by Joseph
Rykwert, Neil Leach, and Robert Tavernor. Cambridge: MIT Press, 1988.

Allen, John. *Lost Geographies of Power.* Malden, Mass.: Blackwell, 2003.

Allen, Roger. "Writings of Members of the Nazli Circle." *Journal of the American
Research Center in Egypt* 8 (1969–70): 79–84.

Allen, William. "Sixty-five Istanbul Photographers, 1887–1914." In *Shadow and
Substance: Essays in the History of Photography*, edited by Kathleen Collins, 127–
36. Bloomfield Hills, Mich.: Amorphous Institute Press, 1990.

Alloula, Malek. *The Colonial Harem.* Translated by Myrna Godzich and Wlad
Godzich. Theory and History of Literature, vol. 21. Minneapolis: University of
Minnesota Press, 1986.

Altoma, Salih J. "The Emancipation of Women in Contemporary Syrian Literature." In *Syria: Society, Culture and Polity*, edited by Richard T. Antoun and
Donald Quataert, 79–96. Albany: State University of New York Press, 1991.

Amin, Qasim. *Al-Mar'a al-jadida*. Cairo, 1900.

———. 1899. *Tahrir al-mar'a*. Cairo: Dar al-Ma'arif, 1970.

And, Metin. *Turkish Miniature Painting*. Ankara: Dost yayinlari, 1974.

Anderson, Amanda. *Tainted Souls and Painted Faces: The Rhetoric of "Fallenness"
in Victorian Britain*. Ithaca: Cornell University Press, 1993.

Apter, Emily. "Female Trouble in the Colonial Harem." *Differences* 4, no. 1 (1992):
205–24.

Arabian Nights. Translated and with a preface by Edward Forster. 5 vols. London:
William Miller, 1802.

Ardener, Shirley. Introduction. In *Women and Space: Ground Rules and Social
Maps*, edited by Shirley Ardener, 1–30. Oxford: Berg, 1997.

Ardener, Shirley, ed. *Women and Space: Ground Rules and Social Maps*. Oxford:
Berg, 1997.

'Arib. *Silat tarikh al-Tabari*. Edited by M. J. De Goeje. Leiden: Brill, 1897.

Arif, Mehmed. "Kanunname-i Al-i Osman." *Tarih-i Osmanî Encümeni Mecmuası*.
Supplement. Istanbul: Tarih-i Osmani Encümeni, 1329/1911–12.

Arkoun, Mohammed. *The Unthought in Contemporary Islamic Thought*. London:
Saqi, 2002.

Arnaud, J. *Les eaux thermales de Korbous près Tunis (Tunisie)*. Paris: Levé, 1912.

Asad, Talal. *Formations of the Secular: Christianity, Islam, Modernity*. Stanford:
Stanford University Press, 1993.

'Ata, Tayyarzade Ahmed Atâullah. *Tarih-i 'Ata*, 5 vols. Istanbul: Yahya Efendi
Matba'asi, 1875–76.

Atil, Esin. *Levni and the Sûrnâme: The Story of an Eighteenth-Century Ottoman
Festival*. Istanbul: Koçbank, 1999.

'Atiya, 'A. *Mudhakkirat 'amil fi biqa' al-'ahirat*. Vol. 2. Cairo: Matba'at Wadi
al-Muluk, n.d.

'Attar, Samar. *Al-Bayt fi sahat 'Arnus*. Sydney: Manshurat Sharbal Bi'ayni, 1988.

———. *The House on Arnus Square*. Translated by the author. Pueblo, Colo.:
Passeggiata, 1998.

Ayalon, Ami. *The Press in the Arab Middle East*. New York: Oxford University
Press, 1995.

Ayyub, Dhu al-Nun. *Al-Athar al-kamila li-adab Dhi al-Nun Ayyub*. Baghdad:
Wizarat al-i'lam, 1978.

Azhari, Abu Mansur Muhammad b. Ahmad al-. *Tahdhib al-lughat*. Edited by
'Abd Allah Darwish and Muhammad 'Ali al-Najjar. 9 vols. Cairo: al-Dar al-
misriyah li'l-ta'lif wa al-tarjamah, 1964–66.

'Azma, Bashir al-. *Jil al-hazima: Bayna al-wahda waal-infisal; Mudhakkirat*. London: Riyad al-Rayyis lil-kutub waal-nashr, 1991.

Babayan, Kathryn. "The ''Aqā'id al-nisā': A Glimpse at Safavid Women in
Local Isfahani Culture." In *Women in the Medieval Islamic World*, edited by
Gavin Hambly, 349–81. New York: St. Martin's, 1998.

Bachelard, Gaston. *The Poetics of Space.* Translated by Maria Jolas. Boston: Beacon, 1969.

Bachrouch, Taoufik. *Le Saint et le Prince en Tunisie: Les Elites Tunisiennes du pouvoir et de la devotion.* Tunis: Publications de la Faculté des Sciences Humaines et Sociales de Tunis, 1989.

Badr, 'Abd al-Muhsin Taha. *Tatawwur al-riwaya al-'arabiyya al-haditha fi Misr, 1870–1938.* Cairo: Dar al-ma'arif, 1963.

Badran, Margot. "Dual Liberation: Feminism and Nationalism in Egypt, 1870s–1925." *Feminist Issues* 8, no. 1 (1988): 15–34.

———. *Feminists, Islam, and Nation: Gender and the Making of Modern Egypt.* Princeton: Princeton University Press, 1995.

———. Introduction. In Huda Sha'rawi, *Harem Years: The Memoirs of an Egyptian Feminist,* 7–22. Translated by Margot Badran. London: Virago, 1986.

Baedeker, Karl. *Baedekers Konstantinopel, Balkanstaaten, Kleinasien, Archipel, Cypern: Handbuch für Reisende.* Leipzig: Karl Baedeker, 1914.

Baer, Gabriel. "Slavery in Nineteenth Century Egypt." *Journal of African History* 8, no. 3 (1967): 417–41.

Bahloul, Joëlle. *The Architecture of Memory: A Jewish-Muslim Household in Colonial Algeria, 1937–1962.* Cambridge: Cambridge University Press, 1996.

Baldwin, Gordon. *Roger Fenton: Pasha and Bayadère.* Los Angeles: J. Paul Getty Museum, 1996.

Balibar, Etienne. "The Nation Form: History and Ideology." In Etienne Balibar and Immanuel Wallerstein, *Race, Nation, Class: Ambiguous Identities,* 86–106. Translated by Chris Turner. London: Verso, 1991.

Barkan, Ömer Lûtfi. *XV ve XVIinci Asırlarda Osmanlı İmparatorluğunda Ziraî Ekonominin Hukukî ve Malî Esaslar: Kanunlar.* Istanbul: Bürhaneddin Erenler Matbaası, 1943.

———. "Kânûn-nâme." In *İslam Ansiklopedisi,* 6:185–96. Istanbul: Milli Eğitim Basımevi, 1977.

———. "Osmanlı Devrinde Akkoyunlu Hükümdarı Uzun Hasan Beye Ait Kanunlar." *Tarih Vesikaları* 1–2 (1941): 91–106; 3 (1941): 184–96.

Baron, Beth. "Readers and the Women's Press in Egypt." *Poetics Today* 15, no. 2 (1994): 217–40.

———. *The Women's Awakening in Egypt.* New Haven: Yale University Press, 1994.

Bates, Daniel. *Nomads and Farmers: A Study of the Yörük of Southeastern Turkey.* Ann Arbor: University of Michigan Press, 1973.

Batur, Sabahattin. "The Harem as an Institution in Ottoman Life." In *The Topkapı Saray Museum: Architecture, the Harem and Other Buildings,* edited by J. Michael Rogers, 19–26. London: Thames and Hudson, 1988.

Bayly, C. A. *The Birth of the Modern World, 1780–1914: Global Connections and Comparisons.* Oxford: Blackwell, 2004.

———. *Empire and Information: Intelligence Gathering and Social Communication in India, 1780–1870.* Cambridge: Cambridge University Press, 1996.

Bayram V, Muhammad. *Safwat al-'itibar bi-mustawda al-amsar wa al-aqtar*. 5 vols. Beirut: Dar Sadir, 1974.

Bayyumi, Muhammad Sa'id al-. *Al-Manazil al-sirriyya*. Cairo: Matba'at Abi Hul, 1919.

Beaulieu, Jill, and Mary Roberts, eds. *Orientalism's Interlocutors: Painting, Architecture and Photography*. Durham: Duke University Press, 2002.

Behdad, Ali. "The Eroticized Orient: Images of the Harem in Montesquieu and His Precursors." *Stanford French Review* 13, 2–3 (1989): 109–26.

Ben Achour, Mohamed El Aziz. *Catégories de la Société Tunisoise dans la deuxième moitié du XIXème siècle*. Tunis: Institut National d'Archeologie et d'Art, 1989.

———. *La Cour du Bey de Tunis*. Tunis: Espace Diwan, 2003.

Bergaoui, Mohamed. *Tourisme et Voyages en Tunisie: Les Années de la Régence*. 3rd ed. Tunis: Simpact, 2005.

Berkes, Niyazi. *The Development of Secularism in Turkey*. New York: Routledge, 1998.

Bernheimer, Charles. *Figures of Ill Repute: Representing Prostitution in Nineteenth-Century France*. Durham: Duke University Press, 1997.

Bey, El-Mokhtar. *Les Beys de Tunis (1705–1957): Hérédité, Souveraineté, Généalogie*. Tunis: Serviced, 2002.

Bey, Fayçal. "Le 1er décembre 1846: Le bey de Tunis chez le roi des français." *Histoire*, March 19, 2004, 68–69.

———. *La Dernière Odalisque*. Paris: Stock, 2001.

Bhabha, Homi K. "Signs Taken for Wonders: Questions of Ambivalence and Authority under a Tree outside Delhi, May 1817." In Homi K. Bhabha, *The Location of Culture*, 101–22. London: Routledge, 1994.

Bianca, Stefano, ed. *Syria: Medieval Citadels between East and West*. Turin: Umberto Allemandi, 2007.

———. *Urban Form in the Arab World, Past and Present*. London: Thames and Hudson, 2000.

Bianca, Stefano A., Jean-Claude David, Giovanni Rizzardi, Yves Beton, and Bruno Chauffert-Yvart. *The Conservation of the Old City of Aleppo: A Report Prepared for the Government of the Syrian Arab Republic by the United Nations Educational, Scientific and Cultural Organization*. Restricted technical report PP/1979-80/4/7.6/05. Paris: UNESCO, 1980.

Bin Hamida, Muhsin. *Al-Baji al-Mas'udi*. Tunis: Maison Tunisienne de l'Edition, 1962.

Blackbourn, David. "'Taking the Waters': Meeting Places of the Fashionable World." In *The Mechanics of Internationalism: Culture, Society, and Politics from the 1840s to the First World War*, edited by Martin H. Geyer and Johannes Paulmann, 435–57. Oxford: Oxford University Press, 2001.

Blecher, Robert. "When Television Is Mandatory: Syrian Television Drama in the 1990s." In *France, Syrie et Liban 1918–1946: Les ambiguïtés et les dynamiques de la relation mandataire*, edited by Nadine Méouchy, 169–80. Damascus: Institut français d'études arabes de Damas, 2002.

Blili, Leila Temime. *Histoire de familles: Mariages, repudiations et vie quotidienne à Tunis, 1875–1930.* Tunis: Script, 1999.

Bluestone, Daniel. "Academics in Tennis Shoes: Historic Preservation and the Academy." *Journal of the Society of Architectural Historians* 58, no. 3 (September 1999): 300–307.

Boer, Inge E. "Despotism from under the Veil: Masculine and Feminine Readings of the Despot and the Harem." *Cultural Critique* 32 (1995–96): 43–73.

Bonebakker, S. A. "Adab and the Concept of Belles-Lettres." In *The Cambridge History of Arabic Literature: Abbasid Belles-Lettres,* edited by Julia Ashtiani, T. M. Johnstone, J. D. Latham, and R. B. Serjeant, 16–30. Cambridge: Cambridge University Press, 1990.

Booth, Marilyn. "Armchair Harems." H-Gender MidEast, posted September 29, 2007. http://h-net.msu.edu/.

———. *Bayram al-Tunisi's Egypt: Social Criticism and Narrative Strategies.* Exeter, Great Britain: Ithaca Press, 1990.

———. "Disruptions of the Local, Eruptions of the Feminine: Local Reportage and National Anxieties in an 1890s Egyptian Daily." Paper presented at the Mediterranean Research Meeting, Robert Schumann Centre of the European University, Montecatini Terme, Italy, March 12–15, 2008.

———. "Fiction's Imaginative Archive and the Newspaper's Local Scandals: The Case of Nineteenth-Century Egypt." In *Archive Stories: Facts, Fictions and the Writing of History,* edited by Antoinette Burton, 274–95. Durham: Duke University Press, 2005.

———. "From the Horse's Rump and the Whorehouse Keyhole: Ventriloquized Memoirs as Political Voice in 1920s Egypt." *Maghreb Review* 32, nos. 2–3 (2007): 233–61.

———. "John Stuart Mill . . . Islamist? Conduct Literature, Islamic Politics, and Gender in Egypt." Unpublished manuscript, 2004.

———. *May Her Likes Be Multiplied: Biography and Gender Politics in Egypt.* Berkeley: University of California Press, 2001.

———. "On Gender, History . . . and Fiction." In *Middle East Historiographies: Narrating the Twentieth Century,* edited by Israel Gershoni, Amy Singer, and Y. Hakan Erdem, 211–41. Seattle: University of Washington Press, 2006.

———. "Un/safe/ly at Home: Narratives of Sexual Coercion in 1920s Egypt." In "Special Issue on Violence, Vulnerability and Embodiment," edited by Shani D'Cruze and Anupama Rao, 744–68. *Gender and History* 16, no. 3 (2004).

Boserup, Ester. *Woman's Role in Economic Development.* New York: St. Martin's, 1970.

Bourdieu, Pierre. *The Logic of Practice.* Translated by Richard Nice. Stanford: Stanford University Press, 1990.

———. *Outline of a Theory of Practice.* Translated by Richard Nice. Cambridge: Cambridge University Press, 1977.

Boutier, Jean. "Un autre Midi: Notes sur les sociétés populaires en Corse (1790–1794)." *Annales Historiques de la Revolution Française* 268 (janvier–mars 1987): 158–75.

Boym, Svetlana. *The Future of Nostalgia*. New York: Basic, 2001.

Bray, Julia. "A Caliph and His Public Relations." *Middle Eastern Literatures* 7, no. 2 (2004): 159–69.

Brown, Marilyn R. "The Harem De-Historicized: Ingres's *Turkish Bath*." *Arts* 61, no. 10 (summer 1987): 58–68.

Bryson, Norman. *Tradition and Desire*. Cambridge: Cambridge University Press, 1984.

Bukhari, Muhammad b. Isma'il al-. *Sahih*. Bilingual ed. Translated by Muhammad Muhsin Khan. 9 vols. Chicago: Kazi, 1979.

Burton, Antoinette. "Reviewed work(s): *Gendering Orientalism: Race, Femininity, and Representation* by Reina Lewis and *Colonial Fantasies: Towards a Feminist Reading of Orientalism* by Meyda Yeğenoğlu." *Signs* 25, no. 1 (autumn 1999): 243–46.

Busquets, Joan, ed. *Aleppo: Rehabilitation of the Old City; The Eighth Veronica Rudge Green Prize in Urban Design*. Cambridge: Harvard Graduate School of Design, 2005.

Cambon, Paul. "Lettres de Tunisie." *Revue des Deux Mondes* 3 (May 1931): 127–50; 373–98.

Cannon, Byron D. "Nineteenth-Century Arabic Writings on Women and Society: The Interim Role of the Masonic Press in Cairo (*al-Lata'if*, 1885–1895)." *International Journal of Middle East Studies* 17, no. 4 (1985): 463–84.

Carlier, Omar. "Le Café maure: Sociabilité masculine et effervescence citoyenne (Algérie XVIIe–XXe siècles)." *Annales: Economies, Sociétés, Civilisations* 45, no. 4 (1990): 975–1003.

Casey, Edward S. "The World of Nostalgia." *Man and World* 20, no. 4 (1987): 361–84.

Cavasino, Agnès. *Emilie de Vialar Fondatrice: Les Soeurs de Saint-Joseph de l'Apparition; Une congrégation missionaire*. Fontenay-sous-Bois, France: Congrégation des Soeurs de Saint-Joseph de l'Apparition, 1987.

Çelik, Zeynep. "Speaking Back to Orientalist Discourse at the World's Columbian Exposition." In *Noble Dreams, Wicked Pleasures: Orientalism in America, 1870–1930*, edited by Holly Edwards, 77–98. Princeton: Princeton University Press, 2000.

Cerasi, Maurice. "The Formation of Ottoman House Types: A Comparative Study in Interaction with Neighboring Cultures." *Muqarnas* 15 (1998): 116–56.

Chapoutot-Remadi, Mounira. "Femmes dans la ville Mamluke." *Journal of the Economic and Social History of the Orient* 38, no. 2 (1995): 145–64.

Chater, Khélifa. *Dépendance et mutations précoloniales: La régence de Tunis de 1815 à 1857*. Tunis: Publications de l'Université de Tunis, 1984.

Chatterjee, Partha. *The Nation and Its Fragments*. Princeton: Princeton University Press, 1993.

Choay, Françoise. *The Invention of the Historic Monument*. Translated by Lauren O'Connell. Cambridge: Cambridge University Press, 2001.

Çizgen, Engin. *Photographer/Fotografçi Ali Sami, 1866–1936*. Istanbul: Haşet Kitabevi, 1989.

————. *Photography in the Ottoman Empire*. Istanbul: Haşet Kitabevi, 1987.

Clancy-Smith, Julia. "The Intimate, the Familial, and the Local in Trans-national Histories of Gender." *Journal of Women's History* 18, no. 2 (2006): 174–83.

————. "Exoticism, Erasures, and Absence: The Peopling of Algiers, 1830–1900." In *Walls of Algiers: Narratives of the City through Text and Image*, edited by Zeynep Celik, Julia Clancy-Smith, and Frances Terpak. Los Angeles: Getty Research Institute and Seattle: University of Washington Press, 2009, 19–61.

————. "Le regard colonial: Islam, genre et identités dans l'Algérie Français." Translated by François Armengaud. *Nouvelles Questions Féministes* 25, no. 1 (2006): 25–40.

————. *Mediterraneans: North Africa and Europe in an Age of Migration, c. 1800–1900*. Berkeley: University of California Press, 2010.

————. "A Visit to a Tunisian Harem." *Journal of Maghrebi Studies* 1–2, no. 1 (spring 1993): 43–49.

Coe, Brian, and Paul Gates. *The Snapshot Photograph: The Rise of Popular Photography*. London: Ash and Grant, 1977.

Cole, Juan R. I. *Colonialism and Revolution in the Middle East: Social and Cultural Origins of Egypt's 'Urabi Movement*. Cairo: American University in Cairo Press, 1999.

————. "Feminism, Class, and Islam in Turn-of-the-Century Egypt." *International Journal of Middle East Studies* 10, no. 2 (1981): 393–405.

————. "Printing and Urban Islam in the Mediterranean World, 1890-1920." In *Modernity and Culture from the Mediterranean to the Indian Ocean*, edited by Leila Tarazi Fawaz and C. A. Bayly, 344-64. New York: Columbia University Press, 2002.

Conklin, Alice L., and Julia Clancy-Smith. Introduction. In "Writing French Colonial Histories," edited by Alice L. Conklin and Julia Clancy-Smith, 497–505. Special issue, *French Historical Studies* 27, no. 3 (summer 2004).

Connelly, Bridget. *Arab Folk Epic and Identity*. Berkeley: University of California Press, 1986.

Cook, Michael A. *Commanding Right and Forbidding Wrong in Islamic Thought*. Cambridge: Cambridge University Press, 2001.

Corbin, Alain. *The Lure of the Sea: The Discovery of the Seaside in the Western World, 1750–1840*. Translated by Jocelyn Phelps. Cambridge: Cambridge University Press, 1994.

Crabbs, Jack A. *The Writing of History in Nineteenth-Century Egypt: A Study in National Transformation*. Detroit, Mich.: Wayne State University Press, 1984.

David, Jean-Claude. "La cour-jardin des maisons d'Alep à l'époque ottomane." *Res Orientales* 3 (1991): 63–72.

————. "Une grande maison de la fin du XVIe siècle à Alep." *Bulletin d'Études Orientales* 50 (1998): 61–96.

————. "Nouvelles architectures domestiques à Alep au XIXe siècle: Expressions locales d'un phénomène régional?" In *La maison beyrouthine aux trois arcs: Une architecture bourgeoise du Levant*, edited by Michael F. Davie, 217–43. Beirut: Centre de recherches et d'études sur l'urbanisation du monde arabe, 2003.

————. "Politique et urbanisme à Alep, le projet de Bab al-Faradj." In *Etat, ville et mouvements sociaux au Maghreb et au Moyen-Orient*, edited by Kenneth Brown, Bernard Hourcade, Michèle Jolé, Claude Liauzu, Peter Sluglett, and Sami Zubaida, 317–24. Paris: L'Harmattan, 1989.

David, Jean-Claude, and Fawaz Baker. "Élaboration de la nouveauté en architecture en Syrie." *Environmental Design* 1-2 (1994–95): 50–75.

David, Jean-Claude, and Dominique Hubert. "Maisons et immeubles du début du XXe siècle à Alep." *Les cahiers de la recherche architecturale* nos. 10–11 (April 1982): 94–101.

Davis, Fanny. *The Ottoman Lady: A Social History from 1718 to 1918.* Westport, Conn.: Greenwood, 1986.

Day, Philippa, ed. *At Home in Carthage: The British in Tunisia.* Tunis: Trustees of St. Georges Church, 1992.

de la Broquière, Bertrandon. *Le Voyage d'Outremer.* Edited by C. Schefer. Paris: E. Leroux, 1892.

De la Puente, Cristina. "Sin linaje, sin alcurnia, sin hogar: Eunucos en el Andalus en época Omeya." In *Identidades Marginales*, edited by Cristina De la Puente, 147–93. Madrid: Consejo Superior de invetigaciones ceintíficas, 2003.

De Lauretis, Teresa. "The Technology of Gender." In Teresa de Lauretis, *Technologies of Gender: Essays on Theory, Film, and Fiction*, 1–30. Bloomington: Indiana University Press, 1987.

Debbasch, Yvan. *La nation française en Tunisie (1577–1835).* Paris: Sirey, 1957.

DelPlato, Joan. "A British 'Feminist' in the Turkish Harem: A Portrait of Lady Mary Wortley Montagu." In *Eighteenth-Century Women and the Arts*, edited by Frederick Keener and Susan Lorsch, 148–63. Westport, Conn.: Greenwood, 1988.

————. "Collecting/ Painting Harem/ Clothing." In *Material Cultures, 1740–1920*, edited by John Potvin and Alla Myzalev, 87–108. Aldershot, England: Ashgate, 2009.

————. "Lefebvre's Critique of Space as Interdisciplinary Paradigm: Desire and Colonialism in Three Harem Paintings by Delacroix, Renoir and Lewis, 1834–70." In *Gendered Landscapes: An Interdisciplinary Exploration of Past Place and Space*, edited by Bonj Szczgiel, Josephine Carubia, and Lorraine Dowler, 66–81. University Park: Pennsylvania State University, Center for Studies in Landscape History, 2000.

————. *Multiple Wives, Multiple Pleasures: Representing the Harem, 1800–1875.* Madison, N.J.: Fairleigh Dickinson University Press, 2002.

Deutsch, Sarah. *Women and the City: Gender, Spaces, and Power in Boston, 1870–1940.* Oxford: Oxford University Press, 2000.

Dialmy, Abdessamad. *Logement, sexualité et Islam.* Casablanca: Éditions Eddif, 1995.

Di-Capua, Yoav. "The Thought and Practice of Modern Egyptian Historiography, 1890–1970." Ph.D. diss., Princeton University, 2004.

Domosh, Mona, and Joni Seager. *Putting Women in Place: Feminist Geographers Make Sense of the World.* New York: Guilford, 2001.

Dorys, Georges. *The Private Life of the Sultan of Turkey.* Translated by Arthur Hornblow. New York: Appleton, 1902.

Duben, Alan, and Cem Behar. *Istanbul Households: Marriage, Family and Fertility, 1880–1940.* Cambridge: Cambridge University Press, 1991.

Duda, Dorothea. *Innenarchitektur syruscher Stadthäuser des 16.-18. Jh.: Die Sammlung Henri Pharaon in Beirut.* Beirut: Franz Steiner, 1971.

Dunant, J. Henry. *Notice sur la Régence de Tunis.* Geneva: Jules Fick, 1858.

Duncan, Nancy. "Renegotiating Gender and Sexuality in Public and Private Spaces." In *Bodyspace: Destabilizing Geographies of Gender and Sexuality,* edited by Nancy Duncan, 127–45. London: Routledge, 1996.

Düzdağ, M. E. *Şeyhülislam Ebussuâd Efendi Fetvaları Işığında 16: Asır Türk Hayatı.* Istanbul: Erdoğan Kitabevi, 1983.

Early, Evelyn A. "Syrian Television Drama: Permitted Political Discourse." In *Everyday Life in the Muslim Middle East,* edited by Donna Lee Bowen and Evelyn A. Early, 322–34. 2nd ed. Bloomington: Indiana University Press, 2002.

El Cheikh, Nadia Maria. "Revisiting the Abbasid Harems." *Journal of Middle East Women's Studies* 1, no. 3 (fall 2005): 1–19.

———. "Women's History: A Study of al-Tanukhi." In *Writing the Feminine: Women in Arab Sources,* edited by Manuela Marin and Randi Deguilhem, 129–48. London: I. B. Tauris, 2002.

Eldem, Sedad H., and Feridun Akozan. *Topkapı Sarayı: Bir Mimari Araştırma.* Istanbul: Kültür ve Turizm Bakanlığı, 1982.

El-Hibri, Tayeb. *Reinterpreting Islamic Historiography: Harun al-Rashid and the Narrative of the 'Abbasid Caliphate.* Cambridge: Cambridge University Press, 1999.

El-Rouayheb, Khaled. *Before Homosexuality in the Arab-Islamic World, 1500–1800.* Chicago: University of Chicago Press, 2005.

Encyclopaedia Britannica. 11th ed. Cambridge: Cambridge University Press, 1910–11.

Encyclopaedia of Islam. New ed. Edited by H. Gibb et al. Leiden: Brill, 1960–2008. [Cited as *EI²*.]

Entrikin, J. Nicholas. *The Betweenness of Place: Towards a Geography of Modernity.* Baltimore: Johns Hopkins University Press, 1991.

Fahmy, Khaled. "Prostitution in Egypt in the Nineteenth Century." In *Outside In: On the Margins of the Modern Middle East,* edited by Eugene Rogan, 77–103. London: I. B. Tauris, 2002.

Farid, Mahmud Kamil. *Asrar al-shawari' wa al-qusur: Riwaya adabiyya misriyya akhlaqiyya 'asriyya.* Cairo [distributed by Idarat matba'at al-ma'ahid], n.d.

Fatima, Altaf. *The One Who Did Not Ask.* Translated by Rukhsana Ahmad. Oxford: Heinemann, 1993.

Fay, Mary Ann. "Women and Waqf: Toward a Reconsideration of Women's Place in the Mamluk Household." *International Journal of Middle East Studies* 29 (1997): 33–51.

Fayruzabadi al-Shirazi, Majd al-Din Muhammad b. Ya'qub al-. *Qamus al-muhit.* 4 vols. Cairo: al-Matba'ah al-Kustaliyah, 1289 [A.H.].

Finn, Robert. *The Early Turkish Novel, 1872–1900*. Istanbul: Isis, 1984.

Fishman, Robert. *Bourgeois Utopias: The Rise and Fall of Suburbia*. New York: Basic, 1987.

Ford, Colin, and Karl Steinorth, eds. *You Press the Button, We Do the Rest: The Birth of Snapshot Photography*. London: Nishen, 1988.

Foucault, Michel. *Discipline and Punish: The Birth of the Prison*. Translated by Alan Sheridan. New York: Vintage, 1979.

———. *History of Sexuality*. Vol. 1, *Introduction*. Translated by Robert Hurley. New York: Vintage, 1978.

———. "Of Other Spaces." Translated by Jay Miskowiec. *Diacritics* 16, no. 1 (1986): 22–27.

Friès, Franck. "Les plans d'Alep et de Damas, un banc d'essai pour l'urbanisme des frères Danger (1931–1937)." *Revue du Monde Musulman et de la Méditerranée* 73–74 (1994): 311–25.

Gabrieli, Francesco. "Il valore letterario e storico del farag ba'da s-sidda di Tanūhı." *Revista Degli Studi Orientali* 19 (1940–41): 16–44.

Gallant, Thomas W. *Experiencing Dominion: Culture, Identity, and Power in the British Mediterranean*. Notre Dame, Ind.: University of Notre Dame Press, 2002.

Ganiage, Jean. *Les Origines du Protectorat Français en Tunisie (1861–1881)*. Tunis: Maison Tunisienne de l'Edition, 1968.

Gaube, Heinz, and Eugen Wirth. *Aleppo: Historische und geographische Beiträge zur baulichen Gestaltung, zur sozialen Organisation und zur wirtschaftlichen Dynamik einer vorderasiatischen Fernhandelsmetropole*. Wiesbaden, Germany: L. Reichert, 1984.

Gautier, Théophile. *Constantinople*. 1853. Translated by Robert Howe Gould. New York: Henry Holt, 1875.

———. *Critique d'Art, Extraits des Salons (1833–1872)*. Edited by Marie-Hélène Girard. Paris: Séguier, 1994.

Georgeon, François. "L'Économie politique selon Ahmed Midhat." In *Des Ottomans aux Turcs: Naissance d'une nation*, edited by François Georgeon, 223–40. Istanbul: Isis, 1995.

Gerbod, Paul. "Une forme de sociabilité bourgeoise: Le thermalisme en France, en Belgique et en Allemagne, 1800–1850." In *Sociabilité et société bourgeoise en France, en Belgique et en Allemagne, 1750–1850*, edited by Étienne François, 105–22. Paris: La Documentation Française, 1986.

Ghazali, Abu Hamid Muhammad b. Muhammad, al-. *Ihya' 'ulum al-din*. 5 vols. Cairo: Mu'assasat al-Halabi, 1967–68.

Ghazzi, Kamil al-. *Kitab nahr al-dhahab fi tarikh Halab*. 1923–26. Edited by Shawqi Sha'th and Mahmud Fakhuri. 3 vols. 2nd ed. Aleppo: Dar al-qalam al-'arabi, 1991–93.

Göle, Nilufer. *The Forbidden Modern: Civilization and Veiling*. Ann Arbor: University of Michigan Press, 1997.

Gonnella, Julia. *Ein christlich-orientalisches Wohnhaus des 17. Jahrhunderts aus Aleppo (Syrien): Das "Aleppo-Zimmer" im Museum für Islamische Kunst, Staat-*

liche Museen zu Berlin-Preussischer Kulturbesitz. Mainz, Germany: Museum für Islamische Kunst, 1996.

———. "The Citadel of Aleppo: Recent Studies." In *Muslim Military Architecture in Greater Syria: From the Coming of Islam to the Ottoman Period,* edited by Hugh Kennedy, 165–75. Leiden: Brill, 2006.

Goody, Jack. "Polygyny, Economy and the Role of Women." In *The Character of Kinship,* edited by Jack Goody, 175–90. Cambridge: Cambridge University Press, 1973.

Gövsa, İbrahim. "Ahmet Midhat Efendi." In *Türk Meşhurları,* 21–22. Istanbul: Yedigün Neşriyatı, n.d.

Grabar, Oleg. *The Formation of Islamic Art.* New Haven: Yale University Press, 1987.

Graham-Brown, Sarah. *Images of Women: The Portrayal of Women in Photography of the Middle East 1860–1950.* London: Quartet, 1988.

Green, Arnold H. *The Tunisian Ulama, 1873–1915: Social Structure and Response to Ideological Currents.* Leiden: Brill, 1978.

Grosrichard, Alain. *The Sultan's Court: European Fantasies of the East.* Translated by Liz Heron with an introduction by Mladen Dolar. London: Verso, 1998.

Guha-Thakurta, Tapati. *Monuments, Objects, Histories: Institutions of Art in Colonial and Post-colonial India.* New York: Columbia University Press, 2004.

Gurlitt, Cornelius. *Die Baukunst Konstantinopels.* Berlin: E. Wasmuth, 1912.

Habermas, Jürgen. *The Structural Transformation of the Public Sphere: An Inquiry into a Category of Bourgeois Society.* Translated by Thomas Burger. Cambridge: MIT Press, 1998.

Hallaj, Omar Abdulaziz. "The Process of Valuation of Urban Heritage: Comparative Analysis of Aleppo, Syria, and Shibam, Yemen." In *États et sociétés de l'Orient Arabe en quête d'avenir, 1945–2005,* edited by Gérard D. Khoury and Nadine Méouchy, 2:195–208. Paris: Geuthner, 2007.

Hanioğlu, M. Şükrü. *Preparation for a Revolution: The Young Turks, 1902–1908.* Oxford: Oxford University Press, 2001.

Hanson, Susan, and Geraldine Pratt. *Gender, Work and Space.* London: Routledge, 1995.

Hathaway, Jane. *Beshir Agha: Chief Eunuch of the Ottoman Imperial Harem.* Oxford: One World, 2005.

———. "The Wealth and Influence of an Exiled Ottoman Eunuch in Egypt: The *Waqf* Inventory of Abbas Agha." *Journal of the Economic and Social History of the Orient* 37, no. 4 (1994): 293–317.

Hayden, Dolores. *The Grand Domestic Revolution.* Cambridge: MIT Press, 1980.

———. *Redesigning the American Dream: Gender, Housing and Family Life.* New York: Norton, 2002.

Hegland, Mary E. "Political Roles of Aliabad Women: The Public-Private Dichotomy Transcended." In *Women in Middle Eastern History: Shifting Boundaries in Sex and Gender,* edited by Nikki R. Keddie and Beth Baron, 215–30. New Haven: Yale University Press, 1991.

Herbert, Lady Mary E. *A Search after Sunshine, or Algeria in 1871*. London: Bentley, 1872.

Hesse-Wartegg, Baron Ernst von. *Tunis: The Land and the People*. London: Chatto and Windus, 1882.

Heyd, Uriel. *Studies in Old Ottoman Criminal Law*. Oxford: Clarendon Press of Oxford University Press, 1973.

Hibbert, James. *Catalogue of the Pictures and Drawings of the Newsham Bequest to the Corporation of Preston*. Preston, England: R. Parkinson, 1884.

Hilal, 'Imad. *Al-Baghaya fi Misr: Dirasa tarikhiyya ijtima'iyya (min 1834 — 1949)*. Cairo: al-'Arabi lil-nashr wa al-tawzi', 2001.

Hill, Jane. "'Today There Is No Respect': Nostalgia, 'Respect,' and Oppositional Discourse in Mexicano (Nahuatl) Language Ideology." In *Language Ideologies: Practice and Theory*, edited by B. Schieffelin, K. Woolard, and P. Kroskrity, 68–86. New York: Oxford University Press, 1998.

Hillenbrand, Robert. *Islamic Architecture*. New York: Columbia University Press, 1994.

Himsi, Qustaki al-. *Udaba' Halab dhu al-athar fi al-qarn al-tasi' 'ashar*. Aleppo: al-Matba'a al-maruniyya, 1925.

Hivernel, Jacques. "Bab al-Nayrab, un faubourg d'Alep, hors de la ville et dans la cité." *Etudes rurales* 155–56 (2000): 215–38.

Hoffner, Harry A., Jr. "Legal and Social Institutions of Hittite Anatolia." In *Civilizations of the Ancient Near East*, edited by J. Sasson, 1:555–69. New York: Scribners, 1995.

Hollander, Anne. *Fabric of Vision*. London: National Gallery, 1992.

———. *Seeing through Clothes*. Berkeley: University of California Press, 1993.

Hossain, Rokeya Sakhawat. *Sultana's Dream: A Feminist Utopia, and Selections from The Secluded Ones*. Edited and translated by Roushan Jahan. Afterword by Hanna Papanek. New York: The Feminist Press at the City University of New York, 1988.

Hourani, Albert. *Arabic Thought in the Liberal Age, 1798–1939*. London: Oxford University Press, 1962.

Hugon, Henri. "Une ambassade tunisienne à Paris en 1825 (Mission de Si Mahmoud Kahia)." *Revue Tunisienne* nos. 13–14 (1933): 108–14.

Hunter, James Davison. *Evangelicalism: The Coming Generation*. Chicago: University of Chicago Press, 1987.

Husri, Sati' al-. *Abhath mukhtara fi al-qawmiyya al-'arabiyya*. Cairo: Dar al-ma'arif, 1964.

Ibn 'Abd al-Barr, Yusuf b. 'Abdallah. *Al-Isti'ab fi ma'rifat al-ashab*. Beirut: Dar al-kutub al-'ilmiyya, 1415/1995.

Ibn 'Abd Rabbih. *Al-'Iqd al-farid*. Edited by Abd al-Majid al-Tarhini. 9 vols. Beirut: Dar al-Kutub al-Ilmiyya, 1983.

Ibn Abi Diyaf, Ahmad [Ahmad Ben Diyaf]. *Ithaf ahl al-zaman bi akhbar muluk Tunis wa 'ahd al-aman*. Edited by Ahmed Abdesselem. 8 vols. Tunis: Tunisian Printing Office, 1989.

Ibn al-Hajj. *Al-Madkhal ila tanmiyat al-a'mal bi-tahsin al-niyyat*. Cairo: al-Matba'a al-misriyya, 1929.

Ibn al-Jawzi. *Ahkam al-nisa.'* Edited by Ahmad Shuhan. Damascus: Maktabat al-turath, 1411/1991.

———. *Al-Muntazam fi tarikh al-umam wa al-muluk*. Edited by Muhammad 'Ata and Mustafa 'Ata. 8 vols. Beirut: Dar al-kutub al-'ilmiyya, 1992.

Ibn Bassam al-Shantarini. *Al-Dhakhira fi mahasin ahl al-Jazira*. Edited by Ihsan 'Abbas. 8 vols. Tunis: al-Dar al-'arabiyya li al-kitab, 1975–79.

Ibn Battuta. *The Travels of Ibn Battuta*. Edited and translated by H. A. R. Gibb. Volume 2. Hakluyt Series 117 (2nd series), Cambridge: Cambridge University Press, 1962.

Ibn Darraj al-Qastali. *Diwan Ibn Darraj al-Qastali*. Edited by Mahmud 'Ali Makki. Damascus: al-Maktab al-islami, 1961.

Ibn Hajar al-'Asqalani, Ahmad b. 'Ali. *Al-Isaba fi tamyiz al-sahaba*. 8 vols. Beirut: Dar al-kutub al-'ilmiyya, n.d.

Ibn Hanbal. *Ahkam al-nisa.'* Edited by 'Abd al-Qadir Ahmad 'Ata. Cairo: Dar al-turath al-'arabi, 1980.

Ibn Hazm al-Andalusi ['Ali b. Ahmad Ibn Hazm]. *Tawq al-hamama*. Edited by Ihsan 'Abbas. Beirut: al-Mu'assassa al-'arabiyya li-al-tawzi' wa al-nashr, 1993.

Ibn Hazm, 'Ali b. Ahmad. *Al-Muhalla*. Edited by Hasan Zaydan Tilba. 12 vols. Cairo: Maktabat al-Jumhuriyya al-'Arabiyya, 1970.

Ibn Hisham, 'Abd al-Malik. *Al-Sira al-nabawiyya*. Edited by Suhayl al-Zakkar. 2 vols. Beirut: Dar al-fikr, 1992.

Ibn Kathir, Isma'il b. 'Umar. *Tafsir al-Qur'an al-'azim*. 4 vols. Cairo: Dar al-jil, n.d.

Ibn Manzur, Abu al-Fadl Jamal al-Din Muhammad b. Mukarram. *Lisan al-'Arab al-muhit*. 3 vols. Beirut: Dar lisan al-'Arab, 1970.

[Ibn Qayyim al-Jawziyya?]. *Akhbar al-nisa'*. Edited by 'Abd al-Majid Tu'ma al-Halabi. Beirut: Dar al-ma'rifa, 1997.

Ibn Qutayba ['Abd Allah b. Muslim]. *'Uyun al-akhbar*. 4 vols. Cairo: Dar al-kutub al-misriyya, 1930.

Ibn Sa'd, Muhammad. *Al-Tabaqat al-kubra*. Edited by Muhammad 'Abd al-Qadir 'Ata. Beirut: Dar sadir, 1418/1997.

İnalcık, Halil. "Suleiman the Lawgiver and Ottoman Law." *Archivum Ottomanicum* 1, no. 1 (1969): 105–38.

Isfahani, Abu al-Faraj al-. *Kitab al-aghani*. Edited by Ibrahim al-Abyari. 31 vols. Cairo: Dar al-sha'b, 1969.

Jabarti, 'Abd al-Rahman b. Hasan al-. *'Aja'ib al-athar fi al-tarajim wa al-akhbar*. Edited by 'Abd al-Rahman 'Abd al-Rahim 'Abd al-Rahman. 4 vols. Cairo: Dar al-kutub al-misriyya, 1998.

Jahiz, al- [Abu 'Uthman 'Amr b. Bahr]. *Al-Bayan wa al-tabyin*. Edited by 'Abd al-Salam Harun. 4 vols. Cairo: Maktabat al-Khanji, 1985.

[Jawhari, Isma'il b. Hammad al-]. *Mukhtar al-sihah*. Abridged by Muhammad b. Abi Bakr b. 'Abd al-Qadir al-Razi. Cairo: Matba'at Wadi al-Nil, 1287 A.H.

Jayawardena, Kumari. *Feminism and Nationalism in the Third World*. London: Zed, 1986.

Jennings, Eric T. *Curing the Colonizers: Hydrotherapy, Climatology, and French Colonial Spas*. Durham: Duke University Press, 2006.

Jokilehto, Jukka. *A History of Architectural Conservation*. Oxford: Butterworth-Heinemann, 1999.

Juha, Farid. *Al-Hayat al-fikriyya fi Halab fi al-qarn al-tasiʿ ʿashar*. Damascus: Al-Ahali, 1988.

Juynboll, G. H. A. "Some *Isnad*-analytical Methods Illustrated on the Basis of Several Woman-demeaning Sayings from *Hadith* Literature." In *Studies on the Origins and Uses of Islamic Hadith*, article 6. Aldershot, England: Variorum, 1996.

Kahf, Mohja. *Western Representations of the Muslim Woman: From Termagant to Odalisque*. Austin: University of Texas Press, 1999.

Kammen, Michael. *Mystic Chords of Memory*. New York: Vintage, 1991.

Kawakibi, Salam. "Le rôle de la télévision dans la relecture de l'histoire." *Maghreb/Machrek* 158 (October–December 1997): 47–55.

Kayali, Hasan. *Arabs and Young Turks: Ottomanism, Arabism, and Islamism in the Ottoman Empire, 1908–1918*. Berkeley: University of California Press, 1997.

———. "Elections and the Electoral Process in the Ottoman Empire, 1876–1919." *International Journal of Middle East Studies* 27, no. 3 (1995): 265–86.

Keddie, Nikki R. "Introduction: Deciphering Middle Eastern Women's History." In *Women in Middle Eastern History: Shifting Boundaries in Sex and Gender*, edited by Nikki R. Keddie and Beth Baron, 1–22. New Haven: Yale University Press, 1991.

Keith, Michael, and Steve Pile. "Introduction, Part 2: The Place of Politics." In *Place and the Politics of Identity*, edited by Michael Keith and Steve Pile, 22–40. London: Routledge, 1993.

Kennedy, Dane. *The Magic Mountains: Hill Stations in the British Raj*. Berkeley: University of California Press, 1996.

Kennedy, Hugh. *The Court of the Caliphs: The Rise and Fall of Islam's Greatest Dynasty*. London: Weidenfeld and Nicholson, 2004.

Kenny, L. M. "East versus West in *al-Muqtataf*, 1875–1900: Image and Self-Image." In *Essays on Islamic Civilization Presented to Niyazi Berkes*, edited by D. P. Little, 140–54. Leiden: Brill, 1976.

Kermeli, E., and O. Özel, eds. *The Ottoman Empire: Myths, Realities, and Black Holes, Contributions in Honour of Colin Imber*. Istanbul: Isis, 2006.

Khalidi, Tarif. *Arabic Historical Thought in the Classical Period*. Cambridge: Cambridge University Press, 1994.

Khayr al-Din al-Tunisi. "A mes enfants. Mémoires de ma vie privée et politique." In *Kheredine: Homme d'état; Documents historiques annotés*, edited by Mohamed-Salah Mzali and Jean Pignon, 15–105. Tunis: Maison Tunisienne de l'Edition, 1971.

Khechen, Mona. "Spatial Patterns in Transformation: A Rehabilitation Framework for Old Aleppo." Doctor of design thesis, Harvard University, 2004.

Khouri, Dina Rizk. "Drawing Boundaries and Defining Spaces: Women and Space in Ottoman Iraq." In *Women, the Family, and Divorce Laws in Islamic*

History, edited by Amira El Azhary Sonbol, 173–87. Syracuse, N.Y.: Syracuse University Press, 1996.

Kilpatrick, Hilary. "Some Late 'Abbasid and Mamluk Books about Women: A Literary Historical Approach." *Arabica* 42 (1995): 69–75.

Kirshenblatt-Gimblett, Barbara. *Destination Culture: Tourism, Museums, and Heritage*. Berkeley: University of California Press, 1998.

———. "From Ethnology to Heritage: the Role of the Museum." Keynote address, 8th congress of the Societé Internationale d'Ethnologie et de Folklore, Marseilles, April 28, 2004.

Köseoğlu, Cengiz. "A Tour of the Harem Apartments of the Topkapı Saray." In *The Topkapı Saray Museum: Architecture, the Harem and Other Buildings*, edited by J. Michael Rogers, 27–36. London: Thames and Hudson, 1988.

Köymen, Oya. "The Advent and Consequences of Free Trade in the Ottoman Empire: Nineteenth Century." *Etudes Balkaniques* 2 (1971): 47–55.

Kurdi, Fatina. "Al-Tatawwur al-'umrani li-Halab fi muwajaha al-ta'thirat al-Urubbiyya." *Bulletin d'Études Orientales* 52 (2000): 347–56.

Lacan, Jacques. "The Instance of the Letter in the Unconscious." In Jacques Lacan, *Ecrits: A Selection*, 138–68. Translated by Bruce Fink. New York: Norton, 2002.

———. "The Signification of the Phallus." In Jacques Lacan, *Ecrits: A Selection*, 271–80. Translated by Bruce Fink. New York: Norton, 2002.

Lal, Ruby. *Domesticity and Power in the Early Mughal World: Historicizing the Harem*. Cambridge: Cambridge University Press, 2005.

———. "Historicizing the Harem: The Challenge of a Princess's Memoir." *Feminist Studies* 30, no. 3 (2004): 590–616.

Lallemand, Charles. *Tunis au XIXe siècle*. Paris: Maison Quantin, 1890.

Lane, Edward William. *An Account of the Manners and Customs of the Modern Egyptians*. 1836. Reprint, London: J. M. Dent, 1936.

———, ed. *Selections from the Kur-an*, ed. and trans. Edward William Lane. London: James Madden, 1843.

Lane-Poole, Stanley. *The Story of Cairo*. 1902. Reprint, Liechtenstein: Nendeln, 1971.

Larguèche, Dalenda. "Femme et don pour la ville: Aziza 'Uthmana entre histoire et mémoire." In *Femmes en villes*, edited by Dalenda Larguèche, 35–53. Tunis: Cahiers du Cérès, 2005.

———. "Loisirs, sociabilité et mutations culturelles dans la régence de Tunis à l'époque Ottomane." In *Mélanges Méditerranéens d'amitié et de reconnaissance à André Raymond*, edited by Abdeljelil Temimi, 1:155–65. Tunis: Fondation Temimi, 2004.

Laroui, Abdallah. *The Crisis of the Arab Intellectual: Traditionalism or Historicism?* Berkeley: University of California Press, 1976.

Leder, Stefan, and Hilary Kilpatrick. "Classical Arabic Prose Literature: A Researcher's Sketch Map." *Journal of Arabic Literature* 22, no. 1 (1992): 2–25.

Lefebvre, Henri. *The Production of Space*. Translated by Donald Nicholson-Smith. Oxford: Blackwell, 1991.

Lehmann, Ulrich. *Tigersprung: Fashion in Modernity*. Cambridge: MIT Press, 2000.

Lejeune, Philippe. *Le pacte autobiographique*. Paris: Éditions de Seuil, 1975.

Lewis, Reina. *Gendering Orientalism: Race, Femininity and Representation*. London: Routledge, 1996.

———. *Rethinking Orientalism: Women, Travel and the Ottoman Harem*. London: I. B. Tauris, 2004.

Lewis, Reina, and Nancy Micklewright, eds. *Gender, Modernity and Liberty: Middle Eastern and Western Women's Writings; A Critical Sourcebook*. London: I. B. Tauris, 2006.

Lipstadt, Hélène. "'There Is [Almost] No Occurrence of the Berber House in This Document': For the 'Good Use' of Bourdieu's Anthropology for Architecture." Paper presented at the annual meeting of the Society for Architectural Historians, Denver, Colorado, April 23–27, 2003.

Lorcin, Patricia. "Rome and France in Africa: Recovering Colonial Algeria's Latin Past." *French Historical Studies* 25 (spring 2002): 295–329.

Low, Setha M., and Denise Lawrence-Zúñiga, eds. *The Anthropology of Space and Place: Locating Culture*. Malden, Mass.: Blackwell, 2003.

Lowe, Lisa. "Rereadings in Orientalism: Oriental Inventions and Inventions of the Orient in Montesquieu's '*Lettres persanes*.'" *Cultural Critique* no. 15 (1990): 115–43.

Lowenthal, David. *The Past Is a Foreign Country*. Cambridge: Cambridge University Press, 1985.

———. *Possessed by the Past: The Heritage Crusade and the Spoils of History*. New York: Free Press, 1996.

Lutfi, Hoda. "Manners and Customs of Fourteenth-Century Cairene Women: Female Anarchy versus Male Shar'i Order in Muslim Prescriptive Treatises." In *Women in Middle Eastern History: Shifting Boundaries in Sex and Gender*, edited by Nikki R. Keddie and Beth Baron, 99–118. New Haven: Yale University Press, 1991.

———. "Al-Sakhawi's *Kitab al-Nisa*' as a Source for the Social and Economic History of Muslim Women during the Fifteenth Century A.D." *Muslim World* 71 (1981): 104–24.

Mabro, Judy. *Veiled Half-Truths: Western Travellers' Perceptions of Middle Eastern Women*. London: I. B. Tauris, 1991.

Macfarlane, Alan. *The Savage Wars of Peace: England, Japan and the Malthusian Trap*. Oxford: Blackwell, 1997.

MacKenzie, John. *Orientalism: History, Theory and the Arts*. Manchester, England: Manchester University Press, 1995.

Malinas, Albert. *Notice sur le groupe hydro-minéral de Korbous (Tunisie)*. Tunis: Rapide, 1909.

Marmon, Shaun. *Eunuchs and Sacred Boundaries in Islamic Society*. Oxford: Oxford University Press, 1995.

Martel, André. *Luis-Arnold et Joseph Allegro: Consuls du Bey de Tunis à Bône*. Paris: Presses Universitaires de France, 1967.

Massey, Doreen. *For Space*. London: Sage, 2005.

———. *Space, Place, and Gender*. Minneapolis: University of Minnesota Press, 1994.

———. *Spatial Divisions of Labor: Social Structures and the Geography of Production*. London: Macmillan, 1984.

Mas'udi, Abu al-Hasan al-. *Muruj al-dhahab wa ma'adin al-jawhar*. Edited by Charles Pellat. 7 vols. Beirut: Publications de l'université libanaise, 1973–74.

———. *Muruj al-dhahab wa ma'adin al-jawhar*. Edited by Mufid Muhammad Qumayha. 4 vols. Beirut: Dar al-kutub al-'ilmiyya, 1986.

McDowell, Linda. *Gender, Identity and Place: Understanding Feminist Geographies*. Minneapolis: University of Minnesota Press, 1999.

McDowell, Linda, and Joanne P. Sharp, eds. *Space, Gender, Knowledge: Feminist Readings*. London: Arnold, 1997.

Melek Hanım. *Thirty Years in the Harem*, 1872. Facsimile reprint with an introduction by İrvin C. Schick. Cultures in Dialogue Series 1, vol. 1. Piscataway, N.J.: Gorgias Press, 2005.

Melman, Billie. *Women's Orients: English Women and the Middle East, 1718–1918; Sexuality, Religion, and Work*. Ann Arbor: University of Michigan Press, 1992.

Meriwether, Margaret L., and Judith Tucker. Introduction. In *A Social History of Women and Gender in the Modern Middle East*, edited by Margaret L. Meriwether and Judith Tucker. Boulder, Colo.: Westview, 1999.

Mernissi, Fatima. *Dreams of Trespass: Tales of a Harem Girlhood*. Reading, Mass.: Addison-Wesley, 1994.

———. *Le harem et l'occident*. Paris: Albin Michel, 2001.

———. *The Veil and the Male Elite: A Feminist Interpretation of Women's Rights in Islam*. Translated by Mary Jo Lakeland. Reading, Mass.: Addison-Wesley, 1991.

Meyer, Eric. "'I Know Thee Not, I Loathe Thy Race': Romantic Orientalism in the Eye of the Other." ELH 58, no. 3 (1991): 657–99.

Micklewright, Nancy. *A Victorian Traveler in the Middle East: The Photography and Travel Writing of Annie Lady Brassey*. London: Ashgate, 2003.

Milani, Farzaneh. "The Mediatory Guile of the Nanny in Persian Romance." In "The Uses of Guile: Literary and Historical Moments," 181–201. Special issue, *Iranian Studies* 32, no. 2 (spring 1999).

Miskawayh, Ahmad b. Muhammad. *The Eclipse of the Abbasid Caliphate*. Translated by H. F. Amedroz and D. S. Margoliouth. 4 vols. Oxford: Basil Blackwell, 1921.

———. *Tajarib al-umam*. Edited by H. F. Amedroz. 6 vols. Oxford: Basil Blackwell, 1920.

Mitchell, Don. *Cultural Geography: A Critical Introduction*. Malden, Mass.: Blackwell, 2000.

Mitchell, Timothy. *Colonising Egypt*. Berkeley: University of California Press, 1988.

Moalla, Asma. *The Regency of Tunis and the Ottoman Porte, 1777–1814: Army and Government of a North-Africa Ottoman Eyalet at the End of the Eighteenth Century*. London: Routledge, 2005.

Momsen, Janet Henshall, and Janet G. Townsend, eds. *Geography of Gender in the Third World*. Albany: State University of New York Press, 1987.

Monchicourt, Charles. *Relations inédites de Nyssen, Filippi et Calligaris (1788, 1829, 1834)*. Paris: Société d'éditions géographiques, maritimes et coloniales, 1929.

Montagu, Lady Mary Wortley. *Letters*. Edited by Isobel Grundy. London: Penguin, 1997.

Montesquieu, Baron de la Brède et de. *The Persian Letters*. Translated by George R. Healy. Indianapolis: Hackett, 1999.

Moosa, Matti. *The Origins of Modern Arabic Fiction*. 2nd ed. Boulder, Colo.: Lynne Rienner, 1997.

Mortimer, Mildred. "Whose House Is This? Space and Place in Calixthe Beyala's *C'est le soleil qui m'a brûlée* and *La Petite Fille du réverbère*." *World Literature Today* 73, no. 3 (summer 1999): 467–73.

Mouradgea d'Ohsson, Ignace. *Tableau général de l'empire othoman*. 7 vols. Paris: De L'imprimerie de Monsieur Firmin Didot, 1787–1824.

Mudiriyya al-'amma lil-athar wa al-matahif, al-. *Dalil al-matahif wa al-mawaqi' al-athariyya fi Suriyya*. Damascus: Al-Mudiriyya al-'amma lil-athar wa al-matahif, 1979.

Muhammad, Zaynab. *Asrar wasifa misriyya*. Cairo: Maktabat al-nashr wa al-ta'lif, 1927.

———. *Mudhakkirat wasifa misriyya*. Cairo: Maktabat al-nashr wa al-ta'lif, 1927.

Musa, Salama. *Al-Yawm wa al-ghad*. Cairo: Salama Musa nashr wa tawzi', 1927.

Musallam, Basim. *Sex and Society in Islam*. Cambridge: Cambridge University Press, 1983.

Najmabadi, Afsaneh. "Reading 'Wiles of Women' Stories as Fictions of Masculinity." In *Imagined Masculinities: Male Identity and Culture in the Modern Middle East*, edited by Mai Ghoussoub and Emma Sinclair-Webb, 147–68. London: Saqi, 2000.

Nead, Lynda. *Female Nude: Art, Obscenity and Sexuality*. London: Routledge, 1992.

Necipoğlu, Gülru. *Architecture, Ceremonial, and Power: The Topkapi Palace in the Fifteenth and Sixteenth Centuries*. Cambridge: MIT Press, 1991.

———. "Framing the Gaze in Ottoman, Safavid and Mughal Palaces." *Ars Orientalis* 23 (1993): 303–42.

Niranjana, Seemanthini. *Gender and Space: Femininity, Sexualization and the Female Body*. New Delhi: Sage, 2001.

Nochlin, Linda. "The Imaginary Orient." *Art in America* 71 (May 1983): 118–31, 187–91.

Noorani, Yaseen. "Heterotopia and the Wine Poem in Early Islamic Culture." *International Journal of Middle East Studies* 36, no. 3 (2004): 345–66.

Nord, Deborah Epstein. *Walking the Victorian Streets: Women, Representation, and the City*. Ithaca: Cornell University Press, 1995.

Nusayr, 'Ayda Ibrahim. *Al-Kutub al-'arabiyya alati nushirat fi Misr bayna 'amay 1926–1940*. Cairo: American University in Cairo Press, 1980.

Ockman, Carol. *Ingres's Eroticized Bodies: Tracing the Serpentine Line*. New Haven: Yale University Press, 1995.

O'Donnell, Joseph Dean. *Lavigerie in Tunisia: The Interplay of Imperialist and Missionary.* Athens: University of Georgia Press, 1979.

Oestrup, J. "Ahmed Midhat." In *The Encyclopedia of Islam,* edited by M.Th. (Martijn Theodoor) Houtsma, 1:199–200. 9 vols. Leyden: Brill, 1913–38.

Owen, Roger. "The 1838 Anglo-Turkish Convention: An Overview." *New Perspectives on Turkey* 7 (spring 1992): 7–14.

Özendes, Engin. *Sébah & Joaillier'den Foto Sabah'a: Fotoğrafta Oryantalizm.* Istanbul: Yapı Kredi Yayınları, 1993.

Patterson, Orlando. *Slavery and Social Death.* Cambridge: Harvard University Press, 1982.

Peakman, Julie, ed. *Whore Biographies 1700–1825.* 4 vols. London: Pickering and Chatto, 2006.

Peirce, Leslie. *The Imperial Harem: Women and Sovereignty in the Ottoman Empire.* Oxford: Oxford University Press, 1993.

———. "'The Law Shall Not Languish': Social Class and Public Conduct in Sixteenth-Century Ottoman Legal Discourse." In *Hermeneutics and Honor: Negotiating Female 'Public' Space in Islamic/ate Societies,* edited by Asma Afsaruddin, 140–58. Harvard Middle Eastern Monographs. Cambridge: Harvard University Press for the Center for Middle Eastern Studies, Harvard University, 1999.

———. *Morality Tales: Law and Gender in the Ottoman Court of Aintab.* Berkeley: University of California Press, 2003.

Penzer, Norman M. *The Harēm: An Account of the Institution as It Existed in the Palace of the Turkish Sultans with a History of the Grand Seraglio from Its Foundation to Modern Times.* London: Harrap, 1936.

Perkins, Kenneth J. "So Near and Yet So Far: British Tourists in Algiers, 1875–1914." Paper presented at the annual meeting of the Middle East Studies Association, Boston, 2006.

Perniola, Mario. "Between Clothing and Nudity." In *Fragments for a History of the Human Body,* pt. 2, edited by Michel Feher, 236–65. New York: Zone, 1989.

Perrot, Philippe. *Fashioning the Bourgeoisie: A History of Clothing in the Nineteenth Century.* Princeton: Princeton University Press, 1994.

Petry, Carl F. "Class Solidarity versus Gender Gain: Women as Custodians of Property in Later Medieval Egypt." In *Women in Middle Eastern History: Shifting Boundaries in Sex and Gender,* edited by Nikki R. Keddie and Beth Baron, 122–42. New Haven: Yale University Press, 1991.

Petzen, Barbara. "'Matmazels' nell'harem: Le governanti europee nell'Impero ottomano." *Genesis* 1, no. 1 (2002): 61–84.

Philipp, Thomas. *Gurgi Zaydan: His Life and Thought.* Beirut: Orient-Institut der Deutshe Morgenländ Gesellschaft, 1979.

———. "National Consciousness in the Thought of Jurji Zaydan." *International Journal of Middle East Studies* 4, no. 1 (1973): 3–22.

Pons, Monsignor A. *La nouvelle église d'Afrique: Ou le Catholicisme en Algérie, en Tunisie et au Maroc depuis 1833.* Tunis: Namura, 1930.

Pulaha, Selami, and Yaşar Yücel. *1. Selim Kânûnnâmeleri (1512–1520)*. Ankara: Türk Tarih Kurumu Basımevi, 1995.

Qattan, Najwa al-. "Dhimmis in the Muslim Court: Legal Autonomy and Religious Discrimination." *International Journal of Middle East Studies* 31 (1990): 429–44.

Qudsi, Adli. "Aleppo: A Struggle for Conservation." *Mimar* 12 (1984): 18–23.

Qurtubi, Abu 'Abdullah Muhammad b. Ahmad al-Ansari al-. *Al-Jami' li-ahkam al-Qur'an*. 20 vols. Cairo: Dar al-kutub al-misriyah, 1364.

Raghib al-Isfahani, al-. *Muhadarat al-udaba.'* Edited by 'Umar al-Tabba.' Beirut: Dar al-Arqam b. Abi al-Arqam, 1999.

Raymond, André. *Chronique des rois de Tunis et du pacte fundamental*. 2 vols. Tunis: Alif, 1994.

Redhouse, James W. *A Turkish and English Lexicon*. London: Bernard Quaritch, 1861.

Reid, Donald Malcolm. "Cairo University and the Orientalists." *International Journal of Middle East Studies* 19, no. 1 (1987): 51–75.

———. *The Odyssey of Farah Antun: A Syrian Christian's Quest for Secularism*. Minneapolis: Bibliotheca Islamica, 1975.

———. "The Syrian Christians and Early Socialism in the Arab World." *International Journal of Middle East Studies* 5, no. 2 (1974): 177–93.

———. "Syrian Christians, the Rags-To-Riches Story, and Free Enterprise." *International Journal of Middle East Studies* 1, no. 4 (1970): 358–67.

Repp, Richard. *The Müfti of Istanbul: A Study in the Development of the Ottoman Learned Hierarchy*. London: Ithaca, 1986.

Ribeiro, Aileen. *Ingres in Fashion: Representations of Dress and Appearance in Ingres's Images of Women*. New Haven: Yale University Press, 1999.

Rizas, G. *Abdul Hamid: Sa vie politique et intime, 33 ans de tyrannie, tous les secrets de la camarilla dévoilés, prodigieux efforts du parti Jeune-Turc*. 2nd ed. Istanbul: E. Pallamary, 1909.

Roberts, Mary. "Cultural Crossings: Sartorial Adventures, Satiric Narratives, and the Question of Indigenous Agency in Nineteenth-Century Europe and the Near East." In *Edges of Empire: Orientalism and Visual Culture*, edited by Jocelyn Hackforth-Jones and Mary Roberts, 70–94. London: Blackwell, 2005.

———. *Intimate Outsiders: The Harem in Ottoman and Orientalist Art and Travel Literature*. Durham: Duke University Press, 2007.

Roded, Ruth. *Women in Islamic Biographical Collections: From Ibn Sa'd to Who's Who*. Boulder, Colo.: Lynne Rienner, 1994.

Rogers, J. Michael, ed. *The Topkapı Saray Museum: Architecture, the Harem and other Buildings*. London: Thames and Hudson, 1988.

Rose, Gillian. *Feminism and Geography: The Limits of Geographical Knowledge*. Minneapolis: University of Minnesota Press, 1993.

Rose, Susan D. "Christian Fundamentalism: Patriarchy, Sexuality, and Human Rights." In *Religious Fundamentalisms and the Human Rights of Women*, edited by Courtney W. Howland, 9–20. New York: St. Martin's, 1999.

Rosenthal, Donald A. *Orientalism: The Near East in French Painting 1800–1880.*
   Rochester, N.Y.: Memorial Art Gallery of the University of Rochester, 1982.
Ruskin, John. *Works of John Ruskin.* Edited by E. T. Cook and Alexander
   Wedderburn. 39 vols. New York: George Allen, 1903–12.
Sabaï, Nadia. *Mustapha Saheb Ettabaa: Un haut dignitaire beylical dans la Tuni-
   sie du XIXe siècle.* Preface by El-Mokhtar Bey. Carthage: Editions Cartaginoi-
   series, 2007.
Sabi', Hilal al-. *Kitab tuhfat al-umara' fi tarikh al-wuzara'.* Edited by H. F. Ame-
   droz. Beirut: Catholic Press, 1904.
———. *Rusum dar al-Khilafa.* Edited by Mikha'il 'Awwad. Baghdad: Matba'at
   al-'Ani, 1964.
Sa'id, Amina al-. "Hal ta'udu al-mar'a ila 'asr al-harim?" *al-Hilal,* September 1987,
   30–35.
Said, Edward. *Orientalism.* New York: Pantheon, 1978.
Salamandra, Christa. "Moustache Hairs Lost: Ramadan Television Serials and
   the Construction of Identity in Damascus, Syria." *Visual Anthropology* 10, nos.
   2–4 (1998): 227–46.
———. *A New Old Damascus: Authenticity and Distinction in Urban Syria.*
   Bloomington: Indiana University Press, 2004.
Saler, Michael. "Modernity and Enchantment: A Historiographic Review."
   American Historical Review 111, no. 3 (June 2006): 692–716.
Sauvaget, Jean. *Alep: Essai sur le développement d'une grande ville syrienne, des ori-
   gines au milieu du XIXe siècle.* 2 vols. Paris: Geuthner, 1941.
al-Sayyid-Marsot, Afaf Lutfi. "The Revolutionary Gentlewoman in Egypt." In
   Women in the Muslim World, edited by Lois Beck and Nikki Keddie, 261–76.
   Cambridge: Harvard University Press, 1978.
Schacht, Joseph. *An Introduction to Islamic Law.* Oxford: Clarendon Press of
   Oxford University Press, 1954.
Schechter, Relli. *Transitions in Domestic Consumption and Family Life in the Mod-
   ern Middle East.* New York: Palgrave Macmillan, 2003.
Schick, İrvin C. *The Erotic Margin: Sexuality and Spatiality in Alteritist Discourse.*
   London: Verso, 1999.
Schimmel, Ann Marie. "Celestial Garden in Islam." In *The Islamic Garden,* edited
   by Elisabeth B. MacDougall and Richard Ettinghausen. Washington, D.C.:
   Dumbarton Oaks, 1976, 13–39.
Schumann, Christoph. "The Generation of Broad Expectations: Nationalism,
   Education and Autobiography in Syria and Lebanon, 1930–58." *Die Welt des
   Islam* 41, no. 2 (2001): 174–205.
———. *Radikalnationalismus in Syrien und Libanon; Politische Sozialisation und
   Elitenbildung, 1930–1958.* Hamburg: Deutsches Orient Institut, 2001.
Scott, David, and Charles Hirschkind, eds. *Powers of the Secular Modern: Talal
   Asad and His Interlocutors.* Stanford: Stanford University Press, 2006.
Seng, Yvonne. "Standing at the Gates of Justice: Women in the Law Courts of
   Early-Sixteenth-Century Üsküdar, Istanbul." In *Contested States: Law, Hege-*

mony, and Resistance, edited by M. Lazarus-Black and S. F. Hirsch, 184–206. New York: Routledge, 1994.

Şeref, 'Abdurrahmān. "Topkapu Sarāy-i Hümāyūnı." In *Tārīh-i 'Osmānī Encümenī Mecmū'asi* (1910–12), nos. 5–12. Istanbul: Mekteb-i Mülkiye-i Şahane Destgâhı.

Shaarawi, Huda. *Harem Years: The Memoirs of an Egyptian Feminist*. Translated with an introduction by Margot Badran. London: Virago, 1986.

Shafi'i, al- [Muhammad b. Idris]. *Kitab al-Umm*. Edited by Muhammad Badr al-Din Hassun. 10 vols. Beirut: Dar Qutayba, 1996.

Shafiq, Ahmad. *Al-Riqq fi al-islam*. Cairo: al-Matba'a al-Ahliyya al-Amiriyya bi-Bulaq, 1892.

Sha'rawi, Antwan. "Al al-Marrash wa al-salunat al-adabiyya fi Halab fi al-nisf al-thani min al-qarn al-tasi' 'ashar." *Majallat al-Dad* 65, no. 9 (September 1995): 23–65.

Sha'rawi, Huda. *Mudhakkirat*. Cairo: Dar al-Hilal, 1981.

Sheehi, Stephen. "Doubleness and Duality: Jurji Zaydan's *Al-Mamluk al-Sharid* and Allegories of Becoming." *Journal of Arabic Literature* 30, no. 1 (1999): 90–105.

———. *Foundations of Modern Arab Identity*. Gainesville: University Press of Florida, 2004.

Sibley, David. *Geographies of Exclusion: Society and Difference in the West*. London: Routledge, 1995.

———. "Outsiders in Society and Space." In *Inventing Places: Studies in Cultural Geography*, edited by Kay Anderson and Fay Gale, 107–22. Melbourne, Australia: Longman Cheshire, 1992.

Simmel, Georg. "The Ruin." In *Georg Simmel, 1858–1918: A Collection of Essays, with Translations and a Bibliography*, edited by Kurt H. Wolff, 259–66. Columbus: Ohio State University Press, 1959.

Siyavuşgil, Sabri Esat. "Ahmed Midhat Efendi." In *İslâm Ansiklopedesi*, 1:184–87, edited by M.Th. (Martijn Theodoor) Houtsma. Ankara: Milli Eğitim Basımevi, 1950–. 13 vols.

Soja, Edward. *Postmodern Geographies: The Reassertion of Space in Critical Social Theories*. London: Verso, 1989.

———. *Thirdspace: Expanding the Geographical Imagination*. Oxford: Blackwell, 1996.

Solomon-Godeau, Abigail. "Problems and Pleasures for Feminists." *Art in America* 84, no. 7 (July 1996): 27–31.

Sourdel, Dominique. *Le vizirat Abbaside de 749 à 936*. Vol. 1. Damascus: Institut français de Damas, 1959–60.

Spain, Daphne. *Gendered Spaces*. Chapel Hill: University of North Carolina Press, 1992.

Sperl, Stefan. *Mannerism in Arabic Poetry*. Cambridge: Cambridge University Press, 1989.

Staeheli, Lynn. "Publicity, Privacy and Women's Political Action." *Environment and Planning D: Society and Space* 14, no. 5 (1996): 601–19.

Stallybrass, Peter, and Allon White. *The Politics and Poetics of Transgression*. London: Methuen, 1986.

Stetkevych, Jaroslav. *The Zephyrs of Najd*. Chicago: University of Chicago Press, 1993.

Stetkevych, Suzanne. *The Mute Immortals Speak*. Ithaca: Cornell University Press, 1993.

———. *The Poetics of Islamic Legitimacy*. Bloomington: Indiana University Press, 2002.

Stewart, Kathleen. "Nostalgia: A Polemic." *Cultural Anthropology* 3, no. 3 (1988): 227–41.

Stewart, Mary Lynn. *For Health and Beauty: Physical Culture for Frenchwomen, 1880s–1930s*. Baltimore: Johns Hopkins University Press, 2001.

Stockdale, Nancy L. *Colonial Encounters among English and Palestinian Women, 1800–1948*. Gainesville: University Press of Florida, 2007.

Stowasser, Barbara. *Women in the Qur'an, Traditions, and Interpretation*. Oxford: Oxford University Press, 1994.

Suli, Abu Bakr al-. *Ma lam yunshar min awraq al-Suli: Akhbar al-sanawat 295–315*. Edited by Hilal Naji. Beirut: 'Alam al-kutub, 2000.

Süreyya Bey, Mehmed, *Sicill-i Osmani: the Ottoman National Biography*. Westmead, Farnborough, England: Gregg International Publishers, 1971.

Tabari, Abu Ja'far Muhammad ibn Jarir, al-. *Jami'at al-bayan fi ta'wil al-Qur'an*. 12 vols. Beirut: Dar al-kutub al-'ilmiyya, 1418/1997.

Tabbakh, Raghib al-. *I'lam al-nubala' bi-tarikh Halab al-shahba.'* 1923–26. 7 vols. Edited by Muhammad Kamal. Aleppo: Dar al-qalam al-'arabi, 1988–92.

Tanpınar, Ahmet Hamdi. *XIX Asır Türk Edebiyatı Tarihi*. Istanbul: Çağlayan Kitabevi, 1956.

Tanukhi, Abu 'Ali al-Muhassin al-. *Kitab al-faraj ba'da al-shidda*. Edited by 'Abbud al-Shalji. 5 vols. Beirut: Dar Sadir, 1978.

———. *Nishwar al-muhadara wa akhbar al-mudhakara*. Edited by 'Abbud al-Shalji. 8 vols. Beirut: Dar Sadir, 1971.

Tarazi, Filib di. *Tarikh al-sihafa al-'arabiyya*. 1913. Reprint, Beirut: Dar Sadir, 1967. 2 vols.

Temple, Major Sir Grenville T. *Excursions in the Mediterranean. Algiers and Tunis*. 2 vols. London: Saunders and Otley, 1835.

Thompson, Elizabeth. "Public and Private in Middle Eastern Women's History." *Journal of Women's History* 15 (spring 2003): 52–69.

Thornton, Arland. "The Developmental Paradigm, Reading History Sideways, and Family Change." *Demography* 38, no. 4 (2001): 449–65.

Tietze, Andreas. "Mustafa 'Ali on Luxury and the Status Symbols of Ottoman Gentlemen." In *Studia Turcologica Memoriae Alexis Bombaci Dictata*, edited by Aldo Galotta and Ugo Marazzi, 557–90. Naples: Instituto Universitario Orientale, 1982.

Toledano, Ehud R. "Late Ottoman Concepts of Slavery (1830s–1880s)." *Poetics Today* 14, no. 3 (1993): 477–506.

————. *The Ottoman Slave Trade and Its Suppression, 1840–1890*. Princeton: Princeton University Press, 1982.

————. *Slavery and Abolition in the Ottoman Middle East*. Seattle: University of Washington Press, 1998.

Troutt Powell, Eve M. *A Different Shade of Colonialism: Egypt, Great Britain, and the Mastery of the Sudan*. Berkeley: University of California Press, 2003.

Tuan, Yi-Fu. *Space and Place: The Perspective of Experience*. Minneapolis: University of Minnesota Press, 1977.

Tucker, Judith. *Women in Nineteenth-Century Egypt*. Cambridge: Cambridge University Press, 1985.

Turjuman, Siham. *Daughter of Damascus, Taken from Ya mal al-Sham*. Translated by Andrea Rugh. Austin: University of Texas Press, 1994.

————. *Ya Mal al-Sham*. Damascus: Matabi' idarat al-tawjih al-ma'nawi, 1969.

Tveritinova, Anna S. *Sultan I. Selim'in Kanun-namesi*. Moscow: Nauka, 1969.

Udovitch, Avram. "Islamic Law and the Social Context of Exchange in the Medieval Middle East." *History and Anthropology* 1 (1985): 445–65.

Ülken, Ziya Hilmi. *Türkiye'de Çağdaş Düşünce Tarihi*. Istanbul: Ülken Yayınları, 1992.

Uluçay, M. Çağatay. "II. Bayezid'in Ailesi." *Tarih Dergisi* 10 (1959): 105–24.

————. *Padişahların Kadınları ve Kızları*. Ankara: Türk Tarih Kurumu Basımevi, 1980.

'Umar b. Abi Rabi'a. *Sharh Diwan 'Umar b. Abi Rabi'a*. Edited by Muhyi al-Din 'Abd al-Hamid. Beirut: Dar al-Andalus, 1983.

Uzuncarşılı, I. H. *Osman Devletinin Saray Teşkilāti*. Ankara, 1945.

Vadet, Jean Claude. "Les grands themes de l'adab dans le Rabi' al-abrar d'al-Zamakhshari." *Revue des études islamiques* 58 (1990): 189–205.

Vaka Brown, Demetra. *Haremlik: Some Pages from the Life of Turkish Women*. 1909. Facsimile reprint with an introduction by Yiorgos Kalogeras. Cultures in Dialogue Series 1, vol. 2. Piscataway, N.J.: Gorgias Press, 2005.

van Nieuwkerk, Karin. *"A Trade Like Any Other": Female Singers and Dancers in Egypt*. Austin: University of Texas Press, 1995.

Wahidi, al-. *Asbab al-nuzul*. Edited by al-Sayyid al-Jumayli. Beirut: Dar al-kitab al-'arabi, 1414/1994.

Washsha', al-. *Al-Muwashsha*. Edited by 'Abd al-Amir 'Ali Muhanna. Beirut: Dar al-fikr al-lubnani, 1990.

Watenpaugh, Heghnar Z. "Knowledge, Heritage, Representation: The Commercialization of the Courtyard House in Aleppo." In *États et sociétés de l'Orient Arabe en quête d'avenir, 1945–2005*, edited by Gérard D. Khoury and Nadine Méouchy, 2:209–18. Paris: Geuthner, 2007.

————. "Museums and the Construction of National History in Syria and Lebanon." In *The British and French Mandates in Comparative Perspective*, edited by Nadine Méouchy and Peter Sluglett, 185–202. Leiden: Brill, 2004.

Weintraub, Jeff. "The Theory and Politics of the Public/Private Distinction." In *Public and Private in Thought and Practice: Perspectives on a Grand Dichotomy*, edited by Jeff Weintraub and Krishan Kumar, 1–42. Chicago: University of Chicago Press, 1997.

Weisman, Leslie Kanes. *Discrimination by Design: A Feminist Critique of the Man-Made Environment.* Urbana: University of Illinois Press, 1992.

Wensinck, A. J. *Concordance et indices de la tradition Musulmane.* 2d edition. 8 vols. Leiden: Brill, 1992.

Wigh, Leif. *Fotografiska Vyer Från Bosporen Och Konstantinopel / Photographic Views of the Bosphorus and Constantinople.* Stockholm: Fotografiska Museet, 1984.

Wigley, Mark. "Untitled: The Housing of Gender." In *Sexuality and Space,* edited by Beatriz Colomina, 328–89. Princeton: Princeton Architectural Press, 1992.

Windler, Christian. *La diplomatie comme expérience de l'autre: Consuls français au Maghreb (1700–1840).* Geneva: Droz, 2002.

Xenophon. *The Education of Cyrus.* Translated by Wayne Ambler. Ithaca: Cornell University Press, 2001.

Yaqut Ibn 'Abdullah al-Hamawi. *Mu'jam al-Buldan.* 5 vols. Beirut: Dar Sadir, 1984.

Yeazell, Ruth B. *Harems of the Mind: Passages of Western Art and Literature.* New Haven: Yale University Press, 2000.

Yeğenoğlu, Mayda. *Colonial Fantasies: Towards a Feminist Reading of Orientalism.* Cambridge: Cambridge University Press, 1998.

Yusuf, Muhammad Ahmad. *Yawmiyyat saqita.* Cairo: Matba'at al-Qahira, n.d.

Zabidi, Muhammad Murtada al-. *Taj al-'arus min jawahir al-qamus.* 10 vols. Beirut: Dar maktabat al-hay'ah, n.d.

Zannad [Bouchrara], Traki. *Symboliques corporelles et espaces musulmans.* Tunis: Cérès Productions, 1984.

Zaydan, Jurji. *Al-'Abbasa ukht al-Rashid aw nakbat al-baramika.* 1911. Cairo: Dar al-Hilal, 1965.

———. *Asir al-Mutamahdi.* 1891. 2nd ed. Cairo: Dar al-Hilal, 1901.

———. *The Autobiography of Jurji Zaydan.* Edited and translated by Thomas Philipp. Boulder, Colo.: Lynne Rienner, 1990.

———. *Al-Inqilab al-'uthmani.* 1911. Cairo: Dar al-Hilal, 1966.

———. *Istibdad al-mamalik.* Cairo: Dar al-Hilal, 1965.

———. *Jihad al-muhibbin.* 3rd ed. Cairo: Dar al-Hilal, 1909.

———. *Al-Mamluk al-sharid.* 1891. Cairo: Dar al-Hilal, 1965.

———. *Shajarat al-Durr.* 1914. Cairo: Dar al-Hilal, 1965.

———. *Ta'rikh al-tamaddun al-islami.* 2 vols. Cairo: Dar al-Hilal, 1968.

Zeyneb Hanoum. *A Turkish Woman's European Impressions.* 1913. Facsimile reprint with an introduction by Reina Lewis. Cultures in Dialogue Series 1, vol. 3. Piscataway, N.J.: Gorgias Press, 2005.

Ziegler, Antje. "Al-Haraka Baraka! The Late Rediscovery of Mayy Ziyada's Works." *Die Welt des Islams* 39, no. 1 (1999): 103–15.

Ziyada, Mayy. *'A'isha al-Taymur: Sha'irat al-tali'a.* Cairo: Dar al-Muqtataf, 1926.

Zonana, Joyce. "The Sultan and the Slave: Feminist Orientalism and the Structure of *Jane Eyre.*" *Signs* 18, no. 3 (1993): 592–617.

CONTRIBUTORS

ASMA AFSARUDDIN is professor of Islamic studies in the Department of Near Eastern Languages and Cultures at Indiana University, Bloomington, and previously taught at the University of Notre Dame, Harvard University, and Johns Hopkins University. She is the author of *The First Muslims: History and Memory* (2008) and *Excellence and Precedence: Medieval Islamic Discourse on Legitimate Leadership* (2002); the editor of *Hermeneutics and Honor: Negotiating Female "Public" Space in Islamic/ate Societies* (1999); and a co-editor of *Humanism, Culture, and Language in the Near East: Studies in Honor of Georg Krotkoff* (1997). Her research has been funded by the Guggenheim Foundation and the Carnegie Corporation, which named her a Carnegie Scholar for 2005.

ORIT BASHKIN is assistant professor of Middle Eastern studies and history in the Department of Near Eastern Languages and Civilizations at the University of Chicago. Her Ph.D. dissertation looks at the construction of the Iraqi public sphere and the emergence of democratic discourses in Iraq during the interwar period. Her research interests include Arab intellectual history, Arabic literature, modern Iraqi history, and the history of Arab Jews in Iraq and Israel. She is the author of *The Other Iraq: Pluralism and Culture in Hashemite Iraq, 1921–1958* (2008).

MARILYN BOOTH holds the Iraq Chair in Arabic and Islamic studies at the University of Edinburgh. Previously she was director of the Center for South Asian and Middle Eastern Studies, and associate professor in the Program in Comparative and World Literature, at the University of Illinois Urbana-Champaign. The author of *May Her Likes Be Multiplied: Biography and Gender Politics in Egypt* (2001) and *Bayram al-Tunisi's Egypt: Social Criticism and Narrative Strategies* (1990), she has also translated many works of fiction from Arabic. She has published essays on memoirs, vernacular poetry, censorship and literature, gender and modern Arabic fiction, biography and constructions of masculinity in early Arabic gender discourse, and the theory and practice of literary translation. She has also taught at Brown University and the American University in Cairo.

JULIA CLANCY-SMITH is professor of Middle Eastern history at the University of Arizona. Her work has focused on colonialism and gender in North Africa. She is author of *Rebel and Saint: Muslim Notables, Populist Protest, Colonial Encounters (Algeria and Tunisia, 1800–1904)* (1994), *Mediterraneans: North Africa and Europe in an Age of Migration, 1800–1900* (2010), and *Exemplary Women and Sacred Journeys: Women and Gender in Judaism, Christianity, and Islam* (2006). She has edited or co-edited volumes on North Africa, women, and colonial histories, most recently with Zeynep Çelik and Frances Terpak, *Walls of Algiers: Narratives of the City through Text and Image* (Los Angeles and Seattle: Getty Research Institute and the University of Washington Press, 2009). Her current book project focuses on girls' education in colonial North Africa.

JOAN DELPLATO, professor of art history at Bard College at Simon's Rock, is the author of *Multiple Wives, Multiple Pleasures: Representing the Harem, 1800–1875* (2002), which was awarded a Millard Meiss publication grant from the College Art Association. With co-editor Julie Codell, she is preparing "Oriental Erotics: The Middle-Eastern Body, Visual Culture, and Modernity."

NADIA MARIA EL CHEIKH is professor of history at the American University of Beirut, where she has also been the director of the Center for Arab and Middle Eastern Studies. She is the author of *Byzantium Viewed by the Arabs* (2004). Her latest project explores the workings of the Abbasid court through an examination of the interaction of harem and court in the early fourth/tenth century. Among her most recent contributions in this area are "Servants at the Gate: Eunuchs at the Court of al-Muqtadir," *Journal of the Social and Economic History of the Orient* 48, no. 2 (2005): 234–52; and "The Court of al-Muqtadir: Its Space and Its Occupants," *Proceedings of the Seventh Conference of the School of 'Abbasid Studies*, Orientalia Lovaniensia Analecta, no. 177 (forthcoming).

JATEEN LAD is an architect, writer, and photographer based in London and Pondicherry, India. He studied at the University of Cambridge, Harvard University, and the Massachusetts Institute of Technology, where his research explored the harem and haram as forbidden and guarded sanctuaries in both ritual and palatial contexts. He is currently working on the notions of display and multi-plicity at the Hawa Mahal in Jaipur, which was the subject of his widely exhibited photographic narrative, Labyrinths, Jalis and the Gaze: The Changing Zenana of Royal Jaipur.

NANCY MICKLEWRIGHT is head of scholarly programs and publications at the Freer and Sackler Galleries in Washington, D.C. Before joining the Freer and Sackler, she was senior program officer at the Getty Foundation for nine years. Prior to her move to the Getty Foundation she was a professor of the history of Islamic art and architecture and the history of photography at the University of Victoria, in British Columbia, Canada. She has a long-standing interest in gender as a category of analysis and has used it in her writings on aspects of late Ottoman art (painting, dress, and photography). She is the author of *A Victorian Traveler in the Middle East: The Photography and Travel Writing of Annie Lady Brassey* (2003) and the editor, with Reina Lewis, of *Gender, Modernity and Liberty: Middle Eastern and Western Women's Writings; A Critical Sourcebook* (2006). The history of photography in the late Ottoman world is one of her continuing research interests.

YASEEN NOORANI is assistant professor of Near Eastern studies at the University of Arizona, specializing in comparative literature (Arabic and Persian). He is interested in the relationship between premodern and modern normative ideals in the Middle East. He is the author of *Culture and Hegemony in the Colonial Middle East* (2010) and the co-editor of *Counterhegemony in the Colony and Postcolony* (2007).

LESLIE PEIRCE is Silver Professor of History at New York University, where she teaches Ottoman studies and the history of the premodern Middle East. She previously taught in the Departments of History and Near Eastern Studies at the University of California, Berkeley. She is the author of *The Imperial Harem: Women and Sovereignty in the Ottoman Empire* (1993) and *Morality Tales: Law and Gender in the Ottoman Court of Aintab* (2003). Both books won the Turkish Studies Association's biannual Köprülü Book Prize, and the second the Albert Hourani Book Prize of the Middle East Studies Association. She is currently working on a study of abduction in Ottoman political life, folk epic, and law.

İRVİN CEMİL SCHICK has taught at Harvard University and the Massachusetts Institute of Technology, and is currently at Istanbul Şehir University. His books include *The Erotic Margin: Sexuality and Spatiality in Alteritist Discourse* (1999), *Çerkes Güzeli: Bir Şarkiyatçı İmgenin Serüveni* (the fair Circassian: adventures of an orientalist motif; 2004), *Avrupalı Esireler ve Müslüman Efendileri: "Türk" İllerinde Esaret Anlatıları* (European female captives and their Muslim masters: narratives of captivity in "Turkish" lands; 2005), and *İslam, Cinsiyet, Kültür Üzerine Yazılar* (writings on Islam, gender, and culture, forthcoming). He is also a co-editor (with Amila Buturović) of *Women in the Ottoman Balkans: Gender, Culture and History* (2007).

A. HOLLY SHISSLER is associate professor in the Department of Near Eastern Languages and Civilizations at the University of Chicago, specializing in late Ottoman history. She is the author of *Between Two Empires: Ahmet Ağaoğlu and the New Turkey* (2002). Her recent research focuses on women and social engineering in the early years of the Turkish Republic.

HEGHNAR ZEITLIAN WATENPAUGH is associate professor of art history at the University of California, Davis. She has published on early modern Islamic urbanism, issues of gender and space, and the preservation and commodification of architecture in the era of colonialism and nationalism in modern Middle Eastern societies. Her *The Image of an Ottoman City: Imperial Architecture and Urban Experience in Aleppo in the Sixteenth and Seventeenth Centuries* (2004) received the Spiro Kostof Book Award from the Society of Architectural Historians. She has received fellowships and awards from the J. Paul Getty Trust, the National Endowment for the Humanities, and the Center for Advanced Study in the Visual Arts at the National Gallery of Art. She has taught at Rice University, and she held the Aga Khan Career Development Professorship at the Massachusetts Institute of Technology from 2001 to 2005.

INDEX

Where "Hanım" or a variant appears as an honorific, it follows
the indexed name: for example, Layla Hanım, Zeyneb Hanoum.

Byzantine Empire and subjects, 92, 107, 120, 130, 308

Cairo, 6, 11, 16, 190, 225, 227, 301, 348, 353, 355–58, 364

Caliphs, 39, 90–91, 95, 160, 294. *See also* Harem: caliphal or imperial; Mother of the ruler; *names of individual caliphs*

Cariye (jariya), 139, 150–51, 155, 161–62, 324, 330–31, 335–36. *See also* Concubinage and concubines; Slavery and slaves

Castration, 114–15, 119, 124, 127, 171 nn. 3–4

Çelik, Zeynep, 256–57

Charity: eunuchs and, 167; reformers and, 320; women and, 65, 190, 368 n. 1

Childbearing and child rearing, 46 n. 30, 90–91, 102 n. 27, 139, 160, 175 n. 31, 190, 225, 227, 297, 299, 323, 327–28, 335. *See also* Children

Children, 34, 53, 182, 191–92; as category (social or legal), 5, 63, 117, 130, 220, 334; fathering, 99, 125, 128–30, 154, 161, 300, 334, 349–53, 359–61, 364–65; as harem or household members, 5, 73, 89–92, 99, 116, 154, 174 n. 29, 176 n. 48, 197, 199, 227, 240, 309, 313, 317–18 n. 92, 345; literary representation of, 16, 60–63, 225, 231, 297, 300, 307, 323, 349–51; as readers, 292. *See also* Childbearing and child rearing

Christianity and Christians, 76–77, 110, 112–14, 125, 134 n. 37, 143, 154, 178, 181, 188, 198, 324, 325–26, 331, 354; Syrian, 221, 226, 258 n. 5, 290–92, 300, 303, 347, 349. *See also* Missionaries

Clancy-Smith, Julia, 13, 86

Cleanliness, 41, 185. *See also* Baths; Hygiene

Clothing. *See* Dress

Colonialisms and colonial discourses, European, 16, 18, 73, 178, 182, 185, 201–5, 216, 264–65, 268, 290, 303, 307, 312–13, 342, 352–55, 357, 365–66

Concubinage and concubines, 88, 91–92, 95, 101, 102 n. 27, 109, 139, 141, 150, 161, 174 n. 29, 181, 296–303, 305–6, 308, 312, 324, 327–30, 335–36, 358; representations of in European art, 263–70. *See also* Slavery and slaves

Conduct manuals, 10–11, 25, 39–43, 346

Conservation of buildings. *See* Preservation

Constantinople (N. E. Maurin), 272–76, 282–84

Constitutional revolution (Turkey, 1908), 293, 296–300, 312

Consumption, 372 n. 49; of European art, 268–72, 278–79, 283–84, 285 n. 8; of novels, memoir, and periodicals, 250, 257, 291–93, 297, 315 n. 36, 344–47, 357, 360; of popular literature, 294; women and, 292, 297, 315 n. 36, 357, 371 n. 43. *See also* Orientalism

Costume. *See* Dress

Criminality, 108–32. *See also* Dulkadir Kanunname; *Kanunname-i Osmani*; Law

Cross-dressing, 248–49, 281

Damascus, 217–21, 224–25, 232

Dar, 31, 52, 64, 70, 90–91, 98, 178, 187

Daughters, 31, 89, 99, 106, 110, 114, 116, 120, 125, 127, 156, 181, 191, 225, 250–51, 322–26, 336–37, 349–53, 356–61, 365–66

De Lauretis, Teresa, 73

DelPlato, Joan, 9, 14, 82 n. 18, 237

Dernschwam, Hans, 104, 122

Desire, 50, 54–62, 269–72, 274–75, 281–82, 328–29, 332, 362–63

Devşirme, 154

Dialmy, Abdessamad, 80

Diplomacy, 13, 178–80, 186–99, 203–4

Divorce, 91, 98, 284 n. 2, 301, 350, 357, 364; and adulterous wives, 112–13, 116, 124, 128, 134 n. 37; legal discourses and practices, 112, 116–17, 119, 129–30, 134 n. 37

Domestic interiors, 249–58, 272–73, 276. *See also* Harems: decor of

Domesticity, as cult, ideology, or ideal, 8, 23, 47 n. 52, 50, 52, 63, 76–77, 291–93, 352

Dowry system, 325, 331

Dress, 8–9, 14, 16–17, 34, 40–41, 72, 80–81, 89, 98–99, 136, 191–94, 229–30, 259 n. 11, 356; in European visual art, 262–72, 275–83, 284 n. 1; in novels and memoirs, 297, 309, 323, 325–26, 329, 331, 335, 357–59, 367–68, 372 n. 49; in photography, 237, 243–45, 247–49, 251–52, 254–55, 257, 260 n. 22, 289 n. 73. *See also Hijab*

Duben, Alan, 71

Dulkadir Kanunname, 121–28, 130–31; relation to Ottoman Kanunname, 125–26, 134 n. 31

Duncan, Nancy, 77–78

Ebu Suud (Ottoman chief mufti), 104–5, 119, 129, 131

Edib Adivar, Halide, 3

Education, 15, 17, 293, 312, 357; girls and, 225–28, 302, 324, 346, 349–50, 352–53, 357, 360, 368 n. 1

Egypt, 7, 14, 190, 207 n. 14, 264–65, 279, 290–95, 342–49; ancient, 351; slavery in, 307–8. *See also* Cairo

El Cheikh, Nadia Maria, 12, 66 n. 11, 85–86, 294, 315 n. 16

England and its subjects, 2, 7–8, 50–51, 187, 192, 197, 198, 242, 262, 277–79, 284 n. 2, 313, 324, 346. *See also* Victorian practices; Women: British

Eunuchs, 12–13, 76, 86, 88, 90–91, 93–94, 96, 98, 100–101, 136–70, 171 n. 3, 173 nn. 18–20, 180, 203, 284

n. 2, 294; Abbasid chief eunuch, 91, 93–94; Ottoman chief eunuch (*kızlar ağası*), 139, 142–43, 153, 156, 163–69, 172 n. 9

Europeans and Americans in the Middle East, 177–82, 184, 186; as development experts, 217. *See also* Christianity and Christians; Colonialisms and cultural discourses; Missionaries; Photography; Women: British; Women: European

Fallenness, 263, 331, 337–38, 342–45, 348–49, 353–54, 359–60, 363–65, 369 n. 4

Family: caliphal, 90–92; in law, 104–32; market forces and, 15, 320–25, 329–37; Ottoman imperial, 104, 136–70; Ottoman, photographic representations of, 249–55; as social unit, 16, 50–51, 76–77, 86, 100, 118, 178, 182–83, 206 n. 5, 224, 320–21; textual representations of, 11, 16, 39–40, 50–51, 59–61, 66 n. 4, 199, 206 n. 5, 299–302, 307, 320–40, 366. *See also* Architecture, domestic; Children; Criminality; Marriage; Men; Women

Fathering. *See* Children; Men

Fatwa (legal opinion), 8, 59, 105–6, 134 n. 31

Felâtun Bey ile Râkım Efendi (Ahmet Midhat), 321, 323–25, 327–30, 334–36, 340

Femininity, 44, 57–59, 62–65, 77, 79, 227, 262–63, 308–9, 342, 352, 356. *See also* Women

Feminism: activism and, 292, 312, 352–55, 359–60, 365–68, 368 n. 1, 373 n. 67; spatial thinking and, 7, 72–75, 342

Fenton, Roger, 241–43, 257

Foucault, Michel, 73–74, 115, 162, 165–66, 281, 309

France and its subjects, 51, 182–83, 185–89, 193–202, 205, 206 n. 5, 216,

MARILYN BOOTH holds the Iraq Chair in Arabic and Islamic studies at the
University of Edinburgh.

Library of Congress Cataloging-in-Publication Data

Harem histories : envisioning places and living spaces / Marilyn Booth, editor.
p. cm.
Includes bibliographical references and index.
ISBN 978-0-8223-4858-0 (cloth : alk. paper)
ISBN 978-0-8223-4869-6 (pbk. : alk. paper)
1. Harems. I. Booth, Marilyn.
HQ1170.H288 2010
306.84′23091767 — dc22
2010024127